Integrated Series in Information Systems

Volume 31

Series Editors

Ramesh Sharda
Oklahoma State University, Stillwater, OK, USA

Stefan Voß
University of Hamburg, Hamburg, Germany

For further volumes:
http://www.springer.com/series/6157

J. Ramon Gil-Garcia

Enacting Electronic Government Success

An Integrative Study of Government-wide Websites, Organizational Capabilities, and Institutions

Springer

J. Ramon Gil-Garcia
Department of Public Administration
Centro de Investigación y Docencia
Economicas
Carretera Mexico-Toluca 3655
Col. Lomas de Santa Fe
01210 Mexico, D.F.
Mexico

ISSN 1571-0270
ISBN 978-1-4614-2014-9 e-ISBN 978-1-4614-2015-6
DOI 10.1007/978-1-4614-2015-6
Springer New York Heidelberg Dordrecht London

Library of Congress Control Number: 2012930905

Printed on acid-free paper

Springer is part of Springer Science+Business Media (www.springer.com)

This book is dedicated to Nadia, Dante, and Julieta; with all my love

Foreword

Over the past 20 years, governments of all types and sizes have enthusiastically adopted a variety of information and communication technologies. They have done so for many reasons—to drive modernization and efficiency, to be more responsive and available to the public, to better manage ever-growing complexity in public problems and programs, to handle burgeoning kinds and amounts of information, to innovate, and more.

Today, governments spend billions on ICTs for internal management, citizen services, and regulatory activities. National, regional, and municipal governments world-wide continue to adopt and adapt technologies in the hope and expectation of civil, social, and economic benefits. Sometimes these goals are achieved, often they are not. Despite studies that document poor performance and frequent failure, well-publicized benchmark studies strongly suggest that the top rated countries or cities offer best practices that could or should be adopted elsewhere. However, can Sweden's strategy be realistic in Africa? Can the Korean model be replicated in Latin America? Popular strategies implemented in one place may or may not work in others, even when they seem similar on the surface. If an initiative to improve the management of health records works in California, should not it also work in New York? If a strategy for e-government development improves government transparency in Mexico should not it do the same in Colombia? The fact is they might, but often they don't. The fundamental question for both scholars and leaders is "why?"

In this book, Ramon Gil-Garcia offers a carefully constructed theoretical foundation for studying e-government success that draws from the research on information systems in organizations, socio-technical systems, and institutional theory as well as public management. It investigates the mutual shaping of government ICT initiatives and their organizational, institutional and societal contexts. The particular strength of his work lies in the way it integrates policy, organizational, and technological factors within a larger institutional and societal environment. The empirical, multi-method study offers important contributions to the emerging field of digital government research as well as to more fundamental aspects of organization studies, public administration, and public policy. It takes e-government portals as the focus for empirical investigation, but the theoretical framework and its practical implications have value far beyond one kind of ICT implementation. In addition, by focusing on the state level of government, the study begins to fill an enormous gap in knowledge about public management at other than the national level.

Using sophisticated quantitative and qualitative analysis, the book presents a model for better understanding that elusive goal—e-government success. The research was conducted in a carefully constructed nested design that is both novel and powerful. It employs quantitative analysis to build and test a preliminary conceptual model of e-government success using PLS techniques and published data about all 50 states. The second stage of the study comprised two qualitative case studies of Indiana and New York, a pair of states with similar ratings on key published indicators of success. However, one state fit the model well and the other poorly. The case studies probed for the actions, policies, and strategies that led these two states to successful outcomes and discovered how the same set of variables operates in different ways to produce state-specific—that is, context-specific—results. While government-wide portals may or may not remain distinguishing artifacts of e-government development in the future, the challenges of choosing, using, and evaluating ICTs in government will surely persist. Researchers, government professionals, and students will therefore all benefit from the integration of ideas presented in this work.

As a field of research, e-government is both multi-disciplinary and practice-based. As a field of practice, it is multi-dimensional and open to advice grounded in real experience and honed by rigorous examination. The practice of e-government and research on e-government can therefore benefit substantially from mutual engagement in applied research that generates new knowledge in both practical and academic domains. In this book, Ramon Gil-Garcia contributes a thoroughly researched and cogent argument about the complexities that challenge every government effort to use technology in new and effective ways. He offers a sophisticated understanding of the factors and interactions that lead to different degrees of success in different environments. The work does what I have always sought to do in my own work—to expand our knowledge and understanding of important public sector phenomena in a way that offers not only better theories, but better government.

Sharon S. Dawes
University at Albany,
State University of New York, USA

Foreword

It is an honor to pen a few thoughts on Ramon Gil-Garcia's searching and persuasive study of e-government success. It examines and extends technology enactment, a conceptual framework I developed and described in Building the Virtual State in 2001. Gil-Garcia moves beyond the initial statement of the model, which was motivated by design strictly within institutional perspectives drawn from organization theory and political science. Through careful, detailed conceptual analysis, he connects technology enactment to key constructs and processes within a family of socio-technical perspectives, including ensemble views, of information systems and organization.

We have before us a study that presents a paradox of sorts. Many institutionalists and socio-technical researchers use qualitative and interpretive analysis to engage with the intricate and emergent nature of technologies as social artifacts and with the myriad direct, indirect and recursive influences on and of socio-technical systems in complex social environments. In this view, positivism and quantification are eschewed in order to resist decontextualizing complex social and technical dimensions and the relationships among these dimensions to what some critics have called reductionist "boxes and arrows." Interpretivists focus on tacit, emergent, multi-faceted constructions of meaning and on subjective and inter-subjective understandings and instantiations of meaning in practice.

Paradoxically, Gil-Garcia embraces constructivism but resists its opposition to quantification. By contrast, he provides the reader with an extensive categorization and operationalization of constructs and a structural equation analysis of constructs that he claims influence and are influenced by e-government socio-technical systems. The study undertakes "one of the first applications of partial least squares … to an e-government success study." Partial least squares is a technique within structural equation modeling for measuring complex multivariate relationships among observed and latent variables. It allows the researcher simultaneously to test the structural model, that is, the relationships among constructs, and the measurement model, or the relationships between indicators and their associated constructs. Gil-Garcia measures relationships between e-government success and a range of constructs and also can measure relationships among the constructs themselves. This modeling is intended to complement and strengthen qualitative approaches that predominate in interpretivist and constructivist research.

Thus, the study embraces both positivism and constructivism both in the theoretical exposition and in the multiple methods employed for empirical research. While it is not unusual to find quantitative analysis combined with in-depth case studies, the study is exceptional in its operationalization of interpretivist constructs. Readers may disagree (as always) with the choice and precise operationalization of constructs, but the effort itself deftly makes space for epistemological shifts in the study between constructivism and positivist, but not linear, quantitative modeling of latent and observed variables.

Some readers will be uncomfortable with the deep interpretivist epistemology that underlies the construction of the model; others will be uncomfortable, or simply will ignore, the highly complex structural equation model that is developed and tested in the study. The attentive reader will engage both epistemologies. Can we resolve the paradox between them? The reader need not side with qualitative or quantitative analysis or with constructivism or positivism but is invited to examine how the sustained use of multiple, and seemingly conflicting, perspectives and methods can deepen an understanding of e-government developments.

Beyond engaging this paradox, the study undertakes to examine technology enactment in the development, implementation and use of state-level e-government websites in Indiana and New York. The aim is both theory building and testing as well as generation of practical lessons for public management and policymaking. It is easy for management pundits to challenge decision makers with dramatic statements such as "Change or die," but it is more difficult and much more useful systematically to develop and validate findings in order to offer fine-grained guidance to those in public organizations and governments in their pursuit of "e-government success."

The problem of bringing greater specificity and measurement to technology enactment, originally a heuristic model, was one motive for the study. But a more important motive, and a considerable contribution made by the present study, is the connection made between technology enactment and conceptual frameworks squarely in the socio-technical perspective. Connecting these conceptualizations is a major act of synthesis and makes useful guidance to decision makers possible. Gil-Garcia expands the original technology enactment framework specifically to better account for environmental dimensions, to describe and explain processes of organizational change, and to highlight the importance of "management strategies and practices" for e-government success.

In the end, the study concludes that organizational features directly affect e-government success while institutional arrangements, as technology enactment sketches, affect e-government success indirectly. Gil-Garcia is able to describe and measure the importance and role of a host of important institutional, organizational, and management practice dimensions. While testing relationships among constructs in a structural equation model is not strictly equivalent to a depiction of the dynamic interplay or complex recursive relationships across social, organizational, cultural, political and technological arrangements, it is refreshing and important to see these different epistemological stances placed side by side.

In the course of the book the reader comes to appreciate that the contributions of the study extend far beyond lessons about building websites in U.S. state governments. Around the globe, researchers and policymakers are challenged today to find and use lessons learned across vastly different political, economic and cultural settings in which e-government is being enacted. Practical recommendations supported by empirical, measurable research are of the utmost importance to policymakers—and the study does not disappoint in this regard. Yet it is worth repeating here Kurt Lewin's dictum taught to every graduate student but often missing from the study of e-government: "There is nothing so practical as a good theory."

Jane E. Fountain
University of Massachusetts Amherst, USA

Preface

Countries around the world are making heavy resource investments in e-government initiatives. However, few of these projects achieve all of their stated goals and many could easily be considered failures. In addition, several new applications and tools have emerged in recent years, significantly increasing the technical and organizational complexity of these projects. E-government initiatives are not only about efficiency and cost-saving; they are now also designed to realize other important benefits for the public sector such as transparency, openness, policy effectiveness, service quality, and citizen participation. As the goals of e-government expand, understanding its success has become more important and urgent. In order to develop the necessary knowledge about this phenomenon, researchers and government professionals need to identify and assess the main conditions, variables, or factors that have an impact on e-government success. However, before being able to evaluate these impacts, it is necessary to define what e-government success looks like and how it should be measured. This book presents a review of both e-government success measures and e-government success factors. It also provides empirical evidence from quantitative analysis and two in-depth case studies about the success of e-government initiatives. Thus, based on sound theory and rigorous empirical analysis, the book not only contributes to academic knowledge, but also provides some practical recommendations for government officials, public managers, and IT professionals.

Before analyzing e-government success, it is first necessary to clarify what e-government is. E-government could be thought of as a totally new phenomenon triggered by the introduction of the Internet and related technologies. In contrast, e-government could also be understood as a new term to represent the use of information and communication technologies in government settings—or a new label for an old phenomenon with a long history. This book takes this second approach. E-government is considered one of many terms used to represent and describe a complex socio-technical phenomenon that has been studied for several decades. New technologies are continuously emerging and expanding its object of study, but the overall phenomenon is still the same. Following this perspective, this book argues that e-government is a broad concept that includes socio-technical aspects of the selection, design, implementation, and use of any kind of information and communication technology in government, from fax machines and mainframe computers to complex inter-organizational systems, cloud computing, information integration, Web 2.0 tools, social media, and open government applications.

Theoretically, this study draws upon and extends institutional theory—specifically, the technology enactment framework—by incorporating concepts from recent studies on technology and organization, as well as theoretical elements from other integrative approaches. Thus, the book attempts to explain the effects of organizational forms and institutional arrangements on the information technology used by government agencies, which is an alternative approach for the study of electronic government. According to Fountain (1995, 2001a), the technology enactment framework pays attention to the relationships among information technology, organizations, embeddedness, and institutions. The book proposes variables to measure each of the different constructs relevant to institutional theory and tests the relationships hypothesized in Fountain's framework. The study also proposes some adjustments and extensions to the original framework in a theory building effort, leading to a new proposal for using institutional and socio-technical integrative theoretical models to better understand electronic government success. Considering the existence of good work at the federal (Fountain 2001a) and the local (Kraemer et al. 1989) levels, this book applies the proposed framework to state governments, filling an existing gap in the literature and enriching previous knowledge by adding evidence at the state level.

Methodologically, the book reports on one of the first systematic, sequential-explanatory mixed-method studies in the field of e-government success. More specifically, this study uses a nested research design, which combines statistical analysis with two in-depth case studies. The study begins with the statistical analysis, using organizational, institutional, and contextual factors as independent variables, but this analysis also explores some of the relationships between different factors and, therefore, considers some of the complex interactions among the dependent and the independent variables. The result is a new way to quantitatively operationalize Fountain's technology enactment framework. An overall score representing e-government success in terms of the functionality of government-wide websites is the ultimate dependent variable. Based on the statistical results, two cases were selected (New York and Indiana) and case studies were developed using semi-structured interviews and document analysis. Government-wide websites are good cases to use because they include a great variety of IT tools and applications and they are a very pervasive example of an e-government initiative. In the context of this book, they are seen as an instance of a broader e-government phenomenon.

In terms of the statistical analysis, the book presents one of the first applications of partial least squares (PLS) to an e-government success study. PLS is a structural equations modeling (SEM) technique that allows for estimating the measurement model and the structural model simultaneously. The use of this sophisticated statistical strategy helped to test the relationships between e-government success and different factors influencing it, as well as some of the relationships between the factors, thus allowing for the exploration of indirect effects. The ability to explore multiple causal relationships simultaneously helps to understand the e-government phenomenon in more detail, without isolating some relationships that are deeply intertwined in the real world. Therefore, in contrast to previous studies that focus on one or a few single variables and ignore most of the organizational, institutional, and contextual aspects of the phenomenon, this study is able to analyze a complex set of variables and identify their direct and indirect influences on the success of e-government initiatives.

This book is the product of great teamwork and the individual dedicated time of many wonderful people. Some helped me in the design, implementation, and writing of this research. Others supported me, encouraged me, and shared both my good and bad times during the process. Although I am thankful to all, I want to especially mention a few of them, recognizing that their actual contributions were greater than my small tribute in this preface.

First, Sharon S. Dawes worked very closely with me throughout this process. She was always willing to share her formidable knowledge and experience in government information strategy and management and was a truly exceptional mentor. She devoted much time to discuss my ideas and our conversations always ended with improved theoretical and practical insights. I learned from her how to build research that is theoretically sound, but also practically useful. I want to thank Sharon for being a superb scholar and a great model to follow. I also want to thank Richard H. Hall, Jon P. Gant, and R. Karl Rethemeyer. From the beginning to the end of this research endeavor, they were always willing to discuss my ideas, asking me the right questions and helping me to develop a solid research product. From general theoretical discussions to their knowledge about specific cases or methodological approaches, their diverse disciplinary backgrounds and experiences greatly enriched my research and have influenced my academic career since then.

There were other individuals who were influential in this research and I am thankful to them. Jane E. Fountain was very supportive in the final stages of this project. Through fruitful conversations, she helped me to see new angles of the technology enactment framework and generate ideas for my overall conclusions and future research plan. Similarly, Wanda Orlikowski encouraged me to continue using and refining non-traditional and integrative approaches to information technologies in organizational settings. Technically, Wynne Chin and Shobha Chengalur-Smith provided helpful guidance for conducting the PLS analysis for this study. I am also thankful to several excellent colleagues from the digital government research community, especially Theresa A. Pardo, Anthony M. Cresswell, Luis F. Luna-Reyes, Natalie Helbig, Anna Raup-Kounovsky, Taewoo Nam, Rodrigo Sandoval-Almazan, Ignacio Criado, Marijn Janssen, Chris Reddick, Enrico Ferro, Sehl Mellouli, and Mila Gasco. They have always been willing to listen to my ideas and sharing my initial thoughts and further elaborations with them has been extremely helpful for the development and refinement of some of the concepts, theoretical implications, and practical recommendations included in this book.

Equally important, an academic work of such dedication as a book requires strong family support. My wife, Nadia, my son, Dante, and my daughter, Julieta, were essential in this collective effort. They have always been with me in my academic adventures and always support my sometimes too ambitious goals. Their love, support, and encouragement have helped me to achieve very high standards and find meaning in my life. I love them and I am deeply thankful to them.

Several organizations have provided some kind of institutional or financial support for this research. I want to especially mention the Mexican National Council of Science and Technology (CONACYT), the Mexico-United States Commission for Educational and Cultural Exchange (in the form of a Fulbright scholarship), the U.S. National Science Foundation, and the Center for Technology in Government (CTG) at the University at Albany, SUNY, which was my academic home while developing this research. In addition, a doctoral fellowship from the National Center for Digital Government at the John F. Kennedy School of Government, Harvard University was important in conducting the two case studies and completing this project (National Science Foundation Grant No. 0131923 and Grant No. 0630239). Finally, I am very grateful to *Centro de Investigación y Docencia Económicas (CIDE)*, from which I have received not only strong institutional support, but also great encouragement and motivation from my colleagues and friends. CIDE has been a pivotal force in the development and refinement of this book.

For the editorial process and final stages of this book, other individuals were also important. I want to thank Ramesh Sharda and Stefan Voß for their help and support throughout this process as the editors of the *Integrated Series in Information Systems* published by Springer, which this book is included in. My thanks also to my editors at Springer, Neil Levine and Matthew Amboy, who have been significantly involved in the whole process from beginning to end. I am also thankful to my research assistant, Ana Catarrivas, whose hard work, creativeness, and dedication have been essential for the completion and refinement of this book. Finally, Anna Raup-Kounovsky did a wonderful job in editing and improving the content and style of the entire book and I want to thank her for that.

Mexico City, Mexico J. Ramon Gil-Garcia

Contents

Abbreviations

CIO	Chief information officer
DIT	Division of Information Technology
EDARC	Enhance Data Access Review Committee
ESRA	Electronic Signatures and Records Act
FAQs	Frequently asked questions
FMS	Financial management system
G2B	Government to business
G2BMKT	Government to businesses in the market
G2C	Government to citizens
G2E	Government to employees
G2G	Government to Government
G2IP	Government to individual as part of the political process
GSP	Gross state product
HIPAA	Health Information Portability and Accountability Act
HTML	HyperText Markup Language
ICT	Information and Communication Technologies
ISO	Information security officer
IT	Information Technologies
ITOC	Information Technology Oversight Commission
NYS	New York state
OECD	Organization for Economic Cooperation and Development
OFT	Office for Technology
PIO	Public information officer
RSS	Really simply syndication

Introduction

E-government is recurrently mentioned as a powerful tool for government administrative reform (CEG 2001; Fountain 2001a; Garson 2004; Heeks 1999; Jaeger and Bertot 2010; Kramer and King 2003; Lee 2010; Luna-Reyes et al. 2007; Margetts 2009; Reddick 2005; Seifert and Chung 2009). However, it is not always clear why public managers, researchers, graduate students and other individuals should be interested in learning more about this phenomenon. I will start this introduction by briefly telling you why people should be interested in electronic government and how information technologies could affect government agencies and public policies in today's world. First, information technologies could potentially solve many of the problems found in current bureaucratic structures. They could improve transparency, service quality, efficiency, citizen participation, openness, and policy effectiveness, among other important aspects. They do have the potential to facilitate the development of the government apparatus of the twenty first century—a networked and IT-enabled public administration (Pardo et al. 2010).

Second, information technologies also have the potential to go beyond solving today's structural and procedural problems to trigger organizational and policy innovation. For instance, government agencies are increasingly working with other agencies, not-for-profit organizations, and private companies in order to better face complex social problems such as the provision of education, health, or housing. Inter-organizational networks are new forms that can be greatly supported by the intense use of information technologies. In fact, government information technologies are not only, not even mainly, about using computers or developing information systems; they are truly about dealing with social issues and crafting public policies supported by IT that could help to solve the most difficult problems in modern society. Technology should not be seen as an end in itself, but as a means to achieve important public goals in several policy domains.

This potential is probably why public officials, citizens, and academics are interested in information technologies and their effects on government performance, openness, transparency, and democratic participation (Ahn and Bretschneider 2011; Ebbers et al. 2008; Hrdinová et al. 2009; Hughes 2011; Margetts 2009;

Markaki et al. 2010; Rahman 2010; Rashid and Rahman 2010; Reddick 2010; Seifert and Chung 2009). For instance, the e-government section of the European Commission website includes a statement related to this potential: "e-Government promises to deliver better, more efficient public services and improve the relationships between citizens and their governments." The same website also recognizes that technology should be only one of the components of a more ambitious reform agenda: "The resulting benefits to the quality of life, industrial competitiveness and society will only be realized, however, if administrations change the way they operate." Therefore, information technologies together with other important government reforms have the potential to go well beyond efficiency and cost-savings to achieve broader benefits for society as a whole.

Similarly, recent studies propose that most citizens want to receive better public services (Baqir and Iyer 2010; CEG 2001; Gil-Garcia and Helbig 2006; Gurría 2008; Luna-Reyes et al. 2010; Markaki et al. 2010; Rorissa et al. 2010; Sancak and Güleç 2010), and information technologies seem to be a key component of the improvements necessary to deliver them (Baqir and Iyer 2010; Antonio Cordella and Iannacci 2010; Choudhury and Kumar 2009; Dawes and Pardo 2002; Eric et al. 2008; Kim et al. 2009; Peled 2001b; Rowley 2011). Information technologies (IT) are a catalyst for organizational change in both the private and public sectors (Bandyopadhyay and Sattarzadeh 2010; Bannister 2007; Davenport 1993; Hanna 2011; Janssen et al. 2004; Milner 2000; Olbrich 2010; Reddick 2010; Scott and Robbins 2010). They have the potential not only to improve the quality of services, but also to produce cost savings and make government policies and programs more effective (Bourquard 2003; Chwelos et al. 2010; Dawes et al. 1999; Garson 2004; Grönlund 2001; Heeks 2001; Sancak and Güleç 2010). In addition, with the recent recession and its consequences for public budgets, the need to innovate has become a survival skill (Waxer 2011).

What does that innovation look like? In December 2010, a deadly tornado touched Cincinnati, Arkansas. Instead of relying on typical channels like TV and radio, "the Arkansas Homeland Security and Preparedness Agency chose to tweet up-to-the-minute storm reports" (Waxer 2011). As Waxer (2011) explains, agencies are embracing social media tools like LinkedIn, Facebook, YouTube, Twitter, and more to communicate with citizens in real time and to support internal collaboration. The case of Arkansas is far from unusual; recent data shows that 66% of all government agencies use some form of social networking (Saba 2010).

Despite the great potential benefits from e-government, scholars and practitioners think government information technologies have not yet achieved the promise of a more efficient, effective, transparent, and democratic public administration (Ashurst et al. 2008; Cook et al. 2002; Chen et al. 2009; Garson 2004; Joseph 2010; Wu et al. 2010). As new technologies continually emerge, there are new opportunities to innovate and also to underperform. For example, although there is a growing consensus that the use of social networking tools may improve performance, service, and management for customers, government adoption of these tools still lags behind the private sector. In the United States, President Barack Obama has championed the use of social media in government: "Within days of its inauguration, the Obama administration has heralded and pushed forward initiatives for open government, transparency, collaboration, and citizen participation massively utilizing and leveraging advanced Web technologies including social media" (Scholl and Luna-Reyes 2011, p. 1). However, looking across the US, 29% percent of government organizations did not make use of any social networking tools as of 2010 (Saba 2010).

Estimates about the failure rate of IT projects are sobering. For instance, Heeks (2003) points out that the success rate of information and communication technology (ICT) projects in the governments of industrialized countries is very low and that there is no reason to think that the e-government success rate in developing countries is any better. In fact, some characteristics of developing countries, such as the lack of adequate infrastructure, suggest that the success rate of e-government projects should be even lower. Consistent with this finding, a 2003 report from the United Nations, entitled *E-Government at the Crossroads*, estimated that "at least 60% of all e-government projects in developing countries fail, and about half waste taxpayers' money to some extent" (Stevenson 2003). The report also recognizes the complexity of e-government projects in general and mentions that "a too-grandiose approach may result in failures or expensive white elephants" (IDABC 2003; Stevenson 2003). In addition, e-government should not be seen as an end in itself, but as a means to enhance the capacity of the public sector (United Nations 2010).

Despite the high rate of failure, government spending for e-government projects has continually increased over the last few years. For instance, recently, President Obama requested a 1.2% increase for spending on information technology projects, totaling almost $80 billion for fiscal year 2011 (it.usaspending.gov). While more than US $3 trillion was spent on government information systems around the world during the past 10 years (Stanforth 2010), some studies indicate a 60–80% failure rate of e-government projects, leading to "a massive wastage of financial, human, and political resources, and an inability to deliver the potential benefits of e-government to its beneficiaries (Heeks 2006, p. 3). In addition, "progress towards realizing the full potential of eGovernment—using digital technologies to improve public services and government-citizen engagements—has been slower and less effective than the technologies' take-up in spheres such as e-commerce" (Eynon and Margetts 2007, p. 73).

All the complexity noted above demands the development of deep knowledge about e-government projects and the context in which they occur. Therefore, understanding the relationships between e-government success and different organizational, institutional, and environmental factors has become imperative. When mapping this practical concern to theory, it is very important to understand the complex and dynamic relationships between information technologies and the social structures around them. This book proposes such an integrative framework for the study of electronic government success.

Recently, different disciplines have developed interesting theoretical approaches to understanding the complex relationships between information technologies and social structures. Initially, most of this research took a linear perspective and assumed uni-directional causality. For instance, either information technologies were thought to have the capacity to transform organizations and institutions or organizational characteristics and institutional arrangements were seen as key factors in shaping the selection, design, implementation, and use of information technologies (Bretschneider 2003; Fountain and Gil-Garcia 2006b). Recent research recognizes that there is a dynamic interaction between social structures and information technologies (Antonio Cordella and Iannacci 2010; Criado 2010; Fountain 2001a; Leonardi 2009b; Orlikowski 2000, 2008). In this view, information technologies have the potential to radically transform social and organizational structures, while organizational and social structures simultaneously affect the use of information technologies.

However, most of this integrative research has been developed based on private sector organizations and our current understanding of the factors affecting how government uses information technologies, and how information technologies affect the way government works, is still limited. Using a nested research design, this study explores the complex relationships between e-government success (represented in this study by the quality or functionality of government-wide websites) and several organizational, institutional, and contextual factors. Accordingly, this research is guided by two interrelated questions; each question represents one direction of the influence between information technologies and social structures:

1. To what extent are e-government initiatives shaped by different organizational characteristics, institutional arrangements, and environmental conditions?
2. To what extent are organizational characteristics, institutional arrangements, and environmental conditions affected by the existence and characteristics of e-government initiatives?

Applications of IT in government are now pervasive, but few types have been implemented as widely as government websites. By 2010, "98% of states offer some combinations of online business and personal tax filing; 92% of states give automobile owners an online option for renewal license plates; 86% of states offer online business registration services [...]; 78% of states let residents make online requests for copies of birth, death, marriage, divorce, and adoption certificates; 72% of states have launched transparency sites to provide visibility into how they spend taxpayer money; [and] 58% of states accept payments for fines online and offer interactive customer service online" (*State of the portal: a review of the 50 states' Online offerings* 2010, p. 5).

These figures show that web applications are increasingly used for different purposes in government. In addition, government-wide websites are inter-organizational efforts and normally include a great variety of web applications, from information display to transactional services and participation channels. Therefore, they are being used in this study as a case or instance of a much broader e-government phenomenon. In addition, as a socio-technical phenomenon, government-wide websites consist not only of technological tools, applications, and features, but also include all the social relationships around them. Most people look at a website and see an interface to information or services, but they do not see the complex organizational network that supports the website or the rich array of institutions that enable or hinder its success.

Inter-agency websites, such as government-wide portals, are particularly interesting because creating them requires inter-organizational collaboration and significant operational and institutional change; consequently, they represent substantial difficulty in their design and implementation. If you think about government websites on a continuum of complexity, individual agency websites are initiatives that may require limited operational and institutional change are at the low end. At the upper end, information integration among multiple government agencies can be achieved only by instituting substantial changes in operational processes and the institutional framework. In addition, government-wide websites are among the few applications of IT that can be compared across multiple jurisdictions. In the United States all 50 states have had government-wide websites for some time, which allows broad comparative analysis. In addition, government-wide websites' increasing popularity and multi-dimensional objectives make them a powerful way to understand other forms of e-government success (Chircu 2008; Norris and Moon 2005). Finally, in recent years, they have "proven their value [to governments and citizens] since states relied on them to extend services at a time when they cannot afford to do it any other way" (*State of the portal: a review of the 50 states' Online offerings* 2010, p. 5).

The rest of this book is organized in seven chapters and a methodological appendix. While the introduction, the cases, and the conclusions should be interesting and useful for most readers, not every individual will need or want to read the book from beginning to end. For instance, for scholars interested in the details of the research, I lay out the design and variables in Appendix 1 at the end of the book, take the reader through the details of the structural equations analyses in Chap. 3, and summarize their results in Chap. 6. Researchers and graduate students will find Chaps. 1 and 2 useful for their theoretical development and as the basis for future research on related e-government topics. Chapter 2 should be of particular interest to scholars looking for new ways to understand electronic government as a socio-technical phenomenon and from an institutional perspective. For those readers who want practical advice based on the research, the ideas in Chap. 1, the recommendations in Chap. 6, and the conclusions in Chap. 7 will be most useful. The cases described in Chaps. 4 and 5 exemplify two very different paths to e-government success and should be useful for both managers and academics.

Electronic government is not a well-defined theoretical construct. In fact, it can be understood as anything from online services only to any ICT used by government (including telephones and fax machines). Therefore, Chap. 1 presents a review of the existing literature and analyzes three different approaches to e-government (definitional, stakeholder-oriented, and evolutionary) to develop a working definition of e-government. For this book, electronic government is a new label for an old phenomenon with a long practical and academic history: the use of information and communication technologies in government. With this definition in place, the second section of Chap. 1 focuses on e-government success measures. This study reviews different approaches to understanding e-government benefits, outputs, and outcomes as measures of e-government success. Finally, section three of Chap. 1 presents some important factors identified in previous studies that influence the success of IT adoption and implementation. There is important research about the impact of organizational, institutional, and environmental factors on the selection, design, implementation, and use of information technologies. This academic tradition attempts to understand how different variables shape or influence the characteristics of government information technologies and, subsequently, affect the organizational outputs and outcomes.

Several academic fields have made significant contributions to our current understanding of information technologies in government. The study presented in this book takes a holistic approach to the e-government phenomenon. Several integrative perspectives are presented in Chap. 2. There are two main differences between other theoretical traditions and the theories that Orlikowski and Iacono (2001) call the ensemble view of information technology and organization. First, the ensemble-view theories argue that information technologies include not only the technological artifacts, but also the social and organizational structures around those artifacts. Second, these theories recognize that there is a dynamic and complex interaction between social structures and information technologies. Therefore, social structures do not determine the characteristics of information technologies and information technologies do not automatically change social structures. Some examples of these more integrative views are structuration theory, socio-technical systems theory, social informatics, and institutional theory.

After reviewing these different theories that take into consideration the dynamic interplay between information technologies and organizational structures, institutional theory (as represented by the technology enactment framework) was selected as the foundation for this research. Fountain's technology enactment theory is suitable for doing research about different stages or processes such as selection, design, implementation, and use of information technologies. In addition, consistent with its institutional theoretical basis, this framework allows the organization to be the main unit of analysis. Finally, institutions are essential in government settings and relatively few previous studies have developed or applied institutional theory to e-government phenomena. Therefore, this study uses an extension and elaboration of the technology enactment framework to better understand the complex relationships between e-government success (as the enacted technology and its organizational outputs and outcomes) and different organizational, institutional, and contextual variables. The theoretical framework proposed in this book—enacting electronic government success—is based mainly on the technology enactment framework, the process model of computing change, and some important ideas related to the concept of multiple enactments and the social construction of reality perspective.

Methodologically, this study uses a mixed method approach called nested research design. The research design and methods are described in Appendix 1.

Nested research encompasses statistical analysis and case study research. First, a statistical analysis was performed using organizational characteristics and institutional arrangements as independent variables and the functionality of government-wide state websites as the dependent variable. The use of partial least squares (PLS) as the statistical technique allowed the testing of multiple relationships simultaneously, in contrast with previous studies that focused on one or a few variables and had to ignore other important factors and their relationships. Second, from the results of the statistical analysis, two cases were selected based on their relative fitness to the model (residuals) and the functionality of their websites. Finally, case studies were developed for both selected states (New York and Indiana). These cases involved multiple data collection techniques such as analysis of documents and semi-structured interviews. State governments were selected as the cases because there was already good work based on local governments (Kraemer et al. 1989) and federal agencies (Fountain 2001c). Therefore, this study attempts to fill a gap in the literature and enrich previous integrative models, by adding evidence at the state level.

Chapter 3 presents a partial least squares (PLS) analysis using information from all 50 states in the US. This is one of the very few quantitative accounts of institutional development in e-government research. In fact, the study represents probably the first attempt to quantitatively operationalize the technology enactment framework. The chapter contains the operationalization of the constructs, some graphs and descriptive statistics, and the results of the measurement and structural models from the PLS analysis. A theory refinement effort using nested models and a summary of the results are also included in this chapter. The theoretical constructs for this research are electronic government success, organizational structures and processes, institutional arrangements and environmental condition. E-government success is measured in terms of organizational outcomes and outputs and government-wide website functionality. The construct organizational structures and processes is divided into (1) general organizational factors: size of the organization, budget allocation, and special training for professionals; and (2) management strategies and practices: outsourced or in-house development and marketing. The institutional arrangements' construct uses indicators such as the presence of civil service in the IT organization, accessibility standards, authority through executive orders and existence of a legislative specific IT committee. Finally, the environmental conditions refer to demographic characteristics, political orientation and competition, and the overall size of the economy. The statistical analysis found three factors that directly influence e-government success: management strategies and practices, general organizational characteristics, and the availability of resources for government agencies, represented by the overall size of the economy. These and other results are explained in more detail throughout the chapter.

The two case studies, New York and Indiana, are described in detail in Chaps. 4 and 5. The structure of these two chapters is the same and maps to the main theoretical constructs of the enacting e-government success framework. Each chapter begins with a description of the government-wide website functionality, its technical features, and the services it provides, which jointly represent the enacted technology in the state. It also describes the organizational benefits for different stakeholders at the local and state government level. Then the organizational structures and processes are divided into (1) management strategies and practices and (2) general organizational characteristics. Institutional arrangements are then analyzed for each state, looking at accessibility and other standards, the involvement of the legislative branch, the support and authority of the executive, and the civil service policy for IT workers. The last construct, environmental conditions, is described in terms of political orientation, demographic factors, and data about the overall size of the economy. Final comments are also provided for each of the two cases.

Chapter 6 highlights the theoretical and methodological contributions of the study, compares and explains the results in terms of the quantitative and qualitative analyses, and provides some practical recommendations for government professionals. For the presentation of the overall results, this section is organized in terms of the main constructs used in this research: (1) enacted technology, (2) organizational outputs and outcomes, (3) management strategies and practices, (4) general organizational characteristics, (5) institutional arrangements, and (6) environmental conditions. The chapter describes some of the variables and specific mechanisms that help to understand e-government success. It also compares and contrasts some of the results with previous studies. The practical recommendations are derived from both the statistical analysis and the two in-depth case studies. Therefore, they are expected to be general enough to be applied to other realities, but at the same time provide specific examples that could be useful to better understand how to think about and implement each recommendation.

Finally, drawing on the results of the statistical analysis and the two case studies, Chap. 7 presents the overall conclusions of the study and suggests areas for future research. The conclusions of this study are widely applicable to e-government success. For instance, they are relevant and useful to understand new applications and tools, such as Web 2.0, social media, open government, cloud computing, or inter-organizational information integration. They are also applicable to many local governments around the world that are just starting their e-government efforts. Thus, the research is very timely and the lessons presented here are directly relevant to many government agencies (national, regional, and local) in developing countries.

In summary, this research had two complementary and intertwined purposes. First, the study contributes to the development of a sound theoretical framework to understand the complex and dynamic relationships between information technologies and social structures in government settings. Understanding how different social and organizational factors affect and are affected by information technologies contributes to the development of better theoretical models and builds on previous academic research. Second, this improved knowledge should have direct and indirect practical implications for the success of e-government initiatives. Thus, this study also provides practical recommendations about information and technology management and policy in government settings, particularly in relation to e-government success measures and success factors. The book is a small step towards realizing the promises of information technologies for governments, citizens, and society.

Chapter 1
Electronic Government Success: Definition, Measures, and Factors

Practitioners and academics around the world increasingly talk about e-government success and how important it is to understand this concept for better evaluating current government IT efforts. For this book e-government success is represented by the achievement of the initiatives' stated goals, but not only in terms of activities, but also in terms of processes, outputs, and outcomes, which together represent a much broader set of success measures. Therefore, in order to truly comprehend e-government success, it is necessary first to understand what e-government is and what its success measures and success factors are. This chapter starts with a review of e-government conceptualizations and proposes a comprehensive definition of this phenomenon to be used in theory and practice. Then, the chapter identifies several ways to understand e-government success measures and describes them in the context of old, current, and emergent technologies. After this, the chapter explains the importance of key e-government success factors and groups them in a more manageable number of categories. Finally, some gaps in the literature are identified and potential solutions are proposed and briefly explained. The following chapter attempts to solve the two main limitations identified in this chapter.

E-government could be thought of as a totally new phenomenon triggered by the introduction of the Internet and related technologies. In contrast, e-government could also be understood as the new term to represent the use of information and communication technologies in government settings—a new label for an old phenomenon with a long academic history. I take this second approach. My proposal is that e-government is one of many terms used to represent and describe a complex socio-technical phenomenon that has been studied for several decades. New technologies are continuously emerging and expand its object of study, but the overall phenomenon is still the same. Following this perspective, e-government is or should be a broad concept that includes socio-technical aspects of the selection, design, implementation, and use of any kind of information and communication technology in government, from fax machines and mainframe computers to complex websites, Web 2.0 tools, social media, and open government applications. As one of its

J. R. Gil-Garcia, *Enacting Electronic Government Success*, Integrated Series in Information Systems 31, DOI: 10.1007/978-1-4614-2015-6_1,

objectives, this chapter attempts to assess the theoretical concept of e-government from multiple perspectives and to devise a comprehensive working definition to guide this study and to be proposed for other researchers to use in future studies. This definition is specific enough to be used in the development of policies and programs too.

Understanding the concept of e-government is a first important step towards assessing the success of e-government initiatives, but it is not the only necessary one. It is also essential to have measures that help managers and researchers to know if these IT initiatives have accomplished their stated goals and objectives. This chapter includes a series of success measures in terms of characteristics, features, results, benefits, outputs, and outcomes of government IT projects. Each of them is briefly described considering previous studies and their potential applicability for assessing the success of e-government initiatives. It is important to clarify that success measures in the context of this book include elements that go well beyond the efficiency value proposition. Considering the nature and goals of government organizations, they also include other important aspects such as service quality, transparency, openness, accountability, citizen participation, policy effectiveness, and the development of an adequate legal framework, among others.

While e-government success measures help to assess if an initiative has accomplished its initial objectives and goals, they are very limited for identifying the reasons behind this success or recommending how to improve performance. For this more detailed information, we also need to understand e-government success factors. This chapter identifies and explains a series of information, technology, organizational, institutional, and environmental factors that have an impact on the selection, design, implementation, and use of information and communication technologies in government settings. Following is a very brief discussion about the different terms used to describe government use of IT as initial background for the rest of this chapter.

1.1 Many Terms and a Single Phenomenon?

Despite the fact that many people use the term e-government, there is no clear consensus about what electronic government means. What is and is not included in this concept? Why or why not use the term "electronic government" to represent the use of information technologies in government settings? Is there a more appropriate use for this and other similar terms? This book argues that electronic government is simply a new label for a very important phenomenon that has been around in theory and practice for several decades, namely government information and communication technologies. According to this vision, electronic government would include myriad tools and applications from fax machines and mainframe computing to social media and open government strategies. In addition, electronic government does not refer to technological artifacts only, but also to the social and organizational aspects and elements around those artifacts. Electronic government is a socio-technical phenomenon. This section briefly describes some of the terms used to talk about the selection, design, implementation, management, and use of information technologies in government settings.

Not all scholars agree with a broad conceptualization of electronic government. In fact, research articles from diverse disciplines and perspectives use different terms to talk about technology in organizations, and specifically about information technologies in government. Some researchers focus on information systems (Antonio Cordella and Iannacci 2010; Grimsley and Meehan 2007; Kraemer et al. 1989; Meneklis and Douligeris 2010; Petter et al. 2008; Shea and Garson 2010; Southon et al. 1999; Walsham and Han 1991), while others prefer the term information management (Andersen et al. 1994; Banerjee 1984; Fedorowicz et al. 2010; Fourie 2010; Aleš Groznik et al. 2008; Klischewski and Scholl 2008; McNabb and Barnowe 2009).

Another group of authors use the term information technology, which encompasses a great variety of hardware and software applied in organizational settings (Bandyopadhyay and Sattarzadeh 2010; Caves and Walshok 1999; Demeester 1999; Ghapanchi et al. 2008; Gottschalk 2009; Kling and Lamb 2000; Lai and Mahapatra 1997; Roberts and Henderson 2000; Robey and Sahay 1996; Rosacker and Rosacker 2010; Tsai et al. 2009; Ubaldi and Roy 2010). Only in relatively recent publications have scholars and practitioners used the term "electronic government" (or digital government) in reference to the selection, design, implementation, and use of information and communication technologies in government agencies (Baqir and Iyer 2010; Bekkers and Homburg 2005; Chadwick and May 2003; Dawes and Pardo 2002; Fountain 2001a, 2008; Garson 2004; Griffin et al. 2007; Hardy and Williams 2011; Helbig et al. 2009b; Hu et al. 2009; Hwang et al. 1999; Lenk 2006; Luna-Reyes et al. 2010; Margetts 2003; Moon 2002; Pratchett 2004; Rorissa et al. 2010; Seifert and Chung 2009; Silcock 2001; Whitson and Davis 2001; Zouridis and Thaens 2005).

Some authors are now proposing the term e-governance in order to represent more inclusive technology-enabled decision-making in government structures and the relationships between government and other social actors (Bissessar 2010; Chen and Hsieh 2009; Choudhari et al. 2011; Frissen 1999; Gulati et al. 2010; Gupta 2010; Luna-Reyes et al. 2010; Norris 2010; Rahman 2010; Rorissa et al. 2010; Snellen 2002). Similar aspects have been proposed before within the terms electronic democracy or electronic policy as components of a broader conceptualization of e-government or of a digital state (6, 2001; Meghan Cook and LaVigne 2002; Chadwick 2003; Dawes 2002; Fountain 2001a; Gil-Garcia and Luna-Reyes 2006).

At first, these definitional differences seem to be related to the evolution of technology. Early researchers concentrated on information management and information systems, probably because of the adoption of early computers in government and their ability to manage data. Then, with the proliferation of a variety of types of hardware, software, and organizational technologies, focus began to shift to information technologies. The introduction of the Internet and the possibility of having direct transactional relationships with citizens or customers prompted terms such as e-commerce, e-business, and e-government. However, academic publications do not show a clear pattern and many of these terms are still in use. In fact, in some cases they are used to represent very similar phenomena and could be considered synonyms.

Adding to this complexity is the fact that electronic government research comes from at least three different disciplinary traditions: Public Administration, Management Information Systems, and Information Science (Scholl 2009). Even the more general Information Systems field continues to be "haunted by feelings of inadequacy [since it] lacks a theoretic core" (Lyytinen and King 2006, p. 233). Therefore, it is not unexpected that some e-government scholars share these feelings. In addition, there are many important concepts from different disciplines with multiple interrelations to take into consideration. These concepts include open government, social media, Web 2.0, strategy, public information, smart cities, smart communities, cultural aspects, organizational factors, user demand, competitiveness, politics, trust, digital divide, data quality, social impacts of technology, security, privacy, and many more. The multiplicity and diversity of concepts from different disciplines enrich and increase the explanatory power of the emergent interdisciplinary field of e-government, but at the same time generate some important challenges.

1.2 Defining Electronic Government

In order to understand the success of electronic government, it is first necessary to have a good definition of the e-government phenomenon. Within the last decade, the term electronic government and its abbreviations of e-government or e-gov have been used as much in political speech as in journalistic work, and more recently appear in academic writing. There is no clear consensus with respect to what electronic government is and what its main characteristics are (Baqir and Iyer 2010; Hardy and Williams 2011; Heeks 2005; Hu et al. 2010; Luna-Reyes et al. 2010; Margetts 2003; Rahman 2010; Rorissa et al. 2011; Yildiz 2007). Some authors argue that it is almost impossible to fully comprehend the meaning, challenges, and potential of electronic government as a concept (Gil-Garcia and Luna-Reyes 2007; Lenk and Traunmüller 2001; Prins 2001; Schelin 2003).

This section presents conceptual approaches to electronic government and then analyzes their differences, similarities, and conceptual amplitude. Several authors in different countries have developed their own definitions and approaches; some of them are presented here. The main characteristics of the conceptual approaches are then compared and a more comprehensive definition of electronic government is assembled and proposed as a working definition for this study and for other researchers to consider in future research. The definition crafted in this chapter is broad and includes myriad strategies and applications of information technologies to government settings. Each of these individual applications could be considered a good example of electronic government as a socio-technical phenomenon and, therefore, a good case to study. They can be seen as complementary components, but also as individual instances of the e-government phenomenon.

There are three different approaches in the academic literature to understand the concept of electronic government (Gil-Garcia and Luna-Reyes 2003, 2006; Schelin 2003). The first conceptual approach takes an evolutionary perspective: electronic government is defined by referring to the stages that seem to exist in its development. A second view assembles a precise definition, which contains what are, or should be, the main characteristics of electronic government. The third and final conceptual approach entails listing the different variants or applications of e-government in terms of the various stakeholders that governments encounter.

1.2.1 Evolutionary Approach: The Stages of Electronic Government

A first way to define electronic government is by constructing a series of stages through which different governments are journeying (Andersen and Henriksen 2006; Baqir and Iyer 2010; Criado and Ramillo 2003; Gil-Garcia and Martinez-Moyano 2004; Gil-Garcia and Martinez-Moyano 2007; Kim and Grant 2010; Layne and Lee 2001; Markaki et al. 2010; Moon 2002; Ojha et al. 2011; Reddick 2004; Rorissa et al. 2011; Rorissa et al. 2010; Sandoval Almazan and Gil-Garcia 2008; Valdés et al. 2011). This approach contains the assumption that there is an evolution toward electronic government. Some authors contend that each one of the stages is already electronic government, while others limit electronic government to the more advanced stages.

Gil-Garcia and Martinez-Moyano (2007) present a model of seven stages as a summary of several e-government evolutionary models (Hiller and Bélanger 2001; Layne and Lee 2001; UN and ASPA 2002): (1) initial presence, (2) extended presence, (3) interactive presence, (4) transactional presence, (5) vertical integration, (6) horizontal integration, and (7) total integration (see Fig. 1.1). The stages should be considered useful for analytical purposes only as they are not necessarily progressive or mutually exclusive (Gil-Garcia and Martinez-Moyano 2007; Lee 2010; Sandoval Almazan and Gil-Garcia 2008).

Initial Presence. The most basic stage focuses on sorting government information and organizing its presentation through Web pages, mostly developed by single government agencies (Baqir and Iyer 2010; Joseph 2010; Kim and Grant 2010; Layne and Lee 2001; Markaki et al. 2010; Ojha et al. 2011; Rorissa et al. 2011). Many of the first electronic government initiatives (national, regional, or local) began in this stage, and some are still trying to consolidate their presence in cyberspace (Al-Busaidy and Weerakkody 2011; Joseph 2010; Klievink and Janssen 2009a; Lee 2010; Rorissa et al. 2010; Sandoval-Almazan and Gil-Garcia 2010; Tsai et al. 2009). Generally, in this stage there is limited public information, some indexes that facilitate search, and, in the best cases, forms that can be obtained directly from the websites (Layne and Lee 2001). These sites normally

Fig. 1.1 A seven stage model for electronic government evolution (based on Gil-Garcia and Martinez-Moyano 2007)

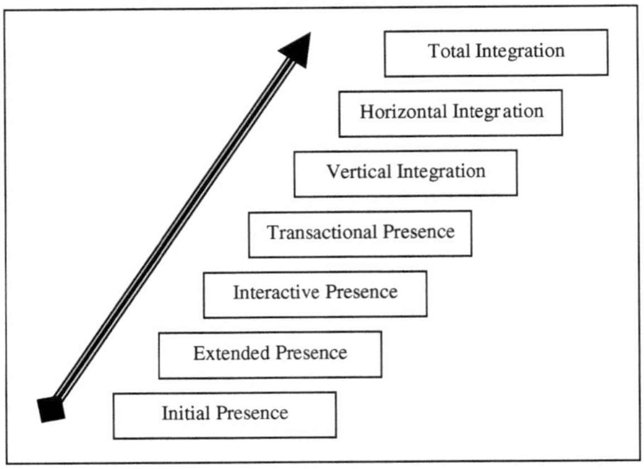

work solely as sources of public information, presenting static pages about the government and its different secretariats, ministries, agencies, directors, etc. On some occasions these sites contain other functions such as "Frequently Asked Questions" or "Additional Information" links (UN and ASPA 2002), but no channels for interaction or transactions.

Extended Presence. In this stage, citizens have access to dynamic and specialized information that is updated through a great number of official government websites (Al Nagia and Hamdan 2009; Baqir and Iyer 2010; Chun et al. 2010; Grönlund 2010; Joseph 2010; Markaki et al. 2010). Sometimes the official website of the national government serves as an entry point that contains links to pages for other branches of government, ministries, secretariats, departments, and sub-national administrations. In this stage, citizens also have access to governmental publications, legislation, and other documents, which they can request electronically through the website or directly download in some standard format. Sometimes they use simple interaction forms such as search engines or electronic mail.

Interactive Presence. This stage is when governments begin to take advantage of the Internet's potential as a useful way to interact with citizens, businesses, and other stakeholders. A government-wide portal normally serves as the initial page where people can find links to the different ministries, secretariats, departments, etc. (Hiller and Bélanger 2001; UN and ASPA 2002). Greater interaction occurs between citizens and government agencies, since users can access information according to their interests and needs (Baqir and Iyer 2010; Ebbers et al. 2008; McNeal et al. 2008; Ojha et al. 2011; Seifert and Chung 2009). In addition, this scheme permits citizens to interact with government any time, at any place. In some cases these sites use passwords as a way to allow for more customized and secure interaction. For Layne and Lee (2001), this stage signals the beginning of electronic government as an authentic way to transform the relationships between government and citizens. This change has the potential to not only improve the quality of services and increase efficiency in government organizations, but it can also promote citizen participation by creating a fast and simple channel for communicating with their authorities (Ahn and Bretschneider 2011; Ebbers et al. 2008; Hughes 2011; Layne and Lee 2001; Markaki et al. 2010; Seifert and Chung 2009).

Transactional Presence. In this stage, citizens have the option of carrying out secure transactions to complete government procedures using government websites (Baqir and Iyer 2010; Joseph 2010; Kim and Grant 2010; Lee 2010; Markaki et al. 2010). Some examples of the processes that can be carried out are visas, passports, death and birth certificates, and licenses, among others. Sometimes, the portal allows users to personalize it and create a consolidated presentation of the governmental services of interest to them. Generally, access is organized according to people's needs instead of government functions or structure. The portal allows users to make electronic payments via secure sites, which facilitates transactions like payment of taxes, fines, and fees (Economides and Terzis 2008; Fedorowicz et al. 2009; Sancak and Güleç 2010; Tan and Benbasat 2009). In addition, in order to perform electronic payments, an institutional framework recognizes and facilitates the use of electronic signatures (Gil-Garcia and Martinez-Moyano 2007).

Vertical Integration. This stage involves the virtual and/or physical integration of government organizations that are responsible for a common function or serve similar clients across the different levels of government (Gil-Garcia and Martinez-Moyano 2007; Gottschalk 2009; Klievink and Janssen 2009b; Moflesh et al. 2009; Ojha et al. 2011; Sancak and Güleç 2010; Ubaldi and Roy 2010). Therefore, this stage refers not only to an incipient integration in the form of government websites, but to the change and reconstruction of processes and governmental structures. According to Layne and Lee (2001), once most services are provided through electronic means, citizens will have higher expectations and vertical integration will become a necessary transformation. Some governmental functions, like criminal justice, health, and education, have developed initiatives that try to obtain, to a certain degree, this type of integration (Antonio Cordella and Iannacci 2010; Cresswell and Connelly 1999; Taylor et al. 2006). Due to the great number and complexity of the services government provides and taking into consideration the small number of government levels, vertical integration is likely to take place before horizontal integration (Layne and Lee 2001).

Horizontal Integration. Layne and Lee (2001) argue that to obtain all the potential of information technologies in government from a citizen perspective, horizontal integration between different government services, agencies, and policy domains is crucial. In order to accomplish this kind of integration, it is necessary to cross organizational boundaries and develop a comprehensive vision of the government as a whole (Assar et al. 2011; Baqir and Iyer 2010; Grönlund 2010; Klievink and Janssen 2009a; Lux Wigand 2010). This stage clearly requires a radical and very complex transformation in the distribution of intra- and inter-organizational power (Bruce Rocheleau 2003). It also relies on the development of trust and creative collaboration models among government agencies (Chen 2010; Gottschalk 2009; Pardo et al. 2006; Ubaldi and Roy 2010; Williams et al. 2010; Zheng et al. 2009).

Total Integration. This is the most advanced stage of this classification. Since citizens typically do not understand the complex organization of government, a totally integrated presence describes when a government provides all services through a single portal that works like an integrated window, a unique window, or a vestibule (Baqir and Iyer 2010; dos Santos and Reinhard forthcoming; Gant et al. 2002; Kim and Grant 2010; Klievink and Janssen 2009b; Lee 2010). Using this window, citizens can access all the information, products, and services they require in their interactions with government. Governments offer all services online and these are grouped according to the different needs of citizens without concern for internal functions, jurisdictions, or other structural and procedural divisions. This stage involves the integration of databases, processes, and, in some cases, government structures. Therefore, governments would need to undertake institutional and administrative reforms that fully employ the potential of information technologies to achieve this stage (Bandyopadhyay and Sattarzadeh 2010; Baqir and Iyer 2010; Bertot et al. 2010; Gil-Garcia et al. 2010; Gil-Garcia and Martinez-Moyano 2007; Hanna 2011; Seongcheol Kim et al. 2009; Navarra 2010; Rahman 2010; Seifert and Chung 2009).

Electronic government entails more than the evolutionary process of systems and technologies, as it results from organizational, institutional, and administrative practices too. In addition, a broad definition of electronic government should consider elements other than websites and the use of Internet. They are clearly an important component and good examples of current e-government initiatives, but they are not the only ones. Therefore, electronic government encompasses a much more complex phenomenon, one that extends well beyond Internet technologies (Gil-Garcia and Luna-Reyes 2008). The following section deals with a different way to conceptualize e-government. This second approach attempts to list and describe the main components or characteristics of electronic government as a concept.

1.2.2 Definitional Approach: The Elements of Electronic Government

The second approach refers to identifying conceptual elements and building an actual definition of electronic government. Various and very diverse definitions were found from a review of the existing literature. Each definition emphasizes particular elements that should be considered in the theoretical distinction between electronic government and similar concepts related to the use of information technologies (Baqir and Iyer 2010; Homburg and Snellen 2007; Hood and Margetts 2007; Hu et al. 2009; Luna-Reyes et al. 2010; Maumbe et al. 2008; Reddick 2010; Rose and Grant 2010; Shareef et al. 2009). Most of the current definitions of electronic government can be summarized with four basic elements. Electronic government is characterized by (a) the use of ICTs (computer networks, internet, telephones, and faxes), (b) the support of governmental actions (to provide information, services, administration, products), (c) the improvement of government relationships with citizens (through the creation of new communication channels or the promotion of citizen engagement in the political or administrative process), and (d) the use of a strategy to add value to the participants in the process (Gil-Garcia and Luna-Reyes 2006). Also, a comprehensive view comprising various conceptual elements of e-government has been recently developed (Hu et al. 2009).

Despite some interesting similarities, there are still important differences between definitions of electronic government (Heeks and Bailur 2007; Hu et al. 2009; Moflesh et al. 2009; Verdegem and Verleye 2009). Grönlund and Horan (2004, p. 714) argue that "all definitions of e-Gov go beyond services to the citizen to include organizational change and the role of government". In contrast, for Zweers and Planqué (2001) electronic government is mainly related to the provision of information, services, or products through electronic means that can be obtained at any time and place through different government agencies, offering added value for all the participants in the transaction (Gil-Garcia and Luna-Reyes 2003). Electronic government can also be seen as the use of information technologies to support government actions and to provide services to citizens (Meghan Cook and LaVigne 2002; LaVigne 2002). Other authors "define e-government simply as the provision of governmental services and information through electronic means, 24 h a day, seven days a week" (Holden et al. 2003, p. 327). More recently, e-government is still defined in very different ways, from "the use of information technology to free movement of information and overcome the physical bounds of traditional paper and physical based systems" to "the use of technology to enhance the access to and delivery of government services to benefit citizens, business partners, and employees." (Pascual 2009; Sancak and Güleç 2010, p. 333). For Grönlund (2001), it is more important to obtain *strategic* use of these information technologies in the public sector.

In addition to internal operations and the provision of services, Dawes (2002) adds that electronic government also encompasses citizen engagement, since the participation of people is very important for political processes. On the same matter, Galindo (2002) argues that electronic government consists of the different relationships that exist between citizens and authorities as a result of the use of electronic tools, specifically the Internet, as a way for citizens to exert their political rights (Ahn and Bretschneider 2011; Gulati et al. 2010; Kang and Gearhart 2010; Reddick 2010). Another way to understand electronic government is as the practical use of innovative information and communication technologies, like the Internet, for efficient and effective provision of services, information, and knowledge (ASPA 2001). From this perspective, e-government entails the use of all types of information and communication technologies, from a fax machine to a cellular network to social media applications, to ease the daily administration of government (UNPAN 2002). In addition, there are different modes of information sharing technologies fueled by the new emergent technology developments in the context of Web 2.0, where website users can collaboratively create content through wikis, forums, and blogs. In this scenario, the information collected by government is increasingly the result of the active participation of citizens and businesses (Gil-Garcia et al. 2009; Hrdinová et al. 2010).

According to a recent study, social networking tools like blogs, wikis, RSS feeds, and social networking sites like Twitter, Facebook and LinkedIN "can help with current challenges facing today's government agencies such as brain drain from a retiring workforce, the need to create inter-agency knowledge sharing, and an increased need to imbed talent tools where the work is done" (Saba 2010, p. 2). But new technologies also come with new challenges. For instance, "as mobile devices become the preferred way to access information and conduct transactions, online government will need to adapt" (*State of the Portal: A Review of the 50 States'Online Offerings* 2010, p. 5).

An additional common definition of electronic government is one that (as in the case of the electronic commerce) relates it almost exclusively to actions conducted through the Internet that improve citizen access to public information and government services (UNPAN 2002). Similarly, for the Organization for Economic Cooperation and Development, e-government is "the use of information and communication technologies, and particularly the Internet, as a tool to achieve better government" (OECD 2003, p. 23). Other organizations' definitions are similar to the OECD's. The European Union clearly addresses e-government as part of its website for the new *i2020* action plan,[1] which states that e-government is "about using the tools and systems made possible by Information and Communication Technologies (ICTs) to provide better public services to citizens and businesses." The Organization of American States describes it in a broader way: "E-government uses information and communication technology to help governments become more accessible to constituents, improve services and efficiency, and become more connected to other parts of the society." Finally, the United Nations (2010), in its recent e-government survey report, addresses e-government as a means of enhancing the capacity of the public sector, together with citizens, to address particular development issues; it is never an end in itself.

Scholl (2002a) mentions different forms of electronic government definitions. Some of them include or solely emphasize the benefit of services through electronic means or a network of computers. Others try to expand the limits of this concept and include the commitment and participation of citizens in the administrative and political processes of government. In his brief overview, there are definitions that encompass very diverse aspects of governmental action: some that consider electronic services as the main or only element of electronic government and others that integrate the improvement of internal management and the promotion of citizen participation as important elements of this concept. More recently, Hu et al. (2009) provide details of a study on the widely shared definitions of e-government and to help scholars–especially young scholars—understand the scope and meaning of the field, scanning e-government research in a 10-year time frame (from 1998 to 2007). They identified six definitional components from a wide array of extant literature defining e-government: (1) these initiatives encompass the management and delivery of information and public services; (2) they include all levels of governments;

---

[1] http://ec.europa.eu/information_society/activities/egovernment/index_en.htm

(3) they are developed on behalf of citizens, business, and other stakeholders; (4) they use multiple tools and applications of the Internet, systems integration, and interoperability; (5) their objective is to enhance the quality and security of services (information, communication, policy making); and (6) they have become a new key strategy or approach (Hu et al. 2009, p. 979).

A similar way to develop an understanding of electronic government is by listing its main elements or components. “E-Government is one of those concepts that means a lot of different things to a lot of different groups” (Grant and Chau 2005, p. 2). Authors like Perri 6 (2001) argue that three groups of activities exist under the label of electronic government: (1) electronic governance, (2) electronic democracy, and (3) electronic services. This author concludes that most of the effort, resources, and political attention of citizens and private organizations have been devoted to the provision of online services. Activities of electronic governance encompass support for policy design and decision-making, institutional development, and administration. Finally, public participation and electronic voting characterize electronic democracy (Gil-Garcia and Luna-Reyes 2006).

Likewise, authors like Cook and LaVigne (2002) and Dawes (2002) assert that the concept of electronic government incorporates four essential dimensions: (1) electronic management, (2) electronic services, (3) electronic commerce, and (4) electronic democracy. Electronic management is the use of information technologies to improve the administrative component of government, contemplating an ample range of possibilities that go from the redesign of work processes to the maintenance of electronic records to the integration of information across different agencies. Electronic services refer to the governmental provision of information, programs, and services, frequently—but not exclusively—through the Internet. Electronic commerce relates to the electronic interchange of money for goods and services such as vehicle registrations, driver’s licenses, and procurement, among others. Finally, electronic democracy is the use of electronic communications to increase citizens’ participation in the public decision-making process (Dawes 2002). Gil-Garcia and Luna-Reyes (2007) propose an alternate category of e-policy instead of e-commerce. In this view, e-commerce and e-services should be in a single category, since a service could imply the electronic interchange of money for goods or not. In contrast, e-policy should be in a separate category, because it refers to the creation of a legal framework (laws, regulations, policies, and other rules) that promotes information intensive initiatives and fosters the knowledge society. It could be related to e-governance in terms of policy design and decision-making.

1.2.3 Stakeholder-Oriented Approach: The Relationships Between Government and Other Entities

A final way to understand e-government is to categorize its components according to the type of relationships that exist between government and other entities (Bandyopadhyay and Sattarzadeh 2010; Brown and Brudney 2004; Fedorowicz et al. 2010; Gil-Garcia and Luna-Reyes 2008; Hiller and Bélanger 2001; Luk 2009; Markaki et al. 2010; Means and Schneider 2000; Moon 2002; Rowley 2011; Schelin 2003; Shareef et al. 2009). This approach relies fundamentally on a commerce-like model and, therefore, concentrates on the use of the Internet as a tool that improves and aids how government functions in its relations with citizens (G2C—Government to Citizen), private organizations (G2B—Government to Business), or other governments (G2G—Government to Government). Describing the concept in another way, Holmes (2001) identifies three main relations that he called the ABC of electronic government: (1) Administration to Citizen, (2) Administration to Business, and (3) Administration to Administration.

Government to Citizen (*G to C*). Perhaps the best-known potential of electronic government is its capacity to improve the variety and quality of the services that governments can provide to their citizens. From this view, the Internet allows governments to serve better, while also promoting greater transparency and clearer accountability. The use of government websites to make public information accessible, to provide services online, and to facilitate the interaction between the citizen and the government are examples of this type of relationship (Ancarani 2005; Holmes 2001; Kanat and Özkan 2009; Lux Wigand 2010; Markaki et al. 2010; Pina et al. 2009; Rahman 2010; Teo et al. 2008).

Government to Business (*G to B*). Private corporations use computers connected to the Internet. This access is especially important in developing countries where the use of personal computers by citizens is very limited, but organizational use is more widespread. Consequently, e-government has enormous potential for improving the relationships between private companies and governments (Bandyopadhyay and Sattarzadeh 2010; Hogrebe et al. 2009; Hussin and Kassim 2010; Liu and Tan 2010; Lu et al. 2010; Lux Wigand, 2010; Markaki et al. 2010; Olbrich 2010). For some authors, this association is not just about the services that government provides to different businesses, but also refers to products and services that the government buys or contracts from private companies.

Government to Government (*G to G*). Often the activities of government require sharing different types of information, products, or services across agencies or jurisdictions. Intergovernmental collaboration is frequently used to provide certain services that require a broad territorial base and detailed processes for the selection of clients, like healthcare or welfare. Electronic government has the potential to facilitate relationships between government agencies, different levels of government, and even among the executive, legislative, and judicial branches (Bandyopadhyay and Sattarzadeh, 2010; Joia 2008; Lux Wigand 2010; Makedon et al. 2010; Moflesh et al. 2009; Zarei and Ghapanchi 2008).

The different categories presented thus far try to capture all the possible relations of government with other entities. Nevertheless, authors like Hiller and Bélanger (2001) believe that due to the importance and peculiarities of certain types of interactions, more specific categories are necessary (see Fig. 1.2). To the previously described relationships, these authors add three more categories: (1) Government to Individuals as Part of the Political Process (G2IP), (2) Government to Companies in the Market (G2BMKT), and (3) Government to Employees (G2E).

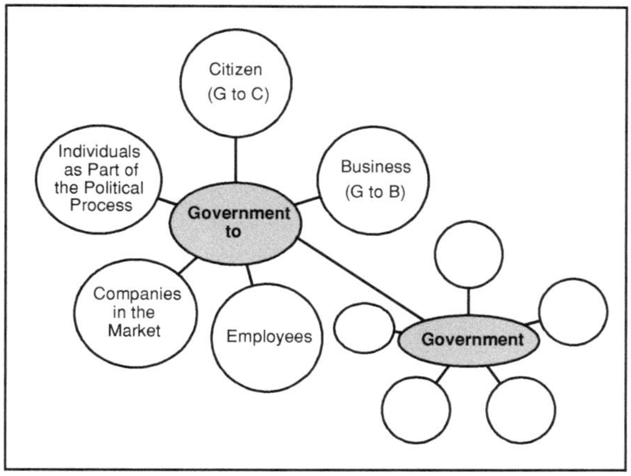

Fig. 1.2 Relationships between a government and other entities

Government to Individuals as Part of the Political Process. The first difference that these authors observe is one derived from the democratic process. The electronic interaction that citizens have with the government when participating in a public policy decision or when voting for their representatives is not the same as the interaction they engage in for the provision of a service. It is essential to understand this difference, since this type of relationship is one that most distinguishes electronic government from any use of information technologies in the private sector. These relationships are clearly related to the emergent concept of electronic democracy (Bandyopadhyay and Sattarzadeh 2010; Brainard and McNutt 2010; Gulati et al. 2010; Kavanaugh et al. 2010; Norris 2010; Rahman 2010).

Government to Companies in the Market. These authors consider the relations between governments and companies to be dual in nature. Companies, like individuals, receive services from government. Nevertheless, the greatest volume of transactions between government and private companies is related to governmental purchases (Badri and Alshare 2008; Ales Groznik and Trkman 2009). There are potential benefits in the use of electronic government for this type of activity, such as savings derived from complete online transactions, better services from suppliers connected to an integrated network, or even greater transparency in procurement processes.

Government to Employees. Hiller and Bélanger (2001) note that the relationships governments have with their employees are very different from the relationships they have with citizens. A government can improve its internal management through better use of information technologies in the workplace (Christensen and Laeliggreid 2010; Gascó 2007; Jun and Weare forthcoming; Seongcheol Kim et al. 2009; Lux Wigand 2010; Olbrich 2010). One example, similar to private companies, is the use of an intranet in order to improve communication with employees (Singh 2009; Williams 2008). Governments could also develop information systems for some human resource management procedures.

In contrast to the definitional approach, this stakeholder-oriented approach is not clear about the main elements of electronic government. It seems that there are different levels of analysis, and each pays attention to different components considered relevant for the study of electronic government. The stakeholder approach tends to expand the components of electronic government beyond the application of electronic commerce to the public sector and include political relationships and democratic mechanisms. However, this approach has a primary focus on the relationships between governments and external entities. A broader definition of electronic government should consider not only external relationships, but also internal improvements through the use of sophisticated information systems.

1.2.4 A Conceptual Foundation for Electronic Government

Certain consistent patterns appear in the literature reviewed above. This final subsection attempts to identify those common elements and construct a working definition of electronic government. First, a definition of electronic government must have solid theoretical bases, but at the same time it must be explicit and easy to implement in practical terms. The definition presented at the end of this section intends to reconcile the tensions between theory and practice. Therefore, it tries to be sufficiently powerful to reflect the theoretical framework that sustains it, and as clear and practical as possible for it to be used in relevant policies and programs (Gil-Garcia and Luna-Reyes 2006).

First, the evolutionary approach refers basically to the web, but e-government is unmistakably more than web applications and the use of the Internet. A broader definition of e-government involves the use of IT to improve a variety of government activities. In addition, this view implies that not all stages should be considered electronic government, when they all represent some form of IT use in government settings (Gil-Garcia and Luna-Reyes 2006). Any use of information technologies in government should be considered when defining electronic government, particularly because it describes a phenomenon that has actually been studied for several decades; that is, the selection, design, implementation, and use of IT (formerly computing) in government organizations.

Second, the stakeholder-oriented approach is mostly about external relationships, or the connections between a government and citizens, businesses, and other governments. However, e-government is more than external relationships. It includes the use of information technologies for improving internal operations and management. In fact, many of the systems used in government are related to internal processes and functions such as human resources, accounting, planning, and continuous improvement. A useful definition of electronic government should include initiatives focused on internal operations and improvements, because many government IT initiatives are of this kind and they should not be ignored. It is clear that the last wave of IT has been driven by Internet-related technologies and external relationships, but other technologies and internal improvements are still very important for government organizations and they should be included in a definition of electronic government.

The definitional approach includes the widest spectrum of e-government applications, elements, and characteristics. Nevertheless, such comprehensiveness makes it difficult to sort and select the essential elements in order to summarize this approach so that the categories and resulting definition make both practical and theoretical sense (Gil-Garcia and Luna-Reyes 2006). Within the definitional approach, several elements arise from the contributions of different authors (Abuali et al. 2010; Amoretti 2007; Kim Viborg Andersen 2006; Bannister and Connolly 2011; Barzilai-Nahon and Scholl 2010; John Carlo Bertot and Jaeger 2006; Bertot et al. 2010; Finger 2010; Fleming et al. 2010; Grönlund 2010; Hanna 2011; Hassan et al. 2011; Johnson 2007; Joseph and Ezzedeen 2009; Lee et al. 2011; Lee 2010; Morgeson III and Mithas 2009; Reddick 2005; Rowley 2011; Scholl 2002b; Spirakis et al. 2010; Streib and Willoughby 2010; Zissis 2011): electronic services (e-services); electronic management (e-management); electronic commerce (e-commerce); electronic personnel management (e-personnel); electronic procurement (e-procurement); electronic democracy (e-democracy); electronic participation (e-participation); electronic voting (e-voting); electronic governance (e-governance); and electronic transparency (e-transparency), among others.

Nearly every author assumes that the improvement of government services is a foundational element of electronic government. A minor number of practitioners and academics reflect on its potential for enhancing and changing internal operations and management as a primary element of electronic government. Even fewer authors acknowledge the significance of information technologies for promoting and preserving democratic values. And very few of them noticeably relate electronic government to the design of public policies that assist and endorse the development of IT initiatives and the information society: electronic public policy (e-policy) (Gil-Garcia and Luna-Reyes 2008). This situation has been changing in recent years, but some of the trends are still similar.

Rosenbloom (1998) identifies three approaches to Public Administration: managerial, political, and legal. Each of these views emphasizes different, but complementary aspects of government. Using this theoretical framework and mapping onto it the main e-government elements, government use of IT could be reorganized into two categories: e-democracy and e-management, which jointly refer to the political and managerial views (see Table 1.1) (Gil-Garcia and Luna-Reyes 2006). Still, the legal view (e-policy) must also be included. In addition to improving services and operations and promoting democratic values and mechanisms, governments should also craft a regulatory and legal framework to guide the electronic revolution. The need for a legal perspective becomes more pressing in light of the fact that information technology policies have been recognized as key factors in the success of e-government initiatives (Andersen and Dawes 1991; Baqir and Iyer 2010; Dawes 2009; Dawes and Nelson 1995; Fletcher 2004; Gil-Garcia et al. 2009; Gulati et al. 2010; Moflesh et al. 2009; Rashid and Rahman 2010; Reddick 2010; Tsai et al. 2009). Andersen and Dawes (1991) present a vision for the use of information technologies that entails three areas of

Table 1.1 Mapping electronic Government elements to public administration theory

Approaches to public administration	Managerial		Political	Legal
Electronic Government categories	E-services	E-management	E-democracy	E-policy
Electronic Government elements	E-services E-commerce E-transactions	E-management E-personnel E-procurement E-planning E-budgeting	E-democracy E-participation E-voting E-transparency E-accountability	E-policy E-governance E-rulemaking

Adapted from Gil-Garcia and Luna-Reyes (2006). Adapted with permission of the publisher

knowledge: (1) data administration and technical competence; (2) organizational and administrative skills; and (3) acknowledging the need to integrate the policy component and policy design. Complexity arises because these areas progress at different rates. While ICTs change rapidly, organizations take time to adjust, and policies evolve much more slowly (Andersen and Dawes 1991; Gil-Garcia and Luna-Reyes 2008).

A recent example of technology's rapid evolution is the application of social networks and collective content creation commonly known as Web 2.0 (Baumgarten and Chui 2009; Bertot et al. 2010; Chun et al. 2010; Gil-Garcia and Luna-Reyes 2008; Lux Wigand 2010; Misuraca 2009; Reddick 2010; Traunmüller 2010). In reference to e-policy, wiki tools are used for jointly creating documents and are commonly employed as a policy-making platform. These Web 2.0 tools can enhance transparency since the policy development involves not only collaborative writing of the content, but also a process that expresses the reasoning behind it with open dialogues among participants. This new environment introduces new and expanded challenges to government information sharing and integration (Baqir and Iyer 2010; Drogkaris et al. 2010; Gil-Garcia et al. 2009; Mergel et al. 2009; Tsui 2009; Ubaldi and Roy 2010). Fountain (2008) argues that "as these next-generation technologies become more dominant [...] they are likely to have an effect on bureaucratic policymaking processes and other unknown effects on e-government" (p. 21).

Finally, in Rosenbloom's framework, e-services are clearly related to the New Public Management perspective and its customer orientation, but are still part of the managerial view (Rosenbloom 1998). However, most authors consider e-services to be the most important component of electronic government and distinct from managerial concerns, which are generally associated with internal operations improvements and efficiency gains (Gil-Garcia and Luna-Reyes 2006). Therefore, they are kept separate from e-management, but also fall within the managerial approach.

As shown in Table 1.1, in order to build a comprehensive definition of electronic government that is valuable for both government policies and actions and for academic research and development, it must incorporate at least these four categories: e-services, e-management, e-democracy, and e-policy. Thus, *electronic government is the selection, design, implementation, and use of information and communication technologies in government to provide public services, improve managerial effectiveness, and promote democratic values and participation mechanisms, as well as the development of a legal and regulatory framework that facilitates information intensive initiatives and fosters the knowledge society* (Gil-Garcia and Luna-Reyes 2003, 2006, 2008). Accordingly, e-government policies are not only about IT projects in government, but also about creating the conditions for their success, broadly defined. While this definition is not totally comprehensive or useful for every purpose, it accounts for most of the theoretical elements found in the literature and it is pragmatic enough to be used as high-level guidance for electronic government strategies, policies, and programs.

Therefore, the overall success of electronic government should be clearly related to the achievement of goals and objectives regarding the provision of services, the improvement of managerial effectiveness (including efficiency), the promotion of participation and other democratic mechanisms, and the creation of an appropriate legal and regulatory framework (Gil-Garcia and Luna-Reyes 2007). Meeting some of these goals and objectives within an e-government initiative could be seen as being successful. Not all single initiatives will seek all the above-mentioned objectives, but it is expected that they include objectives and goals related to one or more categories. In addition, there are different ways to identify and understand success measures. However, in the public sector, success measures should go beyond efficiency and cost savings. They should include transparency, openness, policy effectiveness, service quality, and citizen participation, among others. The following section describes some of these measures in terms of characteristics, features, results, benefits, outputs, and outcomes derived from the use of information technologies in government.

1.3 Success Measures in Electronic Government Initiatives

Unmistakably, information technologies are acknowledged as one of the leading and most promising ways to change private and public organizations (Bandyopadhyay and Sattarzadeh 2010; Bannister 2007; Antonio Cordella and Iannacci 2010; Davenport 1993; Gil-Garcia and Helbig 2006; Hanna 2011; Janssen et al. 2004; Kunstelj and Vintar 2004; Laudon and Laudon 2003; Luna-Reyes et al. 2010; Olbrich 2010; Reddick 2010; Scott and Robbins 2010). As shown in Fig. 1.3 some authors note the tremendous positive impacts that information technology initiatives potentially have on government organizational structures and functions (Barrett and Greene 2000; Bissessar 2010; Markaki et al. 2010; O'Looney 2002; Olbrich 2010; Rosacker and Rosacker 2010; Seifert and Chung 2009; Streib and Willoughby 2010; van Veenstra et al. 2010). As Schelin (2003) writes, "At least potentially, IT involves the transformation of the organizational culture of government" (p. 125).

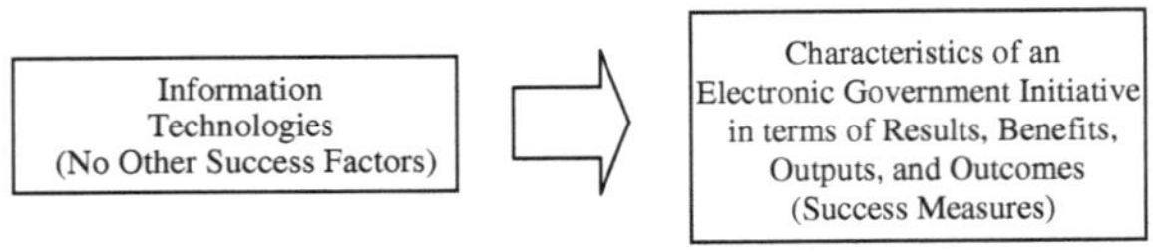

Fig. 1.3 Electronic Government success measures as organizational results, benefits, outputs, and outcomes [Adapted from Gil-Garcia and Helbig (2006). Adapted with permission of the publisher]

Decentralization, improved decision making, high quality services, empowerment, and greater productivity have been mentioned as some of the potential gains from information technology projects (Bandyopadhyay and Sattarzadeh 2010; Baqir and Iyer 2010; Antonio Cordella and Iannacci 2010; Choudhury and Kumar 2009; Seongcheol Kim et al. 2009; Peled 2001a; Rowley 2011; Schuppan 2009). Similarly, with a certain emphasis on IT results, Garson's decentralization/democratization theory states that "for democratization theorists, in the wake of the information revolution comes decentralization, because IT allows dramatic broadening of the span of control, and democratization, because knowledge, which is a critical basis of power, is also dispersed by IT" (Garson 2000b, p. 592).

All the vast literature from this technology-results vision acknowledges the transformational power of information technologies and their effects on organizational structures and outcomes (Andersen et al. 2010; Bandyopadhyay and Sattarzadeh 2010; Barrett and Greene 2000; Heeks 1999; Landsbergen and Wolken 2001; Luna-Reyes et al. 2010; Mergel et al. 2009; O'Looney 2002; Olbrich 2010; Parisopoulos et al. 2009). From this perspective, there seem to be positive results from using information technologies in organizational settings and much research has been dedicated to identifying and analyzing these potential advantages (Bloomfield and Hayes 2009; Dawes 1996; Jarque Uribe 1998; Luna-Reyes et al. 2010; Moon 2002; O'Looney 2002; OECD 2003; Prybutok et al. 2008; van Veenstra et al. 2010). Schelin (2003) argues that this has been the dominant perspective for studying e-government. Benefits from e-government initiatives are manifested in both modifications to current organizational structures and specific organizational outcomes, such as improved service quality or increased policy effectiveness. These potential positive results could be seen as measures of e-government success. The following sections present two different ways to define results from e-government initiatives and the potential problems associated with these different approaches.

1.3.1 Success Measures as Outcomes Only

A basic way to understand the results of an IT initiative is by assessing its final outcomes. From this perspective, positive effects such as transparency, efficiency, effectiveness, or service quality appear to derive directly and almost automatically from the use of IT in organizations (Bandyopadhyay and Sattarzadeh 2010; Baqir and Iyer 2010; Gil-Garcia and Helbig 2006; Luna-Reyes et al. 2010; Lux Wigand 2010; Nour et al. 2008; Rahman 2010; Sancak and Güleç 2010; Smith 2010). These positive results are considered "the reasons for embracing e-government as a means of reforming public management and contributing to broader policy objectives" (OECD 2003, p. 28). They could also be considered primary success measures, because they help to assess if an e-government initiative has achieved certain goals and objectives.

Active public participation and transparency. E-government initiatives are seen as promoting public participation, transparency, and accountability (Gulati et al. 2010; Margetts 2009; Rahman 2010; Reddick 2010). The relationship between governments and citizens involves many very important social and political factors. However, more in some countries than in others, "ICTs can act as an enabler to engage citizens in the policy process, promote open accountable government, and help prevent corruption" (OECD 2003, p. 45). Creating new communication channels is a critical component of participation: "An essential function of e-government is the access and exchange of information. E-government sites allow governments to offer new ways to interact with government, such as email, online meetings and forums for voicing opinion, online transactions, and online voting" (Jaeger 2005, p. 703).

Public participation and transparency are closely related to e-democracy. In fact, e-democracy initiatives involve much more than online voting, referring also to communication exchange between citizens and elected officials (Davis et al. 2002). However, in practice, politicians have noticed that these forums are not very helpful for their re-election purposes, because individuals who make use of electronic channels are frequently not representative of all citizens' interests (Garson 2004). In contrast, Data.gov is a good example of "the current emphasis on opening US government information to the public plus the evolving capability of technological tools for doing so, [which may] offer many opportunities to satisfy the value-creation goal of greater government transparency" (Dawes and Helbig 2010, p. 8). Therefore, the promise of greater public participation and transparency cannot be achieved without the development of easy to use and efficient communication channels between citizens and public officials (Noveck 2009; Yao et al. 2010; Zissis et al. 2009). Public participation, transparency, openness, and accountability should be seen as important ways to measure the success of e-government initiatives (Alshawi and Alalwany 2009; John Carlo Bertot et al. 2008; Chircu 2008; Pina et al. 2009; Pina et al. 2010).

Efficiency and cost reduction. The original implementation and use of information and communication technologies in government has mostly been driven by the persistent need to reduce the draw on resources (Bandyopadhyay and Sattarzadeh 2010; Baqir and Iyer 2010; Chwelos et al. 2010; Markaki et al. 2010; OECD 2003; Rahman 2010). Many of the e-government initiatives related to efficiency fall in the e-management component, such as payment processes, procurement, payroll, and human resources management (Fedorowicz et al. 2009; Fleming et al. 2010; Joseph and Ezzedeen 2009; Langford 2010; Seifert and Chung 2009). In order to obtain greater efficiency benefits from e-government initiatives, a transformation of the related business processes must take place (Baqir and Iyer 2010; Corradini et al. 2010; Kennedy et al. 2010; Pérez-Castillo et al. forthcoming).

But using efficiency as the main or even the sole goal of e-government initiatives presents several problems (OECD 2003): (1) government outcomes are difficult to quantify; (2) we lack an accepted methodology and comparable data to measure the impact of e-government at the scale of the aggregate rather than for individual projects; and (3) we lack a government-wide evaluation of the need for a particular IT service or process. Even more problematic is that initiatives such as e-procurement, once considered a cornerstone of the cost-savings movement, have performed poorly or even been abandoned (Garson 2004; Thomson 2009; Trkman and McCormack 2010). Nevertheless, efficiency and cost savings should still be considered fundamental e-government success measures.

Increased policy effectiveness. In the past, information technologies were mostly related to service quality and cost savings. However, "there is an increasing awareness that e-government initiatives can also help achieve important outcomes in major policy areas such as health, education, anti-crime initiatives, and security." (Luna-Reyes et al. 2010; Markaki et al. 2010; OECD 2003, p. 37; Olbrich 2010; Sancak and Güleç 2010). Information technologies are used not only to improve the quality of services, but also to create interesting possibilities for government, like making programs and policies more effective (Luna-Reyes et al. 2008; Luna-Reyes et al. 2010; Olbrich 2010; Park 2010; Reddick 2009a).

Some studies argue that public managers need to overcome several key challenges in order to improve policy effectiveness using ICTs (Baqir and Iyer 2010; Carter and McBride 2010; De Angelis et al. 2010; Mars and Scott 2010; OECD 2003; Rahman 2010; Rowley 2011). Some relevant examples of these elements are (1) recognition of the fact that capturing the benefits takes time, especially in complex policy areas such as education or welfare; (2) building a framework for identifying and assessing the potential contribution to the relevant policy target; and (3) privacy issues related to sharing information about individuals among different agencies involved in a policy area (OECD 2003). In spite of the difficulty of some of these challenges, increasing the effectiveness of government policies and programs should definitely be considered as a success measure of e-government initiatives.

Improvement of service quality. According to an OECD (2003) study, all the e-government statements reviewed included the primary goal of improving service quality, which is also commonly found in academic literature (Baqir and Iyer 2010; Gil-Garcia and Helbig 2006; Luna-Reyes et al. 2010; Lux Wigand 2010; Markaki et al. 2010; Rorissa et al. 2010; Sancak and Güleç 2010). Some of the specific online initiatives found in this study were (1) online portals that bring together information and transactions relating to a particular topic or group; (2) targeted customization, such as the ability to customize certain services according to individual or organizational characteristics; (3) e-mail listings that provide information about specific topics to certain groups of customers; and (4) authentication tools that help provide identified users with access to specific or customized information and transactions.

Efforts to improve the quality of government services for businesses and individuals have followed customer-oriented strategies (Baqir and Iyer 2010; Chen, 2010; Klievink and Janssen 2009b; Markaki et al. 2010; Mills et al. 2010; Morgeson III and Mithas 2009; Rorissa et al. 2010; Tan and Benbasat 2009). These strategies recognize the potential of e-government initiatives to deliver better services; however, it is imperative to acknowledge how this potential is diminished because of problems of access (Garson 2004). In some countries more than others, social groups such as the poor and certain minorities cannot enjoy the benefits or obtain meaningful value from electronic services (Bandyopadhyay and Sattarzadeh 2010; Baqir and Iyer 2010; Bélanger and Carter 2009; Helbig et al. 2009; Mariscal 2003; Norris 2001; Rahman 2010; Reddick 2010; Rorissa et al. 2010; Schuppan 2009; Warschauer 2003). Overall, it seems clear that improving the quality of government services should continue being an essential success measure for e-government initiatives.

1.3.2 Success Measures as Political, Organizational, and Technical Benefits

Academics and practitioners contend that the potential results from the use of ICTs are more than just final outcomes; they also include a significant alteration in organizational structures and the interactions among individuals inside those organizations (Åkesson and Edvardsson 2008; Bandyopadhyay and Sattarzadeh 2010; Baqir and Iyer 2010; Gil-Garcia et al. 2006; Meneklis and Douligeris 2008; Rose and Grant 2010; van Veenstra et al. 2011). In the words of Kraemer and Dedrick (1997), "The spread of computing technology has had a major impact on how work is done, how decisions are made, how organizations are structured, and how people interact" (p. 94).

In addition, Kraemer and Danziger (1984) identify two different views of the impact of computers on social and organizational structures: (1) a pessimistic view that presents computers as producing an increasingly dehumanized and technocratic world and (2) an optimistic view, which emphasizes how computers could help to produce goods and services with great efficiency and high quality. In some ways, these two visions are complementary instead of contradictory. The pessimistic view highlights the structural consequences of information technologies and the optimistic view pays more attention to the final outcomes of using these IT applications. It seems clear now that information technologies have an impact (at least potentially) on final outputs and outcomes, but also on organizational structures and processes, as well as individual perceptions and behaviors (Bandyopadhyay and Sattarzadeh 2010; Antonio Cordella and Iannacci 2010; Aleš Groznik et al. 2008; Leonardi and Barley 2008; Orlikowski 2008).

From this more comprehensive perspective, myriad results are related to information technology initiatives, such as integrated services, improved decision-making, increased productivity, decentralization, increased revenues, and reduced costs (Benjamin 1984; Chircu 2008; Danziger and Kraemer 1985; Esteves and Joseph 2008; Hong 2009; Jenster 1987; Roldán and Leal 2003). Such positive outcomes tend to vary from one organization to another and according to the distinctiveness of a specific initiative. Still, certain types of benefits are expected in most government IT initiatives (Gil-Garcia and Helbig 2006). According to Dawes (1996), benefits include a combination of transformations to the current organizational and social structures as well as final outcomes and can be sorted into three categories: political, organizational, and technical.

In general, political benefits entail areas of broader public interest. Some examples of these benefits are greater public accountability and comprehensive public information, better appreciation for government-wide policy goals, and integrated service delivery and planning (Andersen and Dawes 1991; Bandyopadhyay and Sattarzadeh 2010; Bissessar 2010; Chircu 2008; Gil-Garcia and Helbig 2006; Langford and Roy 2009; Macintosh et al. 2002; Panagopoulos 2004; Pina et al. 2010; Roy 2009; Ubaldi and Roy 2010). In addition, "the development of computing technology has had an important impact on measuring accountability and presenting this information to the public" (Bruce Rocheleau 2003, p. 37). Public officials may also see political benefits as individual benefits as a result of the use of certain technology applications and characteristics (Fountain 2001a; Kraemer et al. 1989; Pardo et al. 2008a). Political benefits, particularly the ones related to government accountability, comprehensive public information, and integrated service delivery should be considered as fundamental e-government success measures.

An organization needs important changes in order to obtain positive results from e-government initiatives, such as IT training, new IT staff, and new formal channels of communication between original members and the new IT staff. Organizational benefits, also known as firm benefits or business benefits, refer to the augmentation of inter-organizational capabilities and a solution for organization-wide problems (Ashurst et al. 2008; Baqir and Iyer 2010; Dawes and Pardo 2002; Gant 2004; Klievink and Janssen 2009b; Lee 2001; Ubaldi and Roy 2010). Some well-known examples of organizational benefits are cost reductions, improving the decision making process, better coordination, customer satisfaction, and broadened professional networks (Andersen and Dawes 1991; Bandyopadhyay and Sattarzadeh 2010; Gil-Garcia et al. 2009; Gorla et al. 2010; Kuan and Chau 2001; Petter et al. 2008; Roldán and Leal 2003; Walton 1989). Although organizational benefits are treated separately in the literature and as a complement to political and technological benefits (Stowers 2004; Swiss 2003), in order to obtain certain positive outcomes, most organizations require transformations of their internal rules, channels of communications, hierarchical structures, and business processes. Organizational benefits should also be included as important measures of e-government success.

Additionally, "the technical quality of computerized information and computer services are key determinants of even the possibility of payoffs from computerization" (Northrop et al. 1990, p. 507). Technical benefits are related to data processing and information management. It is widely recognized that the use of information technologies may decrease processing time, storage, and duplicate data collection. Consequently, IT can reduce the costs derived from heavy paperwork and data processing found in every public program (Ambite et al. 2002; Barrett and Greene 2000; Caffrey 1998; Dawes 2008; Golubchik 2002; Maumbe et al. 2008). The use of information technologies can also enhance technical standards and help organizations to share technical resources (Bozeman and Bretschneider 1986; Dawes 1996, 2008; Millerand and Baker 2010). Some of these technical benefits are identified in the information systems literature as system-related benefits, like system accessibility, reliability, and usability (Danziger and Kraemer 1985; Gant 2004; Gil-Garcia et al. 2009; Marijn Janssen 2008; Kling 1993; Pardo et al. 2008a). Although not the ultimate goal for most e-government initiatives, technical benefits should be considered as success measures, because they are the basis for other more substantive results.

Benefits are not necessarily or frequently an immediate and direct consequence of information and communication technologies. Social factors and organizational structures interact with technological properties; the final outcomes (positive or negative) are the result of these complex interactions (Antonio Cordella and Iannacci 2010; Criado 2010; Fountain 2001a; Leonardi 2009b; Orlikowski 2000; Orlikowski 2008). Therefore, understanding the potential results of e-government initiatives is only part of the research endeavor. Identifying e-government success measures helps to assess if the initiative has accomplished its initial objectives and goals, but it says very little about the reasons behind its success or how to improve its performance. For this type of analysis, we need to understand e-government success factors. The next section describes and discusses research about different factors that affect the selection, design, implementation, use, and overall success of information technologies in the context of e-government initiatives.

1.4 Electronic Government Success Factors

A strong stream of literature is dedicated to studying the effects of organizational, institutional, and contextual factors on the selection, design, implementation, and use of information technologies (Azad and Faraj 2008; Bandyopadhyay and Sattarzadeh 2010; Bozeman and Bretschneider 1986; Caffrey 1998; Cresswell and Pardo 2001; Dawes and Pardo 2002; Dawes et al. 2004; Detlor et al. 2010; Eynon and Margetts 2007; Garson 2003-b; Gulati et al. 2010; Herrera and Gil-Garcia 2010; Khan et al. 2010; Landsbergen and Wolken 2001; Laudon 1985; Pardo and Scholl 2002; Bruce Rocheleau 1999; Smith 2010; Southon et al. 1999). This academic approach aims to appreciate how different factors impact or transform the resulting government information technology and, subsequently, the resulting organizational outcomes, which together could be seen as e-government success (see Fig. 1.4).

The lack of consensus about the definition of electronic government, as discussed above, leads to different ideas about its success factors. Some authors emphasize the use of administrative tools, such as strategic management or process

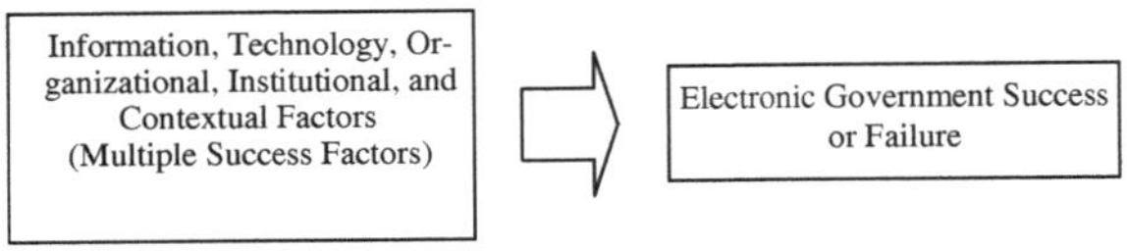

Fig. 1.4 Electronic Government success factors [Adapted from Gil-Garcia and Helbig (2006). Adapted with permission of the publisher]

reengineering, in order to increase an IT initiative's probability of success (Andersen et al. 1994; Bandyopadhyay and Sattarzadeh 2010; Davenport 1993; Gulati et al. 2010; Rahman 2010; Weerakkody and Dhillon 2008; Yu and Janssen 2010). Other authors argue that the key to success is the individual behavior and acceptance of people involved in these technology-related projects (Bandyopadhyay and Sattarzadeh 2010; Davis 1989; Fortin et al. 1997; Aleš Groznik et al. 2008; Joseph 2010; Roberts and Henderson 2000; Rowley 2011; Seddon 1997; Seddon et al. 1999; Streib and Willoughby 2010). A recent study of the e-Mexico initiative shows how institutional arrangements, organizational structures, and managerial processes have promoted or hindered collaboration among organizations and individuals (Luna-Reyes et al. 2007a).

As the debate continues, it remains unclear which factors are the most important in explaining IT success. Nevertheless, serious theoretical efforts have analyzed factors identified as relevant for conceiving information technology in organizations (Bandyopadhyay and Sattarzadeh 2010; Council 2008; Gulati et al. 2010; Markus 2005; Markus and Silver 2008; Remus and Wiener 2010; Rorissa et al. 2010; Rosacker and Olson 2008a, 2008b; Thomas and Fernández 2008). E-government success factors can be classified in five categories (Gil-Garcia and Pardo 2005): (1) data and information factors, such as data definitions, compatibility, and structures referring to the quality and management of data; (2) technology-related factors, related to the unique characteristics of the technology used; (3) organizational factors and the relationship between aspects such as formalization, size, communication channels, centralization, and IT success; (4) institutional factors, which apply to any set of rules, formal and informal, regulations, legislation, and more; and (5) contextual factors, with examples of political, economic, demographic, and social variables.

1.4.1 Data and Information Factors

Various researchers have concentrated on data quality and data accuracy issues (Ballou and Tayi 1999; Kaplan et al. 1998; Klischewski and Scholl 2008; Petter et al. 2008; Prybutok et al. 2008; Redman 1998). Since one principal purpose of an IT initiative is to integrate, share, improve, or disseminate information, the quality of such information is essential and surprisingly it is often taken for granted (Brown 2000; Gonzalez et al. 2010; Klischewski and Scholl 2008). Therefore, data-related problems need to be adequately addressed in order to obtain greater benefits from e-government initiatives. Inconsistencies, inaccuracies, lack of timeliness, and incompleteness of data can all cause problems in information quality (Chutimaskul et al. 2008; Dawes and Pardo 2008; Dawes and Helbig 2010; Madnick et al. 2009; Redman 1998). All these factors affect the overall results of information technology initiatives (Gil-Garcia and Helbig 2006).

In addition, the use of legacy data for decision support systems presents challenges due to the need for "soft" or judgmental data that is not normally required for traditional systems and whose quality needs to be carefully evaluated (Tayi and Ballou 1998). Collaboration and the information sharing associated with it are key aspects of e-government (Cresswell et al. 2002; Dawes and Pardo 2002; Fedorowicz et al. 2010; Gil-Garcia et al. 2007; Gil-Garcia et al. 2009; Joseph 2010; Lux Wigand 2010; Pardo et al. 2001). However, there are important complications present in information sharing initiatives such as incompatible database designs, mismatched data structures, and incongruous data and information distribution (Ambite et al. 2002; Barrett and Greene 2000; Eynon and Margetts 2007; Janssen et al. 2008; Umble et al. 2003). The problems persist even when the involved organizations use the same kind of data, since data definitions and terminology will limit the extent of data and information sharing (Ambite et al. 2002; Dawes 1996; Gil-Garcia and Helbig 2006; Gottschalk 2009; Hovy 2008; Joseph 2010; Maali et al. 2010). Inter-organizational information sharing and integration also face legal, organizational, and political challenges, such as the lack of political support, privacy concerns, and lack of adequate financial resources, among others (dos Santos and Reinhard forthcoming; Ezz et al. 2009; Fedorowicz et al. 2010; Gil-Garcia et al. 2009; Yang and Maxwell 2011).

1.4.2 Technology-Related Factors

All technology characteristics are important for the success of IT initiatives in both private and public organizations. A major challenge for IT-intensive projects is found in technology incompatibility (Baqir and Iyer 2010; Caffrey 1998; Chang et al. 2001; Chengalur-Smith and Duchessi 1999; Eynon and Margetts 2007; Ghapanchi et al. 2008; Joseph 2010; Pardo et al. forthcoming; Tsai et al. 2009; Ubaldi and Roy 2010). The newness and complexity of technology are also constraints that can potentially affect the results of IT projects (Barki et al. 1993; Carroll et al. 2006; Choudhari et al. 2011; Dawes and Nelson 1995; Garson 2003b; Ghapanchi et al. 2008; Gil-Garcia and Helbig 2006; Joseph 2010; Rahman 2010; Sancak and Güleç 2010; Weerakkody et al. 2009).

In addition, similar to projects in non-technology areas, staff skills are very important. The lack of technical skills has been identified as a significant success factor in IT initiatives (Bandyopadhyay and Sattarzadeh 2010; Caffrey 1998; Dawes and Pardo 2002; Ferro and Sorrentino 2010; Ghapanchi et al. 2008; Jain and Kesar 2011; Joseph 2010; Pavlichev 2004; Schelin 2004). Moreover, a totally new project differs greatly from the design to improve an existing system. These "legacy" systems carry additional challenges like compatibility problems, which are not always easy to solve (Baqir and Iyer 2010; Criado 2009; dos Santos and Reinhard forthcoming; Holland et al. 1999; Kelly et al. 1999; Pardo et al. forthcoming; van Veenstra et al. 2011). Duchessi and Chengalur-Smith (1998) studied an example where the conversion of mainframe applications was identified as one of the problems associated with implementing client/server technology. More recently, government adoption of Web 2.0 technologies has raised new issues in technical and semantic interoperability with the existing legacy systems (Charalabidis et al. 2010; Drogkaris et al. 2010; Ojo et al. 2010).

1.4.3 Organizational Factors

Organizational factors refer to characteristics, processes, structures, and relationships that take place within an organizational setting, including the project, organizational, and individual levels. Some examples are understanding strategic goals, a project management approach, the length of the project, the extent of change in business processes, and the lack of implementation guidelines (Angelopoulos et al. 2010; Baqir and Iyer 2010; Chang et al. 2001; Davenport 1993; Gil-Garcia and Helbig 2006; Hossain et al. forthcoming; Joseph 2010; Rorissa et al. 2010; Seneviratne 1999; Umble et al. 2003; Yang and Maxwell 2011). The size of the project and the diversity of the users or organizations involved are two of the most important factors in IT initiatives (Barki et al. 1993; Davis 1982; Dawes and Pardo 2002; Gil-Garcia and Helbig 2006; McFarlan 1981).

There are at least two main problems related to a project's goals and objectives. One is the lack of alignment between the IT project and organizational goals (Dawes and Nelson 1995; Marijn Janssen, forthcoming; Meijer and Thaens 2010; Ubaldi and Roy 2010; Valdés et al. 2011). Information technology is best thought of as part of the strategy of the organization (Andersen et al. 1994). Therefore, IT initiatives should be consistent with the overall mission and goals. A second problem is the existence of multiple, and sometimes conflicting, goals in the public sector as an additional inter-organizational factor (Baqir and Iyer 2010; Bryson et al. 2010; Campbell et al. 2009; Dawes and Pardo 2002; Luna-Reyes et al. 2010; Ubaldi and Roy 2010).

Organizational politics is also an important factor for IT initiatives (Baqir and Iyer 2010; Joseph 2010; Jun and Weare forthcoming; Loukis and Charalabidis 2011; Luna-Reyes et al. 2010; Weissenberger-Eibl and Teufel 2011). Many e-government initiatives require the participation of various public organizations. Additionally, most organizations have multiple stakeholders and multiple goals (Hall 2002). In fact, for some authors, organizations are political entities with different groups competing for power and organizational control (Baer et al. 2010; Heydebrand 1977; Joseph 2010; Newman and Rosenberg 1985; Pache and Santos 2010; Pettigrew 1977; Pfeffer 1982, 1992). Therefore, the multiplicity of stakeholders and goals is even greater in some e-government initiatives and becomes another difficult challenge.

Individual interests and associated behaviors can lead to resistance to change, internal conflicts, and turf issues (Bandyopadhyay and Sattarzadeh 2010; Barki et al. 1993; Barrett and Greene 2000; Bellamy 2000; Best 1997; Bwalya and Healy 2010; Chen 2010; Ebbers and van Dijk 2007; Eynon and Margetts 2007; Gaudino and Moro 2010; Gil-Garcia and Helbig 2006; Hossain et al. forthcoming; Jiang and Klein 2000; Joseph 2010; Leung and Adams 2009; Nasim and Sushil 2010; Bruce Rocheleau 2003). Hence, organizational politics can become a tough challenge to overcome. For example, to overcome resistance and conflict, IT initiatives must understand different social actors and their different perspectives about the impact an information technology could assert on their personal position within the organization (Iivari et al. 1998).

1.4.4 Institutional Factors

Institutional arrangements can be conceived of as laws, norms, and meaning systems (Scott 2001) that constrain the way people act in organizational settings. But in fact, "institutions do not just constrain options: they establish the very criteria by which people discover their preferences" (Powell and DiMaggio 1991, p. 11). Previous theoretical frameworks have used institutional theory to address different aspects of information technologies such as implementation, adoption, and management (Bellamy and Taylor 1996; Butler 2003; Criado 2010; Currie 2009; Gil-Garcia and Hassan 2008; Gulati et al. 2010; Seongcheol Kim et al. 2009; Laudon 1985; Laudon and Westin 1986; Rahman 2010; Wang 2010). It is now widely recognized that institutional arrangements are central elements in understanding how information technologies are selected, designed, implemented, and used in public organizations (Antonio Cordella and Iannacci 2010; Fountain 2008; Heeks and Bailur 2007; Luna-Reyes and Gil-Garcia 2011; Luna-Reyes et al. 2008).

Political Factors and Informal Rules. Political factors seem to be unique to the environment of public organizations, since they refer to the political complexities of every governmental system (Ahn and Bretschneider 2011; Baqir and Iyer 2010; Eynon and Margetts 2007; Lee et al. 2009; Rorissa et al. 2010; Sancak and Güleç 2010). Dawes (1996, p. 381) gives some examples of these factors: (1) external influences over the decision-making process, such as legislative committees, interest groups, civil servants, and other governmental jurisdictions like local governments; (2) the power of agency discretion, which refers to the capacity of expert bureaucrats to influence programs and policies; and (3) the primacy of programs that reinforce vertical connections and create disincentives to horizontal collaboration among agencies.

Institutions are not only laws and regulations, but also norms, actions, or behaviors that people accept as good or take for granted (Gulati et al. 2010; Hossain et al. forthcoming; Khalil 2011; Orlikowski 2000; Sawyer and Tyworth 2006; Scott 2001; Smith 2010; Star and Ruhleder 1996). In this context, additional restrictions and impediments appear in the general institutional framework and the political environment in which government organizations operate. As a recent example present in modern democracies, privacy and security concerns greatly influence government IT initiatives as challenges that must be adequately addressed (Baqir and Iyer 2010; Carter and McBride 2010; Duncan and Roehrig 2003; Joshi et al. 2002; Luna-Reyes and Gil-Garcia 2003b; Milner 2000; Rorissa et al. 2010; Rose and Grant 2010; Sancak and Güleç 2010; Zhao et al. 2010).

Legislation and Regulations. In making any kind of decision, including those about IT projects, public managers must take into consideration a large number of laws and regulations (Bandyopadhyay and Sattarzadeh 2010; Dawes and Nelson 1995; Fletcher 2004; Gil-Garcia and Helbig 2006; Gulati et al. 2010; Harris 2000; Landsbergen and Wolken 2001; NGA 1997; Rosacker and Rosacker 2010; Rose and Grant 2010; Sagheb-Tehrani 2010; Ubaldi and Roy 2010). For instance, in the public sector, the budgeting process embodies one of the most powerful set of rules. Strategies and results of long-term IT initiatives are constrained by one-year budgets, which are common in many national and state governments (Ahn 2011; Bandyopadhyay and Sattarzadeh 2010; Chen and Thurmaier 2008; Dawes and Nelson 1995; Dawes and Pardo 2002; Fountain 2001b; Luna-Reyes et al. 2010; Rorissa et al. 2010; Wyld 2009).

The existence of a federal system, such as in the United States, presents additional challenges that are similar to the ones derived from intergovernmental relationships between different levels of government (Cresswell et al. 2002; Criado 2009; Dawes 2009; Eynon and Margetts 2007; Fedorowicz et al. 2007; Gil-Garcia and Helbig 2006; Jaeger 2002; Kwon et al. 2009; Pardo et al. 2008b). The complexity grows due to the checks and balances among the executive, legislative, and judicial branches (Bellamy 2000; dos Santos and Reinhard forthcoming; Gottschalk 2009; Gulati et al. 2010; Harris 2000; Bruce Rocheleau 2003; Ubaldi and Roy 2010). Another situation presents when agencies attempt to integrate or share information across multiple agencies. IT projects can be constrained by "agency autonomy." Although the United States legal framework does not explicitly mention it, government agencies and programs often act as independent and autonomous units, not taking into account what other public organizations are doing (a situation often referred to as "stove pipes") (Caffrey 1998; Dawes and Pardo 2002; Fountain 2001b; Gøtze et al. 2009; Persson and Goldkuhl 2009; Seifert and Chung 2009; Ubaldi and Roy 2010).

1.4.5 Contextual Factors

Numerous environmental factors constitute the context of organizations. This subsection discusses how academics and experts in organizational theory have developed different ways to understand the impact of the environment on organizations, as well as how organizations attempt to modify their environments (Aldrich 1979; Burke 2011; Gil-Garcia and Helbig 2006; Gulati et al. 2010; Hannan and Freeman 1989; Liao et al. 2011; Pfeffer and Salancik 1978; Scott 1998). Some of the factors identified in the literature are (1) technological,

(2) legal, (3) cultural, (4) political, (5) economic, (6) demographic, and (7) ecological (Clegg and Dunkerley 1980; Hall 2002; Hatch 1997). More specifically, within information systems research, the essential role of environmental variables in shaping the way information technology is designed and used in organizations is widely accepted (Kuan and Chau 2001; Laudon 1985; Menachemi et al. 2011; Rahman 2010; Robey et al. 2008; Sila 2010).

Different authors argue that contextual variables or external pressures such as personnel markets, competition, or politics may affect the results of IT initiatives (Bandyopadhyay and Sattarzadeh 2010; Bellamy 2000; Bozeman and Bretschneider 1986; Chengalur-Smith and Duchessi 1999; Detlor et al. 2010; Laudon 1986; Lee et al. 2011; Lee 2009; Nour et al. 2008; Pina et al. 2009). Environmental determinism posits that external environmental factors shape organizational characteristics and affect the final technology results. In the extreme, this type of determinism does not allow for management intervention (Kraemer et al. 1989). Even without considering this extreme view, the context of organizations is without a doubt an important factor for the success of IT initiatives (Detlor et al. 2010; Hassan et al. 2011; Nour et al. 2008; Sancak and Güleç 2010). Managers with experience in both public and private organizations note that these characteristics are present not only for government agencies, but are also important for private firms. Nevertheless, as we will discuss later in this study, environmental conditions are only one of many important variables to take into consideration.

This section presented different types of factors that have been identified as important determinants of IT success. Most of the research has hypothesized models in which all factors are at the same level of importance, limiting understanding about the complex relationships among different kinds of factors. In addition, these models do not allow more comprehensive and integrative exploration of e-government, largely because of their limited capability to capture indirect and recursive relationships among factors and between success factors and success measures. The next section briefly discusses both of these limitations.

1.5 Current State of Electronic Government Success Research and Practice: What is Missing? What is Needed?

Researchers have gained a great deal of knowledge about the selection, design, implementation, and use of information technologies in government. However, obtaining the potential benefits of IT-related initiatives is still a difficult challenge that involves high risk (Abdel-Hamid and Madnick 1990; Ashurst et al. 2008; Baqir and Iyer 2010; Bissessar 2010; Chen et al. 2009; Joseph 2010; Wu et al. 2010). For example, a 1998 study found that 30 percent of the IT projects surveyed were canceled and 45 percent were late or over budget (Cunningham 1999). Many other studies focus on the difficulties and problems of IT projects, such as cost overruns, project cancellations, limited features, and unintended consequences

(Ashurst et al. 2008; Berlin et al. 2009; Deephouse et al. 1995; Gulati et al. 2010; Keil et al. 1998; Norris 1999; Rahman 2010; Rosacker and Olson 2008b; Weinstein and Jaques 2010). Most of this literature comes from research in the private sector, but government IT initiatives are similarly complex; therefore, public managers need practical tools to make better IT decisions (Bandyopadhyay and Sattarzadeh 2010; Carr 2010; Dawes et al. 1999; Dawes and Préfontaine 2003; Gil-Garcia and Pardo 2005; Hoque et al. 2011). These tools should be developed from well-grounded research and consequentially from good theoretical understanding.

However, our current knowledge about the complex relationships between information technologies and multiple success factors in government settings is still limited. Qualitatively different research is needed in order to improve our understanding. First, we need studies that attempt to develop a better understanding of e-government success by including multiple factors and theorizing about their interrelationships. Second, we need studies based on a more comprehensive view of e-government initiatives. This view should conceptualize information technologies as not only the technological artifacts, but also the social structures around them. This integrative perspective can provide a more accurate picture of how these different factors influence and are influenced by information technologies and, consequently, a better understanding about the relationships among factors and between success factors and success measures.

1.5.1 A Better Understanding of Electronic Government Success Measures and Success Factors

The literature review reveals two categories of studies. One focuses on IT success factors, but relatively few of these focus on government. The other category focuses on government technology projects, but this literature does not delve deeply into the nature of e-government success (represented as quality, functionality, or other outputs and outcomes). Therefore, a major gap in the literature is attention to the determinants of success and failure in e-government projects.

Research is needed to generate a better understanding of the complex and dynamic relationships between e-government success and different organizational, institutional, and contextual factors (Yildiz 2007). It would be equally important to understand how these different factors are interrelated. However, most of the academic work that has been done so far takes a linear view of the relationships between different success factors and information technology (see Fig. 1.5). All the factors are hypothesized to have a direct and linear relationship with information technology success measures and few hypotheses have been made about the relationships among the different success factors themselves. New models should propose relationships among factors and, therefore, direct and indirect effects between success factors and the characteristics of an e-government

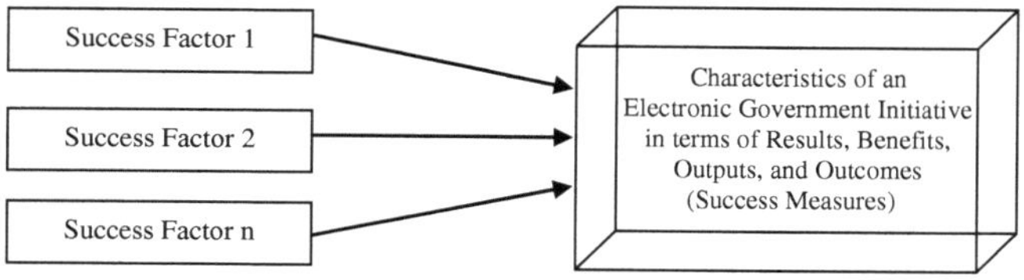

Fig. 1.5 Current models of electronic Government success—mostly direct effects [Adapted from Gil-Garcia (2008). Adapted with permission of the publisher]

initiative (in terms of success measures). This will allow for disentangling the different causal paths and assessing the actual effects of individual success factors.

1.5.2 A More Comprehensive and Dynamic View of Electronic Government as a Socio-Technical Phenomenon

There are two limitations related to the scope of government information technology in previous research. First, previous research overestimated the transformational power of information technologies (Andersen et al. 2010; Kling et al. 1998; Mergel et al. 2009; Parisopoulos et al. 2009; Reddick 2010). ICT were seen as capable of radically transforming organizational and institutional arrangements (Bloomfield and Hayes 2009; Danziger 2004; Dawes 1996; Fountain 2008; Gil-Garcia and Helbig 2006; Prybutok et al. 2008; van Veenstra et al. 2010). From this perspective, the focus of e-government success should be on measuring results, in terms of benefits, outputs, and outcomes.

Later research shows that the relationships between these two constructs are not so simple. For example, referring to organizations in general, Scott (2001, p. 179) mentions that "most contemporary researchers are crafting research designs to examine the complex recursive processes by which institutional forces both shape and are shaped by organizational actions". Similarly, e-government research must explore and analyze the recursive and complex influences between information technologies and the multiple factors that comprise social and organizational structures (see Fig. 1.6).

Second, e-government initiatives need to be understood not only as technological components, but also as the social relationships around the technological artifacts and the interactions among social actors and between these actors and the technological artifacts (Antonio Cordella and Iannacci 2010; Fountain 2008; Gil-Garcia and Helbig 2006; Iannacci 2010; Margetts 2009; Orlikowski 2008; Orlikowski and Scott 2008; Sefyrin and Mörtberg 2009). In order to have a better understanding of e-government, it is necessary to develop a more comprehensive view of the different socio-technical elements and aspects included in this phenomenon. In terms of e-government success, there is a need to understand the complex and dynamic relationships between success factors and success measures.

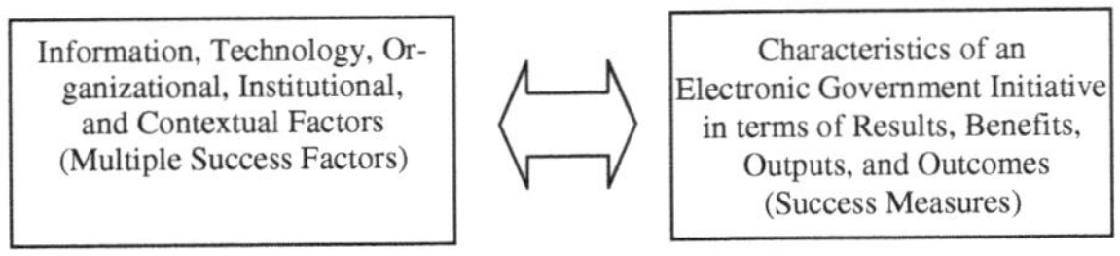

Fig. 1.6 A more comprehensive and dynamic view of electronic Government

Finally, technological artifacts are only one element of a more complex socio-technical environment that includes people, physical spaces, organizational structures, institutions, and social relationships. This more comprehensive view provides the opportunity to better understand not only the technical aspects, but also the social impacts of information technology on individuals and the organization as a whole. Drawing on disciplines such as political science, psychology, anthropology, sociology, and organizational theory, scholars have already adapted some useful ideas and developed theoretical frameworks that account for some of the previously stated limitations. The following chapter presents some of this research and develops an integrative theoretical framework. It shows how digital government researchers can thoughtfully use theoretical advances from other disciplinary traditions. It also presents the work of scholars in the field of electronic government who have developed more comprehensive and dynamic models to understand e-government initiatives.

Chapter 2
Electronic Government Success and the Ensemble View of Information Technology

This chapter reviews some of the more comprehensive and integrative theoretical traditions from information systems (IS) and e-government research. Orlikowski and Iacono (2001) refer to these approaches as the ensemble view of information technologies and organization. This view argues that in order to understand information technologies, it is necessary to analyze not only the technological artifacts, but also the social and organizational aspects around those artifacts. After reviewing several ensemble-view approaches, this chapter develops a theoretical model based primarily on Fountain's (2001a) technology enactment framework and complemented with recent literature on e-government and IT success, ideas from the constructivist approach (including the notions of technologies-in-practice and multiple enactments), and concepts and relationships from other integrative models, particularly the process model of computing change. The chapter ends by explaining the proposed theoretical model, "enacting e-government success," and discussing its initial application to government-wide websites as instances of a much broader e-government phenomenon. Future research should apply this theory to other types of e-government initiatives in order to further assess the usefulness of the model.

2.1 The Ensemble View of Information Technology and Organizations

There are many ways to classify research about information technologies (Davenport 2008; Fulk and Gould 2009; Iivari et al. 1998; Iris et al. 2002; King and Lyytinen 2006; Markus and Robey 1988; Nevo et al. 2009; Newman and Robey 1992; Orlikowski and Baroudi 1991; Orlikowski and Iacono 2001; Robey and Boudreau 1999; Seidel et al. 2010; Somers 2010; Tilson et al. 2010; Yoo et al. 2010). Each of these approaches emphasizes different ontological, epistemological, and methodological characteristics of the research within the IS field. However, most of them agree on the existence of a theoretical approach that emphasizes the social and

J. R. Gil-Garcia, *Enacting Electronic Government Success*,
Integrated Series in Information Systems 31, DOI: 10.1007/978-1-4614-2015-6_2,

complex nature of information systems. This approach proposes a better way to understand the relationships between IT and social structures. This section explains the ensemble view of information technologies and organizations (Orlikowski and Iacono 2001) and lists some of the theories that could be classified in this category.

At present, few scholars argue that technologies are directly responsible for social change (Carugati et al. 2010; Contractor et al. 2011; Fountain 2008; Orlikowski 2007, 2010b; Orlikowski and Iacono 2006; Orlikowski and Scott 2008). Instead, several recent theoretical efforts propose alternative ways to understand the relationships between information technologies and the social systems in which they are deployed (Dutta 2008; Harrison et al. 2007; Meneklis and Douligeris 2010; Pentland and Feldman 2007; Zhang and Scialdone 2010). These more holistic approaches have been called the ensemble view of technology (Orlikowski and Iacono 2001). According to this perspective, technology is only one piece of a more complex socio-technical system (Kling and Lamb 2000; Kraemer et al. 1980; Pasmore 1988). Other components can include training, budgets, policies, laws, and commitment, among others (de Bruijn and Herder 2009; Gil-Garcia and Hassan 2008; Kling and Schacchi 1982; Yaobin Lu et al. 2011; Orlikowski and Iacono 2006; Ribes and Finholt 2009; Ziegenfuss 2011). Therefore, from an ensemble view, information technologies are not only the physical artifacts, but also the social relations around those artifacts (Alter 2010; Davenport and Horton 2006; Fountain 2005; Gil-Garcia et al. 2009; Gil-Garcia and Hassan 2008; Gil-Garcia and Pardo 2006; Orlikowski and Iacono 2006; Rittgen 2008; Shin 2010). According to Orlikowski and Iacono (2001), the ensemble view refers to technology in four different ways: development project, production network, embedded system, and structure.

Some predominant examples of these comprehensive approaches are the following (Gil-Garcia and Hassan 2008): adaptive structuration theory (Robert et al. 2009; DeSanctis and Poole 1994; Miller 2008; Naik and Kim 2010; Niederman et al. 2008; Poole et al. 1998); social informatics (Berleur et al. 2006; Kling 2000; Kling et al. 1998; Stillman and Linger 2009; Strong et al. 2009); the structurational model of technology (Harrison et al. 2007; Hsu et al. 2008; Melin 2009; Meneklis and Douligeris 2010; Orlikowski 1992; Orlikowski and Robey 1991; Zackariasson et al. 2009); the socio-technical systems conceptualization (Baxter and Sommerville 2011; Bostrom and Heinen 1977; Geels 2010; Kraemer and King 1986; Mumford 2000; Walker et al. 2008); and the technology enactment framework (Antonio Cordella and Iannacci 2010; Fountain 1995, 2001a, 2005, 2008; Gil-Garcia and Luna-Reyes 2009; Luna-Reyes and Gil-Garcia 2011; Schellong 2007).

Using different but related theoretical constructions, ensemble view theories argue that there is a dynamic interaction between social structures and information technologies. ICTs have the potential to change social and organizational structures, but at the same time these structures influence the design, implementation, and use of ICTs (Fountain 2008; Gil-Garcia 2005a; Gabriel Puron Cid and Gil-Garcia 2004). In addition, research from this perspective has established the importance of different social actor enactments in understanding this bi-directional relationship (Fountain 2001a, 2005, 2008, 2009; Harrison et al. 2007; Orlikowski 2000; Orlikowski 2008, 2010c).

2.2 Ensemble-View Integrative Models

As mentioned before, several social theories recognize the interplay between social structures and IT, which have been classified as part of the ensemble view (Orlikowski and Iacono 2001). Orlikowski and Iacono (2006, p. 34) argue, "Given the kind of emergent IS phenomena we are witnessing today—open source software, electronic commerce, virtual teams, globally-distributed work, new challenges to privacy and intellectual property rights, etc.—there clearly is scope for more work to be done from an ensemble view". This argument becomes stronger with recent IT developments such as social media, web 2.0, wikis, RSS feeds, and more. However, only a few authors have developed comprehensive and integrative theoretical models that capture the interaction mechanisms between multiple theoretical constructs. This section presents and discusses some ensemble-view integrative models, identifies similarities and differences across them, and offers some theoretical implications from this review. Two of the models were developed from empirical work in government organizations: the technology enactment framework and the process model of computing change. The other two models are more general and considered applicable to any type of organization.

It is important to emphasize that some of these models use similar terms in different ways. For example, within the ensemble view, social structures are generally anything other than the technological artifacts. They could include variables such as organizational structures, the legal framework, environmental forces, and individual behavior, as well as the interrelationships among them (Dawes 2008; Esteves and Joseph 2008; Hornnes et al. 2010; Maxwell and Dawes 2009; Shin 2010; Weigl et al. 2008). In contrast, for Giddens' structuration theory, social structures are only the macro-social rules that we use to behave in society. They do not exist in reality, but are instantiated in social norms, interpretative schemes, and certain facilities and resources. This book uses the term "social structures" in the more general way. The purpose is to help the reader clearly differentiating them from the technological artifacts.

2.2.1 Structuration Theory and Structuring Information Technologies

Giddens identifies a non-static version of the concept of structure, different from what is found in some structuralism or strategic choice models. The author expresses this difference very clearly: "Let us regard the rules of social life, then, as techniques or generalizable procedures applied in the enactment/reproduction of social practices" (Giddens 1984, p. 21). In the structuration view, the structure is formed by what individuals use to interact with other individuals in their daily lives. Therefore, social practices are not the structure, but the result of interactions between individual actions and social structures (Feldman and Orlikowski, forthcoming; Gil-Garcia and Hassan

2008; Orlikowski 2008, 2010a, 2010b, 2010c; Shachaf and Rosenbaum 2010). This subsection explains some of the main concepts of structuration theory and describes the components and logic of two integrative models based on this approach: (1) the structurational model of technology and (2) adaptive structuration theory.

From this perspective, human actions and the broader social world are mutually constitutive (Giddens 1984). At the same time that individual actions are constrained by certain social-level rules, their practices shape or reinforce those social structures (Gerardine DeSanctis et al. 2010; Orlikowski 2008; Shachaf and Rosenbaum 2010; Whittington 2010). These social practices can refer to both relationships between individuals and relationships between individuals and technological artifacts (Gil-Garcia and Hassan 2008). "The basic domain of study of the social sciences, according to the theory of structuration, is neither the experience of the individual actor, nor the existence of any form of societal totality, but social practices ordered across space and time" (Giddens 1984, p. 2).

There is a dynamic interaction between actions and structures and, therefore, there is no clear causality between social structures and individual actions (Elliott 2010; Grgecic and Rosenkranz 2008; Whittington 2010). In fact, "one of the main propositions of structuration theory is that the rules and resources drawn upon in the production and reproduction of social action are at the same time the means of system reproduction (the duality of structure)" (Giddens 1984, p. 19). Following this logic, information technologies can be seen as both a constitutive part of the structures and the result of the interactions between those structures and individual actors (Gil-Garcia and Hassan 2008).

It is necessary to clarify that for the structuration approach, it is important to study social and organizational structures and their relationship with information technologies, but it is more important to understand how users enact different ways to understand and use certain technology (Hunter III 2010; Orlikowski 2008; Orlikowski and Scott 2008; Prasad 2009; Scott 2010b). In relation to this idea, Walsham (1991, p. 81) agrees that "structuration theory is valuable in carrying out empirical studies of IS use and the way in which this modifies social and organizational structures and vice versa". It is not the study of the technological artifacts by themselves, but the objective is to understand the social and technical aspects of information technologies in terms of instantiations of social structures.

According to structuration theory, technologies have the effect of *structuring* the social world in terms of defining the ways people think, options for behavior, and ranges of possible consequences (DeSanctis and Poole 1994; Hunter III 2010; Jones and Karsten 2008; Orlikowski 1992, 2010c). Structuration theory also argues that the social world simultaneously affects technologies. That, regardless of the material capabilities that technologies present, people socially constitute technologies (Fountain 2001a, 2008; Leonardi and Barley 2010; Orlikowski 2000; Orlikowski 2008; Orlikowski and Scott 2008; Shachaf and Rosenbaum 2010). Structuration theory as applied to information technology started with the view that social structures and information technologies affect each other (Orlikowski 1992). In some sense, technology is both an objective force and a socially constructed product (Gil-Garcia and Hassan 2008; Greenhalgh and Stones 2010;

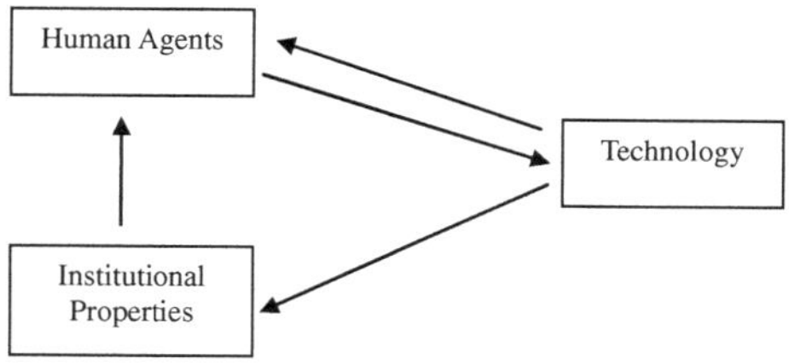

Fig. 2.1 Structurational model of technology. [Adapted with permission from Orlikowski (1992). Copyright 1992, the Institute for Operations Research and the Management Sciences, 7240 Parkway Drive, Suite 300, Hanover, Maryland 21076.]

Leonardi and Barley 2010; Prasad 2009; Shachaf and Rosenbaum 2010). Technology affects both human agents and institutional properties and, at the same time, is affected by human agents (see Fig. 2.1).

The Structurational Model of Technology highlights a duality of technology (Orlikowski 1992). In the model, technology is a product of human action, such as design, development, appropriation, and modification. Technology is also a medium of human action, facilitating and constraining it through the provision of interpretive schemes, facilities, and norms. Institutional conditions surrounding the interaction with technology influence humans in their interaction with it. The consequences of this interaction influence institutional properties of an organization by reinforcing or transforming structures of signification, domination, and legitimation. Therefore, information technologies are socially constructed by users as they select and emphasize some of their properties. In contrast, the features of the technology also affect how actors can use it and what they could use it for.

Orlikowski (1992, p. 406) explains that "technology is physically constructed by actors working in a given social context, and technology is socially constructed by actors through the different meanings they attach and the various features they emphasize and use. However, it is also the case that once developed and deployed, technology tends to become reified and institutionalized, losing its connection with the human agents that constructed it or gave it meaning, and it appears to be part of the objective, structural properties of the organization". Therefore, according to this initial view, information technologies reach stabilization like other technologies (Pinch and Bijker 1987).

DeSanctis and Poole (1994) thought that early structuration models did not fully explain situations resulting from the implementation of advanced information technologies (AIT). There are two central concepts for adaptive structuration theory (AST): structuration and appropriation (DeSanctis and Poole 1994). These two theoretical constructs focus on the dynamic nature of technology adoption and use in organizational settings (see Fig. 2.2). For AST, structuration is the process by which social structures (whatever their source) are produced and reproduced in social life (DeSanctis and Poole 1994, p. 128). AST provides a detailed account of both the structure of advanced technologies and the unfolding of social interaction as these technologies are used. In contrast, appropriation is the immediate visible

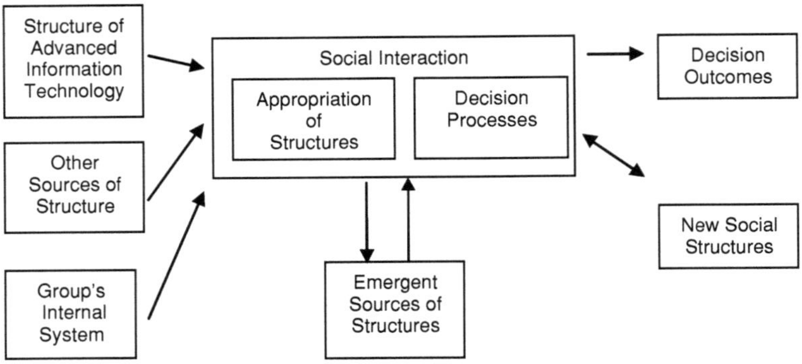

Fig. 2.2 Adaptive structuration theory. [Adapted with permission from DeSanctis and Poole (1994). Copyright 1994, the Institute for Operations Research and the Management Sciences, 7240 Parkway Drive, Suite 300, Hanover, Maryland 21076.]

actions, which are evidence of deeper structuration processes. Appropriations may be faithful or unfaithful, used instrumentally, and used with various attitudes.

AST also proposes two components of the social structures of information technologies: structural features and spirit (DeSanctis and Poole 1994). "Structural features are the specific types of rules and resources, or capabilities, offered by the system. …The spirit is the 'official line,' which the technology presents to people regarding how to act when using the system, how to interpret its features, and how to fill in gaps in procedure which are not explicitly specified" (DeSanctis and Poole 1994, p. 126). Users can appropriate different structural features and adopt or change the spirit of the technologies. They generate different social structures derived from their interactions with the system and with other users, designers, and managers.

As illustrated in Fig. 2.2, the advanced information technology structure (the structural features and the spirit of the technology that outline the expected use of technology within an organization), other sources of structure (task and organizational environment), the group's internal system (styles of interacting, knowledge and experience with structures, perceptions of others' knowledge, and agreement on appropriation), emergent sources of structures (technology outputs, task outputs, and environment outputs), and new social structures (rules and sources) shape social interaction. Social interaction has an impact on the appropriation of structures and decision processes. It creates decision outcomes and influences new social structures (rules and resources) and emergent sources of structures.

2.2.2 Socio-Technical Systems Theory and the Process Model of Computing Change

Socio-technical systems theory recognizes the complexity of the relationship between technologies and social change (Coakes 2011; Dawson and Daniel 2010; Eason 2009; Kling 2000; Kling and Lamb 2000; Luna-Reyes et al. 2005). Not all

Table 2.1 Standard versus socio-technical models

Standard (tool) models	Socio-technical models
IT is a tool	IT is a socio-technical network
Business model is sufficient	Ecological view is needed
One-shot implementation	Implementation is an ongoing social process
Technological effects are direct and immediate	Technological effects are indirect and involve different time scales
Incentives to change are unproblematic	Incentives may require restructuring and may be in conflict with other organizational activities
Politics are bad or irrelevant	Politics are central and even enabling
IT infrastructures are fully supportive. Systems have become user-friendly, people have become "computer-literate," and these changes are accelerating with the "net-generation"	Articulation work is often needed to make IT work, and socio-technical support is critical for effective IT use
Social relationships are easily reformed to take advantage of new conveniences, efficiencies, and business value	Relationships are complex, negotiated, multivalent; the nature of the relationship with the customer makes a difference in what can become digital—including trust
Social effects of IT are large, but isolated and benign	Potentially enormous social repercussions from IT—not just quality of working life, but overall quality of life
Contexts are simple (described by a few key terms or demographics)	Contexts are complex (matrices of businesses, services, people, technology, history, location, etc.)
Knowledge and expertise are easily made explicit	Knowledge and expertise are inherently tacit/implicit

Kling and Lamb (2000), figure Standard versus socio-technical models.

socio-technical models developed by different scholars have exactly the same features, but they share many of the characteristics presented here (Bostrom and Heinen 1977; Dawes 2009; Esteves and Joseph 2008; Kraemer et al. 1989; Lyytinen and Newman 2008; Maxwell and Dawes 2009; Pasmore 1988; Sittig and Singh 2010). This subsection explains the main concepts and theoretical foundations of the socio-technical approach and describes the components and logic of the Process Model of Computing Change, which is an integrative model based on this approach.

Following Kling and Lamb (2000), Table 2.1 shows some of the important differences between the socio-technical view and the tool view of technology. In the socio-technical perspective, information technologies are conceived as socio-technical networks that require an ecological view. Implementation is an ongoing social process rather than a one-shot activity. From a socio-technical view, the effects of technology are not immediate and direct. Incentives may be in conflict with other organizational actions. Politics are not always a barrier; they are central and can be enabling. Usability is important, but it is not enough for successful

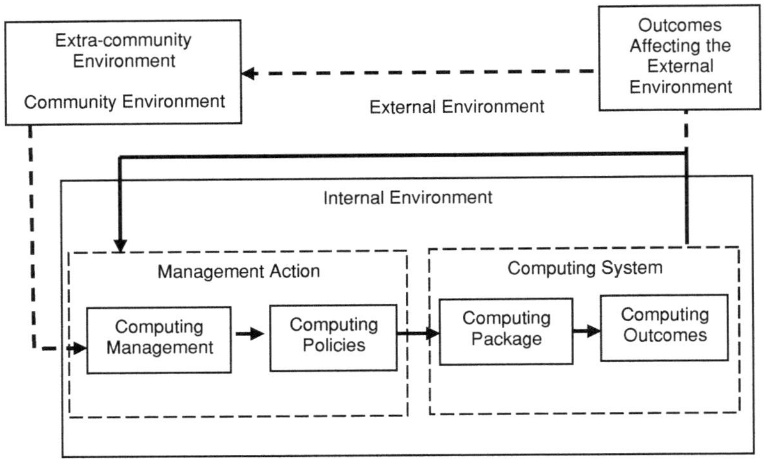

Fig. 2.3 Process model of computing change. [Kraemer et al. (1989). Reprinted with permission of John Wiley and Sons, Inc.]

implementation. IT projects need socio-technical support in addition to IT infrastructures. Social relationships cannot be easily changed according to IT specific requirements; they are complex and have to be negotiated. IT potentially has enormous impacts (positive and negative) on organizations and individuals. Contexts cannot be adequately described by a few key demographics. Finally, it is difficult to make knowledge and expertise explicit, because they are considered inherently tacit and implicit.

Kraemer et al. (1989) propose a model based on this socio-technical perspective, which is called the process model of computing change (see Fig. 2.3). They recognize that both environmental determinism and managerial voluntarism offer partial explanations for the use of IT in organizations. With respect to managerial voluntarism, they state, "After extensive empirical study, we were forced to conclude that the role of managers in computing change in organizations was much less clear than expected. Something other than management policy was playing a major role" (Kraemer et al. 1989, p. 2). Therefore, their model acknowledges the important role of managers, but also the influence of internal and external environmental variables.

The process model of computing change, based on research on local governments, takes many factors into consideration as well as their interrelationships. One of the important concepts in this model is the "computing package." Kraemer et al. (1989, p. 53) use this term to refer to "the system of people, equipment, and techniques involved with computing within an organization." This concept is very similar to that of the socio-technical network that includes and surrounds the technological artifacts. All environmental factors have an impact on the computing package and subsequently on its outcomes. However, this relationship is not direct, but mediated by the actions of managers. Therefore, "the environmental factors first encounter and become altered by computing management" (Kraemer et al. 1989, p. 54).

For Kraemer et al. (1989), environmental effects can be divided into external and internal factors. Examples of external factors are (1) technological availability, (2) vendor marketing practices, (3) funding opportunities, (4) economic conditions, and (5) operational mandates. Complementary, internal factors include (1) competence and continuity of information systems management, (2) structure of the information systems staff, (3) structure of the information systems organization, (4) sophistication of hardware and systems software, (5) pattern of computer applications, (6) organizational structure, and (7) management attributes.

There are two main components of the external environment: the extra-community environment and the community environment. The extra-community environment comprises organizational and technological factors outside the jurisdiction of the local government (Kraemer et al. 1989). Similarly, the community environment includes factors that are present in the community that the government serves. These external factors have an indirect effect on the computing system by means of creating opportunities and constraints to computing management (Kraemer et al. 1989).

Beyond environmental conditions, management objectives and interests are also important to understand the complex relationship between information technology and organization. That becomes evident when we see situations in which managers "initiate action for personal and professional motives, sometimes irrespective of environmental conditions. Often, in fact, when computer managers initiate action on non-environmental grounds, environmental conditions enter into action only as a means of rationalizing and legitimating it" (Kraemer et al. 1989, p. 98). The process model of computing change distinguishes among the environment, management action, and computing conditions (Kraemer et al. 1989). First, as mentioned before, the environment is divided into external and internal components and is hypothesized to have an impact on management action. Environmental conditions also have an indirect influence on the computing package. Second, computing management and computing policies represent management action. Management action has a direct effect on the computing package. Finally, both the computing package and computing outcomes form the computing conditions or computing system.

The main role of managers in this model is to transform environmental opportunities and constraints into computing policies. "Computing policies address both the organizational context and the technological infrastructure of computerization" (Kraemer et al. 1989, p. 105). They constitute both formal and informal rules about computerization and are policies that can be created by top management, the IS department, or other actors within the organization. Their implementation generates the organizational computing package (Kraemer et al. 1989).

As noted above, the technical, resource, and experiential aspects of computing within an organization constitute the computing package (Kraemer et al. 1989). Two of its main elements are its technological sophistication and sociotechnical interface. Both technological sophistication and sociotechnical interface are positively related to computing outcomes (Kraemer et al. 1989). "Computing outcomes are the results of computing package operations that affect the computing system" (Kraemer et al. 1989, p. 106). There are objective and subjective computing outcomes. Objective outcomes are the observed results of the computing package and subjective outcomes are the perceptions and interpretations of those results by different groups within the organization (Kraemer et al. 1989).

Both objective and subjective consequences of computing outcomes can affect the broader organization, the community environment, and the extra-community environment (Kraemer et al. 1989). In addition, computing outcomes and computer management are linked. There are two main feedback mechanisms from outcomes to computer management and they are related to whether the outcomes are considered positive or negative. Positive outcomes generate the desire for more applications for both current users and new areas within the organization. Negative outcomes demand changes to rectify the problems generated by the computing package (Kraemer et al. 1989).

This process model of computing change involves a series of complex and recursive causal relationships. In the words of the authors, "The model of computing change presented above describes a cyclical flow of effects. The environment presents opportunities and constraints, which are filtered by the actions of computing management through its policies, which affect the activities of the computer package and produce outcomes. The consequences of these outcomes, in turn, are fed back to computing management in the form of the needs of the computing package and user demands to support development and mitigate problems" (Kraemer et al., 1989, p. 109). Cordella and Iannacci (2010) found similar dynamics in terms of the relationship between e-government policies and information systems choice and design. The logics embedded in the design of a new technology affect the extant social values inscribed in e-government policies, and vice versa.

2.2.3 Institutional Theory and the Technology Enactment Framework

Institutional theory has been useful in understanding organizational settings (Amenta and Ramsey 2010; Currie 2009; Luna-Reyes et al. 2007b; Mundkur and Venkatesh 2009; Powell and DiMaggio 1991; Scott 2010a; Suddaby 2010). More broadly, institutional frameworks have been developed to study diverse social phenomena in different disciplines such as political science (Amenta and Ramsey 2010; Clegg 2010; Fletcher et al. 1992; March and Olsen 1989; Peters 2001), sociology (Brinton and Nee 1998), economics (North 1999; Rutherford 1999), and more. Institutions can be seen as guidelines for action, but also constraints on those actions (Dover and Lawrence 2010; Scott 2010b; Willmott 2011). Regarding IT initiatives, it is acknowledged they comprise an inscrutable set of interactions and decisions (Hassan and Gil-Garcia 2008). These interactions are constrained by

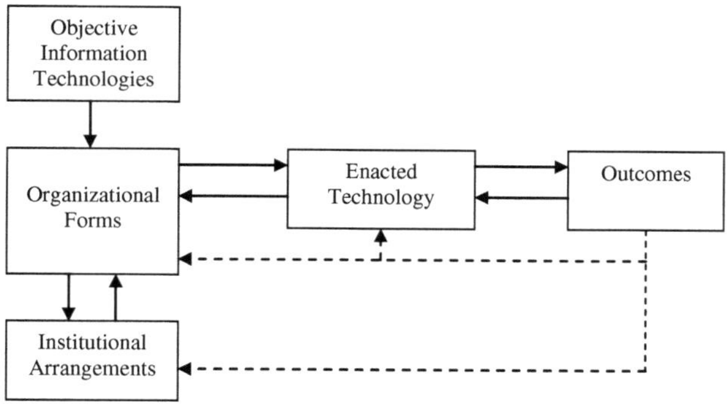

Fig. 2.4 Technology enactment framework [Fountain (2001a), Reprinted with permission of the publisher]

institutional arrangements, but at the same time institutions "frame how those constraints operate" (Fountain 2001a p. 92). Therefore, institutions also influence the specific constraining mechanisms. This subsection provides a brief review of institutional theory and explains the technology enactment framework.

Based on the institutional tradition, the technology enactment framework attempts to understand the influence of institutional arrangements and organizational forms on the selection, design, implementation, and use of information technologies in government agencies (Antonio Cordella and Iannacci 2010; Hassan and Gil-Garcia 2008). According to Fountain (1995, 2001a, 2008), the technology enactment framework pays attention to the relations among information technology, organizations, embeddedness, and institutions (see Fig. 2.4). Institutional theory "offers students of technology a less constrained vantage point from which to examine the role of macrosocial forces" (Barley 1990, p. 62). Institutionalism has the potential not only to identify power structures and their alignment to technological systems, but also to suggest some modifications to the institutional environment that might influence both organizational structures and technological features (Battilana et al. 2009; Yuan Lu et al. 2008; Scott 2010b; Wry et al. 2010). Institutional theory can help explain how information technologies influence organizational and institutional arrangements, as well as how these arrangements affect the way information technologies are selected, designed, implemented, and used (Currie 2009; Fountain 2001a; Jayatilaka and Hirschheim 2009; Phang et al. 2008).

According to the technology enactment framework, objective information technologies are in some way modified by organizational and inter-organizational factors to become enacted technologies (Antonio Cordella and Iannacci 2010; Feldman and Horan forthcoming; Gil-Garcia 2006; Herrera and Gil-Garcia 2010; Lee et al. 2009; Luna-Reyes and Gil-Garcia 2011; Tsai et al. 2009; Yildiz 2007). Fountain (2001a) contends that enacted technology can be understood as the perception, design, and use of objective technologies, such as the Internet and different pieces of hardware and software. Objective technology also includes all other features that could potentially be selected as part of the enacted technology, but for some reason are not included in the information technologies actually in use (Gil-Garcia and Luna-Reyes 2009; Gabriel et al. 2004). Therefore, two elements could represent the enacted technology: the technological features of the current system and the way in which different users take advantage of the technology's characteristics (Fountain 2001a; Hassan and Gil-Garcia 2008). In other words, "the embeddedness of government actors in cognitive, cultural, social, and institutional structures influences the design, perceptions, and uses of the Internet and related IT" (Fountain 2001a, p. 88).

Organizational forms include structural characteristics, such as centralization, formalization, and communication channels. According to Fountain (1995), several bureaucratic characteristics of the organizations that design, implement, or use the technology are contained in this construct. Organizational and organizational network factors have a direct effect on the enacted technology. In contrast, institutional arrangements, represented by laws, regulations, and other cognitive, cultural, or socio-structural constraints found in government contexts, have an indirect effect. According to the technology enactment theory, institutional arrangements influence organizational forms and thereby indirectly impact the enacted technology (Antonio Cordella and Iannacci 2010; Chen and Hsieh 2009; Gil-Garcia 2005b, 2006; Luna-Reyes and Gil-Garcia 2011). Recent research has demonstrated that a direct effect may also exist (Luna-Reyes et al. 2008).

Further, the resulting enacted technology produces certain organizational outcomes. These outcomes (good or bad) produce modifications to the technology itself, but may ultimately lead to transformations in the organizational forms or even the institutional arrangements in the long run (Fountain 2001a, 2008; Gil-Garcia 2005b, 2006; Gil-Garcia and Luna-Reyes 2009). Thus, the technology enactment framework recognizes the complex relations between information technology and social structures, including organizational characteristics, institutional arrangements, and other external forces (Antonio Cordella and Iannacci 2010; Chen and Hsieh 2009; Feldman and Horan forthcoming; Gil-Garcia 2006; Gil-Garcia and Luna-Reyes 2009; Herrera and Gil-Garcia 2010).

Some weaknesses of the framework have been previously suggested and discussed. First, the framework has been considered too abstract and general to be used for prediction and hypothesis testing (Bretschneider 2003; Danziger 2004). Second, Fountain's original piece (*Building a Virtual State*) that introduced the framework makes connections between a case and a set of main arguments in a somewhat too ambitious way—without enough evidence, using examples in limited contexts (only from the US federal government) (Bretschneider 2003) (Garson 2003b; Norris 2003). The original framework does not consider other government contexts such as regional or local; therefore, some potentially important variables could be left out (Yildiz 2007). Third, the framework works better for explaining organizational politics rather than information technology and institutional change. Fourth, the framework's adoption of neo-institutional theory fails to explain how agents overcome institutional barriers (Yang 2003, p. 432), while a more nuanced discussion of institutional theory could be useful (Danziger

2004, p. 109). Finally, in the initial presentation of her framework, Fountain (2001a) ignores previous integrative theories such as the socio-technical approach, which already proposed to study both the technology and the social and organizational relationships around it (Bretschneider 2003; Danziger 2004; Schellong 2007). In this sense, according to some authors, the original technology enactment framework has some important limitations.

In contrast, researchers have also argued that the technology enactment framework has important advantages in comparison with previous research. For example, Bretschneider (2003) says that Fountain's framework is valuable because it attempts to explain the interrelationships between technology, organizations, and institutions. Few previous studies incorporated institutions as an important variable. Similarly, Dawes (2002) explains that the technology enactment framework is important because it uses institutional theory to explain the use of information technology in government, in contrast with studying the government as a regulator of the use of information technologies by other social actors. This author also highlights the relevance of studying practical cases for long periods of time, given the huge investments in information technologies, particularly the Internet. Finally, for some scholars the technology enactment framework is potentially useful in practical terms because it could help public managers to plan, design, and implement e-government initiatives (Danziger 2004; Garson 2003b).

2.3 Social Construction of Information Technology

This section briefly explains the social constructivism approach, describes some of its applications in information systems research, and introduces the concept of multiple enactments as a way to understand the perspectives of different social actors and social groups. Pfeffer (1982) states that social constructionist views are more interactive in their explanations of individual actions; that is, they acknowledge mutual causality and multiple determinations of outcomes (Holstein and Gubrium 2008; Irwin 2011; Lock and Strong 2010). He identifies two main perspectives within this theoretical tradition (Pfeffer 1982, p. 209): (1) an interactionist approach, growing out of either the symbolic interactionists (Blumer 1962; Denzin 2008; Manning and Smith 2010; Mead 1938; Stryker 2008) or the ethnomethodological tradition (Cicourel 1964, 1974; Cunliffe 2010; Garfinkel 1967; Mitev 2009; Ross and Chiasson 2005; Schutz 1967) and (2) a structuralist approach (Berger and Luckmann 1966; Dickerson 2010; Goffman 1961, 1974; Holtzner and Marx 1979; Lock and Strong 2010).

The interactionist approach recognizes that individuals derive meaning through social interaction with others and that meaning is interpreted differently by each individual. In contrast, the structuralist approach sees reality as existing on its own account independently of the way in which it is perceived and reaffirmed by people in everyday activities. A pure structuralist position weighs in on the side of social structure and is commonly associated with gestalt theories. As should be clear for the reader, these two perspectives focus on particular and different aspects of the relationship between individual interactions and social structures. They could be seen as complementary approaches.

2.3.1 Technology and the Social Construction of Reality

According to Berger and Luckmann (1966), what people experience as objective reality is actually socially constructed. Individuals and groups interacting together in a social system form concepts of each other's actions, and these concepts eventually become habituated into reciprocal roles the actors play in relation to each other. When these roles are made available to other members of society to enter into and play out, the reciprocal interactions are said to be institutionalized. In the process of this institutionalization, people's conceptions and beliefs of what reality is become embedded in the institutional fabric of society. Social reality is therefore said to be socially constructed (Berger and Luckmann 1966). Following this logic, the interpretation of social reality depends on individuals' backgrounds and positions within the social setting (Schutz 1967). Intersubjectivity is a very important concept for some constructivist approaches (Dimaggio and Markus 2010; Harklau 2011; Miranda and Saunders 2003). It is through intersubjectivity that "meaning derives from interactive interpretation by multiple persons, not simply from the cognition of a single individual" (Miranda and Saunders 2003, p. 88). Therefore, individuals have different perceptions of social reality, but through their interactions they could build collective meanings and have more similar understandings (Harrison et al. 2007).

Sociologists of technology have adopted a social constructivist approach to understand how technologies are adopted in complex social and organizational systems (Bijker et al. 1987; Bijker and Law 2000; Collins 1987; Johnson and Wetmore 2009; Sismondo 2009; Tatnall 2010). They contend that linear models are not capable of accounting for complex social relationships. Pinch and Bijker (1987) argue that a multidirectional view is necessary for a social constructivist understanding of technological systems (see Fig. 2.5). The first step is to identify the relevant social groups. These are the groups that are concerned with the technological artifact and their interpretations will be relevant for the analysis: "The key requirement is that all members of a certain social group share the same set of meanings, attached to a specific artifact" (Pinch and Bijker 1987, p. 30). The members of each social group have certain common characteristics (background, position in the organization, formal education, experience, etc.) that make them perceive the social reality, including the technological artifact, in a very similar way.

A second step is to identify problems that each group has with respect to certain artifacts. It is also necessary to discover the solutions available for each problem. At this point, it should be evident that conflicts exist between technical requirements and potential solutions for the different social groups (Pinch and Bijker 1987). Complex interactions between problems and solutions of the different social groups

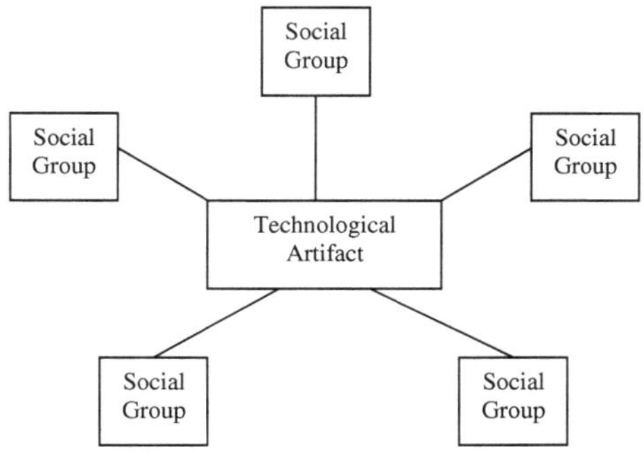

Fig. 2.5 Relationship between technological artifact and relevant social groups (Bijker et al. 1987, © 1987 Massachusetts Institute of Technology, by permission of The MIT Press)

take place and certain artifacts become *stabilized*. Stabilization means that by the end of a certain period of time, certain characteristics of the technical artifacts can be taken for granted. All the relevant groups share the meaning of certain artifacts and their implicit characteristics (Pinch and Bijker 1987). However, the meanings are also shaped by some of the social actors interacting with the technological artifact: "Because IT artifacts are designed, constructed, and used by people, they are shaped by the interests, values, and assumptions of a wide variety of communities of developers, investors, users, etc." (Orlikowski and Iacono 2006, p. 36). In fact, in the case of information technologies, some authors argue that their characteristics continue to be dynamic and emergent as the users interact with the technologies; implying that there is no stabilization for them (Contractor et al. 2011; Leonardi 2009a; Leonardi and Barley 2010; Orlikowski 2000; Orlikowski 2010b; Prasad 2009). Recent studies consider the sociomateriality of organizational life in interacting with technology, thereby accounting for the multiple and dynamic ways in which the social and the material are constitutively entangled in everyday life (Contractor et al. 2011; Orlikowski 2010a; Orlikowski and Scott 2008).

2.3.2 The Social Construction of Reality in Information Systems

According to Orlikowski (1992, p. 401), the social constructivist perspective in information systems research can help to understand "how shared interpretations around a certain technology arise and affect the development of and interaction with that technology". In fact, one of the main advantages of a social constructivist approach is that it takes into consideration the perspectives of different social groups for the analysis (Bartis and Mitev 2008; Howcroft and Light 2010; Stahl 2008). This corpus of research is based mostly on interpretative approaches (Boland 1985; Klein and Hirschheim 1983; Leonardi and Barley 2010; Pinch and Bijker 1987). In contrast to positivism, interpretative approaches represent a philosophical tradition based on the interpretative nature of knowledge. What we know does not exist independently of consciousness, but rather knowledge is a culturally bound social construction (Heshusius and Ballard 1996; Mölder 2010; Packer 2011, pp. 123-166; Riccucci 2010, p. 66).

Doing this kind of analysis requires some specific considerations. Klein and Hirschheim (1983) propose three steps to follow in doing research, using what they call "a consequentialist perspective." First, it is necessary to establish that in principle it is possible to identify the actual consequences (in this case, of an information system). Second, the researcher has to select certain consequences that in principle are predictable. Finally, the predicted and perceived consequences have to be evaluated according to certain criteria. They argue that this process leads to more valuable lessons than a factor approach: "Instead of ending up with a list of technological applications and their possible consequences spelled out in detail, the hermeneutic procedure came up with a better understanding of the conflict-laden nature of changing office technology—a qualitatively totally different kind of knowledge, but one that nevertheless is highly pertinent to the issue at hand" (Klein and Hirschheim, 1983, p. 39).

Information systems have gained much attention from social constructionist approaches. The approaches suggest that interpretation of different social groups shape the characteristics and features of information systems (Howcroft and Light 2010; Huang and Galliers 2011; Iivari et al. 2009; Leonardi and Barley 2010; Vannoy and Salam 2010). However, social constructivist approaches are not necessarily in opposition to positivistic approaches (Friedman and Rogers 2009; Heshusius and Ballard 1996; Shay 2008). Both approaches can contribute to a more comprehensive understanding of the relationships between information technologies and social structures, because they highlight different aspects of social phenomena (Bartis and Mitev 2008; Jackson and Klobas 2008; Mukherjee 2008; Orlikowski and Baroudi 1991; Orlikowski and Iacono 2001). Together, they have the potential to offer a richer and more complete explanation of social phenomena.

In an attempt to conciliate objective and subjective realities, Sarker (2000) developed a model that considers culture, sub-cultures, and frames as social filters through which different social groups subjectively experience the objective reality (see Fig. 2.6). His work is mainly based on Leavitt's (1965) diamond model (Bostrom and Heinen 1977; Markus 1983; Robey 1987) and the work of Berger and Luckmann (1966). Unlike most previous views, this socio-technical model recognizes the importance of multiple elements in a technological system such as structure, tasks, people, and technology.

However, according to Sarker (2000) this socio-technical view offers limited understanding of organizational politics (Alter 2010; Bellamy 2000; Garson 2000a; Leonardi and Barley 2010; Mansell and Silverstone 1996; Newman and Rosenberg 1985; Zanko et al. 2008); and institutional realities (Butler 2003; Gil-Garcia 2006; Hirschheim and Newman 1991; Luna-Reyes et al. 2005, 2007; Orlikowski and Gash 1994; Prasad 1993; Wiredu 2010). In order to account for these factors, it is necessary to take into consideration the subjective experiences of different actors. Sarker (2000) argues that "prior conceptualizations of organizations have recognized only 'objective realities,' which has led to an

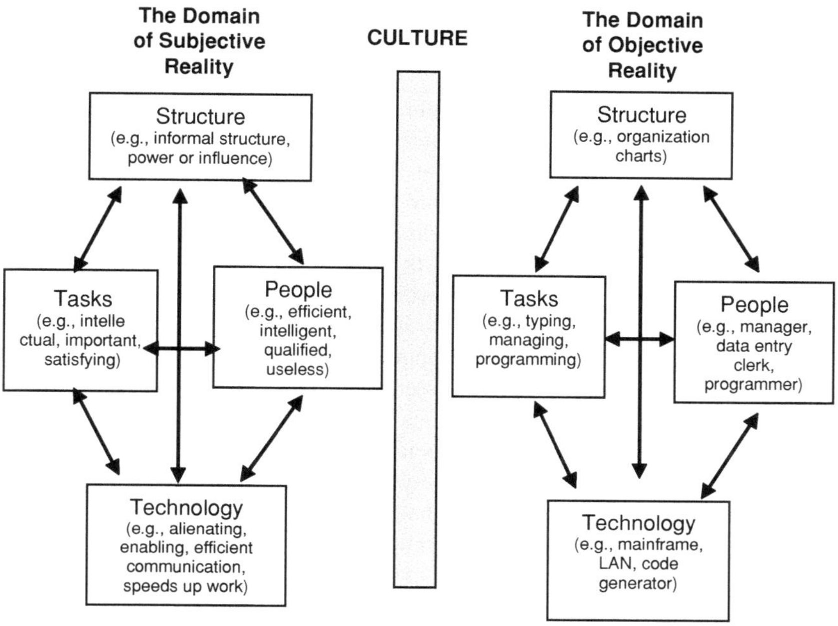

Fig. 2.6 Sarker's organizational model. [Sarker (2000). Reprinted with permission of the publisher]

incomplete understanding of implementation; by including the analysis of 'subjective realities' in the organization, a better understanding of political and institutional forces and of organizational resistance arising from them may be gained" (p. 197). In Sarker's model, organizations are socially constructed, but there are "objective real" and "subjective real" aspects to them.

According to Sarker (2000), objective realities are socially constructed, but their degree of institutionalization makes social actors take them for granted as if they were part of the natural world. In this model, tasks, structures, technologies, and individuals are experienced as objective realities. In contrast, subjective realities are affected by an individual's background, position, culture, and role in the organization. They refer to how individuals give differentiated meanings to what may appear to be the same objective reality. Thus, "individuals socialized into different occupations and roles, and belonging to cultural and interest groups tend to experience the *same* 'objective reality' as *different* 'subjective realities'" (Sarker 2000, p. 199).

Sarker's model is similar to and different from Orlikowski's conceptualization of sociomateriality (Orlikowski 2010b). Subjective reality and objective reality match the social and the material, but sociomateriality emphasizes that the social and the material are constitutively entangled in everyday life. They could be distinctively separated for analysis, but in reality they are profoundly entangled and embedded in social relations. Therefore, sociomateriality has a similar, but distinctive logic in comparison to Sarker's model. The entanglement between both aspects and the deep intermingling of materiality within practice are of central importance.

Recognizing the effect of these different perceptions is not unique to constructivist work and can be clearly appreciated in the following two passages. Kraemer et al. (1989, p. 8) mention that "management action becomes itself an artifact of the social movements, social structures, work-group folkways and mores, ideological perceptions, and administrative hierarchies surrounding the managers". However, the perception of these effects in the organization could be different for different social actors, according to their organizational roles, formal education, previous experiences, and background. Similarly, Reeve and Petch (1999, p. 2) affirm that "purchasing computers for organizations usually involves a hidden agenda of personal interests, career ambitions, and inter-group politics, as well as rational, dispassionate evaluations of organizational needs". The specific interests and perceptions of different social actors have a differentiated influence on the way they interact with the technology and with other actors in the organization. This body of work suggests that both objective and subjective realities are important in understanding organizational dynamics in general and government IT initiatives in particular (Hossain et al. forthcoming; Ruuska and Teigland 2009; Scholl 2008; Tsai et al. 2009; Tseng 2008).

2.3.3 Multiple Enactments of Information Technologies

Orlikowski (2000) proposes a different way to study the relationships between social structures and information technologies; one that is related to social constructivist approaches. Her work argues that past efforts missed some characteristics of information technologies. She relies on Gidden's (1984) original work to introduce a new way to report these two essential conflicts: emergent structures and the enactment of structures (Gil-Garcia and Hassan 2008). This practice lens, as she calls it, and its basic arguments are still strongly rooted in structuration theory and the assumption of causal recursiveness between social structures and information technology (Grgecic and Rosenkranz 2008; Jones and Karsten 2008; Lyytinen and Newman 2008; Orlikowski 1992; Paré et al. 2008; Pinch and Bijker 1987). Orlikowski (2000, p. 406) explains, "Through repeated interaction, certain technology's properties become implicated in an ongoing process of structuration. The resulting recurrent social practice produces and reproduces particular structures of technology use". These structures of technology use would be different for social groups with differentiated characteristics in terms of background, social context, organizational position, professional experience, or formal education.

Orlikowski's approach acknowledges that all interactions are situational; different groups can enact different properties of the technologies according to their own norms, facilities, and interpretative schemes (Harrison et al. 2007; Orlikowski 2000). Building on this idea, different enactments can result from what may appear

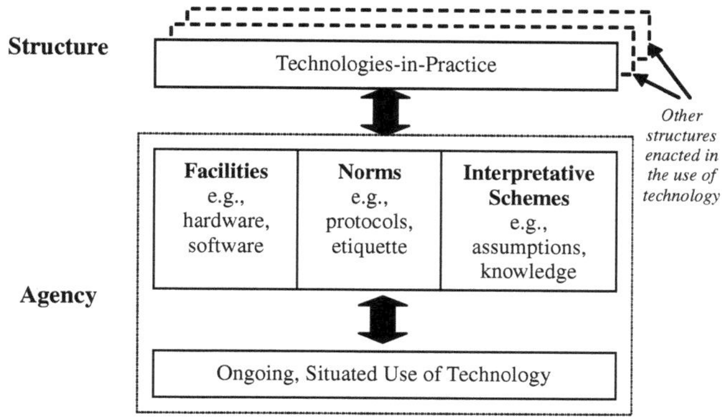

Fig. 2.7 Enactment of technologies-in-practice: one social group [Adapted with permission from Orlikowski (2000). Copyright (2000), the Institute for Operations Research and the Management Sciences, 7240 Parkway Drive, Suite 300, Hanover, Maryland 21076]

to be the same technological properties (see Fig. 2.7). Therefore, social groups with different job positions, personal interests, and professional backgrounds are expected to enact differentiated "technologies in practice," even when the technological artifact could be seen as essentially the same (Gil-Garcia and Hassan 2008; Hardy 2010; Leonardi 2010; Leonardi and Barley 2008; Meneklis and Douligeris 2008; Orlikowski 2008).

This framework also allows for a better understanding of the emergence of information technologies in use—as people interact with certain structural properties of the system—without any assumption about the stability and relative completeness of the technologies (Gil-Garcia and Hassan 2008; Jarrahi 2010; Orlikowski 2000; Zillien and Hargittai 2009). "Instead, the focus is on what structures emerge as people interact recurrently with whatever properties of the technology are at hand, whether these were built in, added on, modified, or invented on the fly" (Orlikowski 2000, p. 407). This implies that technological artifacts do not necessarily reach stabilization as was initially proposed by sociologists of technology (Bijker and Law 2000; Pinch and Bijker 1987), "IT artifacts are neither fixed nor independent, but they emerge from ongoing social and economic practices" (Orlikowski and Iacono 2006, p. 36).

The social and economic practices are dynamic and context-specific. Therefore, different social groups will enact different technologies-in-practice, but the same social group will also enact different technologies-in-practice at different times and spaces (e.g., past, present, future) (see Fig. 2.8). For instance, Harrison and colleagues (2007) analyze the different enactments of geographic information technologies (GIT) during the response and aftermath of the World Trade Center attacks of September 11. They found that the perceptions of different social groups involved were affected by their previous backgrounds and organizational positions, leading to different technologies-in-practice. They also found that through their intensive interactions, the groups started sharing some of their perceptions and

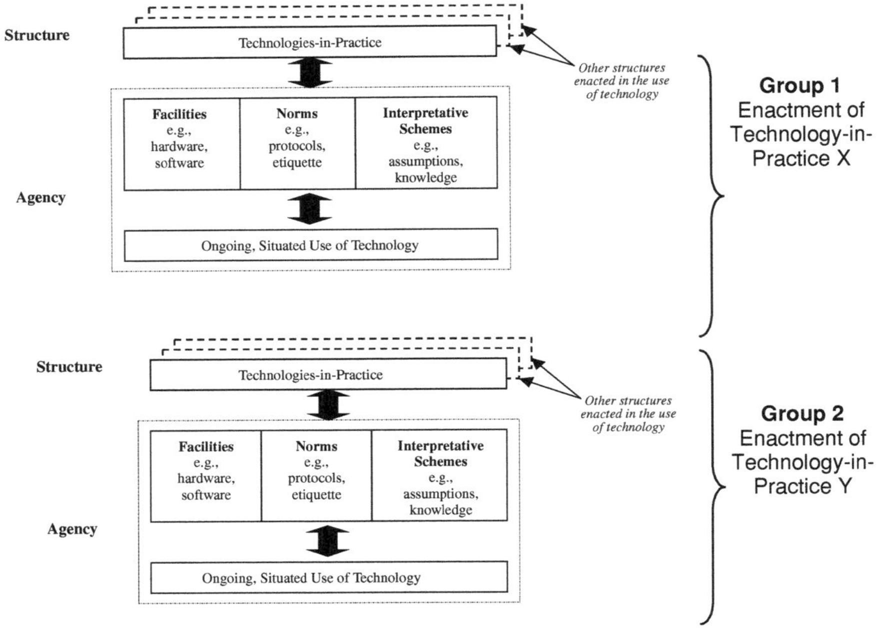

Fig. 2.8 Enactment of technologies-in-practice: two social groups. [Adapted with permission from Orlikowski (2000). Copyright (2000), the Institute for Operations Research and the Management Sciences, 7240 Parkway Drive, Suite 300, Hanover, Maryland 21076]

meanings; at the end, the group enactments of GIT were much more similar to each other than at the beginning (Harrison et al. 2007).

The concept of sociomateriality helps understand the recursive and complex relationships between humans and technologies-in-practice (Orlikowski 2007, 2010b; Orlikowski and Scott 2008). All practices are always sociomaterial, and this sociomateriality shapes the characteristics and possibilities of social and organizational life. Technologies-in-practice become manifestations of organizational practices increasingly entangled with emerging sociomaterialities.

2.4 Enacting Electronic Government Success

After reviewing different theories that take into consideration the dynamic and complex interplay between information technologies and social structures, the technology enactment framework was selected as the foundation of a new integrative model to understand e-government success. First, Fountain's technology enactment theory is suitable for doing research about different stages or processes such as selection, design, implementation, and use of information technologies (Fountain and Gil-Garcia 2006a). Second, consistent with its institutional

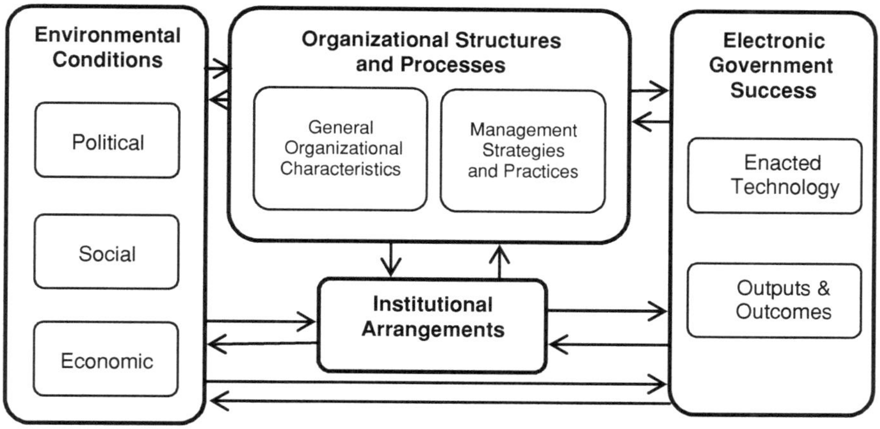

Fig. 2.9 Enacting electronic government success

theoretical basis, this framework allows the organization to be the main unit of analysis (Fountain 2001a, 2001c, 2008), instead of the individual. Third, the theory was developed using empirical data from government agencies and, therefore, takes into consideration some of the particularities of the public sector. Fourth, the theory is flexible enough to be used from a positivist or a non-positivist view. Fifth, related to the previous point, the framework allows for using qualitative and quantitative research strategies. Finally, this framework pays particular attention to institutional arrangements and institutions are essential to understand government phenomena. For these reasons, the technology enactment framework is a strong alternative for the foundation of a new integrative e-government success theory. This subsection presents the development of a new integrative model to understand e-government success. It discusses each of the relevant theoretical constructs and relates them to specific variables found in the literature and already presented in Chap. 1.

Thus, this book proposes a theoretical model to better understand the complex relationships between e-government success and different organizational, institutional, and contextual factors. In order to develop a more comprehensive understanding, the technology enactment theory is complemented with ideas and concepts from recent e-government literature, social constructivism, and other integrative approaches to information technologies (mentioned before in this chapter). I agree that "given the context-specificity of IT artifacts, there is no single, one-size-fits-all conceptualization of technology that will work for all studies" (Orlikowski and Iacono 2006, p. 37) and, therefore, there would not be a one-size-fits-all theoretical model either. However, integrative models could be developed for specific phenomena. This section proposes an integrative theoretical model to understand e-government success (see Fig. 2.9).

As mentioned before, the technology enactment framework belongs to the institutional tradition (Chen and Hsieh 2009; Gil-Garcia and Hassan 2008; Powell and DiMaggio 1991; Scott 2001) and attempts to explain the effects of organizational forms and institutional arrangements on the information technology selected, designed, implemented, and used by government agencies (Antonio Cordella and Iannacci 2010; Gil-Garcia 2005b, 2006; Herrera and Gil-Garcia 2010; Luna-Reyes and Gil-Garcia 2011). According to Fountain (1995, 2001a, 2008), the technology enactment framework pays attention to the relationships between information technology, organizations, embeddedness, and institutions. Therefore, in contrast with other theoretical lenses, this framework does pay special attention to institutions and the role they play in the enactment of government information technologies. This influence is particularly important in government settings, because governments are enabled to act by laws and regulations and the impact of these institutions could be greater than in the private sector.

Being primarily based on Fountain's technology enactment framework, the logic and dynamics of the proposed theoretical model (enacting e-government success) are very similar to the original framework (Fountain 1995, 2001a, 2008). Organizational forms have an impact on the enacted technology and its outcomes. Institutional arrangements have an indirect influence on the enacted technology through their direct influence on organizational forms. Based on the process model of computing change and previous research on IT success, direct impacts from institutional arrangements and environmental conditions are also taken into consideration (Kraemer et al. 1989; Luna-Reyes et al. 2008). Finally, the recursive nature of the relationship between information technologies and social structures is acknowledged in most of the cases with arrows going in the opposite direction, representing bidirectional effects.

By adopting an ensemble view of technology (Orlikowski and Iacono 2001), this theoretical model focuses not only on the enacted technology and organizational outcomes, but also on some of the processes that generate certain organizational structures and processes, as well as certain institutional arrangements. Therefore, it is important to consider the more general environment affecting the technology enactment process. Some of the environmental dimensions identified in previous research (Hall 2002; Herrera and Gil-Garcia 2010; Luna-Reyes and Gil-Garcia 2011; Savvides and Koutrakou 2010; Tsai et al. 2009) can be mapped to the constructs of the technology enactment framework: technological conditions to "objective technology," legal and cultural conditions to "institutional arrangements." However, other important contextual factors are not taken into consideration: political conditions, economic conditions, demographic conditions, and ecological conditions. The proposed model includes the construct "environmental conditions" in order to have a more comprehensive understanding of the relationships between e-government success and its larger environment.

Organizational, institutional, and contextual factors, as well as their multiple interactions, affect the way information technologies are selected, designed, implemented, and used in government organizations (Antonio Cordella and Iannacci 2010; Fountain 2001a, 2008; Gil-Garcia 2005b, 2006; Luna-Reyes and

Gil-Garcia 2011). All these factors produce certain opportunities and constraints: "The mix of opportunities and constraints confronting an organization constitutes the options for action by that part of the government's political-administrative system that constitutes computing management" (Kraemer et al. 1989, p. 104). In this case, computing management is represented by the social actors with decision-making power within a government agency. They can certainly make important decisions about IT, but their decisions are affected and constrained by organizational and institutional variables. As mentioned by Fountain (2001a, p. 193),"The Internet is a revolutionary lever for institutional change. Yet inside the machinery of the state, amid a web of institutional structures that offer perverse incentives for innovation and efficiency gains, the action of this lever is complex, indirect, and mediated significantly by institutional and organizational arrangements".

In the proposed model, the success of e-government is defined and represented in terms of enacted technology (e.g., functional interface and other characteristics of the systems) and organizational outputs and outcomes (e.g., efficiency, effectiveness, and other potential results). More specifically, enacted technology refers to certain characteristics of the e-government initiative such as hardware, software, functionality, usability, or accessibility, but also to the derived social relations and diverse uses. E-government success would also include some of the potential outputs and outcomes stated in the goals and objectives of the e-government initiative such as efficiency, cost-savings, effectiveness, greater service quality, transparency, and/or increased citizen participation, among others.

There is also a dynamic interaction between enacted technology, outputs, and organizational structures and processes. So, it is expected that information technologies have an impact on the organization, but it is also expected that the characteristics of the organization and the individuals within the organization affect the way ICTs are implemented and, consequently, their overall results. This recursive way of thinking about certain "technical" characteristics of information systems has been suggested previously. Kling (1993, p. 4) states that "there is a growing realization, as networks tie users together at a rapidly rising rate, that usability cannot generally be determined without our considering how computer systems are shaped by and also alter interdependencies in groups and organizations". Therefore, information technologies are shaped not only by individual users, but also by the characteristics of the groups and organizations in which those individuals live and work (Leonardi 2010; Leonardi and Barley 2008; Orlikowski 2008, 2010a, 2010c).

The technology enactment framework, the process model of computing change, and other integrative theoretical approaches involve a series of complex and recursive causal relationships. For instance, "the model of computing change... describes a cyclical flow of effects. The environment presents opportunities and constraints, which are filtered by the actions of computing management through its policies, which affect the activities of the computer package and produce outcomes. The consequences of these outcomes, in turn, are fed back to computing management in the form of the needs of the computing package and user demands to support development and mitigate problems" (Kraemer et al. 1989, p. 109). In addition, "information systems quickly become intertwined in hundreds of ways with performance programs, routines, communication modes, and power" (Fountain 2001a, p. 196). Accordingly, IT initiatives are outcomes of a recursive and complex relationship between information technologies and social structures (organizations, institutions, and policies). As a consequence, the results of IT-related activities are highly uncertain and cannot be easily predicted.

Furthermore, the resulting enacted technology produces certain organizational outcomes in terms of efficiency, transparency, effectiveness, participation, and accountability, among others (Gil-Garcia and Luna-Reyes 2007). These outcomes (good or bad) produce modifications in the technology itself, but also in the long run, may lead to transformations in the organizational forms or even the institutional arrangements (Fountain 2001a, 2008). Thus, similar to other ensemble-view approaches, the technology enactment framework recognizes the complex relationships between information technologies and social structures.

The proposed model of enacting e-government success takes into consideration all these different theoretical constructs and hypothesizes their interrelationships. In addition, in order to reach a more comprehensive understanding of this complex phenomenon from different perspectives, this model considers some ideas from social constructivist approaches. Therefore, perspectives of different relevant social groups should be included in the analysis. This inclusion provides the opportunity to learn about both objective and subjective realities, and thus to have a qualitatively different understanding that does not ignore the differences in perceptions and interests among social actors.

Objective reality is represented by contextual, institutional, and organizational factors that are taken for granted by the relevant groups involved in developing, managing, and interacting with e-government initiatives. Characteristics such as state population, state government size, IT organization budget, IT organization size, existence of usability, accessibility, or other types of training for IT professionals, the number of services provided through the website, contact information presented, and others could be perceived as objective reality that exists independently of the social context. This perception is not necessarily true from a third party perspective, but it is true for the groups involved with the technological artifacts and the social relationships around those artifacts. Objective reality could also include the joint perceptions about the success of an e-government initiative; that is, the characteristics that most participants perceive in a very similar way.

In contrast, subjective reality includes the differentiated perceptions of relevant social groups involved with the technological artifacts. Professional background, position within the organization, and work experience will all affect the way different social groups assign meaning to what may appear to be the same objective reality. Perceptions of efficiency, informal networks, importance, and other qualifying characteristics of the different factors (organizational, institutional, and environmental) or the enacted technology are examples of this subjective reality. The proposed model attempts to capture, at least partially, these two domains of reality in order to obtain a more comprehensive understanding of the recursive and complex nature of the relationships between information technologies and social structures.

As mentioned above, previous studies have found evidence supporting different factors as important determinants of e-government success. However, most of this research has hypothesized models in which all factors are at the same level of importance and only as direct effects, limiting understanding about the complex relationships among different kinds of factors (e.g., organizational and institutional) (Gil-Garcia 2008). Therefore, these models do not allow a more comprehensive and integrative exploration of e-government success. In contrast, the model proposed in this book attempts to contribute in this direction by allowing indirect effects and explicitly including some of the interrelationships among organizational, institutional, and environmental variables. Below are descriptions of each component of the proposed theoretical model and some specific research questions associated with them.

2.4.1 Electronic Government Success

E-government means different things to different social actors and in different contexts (Antonio Cordella and Iannacci 2010; Gil-Garcia and Luna-Reyes 2003, 2006; Hardy and Williams 2008; Luna-Reyes and Gil-Garcia 2011; Schelin 2003; Scholl et al. 2006) from internal systems to services provided through the Internet, from hardware to organizational technologies, from personal computers in government offices to highly sophisticated information systems that cross organizational boundaries. Furthermore, there is no consensus about what IT success and e-government success mean and how to measure them (Alshawi and Alalwany 2009; Carbo and Williams 2004; DeLone and Mclean 1992, 2003; Fasanghari and Habibipour 2009; Gil-Garcia and Pardo 2005; Gonzalez et al. 2010; Jun and Weare forthcoming; Morgeson III and Mithas 2009). One way to think about e-government success is in terms of certain success measures. They could be included in the goals and objectives that e-government initiatives attempt to accomplish. Following this logic, an e-government initiative is successful to the extent it achieves its goals and objectives in terms of specific success measures.

Fountain (2001a) contends that the enacted technology can be understood as the perception, design, and use of objective technologies, such as the Internet and different pieces of hardware and software. Therefore, the enacted technology can be represented through the technological features of the current system and the way in which different users take advantage of those technology characteristics (Fountain 2001a; Laudon 1986). These features and potential benefits could be seen as e-government success measures. In contrast, objective technology includes all features that could potentially have been selected as part of the enacted technology, but for some reason are not parts of the information technologies in use (Gabriel Puron Cid and Gil-Garcia 2004).

The perception and use of information technologies within an organization constitute the enacted technology (Fountain 1995, 2001a). The enacted technology construct is similar to what Kraemer et al. (1989) called the computing package. According to these authors, two of its more important elements are its technological sophistication and sociotechnical interface. Both technological sophistication and sociotechnical interface are positively related to computing outcomes (Kraemer et al. 1989): "Computing outcomes are the results of computing package operations that affect the computing system" (Kraemer et al. 1989, p. 106). These results could be direct outputs of the information system or more general organizational outcomes such as efficiency, effectiveness, service quality, increased transparency, and greater citizen participation.

There are objective and subjective computing outcomes that could be used to measure the success of an e-government project. Objective outcomes are the observed results of the computing package and subjective outcomes are the perceptions and interpretations of those results by different groups within the organization (Kraemer et al. 1989). These perceptions could be very different and, in fact, "institutional actors tend to see the world from a particular vantage point colored greatly not by atomistic interests, but by interests and models that derive in part from structural position and ongoing social relations in networks" (Fountain 2001a, p. 83). As a result of the different actors and stakeholders involved in the use of information technologies who have different views and different approaches (Angelopoulos et al. 2010; Foteinou and Pavlidis 2010; Marijn Janssen and Klievink 2010), it is difficult to reach consensus on evaluating the performance of IT projects and information systems. Therefore, understanding and measuring e-government success is not an easy task and faces myriad challenges, from deciding on a measuring technique to incorporating different perspectives on the success of a particular e-government initiative (Angelopoulos et al. 2010; Petter et al. 2008).

2.4.2 Organizational Structures and Processes

According to the technology enactment framework, objective information technologies are, in some way, modified by organizational and inter-organizational factors. In other words, "the embeddedness of government actors in cognitive, cultural, social, and institutional structures influences the design, perceptions, and uses of the Internet and related IT" (Fountain 2001a, p. 88). This is consistent with findings from other studies of public sector information systems (Antonio Cordella and Iannacci 2010; Dawes and Pardo 2002; Ganapati 2011; Herrera and Gil-Garcia 2010; Seongcheol Kim et al. 2009; Kraemer and King 1986; Laudon and Westin 1986; Moon 2002; Mundkur and Venkatesh 2009). Organizational structures and processes could include structural characteristics such as centralization, formalization, and communication channels, among others (Antonio Cordella and Iannacci 2010; Damanpour and Schneider 2009; Lee et al. 2011; Luna-Reyes and

Gil-Garcia 2011; van Veenstra et al. 2010). According to Fountain (1995, 2001a, 2008), several bureaucratic characteristics of the organizations that design, implement, or use the technology are contained in this construct. Organizational and organizational network factors have a direct effect on the enacted technology.

In general terms, organizational factors relate to the organization as a whole and some characteristics of the specific IT initiatives. These factors can include the length of the project, understanding its strategic goals, the extent of change in business processes, the project management approach, and the lack of implementation guidelines (Chang et al. 2001; Davenport 1993; Gil-Garcia et al. 2009; Gil-Garcia and Pardo 2005; Gottschalk 2009; Hussin and Kassim 2010; Reddick 2009b; Seneviratne 1999; Umble et al. 2003). Despite the importance of other organizational factors, adequate funding is undoubtedly one of the most important factors (Barrett and Greene 2000; Caffrey 1998; Dawes and Pardo 2002; Detlor et al. 2010; Edmiston 2003; Fleming et al. 2010; Gonzalez et al. 2010; Harris 2000; Ho 2002; Holden et al. 2003; Moon 2002; NGA 1997; Rose and Grant 2010; West and Berman 2001). The size of the project and the diversity of the users or organizations involved are also two important factors to consider in IT initiatives (Barki et al. 1993; Choudhari et al. 2011; Davis 1982; Dawes and Pardo 2002; Ghapanchi et al. 2008; McFarlan 1981; Melin and Axelsson 2009; Tsai et al. 2009).

In the model proposed in this book, the "organizational structures and processes" construct includes both organizational forms (Fountain 2001a, 2008) and management action (Kraemer et al. 1989). This is consistent with previous integrative models because "computing management is a filter through which environmental opportunities and constraints must pass" (Kraemer et al. 1989, p. 105). This view does not imply that managers always know the exact effects of certain information technologies on the organization, but they have certain expectations about them (Åkesson and Edvardsson 2008; De' and Sarkar 2010; Fountain 2001a; Gil-Garcia 2006; Kraemer et al. 1989; Sarker 2000). Some of the possible expectations are cost reduction, organizational control, operational integration, increased productivity, and power reinforcement (Andersen et al. 2010; Badri and Alshare 2008; Rowley 2011; Srivastava 2011).

Although organizations are influenced by their environmental conditions, management objectives and interests are very important because they act as filters in the environment (Jansen and Løvdal 2009; Nunes et al. 2009). In addition, environmental conditions can serve as ways to justify pre-determined actions that are based on other motivations or incentives. For instance, sometimes managers "initiate action for personal and professional motives, sometimes irrespective of environmental conditions. Often, in fact, when computer managers initiate action on non-environmental grounds, environmental conditions enter into the action only as a means of rationalizing and legitimating it" (Kraemer et al. 1989, p. 98). Thus, organizational structures and processes are important e-government success factors. Organizational forms and management action are expected to have a direct influence on the success of an e-government initiative.

RQ1: To what extent organizational structures and processes have a direct effect on e-government success?

2.4.3 Institutional Arrangements

Institutional arrangements can be conceived of as laws, norms, and meaning systems (Scott 2001). These institutional factors constrain the way people act in organizational settings. In fact, "institutions do not just constrain options: they establish the very criteria by which people discover their preferences" (Powell and DiMaggio 1991, p. 11). Therefore, institutional arrangements are very important elements in understanding how information technologies are selected, designed, implemented, and used in public organizations (Antonio Cordella and Iannacci 2010; Fountain 2001a; Gil-Garcia 2006; Hardy and Williams 2008; Hassan and Gil-Garcia 2008; Herrera and Gil-Garcia 2010; Tsai et al. 2009).

Institutions form guidelines for action, but also constrain those actions (Scott 2001). Information technology initiatives involve a complex set of decisions and interactions. These interactions are constrained by different institutional arrangements, but at the same time institutions "frame how those constraints operate" (Fountain 2001a, p. 92). Previous theoretical frameworks have used institutional theory to explain different aspects of information technologies such as adoption, implementation, and management (Bellamy and Taylor 1996; Butler 2003; Antonio Cordella and Iannacci 2010; Hardy and Williams 2008; Hassan and Gil-Garcia 2008; Laudon 1986; Tsai et al. 2009).

Government organizations are usually created and operate by virtue of a specific formal rule or group of rules. In making any kind of decision, including decisions about IT projects, public managers must take into consideration a large number of laws and regulations (Apostolou et al. 2011; Dawes and Nelson 1995; Fletcher 2004; Ghapanchi et al. 2008; Harris 2000; Landsbergen and Wolken 2001; NGA 1997). Federal systems, as in the United States, present additional challenges derived from the particularities of the intergovernmental relationships between different levels of governments and the diversity of local governments (Megan Cook et al. 2004; Chen and Thurmaier 2008; Ghapanchi et al. 2008; Gil-Garcia et al. 2005; Tolbert et al. 2008; Ubaldi and Roy 2010). The checks and balances among the executive, legislative, and judicial branches also pose challenges (Bellamy 2000; dos Santos and Reinhard forthcoming; Gottschalk 2009; Harris 2000; Bruce Rocheleau 2003).

Other institutional arrangements refer to the political complexities of every governmental system. Some examples of these factors are given by Dawes (1996, p. 381): (1) external influences over the decision-making process, such as legislative committees, interest groups, civil servants, and other governmental jurisdictions like local governments; (2) the power of agency discretion, which refers to the capacity of expert bureaucrats to influence programs and policies; and (3) the great importance of some government programs that reinforces vertical connections and creates disincentives to horizontal collaboration among agencies. For instance, this lack of collaboration can constrain IT projects that attempt to integrate or share information across multiple agencies (Fedorowicz et al. 2009; Fedorowicz et al. 2010; Fountain 2008; Kwon et al. 2009; Pardo et al. 2007; Pardo et al. 2008a; Wenjing 2011).

Institutions are not only laws and regulations, but also norms, actions or behaviors that people accept as good or take for granted (Hossain et al. forthcoming; Khalil 2011; Orlikowski 2000; Sawyer and Tyworth 2006; Scott 2001; Smith 2010; Star and Ruhleder 1996). For example, in modern democracies, privacy, accessibility, and security are seen as very positive and they greatly influence government actions. These are aspects that must be adequately addressed in government IT initiatives (Carter and McBride 2010; Duncan and Roehrig 2003; Joshi et al. 2001; Joshi et al. 2002; Luna-Reyes and Gil-Garcia 2003a; Milner 2000; Rowley 2011; Shareef et al. 2009). In summary, institutional arrangements are represented by laws, regulations, and other cognitive, cultural, or socio-structural constraints found in government contexts. They can both directly and indirectly impact the success of e-government initiatives.

RQ2: To what extent institutional arrangements have a direct effect on e-government success?

RQ3: To what extent institutional arrangements have an indirect effect on e-government success, through their direct effect on organizational structures and processes?

2.4.4 Environmental Conditions

By adopting an ensemble view of technology, this study investigates not only the enacted technology as the technical features and outcomes of government-wide websites, but also the processes that generate certain organizational forms and institutional arrangements. Therefore, it is important to consider the more general environment affecting the technology enactment process and in which the e-government initiatives are embedded. The context of organizations includes very important environmental factors. Some of the environmental dimensions identified in the literature are (1) technological conditions, (2) legal conditions, (3) cultural conditions, (4) political conditions, (5) economic conditions, (6) demographic conditions, and (7) ecological conditions (Clegg and Dunkerley 1980; Hall 2002; Hatch 1997; Meneklis and Douligeris 2010; Schuppan 2009; Srivastava and Teo 2008). Scholars interested in organizational theory have developed different ways to understand the impact of the environment on organizations, as well as how organizations attempt to modify their environments (Aldrich 1979; Burke 2011; Hannan and Freeman 1989; Liao et al. 2011; Pfeffer and Salancik 1978; Scott 1998).

In information systems, researchers have recognized the important role of environmental variables in shaping the way information technology is designed, implemented, and used in organizations (Kuan and Chau 2001; Laudon 1985; Menachemi et al. 2011; Sila 2010). However, the environment is not the only important factor to take into consideration. Environmental determinism posits that external environmental factors shape organizational characteristics and affect the final technology results. In the extreme, this type of determinism does not allow for management intervention (Anderson 2009; Fountain and Gil-Garcia 2006b; Glaser et al. 1983; Kraemer et al. 1989; Myeong and Choi 2010). The context of organizations is without a doubt an important factor for the success of IT initiatives. Nevertheless, as we will discuss later in this study, environmental conditions are only one of many important variables to take into consideration. Some contextual variables or external pressures such as personnel markets, competition, or political factors may affect the results of IT initiatives (Bellamy 2000; Bozeman and Bretschneider 1986; Chengalur-Smith and Duchessi 1999; Detlor et al. 2010; Laudon 1986; Lee et al. 2011; Pina et al. 2009).

Environmental factors have an impact on the enacted technology and subsequently on its outcomes, which are always indeterminate (Fountain 2001a). In addition, this relationship is not always direct, but mediated by managerial, organizational, or institutional variables. Therefore, under certain conditions "the environmental factors first encounter and become altered by computing management" (Kraemer et al. 1989, p. 54). Besides, an organization's context is usually not simple and homogenous. Therefore, a model like this should explore how different contextual factors influence the success of e-government.

RQ4: To what extent environmental conditions have a direct effect on e-government success?

RQ5: To what extent environmental conditions have an indirect effect on e-government success, through their direct effect on organizational structures and processes?

RQ6: To what extent environmental conditions have an indirect effect on e-government success, through their direct effect on institutional arrangements?

The model just described in this section could be used to understand any type of e-government initiative, from the use of personal computers to sophisticated organization-wide information systems, from single agency websites to inter-organizational collaboration and information integration. For the purpose of this book, I will demonstrate the usefulness of the "enacting e-government success" framework by analyzing technical, organizational, institutional, and environmental aspects of government-wide websites. The following section explains the reasons for and advantages of using government-wide websites as the example for this book. It is important to clarify that in my view, while e-government is much more than delivering services through the Internet, the empirical work in this book will focus on government websites as just one example of an e-government initiative and as a good way to discuss e-government success. For this book, government-wide websites are instances of a much broader e-government phenomenon.

2.5 Government-Wide Websites as Instances of the Electronic Government Phenomenon

The Internet has the potential to facilitate the relationships between people and organizations. This result is not exclusive to government agencies: "The possibilities of widespread Internet use have also stimulated substantial development in a variety of applications, such as electronic commerce, distance education, electronic publishing, digital libraries, and virtual communities" (Kling 2000, p. 217). Nevertheless, the promises and problems of information technologies for government reform have been widely recognized (Garson 2004; Heeks 1999; Jaeger and Bertot 2010; Kraemer and King 2003; Lee and Lee 2009; Margetts 2009; Scott and Robbins 2010; Seifert and Chung 2009; Tolbert et al. 2008). This section briefly describes government-wide websites as socio-technical phenomena and interesting instances of e-government. It also explains why they could be useful to understand other forms of electronic government.

Recently, there has been more attention to IT initiatives and specifically to developing websites at all levels of government. The interest in studying websites or web portals has also increased over the last decade (Detlor and Finn 2002; Detlor Hupfer et al. 2009; Fletcher 2002, 2004; Gant et al. 2002; Morgeson III and Mithas 2009; Reddick 2009a; Scavo 2003; Tripathi et al. 2011). Websites have the potential to change the way citizens, businesses, and other stakeholders interact with government. They can help with the provision of services, improve communication, and promote participation, collaboration, and citizen engagement with government policies and programs. However, in order to realize all the potential benefits of government websites, it is necessary to understand the technical and social aspects involved in these e-government initiatives.

Government websites are e-government initiatives that started more than ten years ago and have constantly added tools and applications, becoming more complex in terms of technological sophistication and the variety of applications they include. They have not been substituted, but expanded in many different ways, including social media applications and Web 2.0 tools (Bertot et al. 2010; Chang and Kannan 2008; Hrdinová et al. 2010; Osimo 2008; Tapscott et al. 2008). Therefore, some of the challenges and problems for these websites are also expected to be very similar to the ones previously encountered.

Even if we think of a website just as a complex interface, Kling (1993, p. 4) argues, "Interfaces also involve capabilities beyond the primary information processing features of a technology. They entail ways in which people learn about the systems and ways to manage the diverse data sets that routinely arise in using many computerized systems". Not only do government websites entail a great

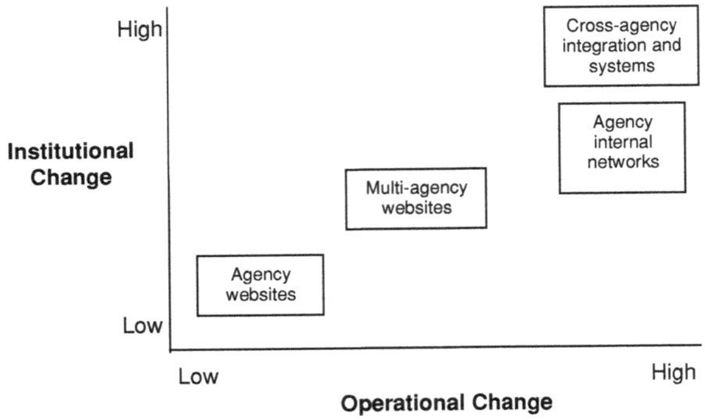

Fig. 2.10 Virtual agencies and ease of implementation [Fountain (2001), Reprinted with permission of the publisher]

variety of applications and tools, but also diverse social aspects and interactions among members of the IT and other government organizations, as well as between government and its users. Therefore, the technology is not simply purchased and plugged in; it is individually and organizationally enacted as "a product of design, negotiation, politics, understanding, social construction, entrepreneurship, and leadership" (Fountain 2001a, p. 195). Unfortunately, when people think about a website, they see an interface, and not the complex organizational network that supports the website and the array of institutions that enable or hinder its capabilities. This book attempts to understand how all these elements come together to achieve e-government success.

The more specific case of government-wide websites is especially interesting due to its inter-organizational nature at the virtual level, but its single-organization nature at the physical level. Most of the time, these websites are managed by a single agency responsible for IT in the state or local government as a whole, but these websites require the participation of most government agencies. As a result of this dual nature, inter-agency websites are e-government initiatives that require moderate operational change and moderate institutional change (Fountain 2001a). They are technically complex and require a certain level of organizational collaboration; they are not as simple as a single-agency website or as complex as information and systems integration across multiple agencies (Estermann et al. 2009; Fountain 2001a; Gil-Garcia 2005a, 2006; Gottschalk 2009; Hanna 2011; Klischewski 2011). Therefore, they are interesting and useful in understanding the success of other e-government initiatives (see Fig. 2.10).

Government-wide websites also represent an interesting potential mixture of information technology applications, from restricted intranets and extranets for specific audiences to open government websites, social media, wikis, blogs, and other emergent technologies. Government-wide websites offer information and services from multiple government agencies in such a way that the user does not need to know what organizations are providing which services or information (Chan et al. 2008; Klievink and Janssen 2009b; Seifert and Chung 2009; Taylor and Lips 2008). Areas of interest form the organizational basis for good websites or web portals, as opposed to administrative structures. Multi-agency government websites can be considered key elements of government reform. They are seen as comprehensive points of access to a great variety of electronic public services.

An inter-agency website is considered a collection of web pages containing a wealth of public information and different services that government agencies provide. As part of broader reform agendas, "groups of agencies linked by common clients, such as students or senior citizens, have developed virtual agencies. These virtual agencies use the connectivity of the web to co-locate the information and transactions of several agencies on one website"(Fountain 2001a, p. 99). Normally, government-wide websites link multiple agencies from the same level of government and with very different missions and audiences (Gottschalk 2009; Ojha et al. 2011; Rorissa et al. 2011). Some authors refer to this as horizontal integration (Gil-Garcia and Martinez-Moyano 2007; Layne and Lee 2001; Wu et al. 2009). Each public audience is served by one or more government agencies, which must collaborate and share information to offer integrated services.

In summary, government-wide websites are moderately complex e-government initiatives that require some level of institutional and operational change. These websites are not disappearing in the short term and are currently integrating new tools and applications, such as social media and Web 2.0, as a way to improve their capabilities and establish better channels of communication with citizens, businesses, and other stakeholders. In addition, government-wide websites are a good representation of the diversity and complexity of some e-government initiatives and most governments around the world have at least informational versions of them. They also face challenges similar to other e-government initiatives, from the lack of adequate financial and human resources to complex legal and policy frameworks, from the complexity of the technology to individual resistance to change. Therefore, they are a good example of the e-government phenomenon as a whole, particularly because the study includes not only their technical aspects, but also their organizational, institutional, and contextual ones. While I acknowledge that these initiatives do not necessarily represent all types of e-government, they are useful for generating lessons about success for other e-government initiatives. Future research should apply the theoretical model proposed in this book to other types of e-government initiatives.

Chapter 3
Identifying Electronic Government Success Factors: A Statistical Analysis

Based on Fountain's technology enactment framework, the process model of computing change, and important concepts from environmental approaches to organizations, this chapter develops a sophisticated statistical model of the influence of organizational, institutional, and contextual factors on the functionality of government-wide websites as an instance of e-government success. Therefore, the key argument of this chapter is that organizational structures and processes, institutional arrangements, and environmental conditions have an impact on the selection, design, implementation and use of information technologies in government settings. As a result, this chapter identifies some of the specific effects and interrelationships between multiple variables and the functionality of government-wide websites.

The proposed theoretical framework could be applied to other types of e-government, but for the purposes of this book, it is applied to the 50 state government-wide websites in the US. Within the context of the framework, organizational factors deal with structural and process-oriented characteristics such as centralization, formalization, size, communication channels, strategies, resources, and management decisions. Institutional arrangements refer to IT- related laws and regulations, as well as other formal and informal rules. Finally, environmental conditions include political, social, and economic variables (Hall 2002).

This chapter is organized into four main sections. Section 3.1 contains the operationalization of the constructs for the theoretical model defined in previous chapters. Section 3.2 provides some graphs and descriptive statistics for the observed variables. For those readers more familiar with statistical analysis, Section 3.3 presents the main results of the PLS path modeling, including the measurement and structural models. Some of the more detailed tests for validity and reliability can be found in Appendix A at the end of the book. Using nested models, Section 3.4 proposes a refined model and assesses its validity and reliability. Finally, Section 3.5 summarizes the main findings of this chapter. Readers not familiar with statistical analysis should still benefit from the operationalization explanation, the graphs and descriptive statistics, and the presentation of the overall results of the analysis at the end of this chapter.

J. R. Gil-Garcia, *Enacting Electronic Government Success*,
Integrated Series in Information Systems 31, DOI: 10.1007/978-1-4614-2015-6_3,

3.1 Operationalization of Theoretical Constructs

Due to the statistical technique used in this study, each theoretical construct is represented by one or more observed variables. This section includes the operationalization of each of the constructs (latent variables) and indicators (observed variables). The main data sources for each of the observed variables are included in Appendix A at the end of the book in Table A.1. According to the theoretical model developed in previous chapters, the relevant constructs for this research are (1) electronic government success, (2) organizational structures and processes, (3) institutional arrangements, and (4) environmental conditions. Based on previous studies and expert judgment, the theoretical constructs were operationalized as follows. A summary table for each of the constructs is also presented in Appendix A.

3.1.1 Electronic Government Success

As mentioned before, this book focuses on government-wide websites as an instance of a broader e-government phenomenon. Previous research has relied on website functionality and technological sophistication as measures of the success of these initiatives (Bandyopadhyay and Sattarzadeh 2010; Brandt and Gregg 2010; Brown and Brudney 2004; Choudrie et al. 2004; Dawes 2010; Gil-Garcia 2008; Ho 2002; Holden et al. 2003; La Porte Demchak and DeJong 2002; Moon 2002; Puron Cid, Gil-Garcia and Pardo 2009; Thomas and Streib 2003; van den Haak et al. 2009). More specifically, at the state level, several studies assess e-government success by analyzing different aspects of functionality such as the degree of customization, e-mail responsiveness, and the number of online services, among others (Gant et al. 2002; Gil-Garcia 2008; Gil-Garcia et al. 2007; Inkinen 2010; La Porte et al. 2002; McClure et al. 2000; Olbrich 2010; Rahman 2010; Wang and Liao 2008; West 2000, 2001, 2002, 2003, 2004, 2005, 2006, 2007, 2008).

Consistent with this view, this study operationalizes the e-government success construct as the government-wide state website functionality measured with four indicators (listed in Table A.2 in Appendix A): overall state e-government ranking score (West 2001), number of e-commerce systems (NASCIO 2002), digital state e-commerce score (Lassman 2002), and number of online services (CSG 2002). The overall state e-government ranking and the digital state e-commerce score are composite scales. Both include several important and distinctive elements such as the availability of specific government forms, number of online services, usability assessment, electronic payments, e-mail responsiveness, types of online information, foreign language access, privacy and security, and democratic outreach (Gil-Garcia 2008; Lassman 2002; West 2001).

It is important to clarify that government-wide websites are just one example of many possible e-government initiatives. From the beginning of this book, I am proposing that e-government is a complex phenomenon involving multiple aspects or elements intertwined in a socio-technical network. I am also aware that there are many other examples of e-government initiatives, but for this study I am using the case of government-wide websites as an instance of a broader e-government phenomenon. I have explained the reasons for this decision in the introduction and with more detail at the end of Chap. 2.

3.1.2 Organizational Structures and Processes

There are some organizational characteristics that are more general and enduring, such as organizational size, formal structures, and budgeting schemes. In contrast, there are organizational factors that are more flexible and particular to a specific initiative; these management practices include the division of labor, marketing, and outsourcing, among others (see Table A.3 in Appendix A). For this study, and consistent with Kraemer et al. (1989), this second category of factors is described as management strategies and practices.

General organizational factors include (1) the number of people working for the IT organization as a measure of size, (2) the percentage of the IT budget's revenue sources from federal funds, (3) whether the state provides accessibility training for IT professionals, and (4) the percentage of the IT office budget devoted to maintenance. Management strategies and practices are represented by (1) the number of marketing outlets used by states and the intensity of these marketing efforts, (2) whether the website services are entirely outsourced or entirely provided by the government, (3) whether the IT organization is the only one directly providing website services, and (4) whether the central IT organization directly manages portal development for other agencies.

3.1.3 Institutional Arrangements

As mentioned earlier, institutional arrangements are laws, regulations, policies, and other rules (cognitive, socio-cultural, etc.) that shape organizational forms and affect both the enacted technology and the organizational outputs and outcomes (Fountain 2001a). In this study, institutional arrangements are represented by (1) the existence of mandatory accessibility standards for state websites, (2) whether state IT professionals are all members of the civil service, (3) whether the state relies entirely on executive orders or directives to establish authority for the CIO office, and (4) whether the state has an IT-specific legislative committee in the Senate as a measure of legislative involvement (see Table A.4 in Appendix A).

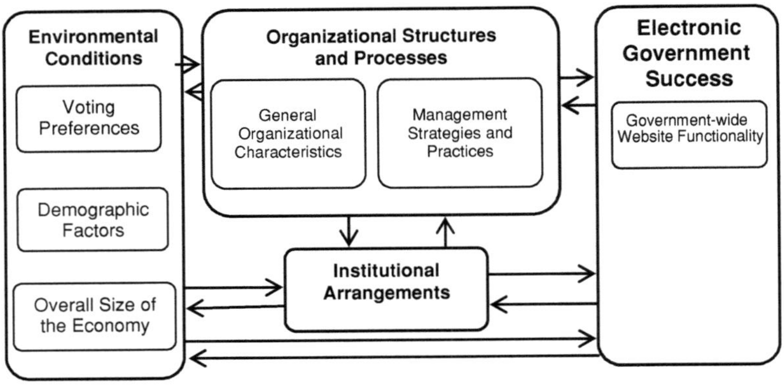

Fig. 3.1 Operationalization of the constructs (statistical analysis)

3.1.4 Environmental Conditions

It is practically impossible to include all of the factors contributing to the environment of an organization in a single research project. Therefore, based on previous studies and considering the availability of data for the period being studied, this research selected three of the most significant factors to represent the environments in which e-government initiatives and organizations are embedded: (1) demographic factors as a proxy for potential e-government demand and citizens' expectations (Ho 2002; La Porte et al. 2002), (2) voting preference as a proxy of a more general political orientation, and (3) overall size of the state economy as a proxy of availability of financial resources for state government agencies (Gil-Garcia 2008).

Demographic factors include measures of education, income, computer ownership, and Internet access (see Table A.5 in Appendix A). Political orientation is represented by the percentage of votes for the Democratic and Republican candidates in the previous gubernatorial election and whether the governor was a Democrat or Republican (see Table A.6 in Appendix A). The size of the state economy was operationalized using government gross state product, total state debt, total state revenue, and the number of jobs and private earnings in several industries such as local government, state government, communication, education, electronic and other electric equipment, and engineering and management services (see Table A.7 in Appendix A).

Given the operationalization of each theoretical construct for the statistical analyses, Fig. 3.1 shows the complete research model for this study with all the variables operationalized at the measurement and structural levels. In summary, (1) environmental conditions are represented by "Voting Preferences", "Demographic Factors", and "Overall Size of the Economy"; (2) organizational structures and processes are represented by "General Organizational Characteristics" and "Management Strategies and Practices"; (3) e-government success is

Table 3.1 Descriptive statistics of manifest variables (electronic government success)

Indicator (manifest variable)	Mean	Standard deviation	Minimum	Maximum
Overall state electronic government ranking (score)	41	4.9	32	52
Digital state e-commerce score	59.6	19.6	16.7	100
Number of e-commerce systems	6.8	2	1	10
Number of online services	5.8	2	2	9

represented by "Government-wide Website Functionality"; and (4) institutional arrangements are kept as a single construct representing formal and informal rules such as laws, norms, and regulations.

3.2 Characterizing Electronic Government in the States: Relevant Data and Descriptive Statistics

This section presents some graphs and descriptive statistics for the observed variables. Its objective is to give the reader a sense of the similarities and differences among the states in terms of the dependent and independent variables. Since 2001 was the only year in which all e-government success measures were available, data for independent variables was collected from several sources in years previous to 2001. Some state characteristics were remarkably different, while others are relatively similar among the 50 states. Table 3.1 shows that the overall e-government ranking (score) ranges from 31.5 points for Wyoming to 52 for Indiana, with a mean of 41.04 points. The digital state e-commerce score has a mean of 59.55 and ranges from 16.67 for Oklahoma to 100 for Maryland. The number of e-commerce systems reported to NASCIO has a range from one for Nevada to ten for Michigan and Texas, with a mean of 6.85. The variable "number of online services" has a mean of 5.76, with four states reporting nine services (Louisiana, Massachusetts, New York, and Virginia) and three states reporting two services (Alabama, Colorado, and Vermont).

The size of the IT organization, represented by the number of employees, varies from 2 in Vermont to 1,058 in New Jersey, with an average of 212.5 employees. Twenty-four states reported that they have accessibility training for IT employees. In 31 states (66%), the central IT organization directly manages portal development for other agencies. Thirteen states do not use any medium to market their state websites. States with a strong marketing strategy include Arizona, Texas, Utah, and West Virginia. In 27 states (59%), only the IT organization directly provides website services. In contrast, only five states (11%) completely outsource website services. The percentage of the IT budget devoted to maintenance ranges from 0.1% in South Carolina to 38% in Alabama, with a mean of 7.73%. The percentage of the IT budget revenue from federal funds has a mean of 3.13% and varies from 0% in 30 states to 38% in Michigan (see Fig. 3.2).

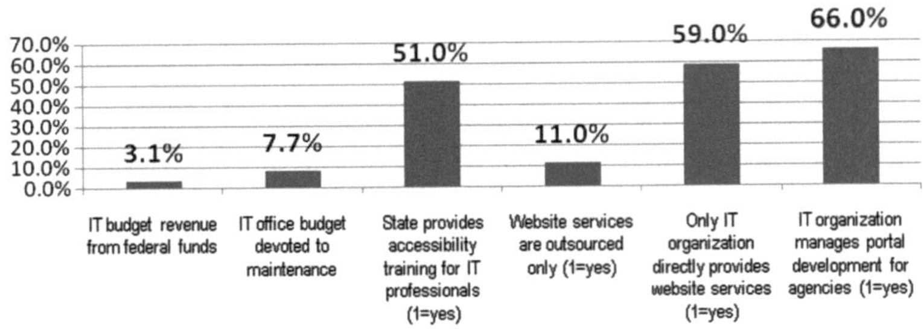

Fig. 3.2 Organizational structures and processes—means or percentages of manifest variables

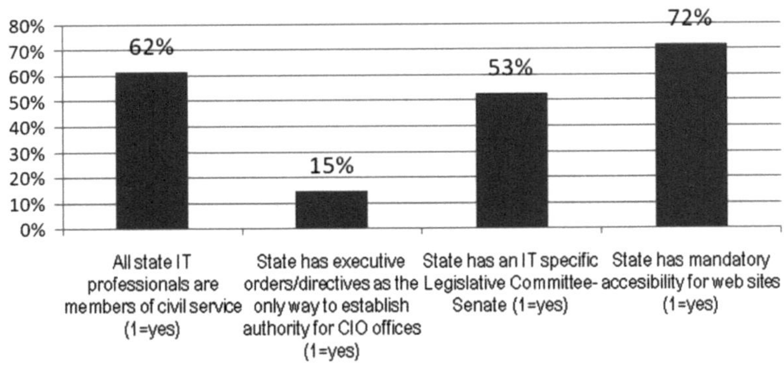

Fig. 3.3 Institutional arrangements—percentages of manifest variables

Twenty-five states have an IT-specific legislative committee in the senate. In 29 states (62%) all state IT professionals are members of the civil service. Only seven states (15%) have executive orders or directives as the only way to establish authority for CIO offices. In 34 states (72%) there are mandatory accessibility standards for state websites (see Fig. 3.3).

Figures 3.4 and 3.5 present some political variables. The percentage of votes for the Democratic Party in the previous gubernatorial election varies from 12% in Maine to 66.1% in New Hampshire, with a mean of 44.83%. In contrast, the percentage of votes for the Republican candidate in the previous gubernatorial election has a mean of 49.2% and ranges from 18% in Alaska to 73.4% in Kansas. In 2000, 18 states had a Democratic governor and 30 states had a Republican governor.

Figure 3.6 presents some demographic factors. Median income per household varies from $29,696 in West Virginia to $55,146 in New Jersey, with a mean of $41,371. Similarly, median income per family ranges from $36,484 in West Virginia to $65,521 in Connecticut, with a mean of $49,241. Income per capita has a mean of $27,139, with a minimum of $20,688 in Mississippi and a maximum of $39,300 in Connecticut. Gross state product per capita has a mean of $31,595, with

Fig. 3.4 Political variables—percentage of votes in the previous gubernatorial election

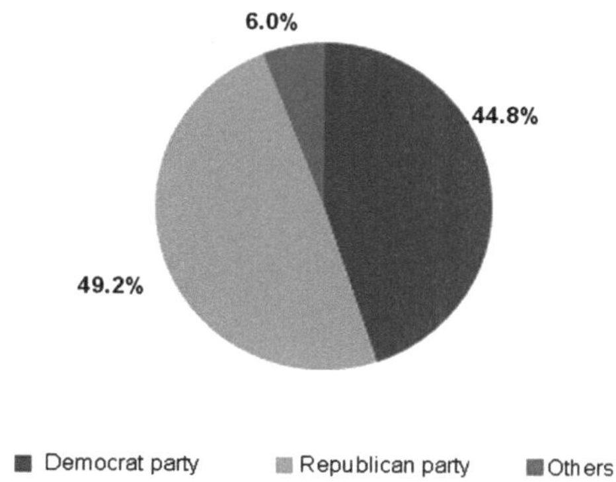

Fig. 3.5 Political variables—governor's party

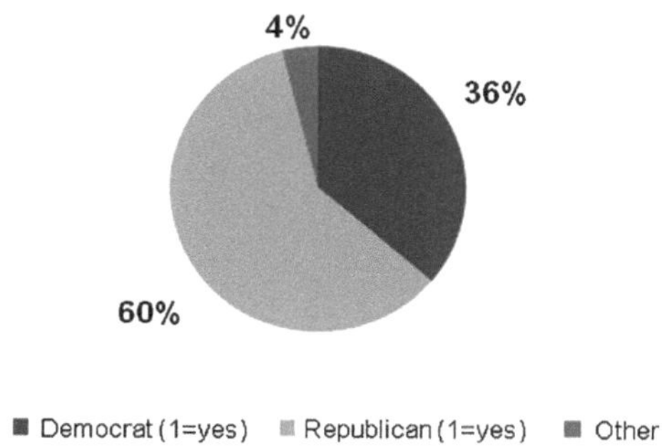

Fig. 3.6 Demographic factors—personal and family income

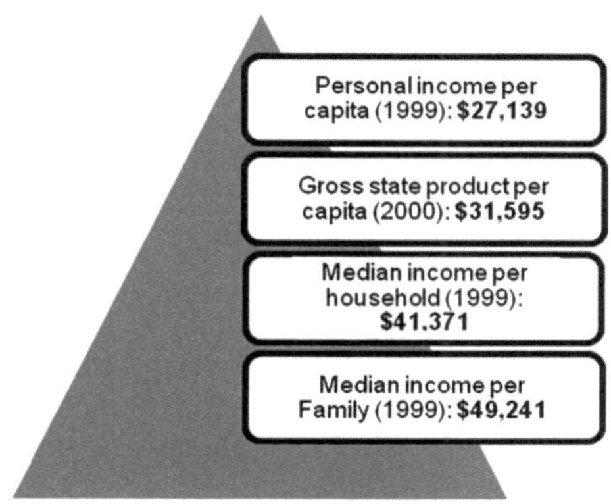

a minimum of $22,498 in West Virginia and a maximum of $44,567 in Connecticut.

The percentage of the population 25 years of age and older with less than a 9th grade education has a mean of 6.7%, with a minimum of 3.2% in Utah and a maximum of 12% in Kentucky (see Fig. 3.7). The percentage of the population

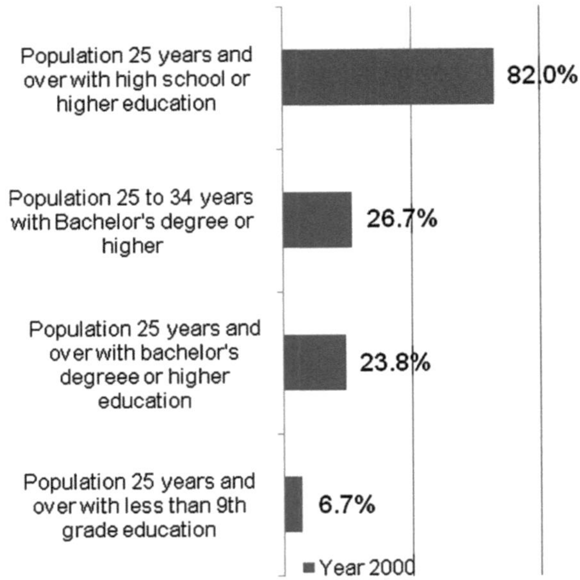

Fig. 3.7 Demographic factors (education)—percentages of manifest variables

25 years of age and older with a high school degree or higher varies from 73% in Mississippi to 88% in Alaska, with a mean of 82%. The percentage of the population 25 years of age and older with a Bachelor's degree or higher has a mean of 23.8%, with a minimum of 15% in West Virginia and a maximum of 33% in Massachusetts. Similarly, the percentage of the population between 25 and 34 years old with a Bachelor's degree or higher varies from 17.3% in Nevada to 41.4% in Massachusetts, with a mean of 26.6%.

The percentage of households with computers has a mean of 42.66% in 1998 and 51.51% in 2000 (see Fig. 3.8). In 1998, it varies from 25.7% in Mississippi to 62.4% in Alaska. For 2000, this percentage has a minimum of 37.2% in Mississippi and a maximum of 66.1% in Vermont. The percentage of households with Internet access has a mean of 26.05% in 1998 and 41.41% in 2000. The minimum value for 1998 was 13.6% in Mississippi and the maximum was 44.1% in Alaska. In 2000, this percentage varies from 26.3% in Mississippi to 56% in New Hampshire. The percentage of the population classified below the poverty line varies from 6.5% in New Hampshire to 19.9% in Mississippi, with a mean of 12%. Similarly, the percentage of families below the poverty level ranges from 4.3% in New Hampshire to 16% in Mississippi and 15.8% in Louisiana (mean = 8.74%).

The number of state government jobs in 2000 varies from about 14,000 in Wyoming to 450,000 in California, with a mean of approximately 99,000 jobs (see Fig. 3.9). In 2000, the number of local government jobs had a mean of about 260,000, with a minimum of 17,400 in Hawaii and a maximum of 1.6 million jobs in California. The total number of jobs in government and government enterprises in 2000 ranges from about 52,800 in Vermont to 2.6 million in California, with a

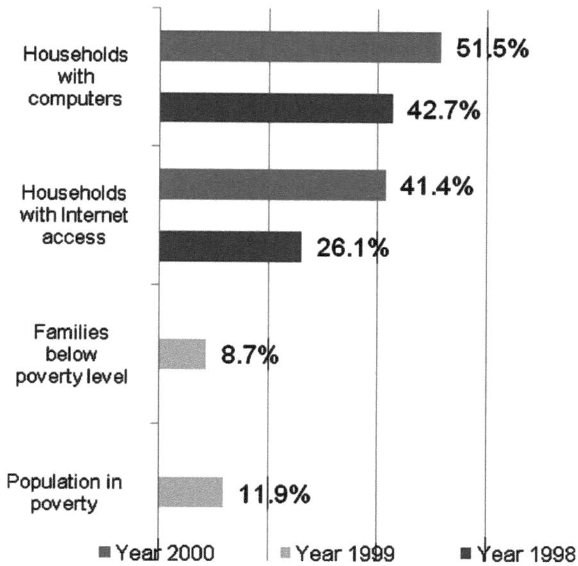

Fig. 3.8 Demographic factors—percentages of manifest variables

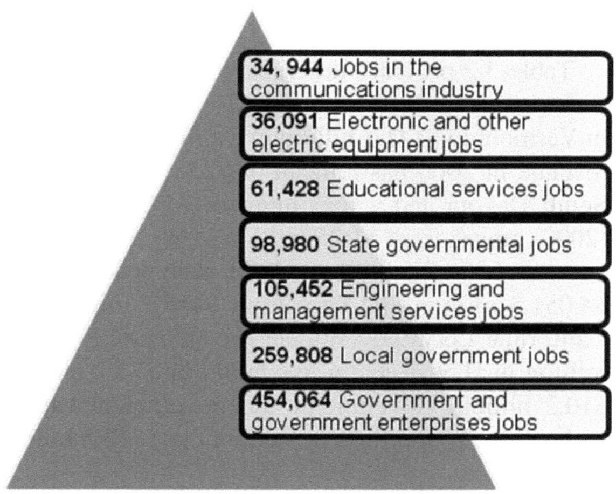

Fig. 3.9 Overall size of the state economy

mean of 454,000 jobs. The number of electronic and other electric equipment jobs in 2000 had a mean of 36,000, with a minimum of 49 in Alaska and a maximum of 280,000 in California. In 2000, the number of jobs in the communications industry ranges from about 2,400 in Wyoming to 201,000 in California, with a mean of about 35,000 jobs. The number of educational service jobs in 2000 had a mean of about 61,400 and varies from 2,600 in Wyoming to 350,000 in New York. In 2000, the number of engineering and management services jobs had a minimum of 7,200

Table 3.2 Overall size of the state economy—descriptive statistics of manifest variables

Indicator (manifest variable)	Mean	Standard deviation	Minimum	Maximum
Local government private earnings (2000)	10.24	13.09	0.80	73.67
Government and government enterprises private earnings (2000)	19.52	21.82	1.93	123.53
State government private earnings (2000)	4.05	3.85	0.45	21.53
Government gross state product (2000)	22.68	24.98	2.33	141.08
State total revenue (2000)	25.19	29.69	2.87	172.48
Engineering and management services private earnings (2000)	4.98	7.24	0.18	41.78
Communications industry private earnings (2000)	2.62	3.58	0.12	17.32
Electronic and other electric equipment private earnings (2000)	2.52	4.41	0.003	28.27
Educational services private earnings (2000)	1.44	2.03	0.03	9.94
Total state debt (2000)	10.95	14.39	1.25	78.61

Note Government gross state product, state total revenue, and private earnings for all industries are presented in billions of dollars. Total state debt is presented in millions of dollars

in Wyoming and a maximum of 820,000 in California, with a mean of about 105,000 jobs.

Table 3.2 provides descriptive statistics for measures of the overall size of the state economy. Government gross state product for 2000 varies from $2.3 billion in Vermont to $141.1 billion in California, with a mean of $22.7 billion. State total revenue in 2000 has a mean of $25.2 billion, with a minimum of $2.8 billion in South Dakota and a maximum of $172.5 billion in California. Total state debt (2000) ranges from $1.25 million in Wyoming to $78.6 million in New York, with a mean of $10.9 million. In 2000, state government private earnings had a mean of $4,051.5 million and vary from $455.7 million in Wyoming to $21.5 billion in California. Local government private earnings in 2000 had a minimum of $803.8 million in Hawaii and a maximum of $73.7 billion in California, with a mean of $10.2 billion. Government and government enterprise private earnings in 2000 varies from $1.9 billion in Vermont to $123.5 billion in California, with a mean of $19.5 billion.

Electronic and other electric equipment private earnings in 2000 range from $2.9 million in Alaska to $28.3 billion in California, with a mean of $2.5 billion. In 2000, private earnings in the communications industry had a mean of $2.6 billion, with a minimum of $116 million in Wyoming and a maximum of $17.3 billion in California. Private earnings from educational service jobs in 2000 vary from $30.2 million in Wyoming to $10 billion in New York, with a mean of $1.4 billion. Finally, private earnings from engineering and management services range from $178.2 million in South Dakota to $41.8 billion in California, with a mean of about $5 billion.

3.3 Results of the Statistical Analysis Using Partial Least Squares

This section presents the results of a statistical model using partial least squares (PLS). First, it describes the constructs and their indicators, including a brief explanation of which ones are formative and which ones are reflective. Then, the results and tests of the measurement model are shown, with a particular emphasis on the differences between formative and reflective constructs. More detailed descriptions of these tests and the respective tables can be found in Appendix A at the end of the book. Finally, the results of the structural model are presented and discussed, including several significance tests, as well as the direct, indirect, and total effects of each construct on e-government success.

Partial least squares (PLS) was the statistical technique used to empirically evaluate the theoretical model.[1] Similar to other structural equations modeling (SEM) methods, PLS can simultaneously test the measurement model (relationships between indicators and their corresponding constructs) and the structural model (relationships between constructs) (Barclay et al. 1995; Hulland 1999).[2] This section presents a quantitative empirical test of an extended model based on Fountain (2001a) and Kraemer et al. (1989). In this case, the structural model has been relatively well defined in previous studies (Cordella 2007; Fountain 1995, 2001a, 2008; Gil-Garcia 2008; Kraemer et al. 1989; Sandfort 2003); therefore, a confirmatory approach is useful. However, the measurement model can be better characterized as exploratory in nature, because there is little guidance about how to quantitatively operationalize the constructs of institutional theory integrative models.

In PLS, the relationship between a construct and its indicators can be modeled as either formative or reflective (Barclay et al. 1995; Gefen, Straub and Boudreau 2000). In this study, state website functionality, voting preferences, demographic factors, and overall size of the economy are reflective constructs with four, four, fourteen, and seventeen indicators, respectively. Management strategies and practices, general organizational factors, and institutional arrangements are

---

[1] PLS analysis was performed using PLS-Graph version 3.00.

[2] Partial least squares (PLS) is a structural equation modeling (SEM) statistical approach for modeling complex multivariable relationships among observed and latent variables (Esposito, Trinchera and Amato 2010). SEM has become the ultimate strategy in validating instruments and testing linkages between constructs (Henseler, Ringle and Sinkovics 2009). SEM attempts to understand the causal relationships between theoretical constructs and how well each construct is captured by its indicators or manifest variables. As a SEM technique, PLS can simultaneously test the structural model (relationships between constructs) and the measurement model (relationships between indicators and their corresponding constructs) (Barclay et al. 1995; Gil-Garcia 2008; Hulland 1999; Tenenhaus, Esposito, Chatelin and Lauro 2005). The PLS technique was considered an appropriate approach due to the nature of the complex relationships among the variables (Gil-Garcia 2005a). For a detailed description of the research design and methods, see Appendix A at the end of the book.

Table 3.3 Constructs and number of indicators for the full model. Gil-Garcia (2008). Adapted with permission of the publisher

Construct	Number of indicators	Type
Government-wide website functionality	4	Reflective
Management strategies and practices	4	Formative
General organizational characteristics	4	Formative
Institutional arrangements	4	Formative
Voting preferences	4	Reflective
Demographic factors	14	Reflective
Overall size of the economy	17	Reflective

formative constructs with four indicators each. Table 3.3 presents a summary of the constructs used in this study.

3.3.1 Measurement Model (Outer Model)

Convergent and discriminant validity were evaluated for the reflective indicators of the measurement model. Convergent validity can be assessed through the examination of indicator reliability, composite reliability, and average variance extracted (Fornell 1982). Table 3.4 shows that all loadings but one were above the 0.7 threshold, suggesting good indicator reliability (Fornell and Larcker 1981). Similarly, composite reliabilities were all greater than 0.7; therefore, all indicators were kept in the model.[3] Appendix A includes several tests for validity and reliability, including the comparison of the square root of the average variance extracted (AVE) with the correlations among reflective constructs (see Table A.8 in Appendix A). All constructs were more strongly correlated with their own measures than with any of the other constructs, suggesting good convergent and discriminant validity. Finally, as suggested by Chin (1998), cross-loadings were calculated and all indicators showed higher loadings with their respective construct than with any other reflective construct (see Table A.9 in Appendix A).

Table 3.5 shows the weights of formative indicators in their respective constructs. These results can be examined to identify the relevance of these indicators for their respective construct and for the model as a whole. For example, the

[3] In addition, there are three reasons to keep this indicator. First, Chin (1998) mentions that loadings as low as 0.5 should be kept as long as there are other good indicators in the scale. In fact, other authors suggest a cut-off of 0.5 (Hair, Anderson, Tatham, and Black 1998) or 0.6 (SAS 1990) for loadings. Second, PLS estimates are consistent at large (Wold 1982). According to this principle "the estimates will approach the 'true' latent variable scores as both the number of indicators per block and the sample size increase." (Chin and Newsted 1999, p. 329). Third, this indicator makes both theoretical and practical sense.

Table 3.4 Loadings of reflective constructs for the full model

Construct	Indicator	Loading
Government-wide website Functionality CR: 0.853	Overall quality of e-government services (2001)	0.8315
	Number of online services provided by states (2002)	0.8267
	Number of e-commerce systems developed by states (2001)	0.7108
	Quality of e-commerce in state governments (2001)	0.7048
Voting preferences CR: 0.911	Governor was democrat in 2000	0.9069
	Governor was republican in 2000	−0.8545
	Percentage of votes for the democratic party in the previous gubernatorial election (1997–2000)	0.8461
	Percentage of votes for the republican party in the previous gubernatorial election (1997–2000)	−0.7794
Demographic factors CR: 0.968	Median income per family (1999)	0.9332
	Median income per household (1999)	0.9217
	Percentage of population for whom poverty status is determined (1999)	−0.8844
	Percentage of households with internet access (2000)	0.8838
	Percent of families below poverty level (1999)	−0.8673
	Percentage of population 25 years and over with bachelor's degree or higher education (2000)	0.8609
	Percentage of households with computers (2000)	0.8393
	Personal income per capita (1999)	0.8253
	Percentage of households with internet access (1998)	0.8206
	Gross state product per capita (2000)	0.7994
	Percentage of households with computers (1998)	0.7784
	Percentage of population 25–34 years with bachelor's degree or higher (2000)	0.7734
	Percentage of population 25 years and over with high school or higher education (2000)	0.7275

(continued)

Table 3.4 (continued)

Construct	Indicator	Loading
	Percentage of population 25 years and over with less than 9th grade education (2000)	−0.6457
Overall size of the economy CR: 0.994	Local government private earnings (2000)	0.9910
	Government and government enterprises private earnings (2000)	0.9903
	State government private earnings (2000)	0.9895
	Government gross state product (2000)	0.9877
	Number of local government jobs (2000)	0.9864
	Number of engineering and management services jobs (2000)	0.9839
	State total revenue (2000)	0.9838
	Number of government and government enterprises jobs (2000)	0.9828
	Engineering and management services private earnings (2000)	0.9778
	Number of state government jobs (2000)	0.9643
	Number of jobs in the communications industry (2000)	0.9554
	Communications industry private earnings (2000)	0.9366
	Number of educational services jobs (2000)	0.9341
	Number of electronic and other electric equipment jobs (2000)	0.9201
	Electronic and other electric equipment private earnings (2000)	0.8888
	Educational services private earnings (2000)	0.8790
	Total state debt (2000)	0.8586

Significant tests were conducted using bootstrapping (200 samples) and all loadings are statistically significant at the one percent level (p-value<0.01). CR= Composite Reliability

Gil-Garcia 2008, Adapted with permission of the publisher

Table 3.5 Weights of formative indicators for the full model

Construct	Indicator	Weight	Significance Level
Management Strategies and Practices	Website services are outsourced only	−0.7843	***
	Number of marketing media and intensity of marketing	0.7203	***
	Only the IT organization directly provides website services	−0.4836	**
	IT organization directly manages portal development for agencies	0.2701	
General Organizational Characteristics	Number of people working for the IT organization (Size)	0.7087	***
	Percentage of the IT budget revenue sources from federal funds	0.5387	**
	State provides accessibility training for IT professionals	0.4406	*
	Percentage of the IT office budget devoted to maintenance	−0.2919	
Institutional Arrangements	State IT professionals are members of the civil service only	0.7185	***
	State has executive orders/directives as the only way to establish authority for CIO offices	−0.5883	***
	State has an IT specific legislative committee—Senate	−0.3712	*
	State has mandatory accessibility standards for state web sites	−0.2904	

Significant tests were conducted using bootstrapping (200 samples). Weights with *** are significant at the 1 percent level, those with ** are significant at the 5 percent level, and those with * are significant at the 10 percent level

Gil-Garcia 2008, Adapted with permission of the publisher

Table 3.6 Summary of research hypotheses for the statistical analysis

Research Hypotheses
H1: Organizational structures and processes are directly associated with the success of electronic government
H2: Institutional arrangements are directly associated with the success of electronic government
H3: Institutional arrangements are indirectly associated with the success of electronic government, through their direct association with organizational structures and processes
H4: Environmental conditions are directly associated with the success of electronic government
H5: Environmental conditions are indirectly associated with the success of electronic government through their direct association with organizational structures and processes
H6: Environmental conditions are indirectly associated with the success of electronic government through their direct association with institutional arrangements

indicators "website services are entirely outsourced" and "central IT organization directly provides all website services" are both negatively related to the formative construct Management Strategies and Practices and, therefore, also negatively related to government-wide state website functionality. Other relationships will be described as part of the results of the structural model.

3.3.2 Structural Model (Inner Model)

The structural model represents the relationships between constructs that were hypothesized in the theoretical model (see Fig. 3.1 at the end of Section 3.1 in this chapter). In PLS there are no well-established overall fit measures. Instead, PLS relies on the statistical and practical significance of paths and the size of the coefficients of determination (R-squares). For the statistical analysis, the research questions presented in Chap. 2. can be seen as testable hypotheses (see Table 3.6). Following this logic, the PLS analysis supported hypotheses 1, 3, 4, 5, and 6. Hypothesis 2 was not supported.

This study did not find a significant direct relationship between institutional arrangements and e-government success represented by government-wide website functionality. The existence of a direct link was tested and found to be neither statistically nor practically significant (a coefficient of at least 0.2). However, institutional arrangements are indirectly associated with the functionality of government-wide state websites through their direct association with general organizational characteristics and management strategies and practices. This finding is consistent with the original technology enactment framework, which presents an indirect relationship between institutional arrangements and the enacted technology. Despite the absence of a direct effect on e-government success, institutional arrangements seem to be important in explaining other constructs in this model (general organizational characteristics and management strategies and practices) and indirectly affect government-wide website functionality (Fig. 3.10).

Similar to multiple regression analysis, all of the following interpretations should take into consideration that all other independent variables in the respective

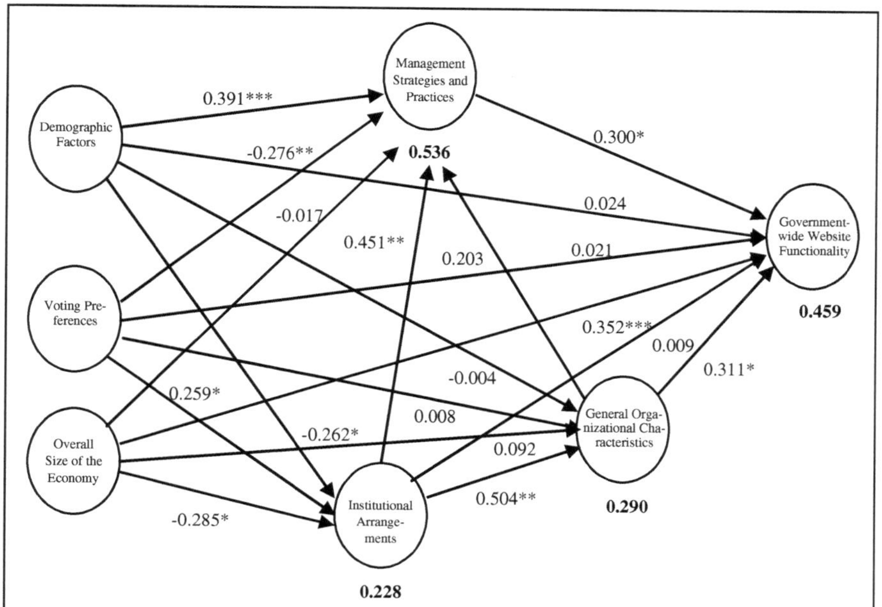

Coefficients followed by *** are significant at the 1 percent level , those followed by ** are sign ificant at the 5 percent level, and those followed by * are significant at the 10 percent level.

Fig. 3.10 PLS structural parameters for the full model [adapted from Gil-Garcia (2005a)]

equation are held constant. Three factors have a significant direct relationship with state website functionality: (1) overall size of the economy, (2) general organizational characteristics, and (3) management strategies and practices. Not surprisingly, states with bigger economies are predicted to have more functional government-wide websites. Organizational factors such as accessibility training, number of employees in the IT organization, percentage of federal resources in the IT organization's budget, and aggressiveness of the marketing strategy are positively associated with state website functionality. In contrast, situations in which website services are either totally outsourced or totally provided by the IT organization are negatively associated with state website functionality.[4] Therefore, a strategy using both outsourcing and in-house development seems to be the most appropriate.

Institutional arrangements is the only construct with a significant direct relationship with general organizational characteristics. For instance, the existence of

[4] Following the logic of dummy variables, the reference category for these three possible outcomes (entirely in-house development, entirely outsourcing, and combination of both) was a combination of both. Therefore, the negative statistically significant coefficients of "entirely in-house development" and "entirely outsourcing" indicates that these two strategies have a negative impact in comparison to the reference category (combination of both).

an IT legislative committee in the state senate and situations in which the authority of the CIO comes mainly from the executive are positively related to enabling organizational factors such as accessibility training, size of the IT organization, and percentage of the IT budget from federal resources. What that means is that states with an IT legislative committee and states in which the authority of the CIO comes from the executive are expected to have bigger IT organizations, more federal resources, and more opportunities for accessibility training. In contrast, situations in which all IT employees are members of the state civil services are negatively related to these organizational enablers. All other paths going to general organizational characteristics are neither statistically nor practically significant, indicating that there is no relevant effect from environmental conditions to general organizational characteristics as represented in this model.

Institutional arrangements, demographic factors, and voting preferences have a significant direct relationship with management strategies and practices. Overall size of the economy is not directly associated with management strategies and practices; this path was not statistically or practically significant. Situations in which all IT employees are members of the state civil service are negatively associated with aggressive marketing strategies and positively associated with situations in which website services are either totally outsourced or totally provided by the IT organization (which are themselves negatively associated with the functionality of the government-wide website). What this means, plainly speaking, is that there is a negative effect of "all IT employees being members of the civil service" on the government-wide website functionality and this effect could take place through multiple organizational variables (Table 3.7).

The existence of an IT legislative committee in the state senate and situations in which the authority of the CIO comes mainly from the executive are positively associated with aggressive marketing strategies and negatively associated with situations in which website services are either totally outsourced or totally provided by the IT organization. Therefore, these two institutional variables (IT legislative committee and executive orders giving authority to the CIO) are positively related to the functionality of government-wide websites.

States with demographics indicating greater potential demand for e-government are predicted to have less aggressive marketing strategies. Potential demand is positively associated with situations in which website services are either totally outsourced or totally provided by the IT organization. In other words, states in which there are more people with adequate conditions to use e-government services are expected to have less functional government-wide websites (however, there are also some indirect positive effects). Similar, states with a more liberal political orientation are predicted to have less aggressive marketing strategies. Liberal orientation is also positively associated with situations in which website services are either totally outsourced or totally provided by the IT organization.

Finally, all three environmental conditions are directly associated with institutional arrangements ($p < 0.1$). States with greater potential demand for e-government (higher incomes, higher levels of education, and higher percentages of computer ownership and Internet access) are predicted to have more enabling

Table 3.7 Structural results for the full model

	Path coefficient	t-statistic	Significance level
Effect on government-wide website functionality (R-sq = 0.4591)			
Management strategies and practices	0.300	1.6565	*
General organizational characteristics	0.311	1.9310	*
Institutional arrangements	0.009	0.0450	
Voting preferences	0.021	0.1639	
Demographic factors	0.024	0.1787	
Overall size of the economy	0.352	3.0195	***
Effect on management strategies and practices (R-sq = 0.5365)			
General organizational characteristics	0.203	1.2840	
Institutional arrangements	−0.451	2.4740	**
Voting preferences	−0.276	2.1644	**
Demographic factors	−0.391	2.7103	***
Overall size of the economy	−0.017	0.1235	
Effect on general organizational characteristics (R-sq = 0.2895)			
Institutional arrangements	−0.504	2.2001	**
Voting preferences	0.008	0.0432	
Demographic factors	−0.004	0.0217	
Overall size of the economy	0.092	0.5983	
Effect on institutional arrangements (R-sq = 0.2281)			
Voting preferences	0.259	1.8968	*
Demographic factors	−0.262	1.7109	*
Overall size of the economy	−0.285	1.9594	*

Significant tests were conducted using bootstrapping (200 samples). Path coefficients with *** are significant at the 1 percent level, those with ** are significant at the 5 percent level, and those with * are significant at the 10 percent level

Gil-Garcia (2005a), Adapted with permission of the publisher

institutional arrangements such as IT legislative committees and situations in which the authority of the CIO comes mainly from the executive. Those states with greater demand are also predicted to be less likely to have all IT employees as members of the civil service.

States with a more liberal political orientation are predicted to be more likely to have all IT employees as members of the civil service and less likely to have an IT legislative committee or for the authority of the CIO to come solely from the executive branch. States with larger economies are predicted to be less likely to have all IT employees as members of the civil service. Overall size of the state economy is positively related to the existence of an IT legislative committee and situations in which the authority of the CIO comes mainly from the executive.

About 46% of the variance in state website functionality was accounted for by its explanatory constructs. Similarly, the model explained about 54% of the variance in web management strategies and practices, 29% of the variance in general organizational characteristics, and 23% of the variance in institutional arrangements. The average explanatory power of endogenous constructs in the model was about 38% ($R^2 = 0.3783$). Falk and Miller (1992) suggest a way to test for significance of these squared multiple correlations. Table 3.8 shows the results of this test when applied to endogenous variables in the full model. All coefficients of multiple determination were significant at the 1 percent level ($p < 0.01$), which means that they are to some extent generalizable.

The change in R-squares is explored to observe whether there is a substantive impact of a particular independent latent variable on a dependent latent variable (see Table 3.8). The effect size, measured using the f^2 statistic, shows some interesting relationships (Chin 1998). Overall size of the economy presents a medium effect ($f^2 = 0.1936$) on government-wide website functionality at the structural level. Institutional arrangements ($f^2 = 0.2526$) and demographic factors ($f^2 = 0.2781$) also present a medium effect on management strategies and practices. Similarly, institutional arrangements ($f^2 = 0.2468$) have a medium effect on general organizational characteristics.

Table 3.9 shows direct, indirect, and total effects. Regarding government-wide website functionality, two situations deserve special attention. First, both general organizational characteristics and overall size of the economy have direct and indirect effects with consistent signs. Therefore, their total effect on government-wide website functionality is greater than their direct effect. What this means, plainly speaking, is that these two constructs are expected to have an impact greater than the one from the regression coefficient, because they have also indirect impacts on the functionality of government-wide websites, through their effect on other variables also included in the model. In contrast, demographic factors have direct and indirect effects with different signs. For instance, indirect effects through management strategies and practices are positive and most indirect effects through institutional arrangements and general organizational characteristics are negative. As a result, the total effect on the functionality of the government-wide website seems very small, when in fact demographic factors have important direct relationships with both management strategies and practices and institutional arrangements.

3.4 Nested Models and Theory Refinement

The previous PLS analysis was conducted to test theory and the results could be thought of as generalizable and contributing to existing knowledge–both theoretical and conceptual. This section identifies some of the most important variables for this specific set of data (US states) in order to provide more specific results and some practical recommendations. The results could also be considered as a new proposed theory to be tested with new datasets and in new situations and national contexts.

After evaluating the full model, analysis of nested models was used to identify structural paths that do not significantly contribute to the explained variance

Table 3.8 F statistic and relative impact of independent variables for the full model

Dependent	Independent	R-sq	F*	W/out	R-sq	f^2
Government-wide website functionality	Management strategies and practices, general organizational characteristics, institutional arrangements, voting preferences, demographic factors, overall size of the economy	0.4591	6.0828 (***)	Management strategies and practices	0.4175	0.0769^{s}
				General organizational characteristics	0.3931	0.1220^{sm}
				Institutional arrangements	0.4591	0
				Voting preferences	0.4588	0.0005
				Demographic factors	0.4585	0.0011
				Overall size of the economy	0.3544	0.1936^{m}
Management strategies and practices	General organizational characteristics, institutional arrangements, voting preferences, demographic factors, overall size of the economy	0.5365	10.1859 (***)	General organizational characteristics	0.5018	0.0748^{s}
				Institutional arrangements	0.4194	0.2526^{ml}
				Voting preferences	0.4686	0.1465^{sm}
				Demographic factors	0.4076	0.2781^{ml}
				Overall size of the economy	0.5363	0.0004
General organizational characteristics	Institutional arrangements, voting preferences, demographic factors, overall size of the economy	0.2895	4.5839 (***)	Institutional arrangements	0.1141	0.2468^{ml}
				Voting preferences	0.2891	0.0005
				Demographic factors	0.2892	0.0004
				Overall size of the economy	0.2903	−0.0011
Institutional arrangements	Voting preferences, demographic factors, overall size of the economy	0.2281	4.5310 (***)	Voting preferences	0.1616	0.0861^{s}
				Demographic factors	0.1611	0.0868^{s}
				Overall size of the economy	0.1554	0.0942^{s}

* Suggested by Falk and Miller (1992, p. 72). All F are statistically significant at the 1 percent level. For f^2, "s" refers to small effect, "m" to medium effect, and "l" to large effect (Chin, 1998). When f^2 has two letters, the first one is the effect size strictly according to Chin (1998), and the second one is the effect size in the context of this research

Table 3.9 Direct and indirect effects for the full model

Dependent	Independent	Direct	Indirect	Total indirect	Total
Government-wide website functionality	Management strategies and practices	0.300		0	0.300
	General organizational characteristics	0.311	0.061	0.061	0.372
	Institutional arrangements	0.009	(−0.135) + (−0.031) + (−0.157)	−0.323	−0.314
	Voting preferences	0.021	(−0.083) + (−0.035) + (−0.008) + (−0.041) + 0.0005 + 0.002	−0.164	−0.143
	Demographic factors	0.024	(−0.117) + 0.035 + 0.008 + 0.041 + (−0.0002) + (−0.001)	−0.034	−0.010
	Overall size of the economy	0.352	(−0.005) + 0.039 + 0.009 + 0.045 + 0.006 + 0.029	0.123	0.475
Management Strategies and Practices	General organizational characteristics	0.203		0	0.203
	Institutional arrangements	−0.451	−0.102	−0.102	−0.553
	Voting preferences	−0.276	(−0.117) + (−0.026) + 0.002	−0.141	−0.417
	Demographic factors	−0.391	0.118 + 0.027 + (−0.0008)	0.144	−0.247
	Overall size of the economy	−0.017	0.129 + 0.029 + 0.019	0.177	0.160
General Organizational Characteristics	Institutional arrangements	−0.504		0	−0.504
	Voting preferences	0.008	(−0.131)	−0.131	−0.123
	Demographic factors	−0.004	0.132	0.132	0.128
	Overall size of the economy	0.092	0.144	0.144	0.236
Institutional Arrangements	Voting preferences	0.259		0	0.259
	Demographic factors	−0.262		0	−0.262
	Overall size of the economy	−0.285		0	−0.285

Table 3.10 Structural paths deleted from the full model

Structural path	f^2 statistic	Significance level	Size of the path	Percentage of variation explained
Overall size of the economy => general organizational characteristics	−0.0011	$p > 0.1$	0.092	0.0234
Institutional arrangements => government-wide website functionality	0	$p > 0.1$	0.009	0.0038
Demographic factors => general organizational characteristics	0.0004	$p > 0.1$	−0.004	0.0006
Overall size of the economy => management strategies and practices	0.0004	$p > 0.1$	−0.017	0.0024
Voting preferences => general organizational characteristics	0.0005	$p > 0.1$	0.008	0.0009
Voting preferences => government-wide website functionality	0.0005	$p > 0.1$	0.021	0.0032
Demographic factors => government-wide website functionality	0.0011	$p > 0.1$	0.024	0.0008

(R-squared) of endogenous constructs. As suggested by Chin (1998), the f^2 statistic was used for this purpose. In addition, three other criteria were taken into consideration. First, a minimum level of statistical significance as suggested by Barclay, Thompson and Higgins (1995) was required; the 10 percent level ($p < 0.1$) was used. Second, a threshold of practical significance of 0.2 (path size) was also used as a criterion (Chin 1998). Third, Falk and Miller (1992) suggest a predictor should account for at least 1.5% of the variance in a predicted variable. Due to the exploratory nature of this study at the measurement level, a more rigorous threshold of 3% of the explained variance was used. Only paths that perform poorly on all four criteria were eliminated from the full model (see Table 3.10).

3.4.1 Measurement Model (Outer Model)

Due to the simultaneous calculation of the measurement and the structural model in PLS, the results of the measurement model are also expected to change, although not radically. Therefore, the measurement model was again evaluated for convergent and discriminant validity. Similar to the full model, reliability of indicators was determined by examining the size and significance of the loadings. Again, all loadings but one were above the recommended threshold (0.70). Composite reliability was also greater than 0.7 for all reflective constructs in this refined model (see Table 3.11).

Table 3.11 Loadings of reflective constructs for the refined model

Construct	Indicator	Loading
Government-wide website functionality CR: 0.853	Overall quality of e-government services (2001)	0.8309
	Number of online services provided by states (2002)	0.8276
	Number of e-commerce systems developed by states (2001)	0.7121
	Quality of e-commerce in state governments (2001)	0.7031
Voting preferences CR: 0.912	Governor was democrat in 2000	0.9052
	Governor was republican in 2000	−0.8635
	Percentage of votes for the democratic party in the previous gubernatorial election (1997–2000)	0.8320
	Percentage of votes for the republican party in the previous gubernatorial election (1997–2000)	−0.7952
Demographic factors CR: 0.969	Median income per family (1999)	0.9240
	Median income per household (1999)	0.9137
	Percentage of households with internet access (2000)	0.8912
	Percent of population for whom poverty status is determined (1999)	−0.8863
	Percent of families below poverty level (1999)	−0.8712
	Percentage of population 25 years and over with bachelor's degree or higher education (2000)	0.8618
	Percentage of households with computers (2000)	0.8509
	Percentage of households with internet access (1998)	0.8306
	Personal income per capita (1999)	0.8107

(continued)

Table 3.11 (continued)

Construct	Indicator	Loading
	Percentage of households with computers (1998)	0.7942
	Gross state product per capita (2000)	0.7842
	Percentage of population 25 to 34 years with bachelor's degree or higher (2000)	0.7672
	Percentage of population 25 years and over with high school or higher education (2000)	0.7437
	Percentage of population 25 years and over with less than 9th grade education (2000)	−0.6596
Overall size of the economy CR: 0.994	Local government private earnings (2000)	0.9909
	Government and government enterprises private earnings (2000)	0.9904
	State government private earnings (2000)	0.9893
	Government gross state product (2000)	0.9879
	Number of local government jobs (2000)	0.9866
	Number of engineering and management services jobs (2000)	0.9846
	State total revenue (2000)	0.9837
	Number of government and government enterprises jobs (2000)	0.9831
	Engineering and management services private earnings (2000)	0.9783
	Number of state government jobs (2000)	0.9645
	Number of jobs in the communications industry (2000)	0.9554

(continued)

Table 3.11 (continued)

Construct	Indicator	Loading
	Communications industry private earnings (2000)	0.9363
	Number of educational services jobs (2000)	0.9331
	Number of electronic and other electric equipment jobs (2000)	0.9217
	Electronic and other electric equipment private earnings (2000)	0.8908
	Educational services private earnings (2000)	0.8777
	Total state debt (2000)	0.8567

Significant tests were conducted using bootstrapping (200 samples) and all loadings are statistically significant at the one percent level (p-value < 0.01).
CR = Composite Reliability

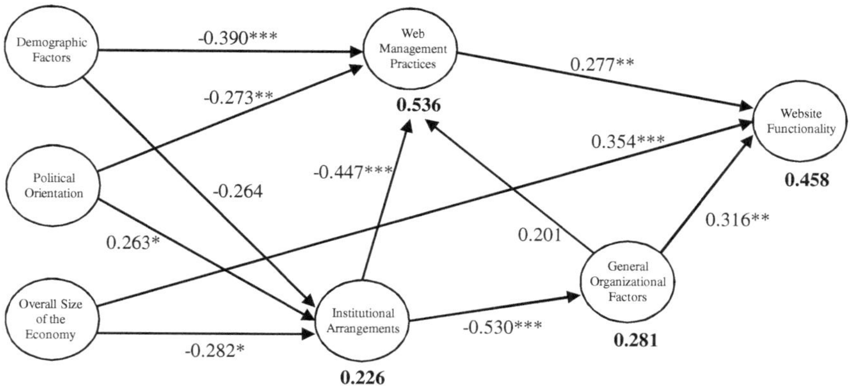

Coefficients followed by *** are significant at the 1 percent level, those followed by ** are significant at the 5 percent level, and those followed by * are significant at the 10 percent level.

Fig. 3.11 PLS structural parameters for the refined model

As expected, the square roots of AVE were greater than the correlations with other constructs in this refined model too (see Table A.10 in Appendix A). In Appendix A, Table A.11 shows loadings and cross-loadings for reflective indicators. All indicators loaded higher on their respective constructs than on all other reflective constructs. As mentioned earlier, formative indicators should not be assessed using traditional measures of convergent and discriminant validity. Table 3.12 presents the weights of the formative indicators. Weight size and statistical significance help to evaluate the relevance of each formative indicator for its respective construct and for the model as a whole. The results of this refined model are very similar to the full model and are also acceptable. Substantive explanations will be provided in the structural model section and the chapter discussing the overall results of this study.

3.4.2 Structural Model (Inner Model)

In this refined model, only hypotheses 1, 3, 4, 5, and 6 are included and, as expected, they were all supported (see Fig. 3.11 and Table 3.13). For instance, for hypothesis 1, general organizational characteristics and management strategies and practices are directly associated with the functionality of government-wide websites. The overall size of the state economy is also directly associated with the functionality of government-wide state websites, giving support to hypothesis 4. These three variables jointly account for approximately 46% of the variance in government-wide website functionality.

Table 3.12 Weights of formative indicators for the refined model

Construct	Indicator	Weight	Significance level
Management strategies and practices	Website services are outsourced only	−0.7899	***
	Number of marketing media and intensity of marketing	0.7142	***
	Only the IT organization directly provide website services	−0.4911	**
	IT organization directly manages portal development for agencies	0.2735	
General organizational characteristics	Number of people working for the IT organization (size)	0.7045	***
	Percentage of the IT budget revenue sources from federal funds	0.5428	**
	State provides accessibility training for IT professionals	0.4450	**
	Percentage of the IT office budget devoted to maintenance	−0.2850	
Institutional arrangements	State IT professionals are members of the civil service only	0.7545	***
	State has executive orders/directives as the only way to establish authority for CIO offices	−0.5432	***
	State has an IT specific legislative committee—senate	−0.3756	*
	State has mandatory accessibility standards for state web sites	−0.2652	

Significant tests were conducted using bootstrapping (200 samples) and loadings with *** are significant at the 1 percent level, those with ** are significant at the 5 percent level, and those with * are significant at the 10 percent level

Institutional arrangements indirectly influence the functionality of government-wide websites through their direct impact on general organizational characteristics and management strategies and practices (supporting hypothesis 3). In addition, institutional arrangements account for about 28% of the variance in general organizational characteristics, and together with demographic factors and voting preferences, about 54% of the variance in management strategies and practices. Therefore, in spite of the lack of direct effects, these results suggest that institutions are crucial factors in understanding e-government success. Theoretical models ignoring institutions could potentially obtain partial and limited explanations of this phenomenon.

Some demographics representing the potential demand for e-government and citizens' expectations (such as education, income, computer ownership, and Internet access) were found to be indirectly associated with the functionality of government-wide websites, through their direct association with institutional arrangements and management strategies and practices (supporting hypotheses 5

Table 3.13 Structural results for the refined model

	Path coefficient	t-statistic	Significance level
Effect on government-wide website functionality (R-sq = 0.4576)			
Management strategies and practices	0.277	2.229	**
General organizational characteristics	0.316	2.232	**
Overall size of the economy	0.354	3.880	***
Effect on management strategies and practices (R-sq = 0.5364)			
General organizational characteristics	0.201	1.288	
Institutional arrangements	−0.447	2.620	***
Voting preferences	−0.273	2.290	**
Demographic factors	−0.390	2.816	***
Effect on general organizational characteristics (R-sq = 0.2811)			
Institutional Arrangements	−0.530	4.225	***
Effect on institutional arrangements (R-sq = 0.2263)			
Voting preferences	0.263	1.745	*
Demographic factors	−0.264	1.635	
Overall Size of the economy	−0.282	1.911	*

Significant tests were conducted using bootstrapping (200 samples). Path coefficients with *** are significant at the 1 percent level, those with ** are significant at the 5 percent level, and those with * are significant at the 10 percent level

and 6). Similarly, political orientation (conservative vs. liberal) is indirectly associated with the functionality of government-wide websites through its significant direct relationship with management practices and institutional arrangements (supporting hypotheses 5 and 6). Demographic factors, political orientation, and overall size of the economy explain about 23% of the variance in institutional arrangements. The average coefficient of determination (R-squared) for the refined model was 0.375 and all determination coefficients were significant at the 1% level (see Table 3.14).

The explanatory power of each independent variable was tested using f^2 and all had at least a small effect on their respective dependent variable (see Table 3.14). Strictly following the recommendations provided by Chin (1998), seven predictors had a small effect ($f^2 > 0.02$) at the structural level and three had a medium effect ($f^2 > 0.15$). Regarding direct and indirect effects, similar to the full model, the total effects of Web management strategies and practices, general organizational characteristics, institutional arrangements, and overall size of the economy on government-wide website functionality is practically significant (>0.2). In contrast, the total effects of political orientation and demographic factors on government-wide website functionality are relatively small. Specifically, demographic factors present positive and negative indirect effects, and therefore the final total

Table 3.14 F statistic and relative impact of independent variables for the refined model

Dependent	Independent	R-sq	F*	W/out	R-sq	f^2
Government-wide website functionality	Management strategies and practices, general organizational characteristics, overall size of the economy	0.4576	12.9360 (***)	Web management factors	0.3970	0.1117^{s}
				General organizational factors	0.3779	0.1469^{sm}
				Overall size of the economy	0.3441	0.2092^{m}
Management strategies and practices	General organizational characteristics, institutional arrangements, voting preferences, demographic factors	0.5364	13.0166 (***)	General organizational factors	0.5018	0.0746^{s}
				Institutional arrangements	0.4132	0.2657^{ml}
				Political orientation	0.4692	0.1449^{sm}
				Demographic factors (demand)	0.4079	0.2772^{ml}
General organizational characteristics	Institutional arrangements	0.2811	18.7686 (***)	N/A	N/A	N/A
Institutional arrangements	Voting preferences, demographic factors, overall size of the economy	0.2263	4.4848 (***)	Political orientation	0.1584	0.0877^{s}
				Demographic factors (demand)	0.1587	0.0874^{s}
				Overall size of the economy	0.1566	0.0901^{s}

* Suggested by Falk and Miller (1992, p. 72). All F are statistically significant at the 1 percent level. For f^2, "s" refers to small effect, "m" to medium effect, and "l" to large effect (Chin, 1998). When f^2 has two letters, the first one is the effect size strictly according to Chin (1998), and the second one is the effect size in the context of this research

effects do not seem practically relevant (−0.023). However, demographic factors have important effects on web management strategies and practices and institutional arrangements. In contrast, all political orientation effects are negative, but they are very small, with a total effect of −0.160.

From the results and effects, it seems clear that different environmental conditions have different relationships with e-government success. For instance, overall size of the state economy has a direct relationship, political orientation has an indirect relationship through its direct relationship with institutional arrangements and web management practices, and potential demand for e-government has an indirect relationship through its direct relationship with management strategies and practices (see Table 3.15).

3.5 Summary of Findings from the PLS Analysis

As the literature review from Chaps. 1 and 2 shows, the use of information technologies has the potential to transform government in terms of how it works and how it interacts with citizens, businesses, and other stakeholders (Gil-Garcia et al. 2008). This study provides evidence that concurs with the emerging literature that recognizes the dynamic interaction between information technologies and social structures (Cordella 2007; Antonio Cordella and Iannacci 2010; Fountain 2008; Gil-Garcia and Helbig 2006; Gil-Garcia and Pardo 2006; Iannacci 2010; Margetts 2009; Orlikowski 2008, 2010c; Orlikowski and Iacono 2006; Orlikowski and Scott 2008; Sefyrin and Mörtberg 2009). This literature argues that there are also impacts from organizational, institutional and environmental variables on the characteristics of information technologies and how they are used in government settings (enacted technology).

The statistical analysis conducted in this chapter found three factors that directly influence the functionality of government-wide websites: (1) management strategies and practices, (2) general organizational characteristics, and (3) overall size of the economy. Therefore, this study suggests that both environmental conditions and management actions are important in understanding e-government success.

Within organizational structures and processes, general organizational characteristics are more enduring and in this study they are represented by (1) size as measured by the number of people working for the IT organization; (2) revenue sources from federal funds; (3) accessibility training for IT professionals; and (4) budget designated to maintenance. In contrast, management strategies and practices are more flexible, since, many times, they are particular to a specific e-government initiative. In this analysis, management strategies and practices focus on (1) the number of outlets used and the intensity of the marketing efforts, (2) whether the IT organization directly manages portal development for agencies, and (3) whether website services are provided directly, outsourced, or a combination of these two strategies.

Table 3.15 Direct and indirect effects for the refined model

Dependent	Independent	Direct	Indirect	Total indirect	Total
Government-wide website functionality	Management strategies and practices	0.277		0	0.277
	General organizational characteristics	0.316	0.056	0.056	0.372
	Institutional arrangements	0	(−0.124) + (−0.167) + (−0.029)	−0.321	−0.321
	Voting preferences	0	(−0.076) + (−0.033) + (−0.044) + (−0.007)	−0.160	−0.160
	Demographic factors	0	(−0.108) + 0.033 + 0.008 + 0.044	−0.023	−0.023
	Overall size of the economy	0.354	0.035 + 0.008 + 0.047	0.090	0.444
Management strategies and practices	General organizational characteristics	0.201		0	0.201
	Institutional arrangements	−0.447	−0.107	−0.107	−0.554
	Voting preferences	−0.273	(−0.118) + (−0.028)	−0.146	−0.419
	Demographic factors	−0.390	0.118 + 0.028	0.146	−0.244
	Overall size of the economy	0	0.126 + 0.030	0.156	0.156
General organizational characteristics	Institutional arrangements	−0.530		0	−0.530
	Voting preferences	0	−0.139	−0.139	−0.139
	Demographic factors	0	0.140	0.140	0.140
	Overall size of the economy	0	0.149	0.149	0.149
Institutional arrangements	Voting preferences	0.263		0	0.263
	Demographic factors	−0.264		0	−0.264
	Overall size of the economy	−0.282		0	−0.282

By looking at the specific sign of each indicator, it is possible to identify the particular effects of individual manifest variables. For instance, some organizational structures and processes such as whether the state provides accessibility training for IT professionals, the number of employees working for the IT organization, the percentage of the IT budget revenue sources from federal funds, the aggressiveness of the marketing strategy, and a certain degree of centralization in the development of the portal are positively associated with government-wide website functionality. In contrast, situations in which website services are either totally outsourced or totally provided by the IT organization are negatively associated with government-wide website functionality. Therefore, strategically combining both outsourcing and in-house development seems to be more appropriate.

In addition, this study shows that management strategies and practices are important, but they are interrelated and partially explained by other success factors, like political orientation and institutional arrangements. Institutional arrangements are also significant predictors of general organizational characteristics. For instance, the existence of an IT legislative committee in the state senate and situations in which the authority of the CIO comes mainly from the executive are positively related to enabling organizational factors such as accessibility training, size of the IT organization, and percentage of the IT budget from federal resources. In contrast, situations in which all IT employees are members of the state civil service are negatively related to these organizational enablers. Similarly, states with all IT employees as members of the civil service are expected to have a less aggressive marketing strategy.

The two organizational constructs appear to be very important in understanding e-government success and institutional arrangements affect both of them. Therefore, understanding institutions and their effects is also a very important task for future research. Theoretical models that do not include institutional variables could potentially lead to partial and limited explanations of e-government success. In addition, in order to have a more comprehensive view of this phenomenon, it is also essential to understand the variables affecting institutions. In this study, institutional arrangements are directly affected by political orientation, the overall size of the economy, and demographic factors. For instance, a more liberal political orientation is positively related to states with all IT employees as members of the civil service and negatively associated with states that have an IT specific committee in the senate and with states that have mandatory accessibility standards. Similar, states with bigger economies are expected to have an IT specific legislative committee and also mandatory accessibility standards for state websites.

Chapter 4
Enacting the Government-Wide New York State Website

While the state of New York is one of the largest and most populous in the US, it was the last major state to create a centralized IT agency (around 1997), following decades of almost complete decentralization of IT functions and services. The New York State (NYS) website demonstrates how a large and diverse state government with a long history of decentralized IT management goes about creating a high-quality government-wide website. In addition to other state governments, the lessons from this case are potentially useful for government agencies at all levels (national, regional, and local) in many developed and developing countries around the world. This chapter describes the strategies, benefits, weaknesses, and challenges of a distributed Web management structure reflecting a hybrid of centralized and decentralized activities (Gil-Garcia and Dawes 2007). It does so following a structure that highlights the main theoretical concepts presented in previous chapters and how they relate to the success of the website. Thus, based on the theoretical framework presented in Chap. 2, this chapter includes the following sections regarding the New York State government-wide website: (1) Enacted Technology, (2) Organizational Outputs and Outcomes, (3) Management Strategies and Practices, (4) Organizational Structures and Processes, (5) Institutional Arrangements, and (6) Environmental Conditions. The chapter ends by providing some final comments regarding the experience of New York State.

4.1 Enacted Technology

NYS agencies began developing Web pages in the early 1990s. However, the effort to create a more centralized and integrated website started in 2000 with a governor's initiative called "Government Without Walls." As of 2005, the state website was more integrated than before, with the development and management activities divided among the Office for Technology (OFT), the Office of the Chief Information Officer, the Governor's Office (in conjunction with a private vendor), and all other

J. R. Gil-Garcia, *Enacting Electronic Government Success*,

Integrated Series in Information Systems 31, DOI: 10.1007/978-1-4614-2015-6_4,

state agencies. This complex arrangement reflected, to a certain extent, the long history of IT decentralization in the state (Gil-Garcia and Dawes 2007).

One of the respondents described the mission of the state website as being "to enable end-users, which in this case would be the citizens of the state, to be able to get to the information they need as quickly and easily as possible." Another respondent said that the mission was "to provide an easy to use... alternative for folks to conduct their business, to live and work, and... grow businesses in New York State. To bring people to New York State, to help them find government rules and regulations and licensing and all those things, and... how to find their way through the maze and do it easily." A different respondent asserted the mission of the website as "to make it easier for citizens to go to one central place to get everything that they need."

In general, respondents agreed that the website's mission was to help citizens, businesses, local governments, state employees, and other stakeholders to get the information and services they need in a more effective and convenient fashion. At the same time, the website provided an opportunity for NYS to save resources and improve citizen satisfaction with state government services and information. In the words of a respondent: "This is the electronic face to the rest of the world... this is New York State, here are our services, here's why it's a good place to do business here, those kinds of things."

In 2005, the NYS OFT had developed the first state government portal. It was built as an index and database in ColdFusion, software developed by Macromedia. It had a search engine that could look for information within the portal database, but could not search for information and services on the agency websites. That is, if the information was contained in the links that agencies included in the portal database, then it could be found with the search engine. By contrast, if the information was on an agency website, but had not been added as a link to the portal database, the search engine would not retrieve it. Part of the NYS website was hosted by private vendors, while the rest was hosted by OFT. Most agency websites were hosted internally and the majority of the content was updated by the respective agencies. The NYS website (see Fig. 4.1) had two different components in 2005: (1) the public website that was accessible to everyone and (2) several password-protected applications for local governments or other specific groups (e.g., real property assessors). These restricted applications were designed for a particular audience and have specific goals and objectives.

The NYS website was organized in five main sections: (1) Governor Pataki, (2) map-NY, (3) e-bizNYS, (4) Citizen Guide, and (5) Search. In addition to the five sections, the portal was organized in categories at the left hand side of the screen, which provided initial guidance to site visitors. Under each of these categories were a number of links to specific information and services. Most of these links went directly to specific applications or forms (e.g., driver's license renewal). The objective of this design was to allow visitors to get to the information or service they needed using the fewest possible number of "clicks." However, the portal was only an indexing tool that included links to agency websites, but attempted to categorize them in useful groups (Gil-Garcia and Dawes 2007). These categories were not mutually exclusive and some links could be found in two or more categories. Agencies decided how to categorize their links on the portal.

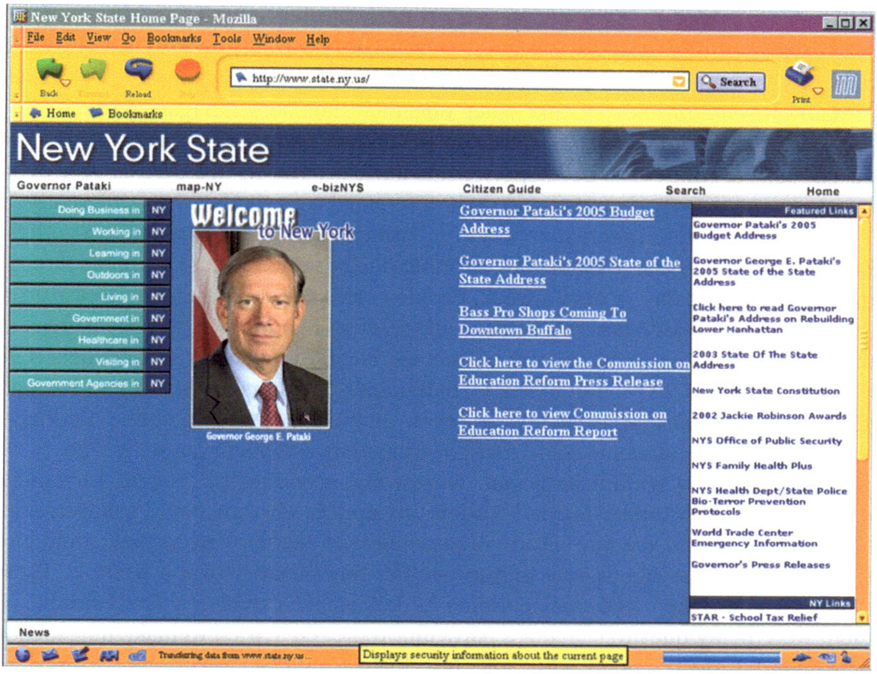

Fig. 4.1 New York State website (April 2005)

The NYS website also included pages that many different agencies within the executive branch had collaboratively developed. The Senate and the Assembly had their own pages, which were also linked to the state portal. Before 2005, most of the online services were provided on the agency websites, but very few agencies accepted credit cards as a payment option. As of 2005, more and more services could be paid using a credit card or other electronic payment method. Many government forms were available as PDF files, but due to accessibility issues they were also usually available in other formats (e.g., HTML) (Gil-Garcia and Dawes 2007). Regarding up-to-date technology, referring to the website, one interviewee stated, "we're at the point now, where it is ready to, in my view, go that next step to start introducing more current technologies into it."

4.2 Organizational Outputs and Outcomes

The NYS portal was initially launched in March of 2001. It was very similar to the portal that existed in 2005; the format and design had some important changes, but the supporting database and overall design remained basically the same. However, one of the advantages of this new design in comparison to the previous structure was its relative ease of use. In 2005, people did not necessarily need to know which agency provided the information or service they wanted in order to find it on the website. Information was organized according to categories and these categories were designed to help citizens, businesses, and other potential audiences navigate through NYS government. Ease of use was identified as a serious challenge by one of the respondents: "It's very difficult to develop a website that can be easily accessed by 95% of the people 'cause everybody's trying to do it differently; everybody thinks differently."

The website offered alternative ways for businesses and citizens to interact with the state government. A large amount of information and services were available through the website 24 h a day, 7 days a week. People could get information more easily and they could find very diverse information and services in one place, thereby increasing the convenience of government for businesses, citizens, and other stakeholders (Gil-Garcia and Dawes 2007). For example, individuals could make reservations for state parks, file their taxes electronically, or renew their driver's license online. Similarly, senior citizens and students could find government programs through the web.

On most pages within the portal, there was an option for citizens to provide feedback using an online form. Through this option, citizens could ask questions about where to find specific information on the website. However, they could also offer their opinions about how to improve the functionality of the website. These opinions were taken into consideration as the website evolved. For example, if there were many questions about a particular topic, OFT tried to make that section of the portal clearer or to add more information. An interviewee said the most important benefit from the state website was that "it gives transparency; people know what you're doing [as state government]."

Businesses had the ability to conduct transactions with the state government electronically. For them, the portal represents an opportunity to get through the necessary "red tape" and perform transactions easily. Further, the website has the potential to promote economic development for the state by providing straightforward access to business opportunities such as state government contracts for vendors (Gil-Garcia and Dawes 2007). On this matter, one respondent said, "If a business wants to do business with the state… in the past they would send in a letter to get on the bidders list and it might take 60 days to get on the bidders list… Today you can do that with the Office of General Services by going online, identifying the products or services that your company provides, and then you are on automatically… that [same] day you can bid for any relevant bids that may be going out."

Local governments also benefited from the website. However, local governments achieve different benefits than citizens do because they do not normally perform one-time transactions (e.g., renewing a driver's license or filing taxes). Local governments were more interested in having online applications that help them with their daily relationships with the state and their respective processes or work flows, which develop slowly.

An important challenge was to make more information and transactions available on the web, made more difficult by New York's fiscal situation, which had been problematic for several years prior to 2005. As budget and workforce demands increased, many viewed the state website as a potential way to improve the efficiency of government agencies. Similar to the private sector, government agencies were looking for online alternatives that could help them to save money and provide better services. A cost-savings justification was important because e-government initiatives were competing for resources with other priorities such as education, health, and public safety, among others.

However, there are other drivers beyond efficiency in the public sector and state agencies had to continue offering services in traditional ways in order to ensure equal access. Offering the same services in multiple channels presented some financial and operational challenges. Even if NYS government had certain services online, it was also required to provide paper-based and walk-in service. Therefore, government could reduce access to other service channels, but had to continue offering several alternatives.

Nevertheless, NYS government achieved important benefits from the website and related Internet technologies, such as efficiency, effectiveness, and citizen satisfaction. A respondent mentioned one benefit from the website: "It would definitely make the state workforce more productive, because the state employees could customize their desktop to use the applications that they truly need on a daily basis." However, cost-savings were not comparable to the private sector, mostly because government could not decide to go totally online, among other restrictions. An essential outcome for state agencies was their ability to communicate with their constituencies in a more effective way. As one respondent noted, "I think all agencies realize that the use of their websites is a very significant communications media for them." More importantly, state portals not only provide electronic services and communicate administrative information; they also have the potential to help government show a more integrated and consistent image to citizens, businesses, and other stakeholders, strengthening democratic values and mechanisms (Gil-Garcia and Dawes 2007). One interviewee clearly pointed out, "You cannot have an effective democracy without an informed electorate. State websites are one element in providing that, providing the electorate with that information."

According to the study entitled "State and Federal E-Government in the United States," developed yearly by Darrell West (2000, 2001, 2002, 2003, 2004), New York had been among the top 15 states in e-government functionality between 2000 and 2004. Among government website rankings, this one takes into consideration the greatest number of elements and attempts to evaluate complete websites. According to this comprehensive measure, New York had a highly functional website, ranking seventh in 2001. However, in more recent years its scores were down, ranking 14th in 2005 (West 2005) and 20th in 2008 (West 2008).

4.3 Management Strategies and Practices

The NYS portal made use of technology to deliver on several outcomes, which are mentioned in the previous paragraphs. The present section describes how management strategies and practices influenced these results. Similar to other states, in the mid-1990s several NYS agencies started their own websites. These were decentralized efforts in which each agency made decisions about content and format. Before 2000, the portal only had an alphabetical list of the state agencies; if people knew which agency they needed, they could click on the respective link and get to the agency's website. When NYS started to develop a more integrated and consistent statewide website, most agencies already had a website and there were over 170 online services and transactions. Therefore, the first statewide goal was not only to create more services, but also to help citizens and businesses find the existing services and information on the web.

The responsibility for achieving this goal fell on the Office for Technology (OFT), which was the state IT agency in New York. OFT helps other agencies use technology to achieve their substantive goals and objectives. As one of the respondents elaborated: "Because we are a technology office, we don't have a separate business and a separate technology plan—it's all one and the same." OFT reported to the Office of the Chief Information Officer (CIO) and its mission was to provide centralized technology services for other state agencies and to a certain extent to local government agencies, with a focus on infrastructure. Computing and networking were the two primary areas in which OFT supported other state agencies, but it also had some responsibilities in the development of IT policies for the state.

OFT, working in conjunction with the Governor's Office, began to develop a more integrated approach for the NYS website in June of 2000. The project began with a review of all the services that individual state agencies offered and the development of a strategy to move them online. The main objective was to have a main page or state portal from which people could have access to information and services provided by NYS agencies. In addition, there was an effort to create the NYS portal and then work with other agencies to establish a process to manage the links to their websites and to keep information up-to-date over time. An additional goal was to reduce the appearance of programmatic stovepipes, at least on the web (Gil-Garcia and Dawes 2007).

Working with many other agencies, OFT identified services that were not online, but that agencies planned or wanted to make available via the portal. OFT prioritized these applications and created a "top 75" list. These 75 applications were tracked over time to evaluate their progress in being offered online. This list was reviewed and modified during quarterly meetings between OFT and state agency representatives for several years. These meetings continue, but after 2005 they are now held annually.

Due to the limited availability of resources, the progress towards phase two—a more integrated and customizable website—has been very slow. However, in 2005 there was a pilot called "Online Permits and Licenses," which was a coordinated effort among multiple agencies to offer a single point of access for all business permits and licenses. The objective was to offer integrated online forms to simplify the processes of opening and managing a business in New York State, which required multiple agencies to coordinate and work together at the back-office level (Gil-Garcia and Dawes 2007).

The NYS website used a decentralized and distributed approach. Agencies introduced their own content to their web pages. Then they went into a back-end system that was linked to the portal and its database. From there, they could add links from the portal to the new content on their agency web pages, including links to new transactions, updated information, or frequently asked questions (FAQs). Agencies could decide the category and sub-category where the link should be classified. They could also decide if the link should be listed in the citizen guide and/or the e-business section and they entered keywords for the search engine to use. By 2005, there was a clear structure to designate which individuals could write and edit links at the agency level (Gil-Garcia and Dawes 2007). Each agency had a publisher, who was often the public information officer (PIO). The publisher approved both new public information and modifications to the existing content. Finally, the information was published overnight when the NYS website was updated.

OFT was responsible for uploading information and keeping it current on several pages of the portal and on its own website. OFT played the role of Web administrator and worked in conjunction with the Governor's Office, which can be considered the content owner of the portal homepage and the Governor's pages on the NYS website (Gil-Garcia and Dawes 2007). Two units at OFT had direct responsibilities over the website. One was responsible for application development, including some applications for the state, small agencies, and internal operations at OFT. The other unit was responsible for content and acted as the liaison between OFT and other agencies in the state government. This coordination took place through the e-commerce/e-government coordinators in each state agency (Gil-Garcia and Dawes 2007).

The decentralized approach allowed OFT to greatly limit the number of full-time staff devoted to website design and maintenance. According to estimates from several interviewees, the total amount of time devoted to the NYS website at OFT in 2005 would be equivalent to no more than one full-time employee. However, at least one person was responsible for the website at every state agency. This person could be the CIO, the Webmaster, or the public information officer (PIO), among others (Gil-Garcia and Dawes 2007).

Regarding troubleshooting and problem resolution, any agency (including OFT) could run reports to identify broken links and other issues. In some cases, the results were discussed between the agencies involved. In addition, some multi-agency groups helped to solve specific problems, such as categories with too many links. One of these joint efforts culminated in the creation of the Small Business Portal, which sits within the NYS portal and helps people to start new small businesses. Agencies could also see how much traffic they were getting from the portal. Most of the communication between OFT and other state agencies regarding the website took place through the e-commerce/e-government coordinators (Gil-Garcia and Dawes 2007). Among many other programs, OFT was responsible for coordinating the e-commerce and e-government efforts of all state agencies, including the development and management of state websites. Other responsibilities were the statewide financial management system (FMS) and several data centers that served most state agencies.

Agencies were responsible for keeping the information current on their respective websites. On this matter an interviewee commented, "If the agencies don't buy into this [the state website] and if they don't enter and update and keep their things current, then people will be searching and they get frustrated and they'll stop coming back." Due to this decentralized approach, all agencies were key players in developing and managing the NYS website (Gil-Garcia and Dawes 2007). OFT played a coordination role in updating information on the portal's main page and acted as the formal liaison between other state agencies, the Governor's Office, and the private vendor. This relationship was more important for some small state agencies than larger ones. However, OFT devoted limited resources to web applications development for agencies, leading many agencies to look for external help in order to develop their web applications.

Due to this distributed approach, the coordination of all the different agencies was not always easy. However, this decentralization also had positive effects, because the workload was dispersed among all agencies. For instance, respondents mentioned that keeping information current on the whole website was one very important challenge. As one of the interviewees mentioned, "Staying current, staying fresh, is very important." The website is the image of the state government and therefore it is extremely important to provide relevant and current information, as well as transactional services. The e-commerce/e-government network coordinators were very helpful in maintaining good communication and improving coordination regarding the website among state agencies.

However, not all agencies had the same technical capabilities and organizational priorities. Therefore, their level of engagement and compliance with the coordination agreements was also lower. Another benefit from decentralization was mentioned by a respondent: "It's a good idea, the way they've done it, to separate out the state portal and then allow agencies to go out and develop their own websites based on their needs. Obviously, the needs of a tourism agency are going to be different from the needs of a revenue agency, which is going to be different from the needs of a health department. So they've allowed each of those agencies to develop their own requirements, their own formatting within their framework."

According to one of the interviewees, various attempts were made to get citizens' opinions and expectations about the initial design of the website. There were focus groups among OFT employees, surveys were conducted, and managers from OFT also tried to get feedback during the Government Technology Conference (GTC East), where they had an informational booth. State agencies were also involved in the initial development of the portal, working with OFT and the Governor's Office in the design of the website and the preparation of a strategy for e-commerce and e-government in New York State. During the development stage, four people at OFT were coordinating content, three or four programmers were working full-time, and there was support from the networks unit in terms of managing bandwidth and potential website traffic.

As of 2005, the NYS website was managed by a combination of outsourcing and in-house development (Gil-Garcia and Dawes 2007). The website was divided for development and management purposes. Most of the web pages, including online transactions, were developed and managed directly by state agencies. No service was provided directly through the portal and the statewide website had not been designed to do so (for example, it lacked the necessary security requirements). OFT did manage the portal categories that were at the left-side navigation column and the major sections that link to other agencies (map-NY, e-bizNYS, and Citizen's Guide). Similar to other state agencies, OFT also had its own website.

As an exception, the Governor's Office managed the front page and the Governor's pages through outsourcing (excluding the static links, such as the New York State Constitution). The formal contractual relationship was between the vendor and the Governor's Office. Nevertheless, OFT had a working relationship with the vendor, which consisted mainly of coordination efforts in relation to the design and content of the website, including technical standards (Gil-Garcia and Dawes 2007).

Website hosting and content management were not centralized in New York State and agencies could make their own decisions about which strategy to follow (in-house, outsourcing, or a combination of both). Overall, the majority of agencies hosted their own sites. In fact, one of the respondents pointed out the fact that there were relatively few instances of agencies outsourcing the hosting of their websites. In addition, an interviewee stated her frustration about OFT's inability to assist agencies in their development efforts due to their huge workload: "Help [for development] is the last thing you're going to get from OFT. No, OFT's, they're not in a position to provide any help." The resources of OFT were clearly not enough to help all the agencies of New York State in developing Web applications.

Outsourced responsibilities for the state website were important because IT initiatives in general and the operations of state websites in particular are often outsourced. In these situations, the contractual requirements and the technical and organizational capability of the vendor had an impact on the characteristics of government websites (Gil-Garcia and Dawes 2007). Some of the New York respondents mentioned that the responsibility for design and management could be in-house, outsourced, or a combination of both. However, it was very important that these responsibilities were clearly defined in order to ensure better coordination. In addition, people involved in website development and management should have a common understanding and goals in order to effectively work together. For instance, one respondent described how "all agencies have to subscribe to the basic accessibility standards. There's [also] content management processes that we have in place that the agencies have to follow and that we follow internally."

In-house responsibilities for the state website were also important because people at agencies could shape the design and content of the website. A clear definition of these responsibilities was crucial in coordinating the work of multiple agencies with different perspectives and goals in relation to the website. Likewise, the commitment of state agencies was reflected in the quality of the information and services provided through the portal. An interviewee mentioned as a management challenge, "Enticing them [agencies] to keep things fresh and current… There are a couple of agencies that just aren't updating and it's just old information like that. So it definitely isn't the technology."

Finally, the marketing strategy strengthened the general goal of building an online state presence. As part of this effort to create a brand for NYS and a homogenous image for the website, a uniform banner was created. The use of this banner on all state websites became a requirement in a statewide policy. State employees participated in a contest to design the banner for the New York State website. The banner was functional and people could click on its picture and four buttons and go to different sections of the state portal. Regarding the use and functionality of the banner, one interviewee explained, "It has that feel and that branding and a connection and the linkage to get back and forth." In addition, there were some guidelines about how agency websites should be structured, but they were flexible and not mandatory for all state agencies.

Apart from the banner, New York State did not aggressively market its website. However, some respondents described marketing as very important so that people would know that the website existed and that they could use it. They mentioned that all agencies should be part of the marketing effort, because OFT does not have the necessary resources to market the website on its own. In contrast, other respondents mentioned that there was nothing to market. For instance, one person said, "We do not market our site, because there is nothing to market. If we wanted to market our website, it would have to be better. It would have to do something else." Likewise, an interviewee stated, "New York State should have a leading website in terms of how it's viewed by the world, in terms of other states, and we don't. So the challenge is to not be frustrated by the fact that we have a functional website that's not exciting."

4.4 General Organizational Characteristics

After describing the management practices and strategies in Section 4.3, the present section focuses on more general organizational characteristics. These include the organization's size, budget issues, and whether IT professionals were specially trained to understand how the organization had an impact on the portal's outcomes. OFT grew out of a 1996 task force and continued growing and taking on new responsibilities. For instance, in 2001 OFT had a total of 600 employees, about three times the US average of 213 employees. Due to the decentralized approach to IT, the number of employees at OFT was most important for some small agencies that rely on OFT for their development efforts. OFT also had many other functions and the website was a very small part of its work. Very few employees at OFT worked on website development and maintenance. In fact, for some respondents, the absolute number of people at the agency was not as important as whether enough people were dedicated to the website and that they could keep it functional.

Similarly, the average budget for a centralized IT organization in the United States was about \$68 million in 2001, while OFT's budget was \$216 million. In 2002, the percentage of OFT's budget devoted to maintenance was 6%, while the national average was about 8%. The maintenance budget is closely related to the ability to keep information and services up-to-date, particularly in terms of adequate staffing. Due to the decentralized approach, website maintenance was important not only for OFT, but also for every state agency.

During the interviews, federal resources were mentioned as something desirable and useful for website development, but no federal resources had been spent on the NYS portal in the years prior to 2005. However, some state agencies developed systems or services using federal grants. Regarding budget issues, one interviewee asserted, "Government is always so behind. And I know why it is—funds. If you don't have the money to keep up with the technology, you've got to work with the technology you've got." But money also seems to be important since it represents support, as an interviewee summarized: "Without money backing from the Governor's Office and from the CIO's Office, the creation and continued enhancement of the state website, it will go nowhere."

Specialized training was identified as an important factor because it is closely related to website design. One of the respondents stated, "You need to be able to develop the skills necessary to design and develop websites. And if you don't have that training and those skills and keep people current, you're not providing the services people are looking for." Website development requires certain skills, such as programming in basic HTML or developing transactional applications in Java, which were not always readily available from the state IT workforce. In addition, specialized training can help to develop accessible websites that are still interesting, flexible, and to certain degree unique. Through training, IT employees learned new ways to design web pages and came to learn that accessibility did not mean that the website had to contain only text, a common misconception. New York State provided accessibility and usability training for IT employees. About half of the states provided these types of trainings.

4.5 Institutional Arrangements

It is clear that OFT, through its practices, strategies, and decisions, shaped the outcomes of the NYS website. Nevertheless, it is crucial to turn now to the institutional arrangements (laws, policies, rules, etc.) that influenced the results of the government-wide website. During one interview, an individual shared that "one of the favorite sayings we have around here is, it's not the technology that's hard; it's getting the policy and getting people on board—that's been a big challenge."

Website accessibility was a very important issue. In 2004, the State Legislature released a statewide policy and standards for web accessibility. These standards were applicable to information available at any public state website and any web-based application that an agency develops. The NYS accessibility standards were partially based on section 508 of the Rehabilitation Act, which is a federal guideline on accessibility (Gil-Garcia and Dawes 2007). Though the act is not a requirement for states, it was useful as a model. These standards were mandatory for all state agencies and established in consultation with several agencies, the state IT professional associations, and the New York State Forum for Information Resource Management. Accessibility standards are so important that a respondent argued it to be "one of the areas where New York State, I think, really excels and conceivably in a sense that almost maybe sets the bar for the rest of the nation, [is] accessibility and all the accessibility rules."

Security was also a significant issue covered by statewide policy. The Office of Cyber Security and Critical Infrastructure Coordination developed an overarching security policy for the state. Additionally, each agency had its own security policy, which in the case of OFT was developed and managed by the information security officer (ISO). The Internet Privacy Act required every state agency website to include a privacy policy, including the portal. OFT created a model policy and many agencies used that model. For instance, if the personal record of an individual was disclosed, that person had to be notified. This situation had implications for government operations in general, but for online information and services in particular. Agencies that collected personal information from citizens, such as the Department of Health, the Department of Motor Vehicles, or Tax and Finance, had to be especially careful in observing privacy requirements. There were also some specific security requirements for agencies in certain public domains, such as criminal justice and law enforcement.

The existence of executive orders regarding the state CIO had the potential to influence the characteristics of the website in at least two different ways. First, the existence of a CIO in the state represented a formal attempt to develop an overarching and more coordinated IT strategy. This coordination could take place through some degree of managerial centralization and through the creation of statewide policies and standards. Second, the fact that the authority of the CIO came from executive orders may indicate strong support from the Governor. This perception of support could provide the CIO with greater authority to enforce directives and policies in relation to website development and maintenance.

In addition to standards and influence from the executive branch, the NYS legislature had the power to mandate the provision of certain information or services online and to impose standards about privacy, security, accessibility, usability, etc. Apart from these mandates, the involvement of the legislature was very low. "We are kind of below the radar with regard to legislation," a respondent stated. While some specific legislation was passed leading up to 2005, there were no specific committees for IT in either house of the legislature.

Despite limited involvement from the state legislature, state and federal regulations had a significant effect on the website. At the state level, the Electronic Signatures and Records Act (ESRA) had some important implications for IT applications in general. It stated that any information that a state agency puts in electronic format must still be available in a paper form. For example, if there was an application for a telephone directory available on the web, the number of printed versions could be greatly reduced, but not totally eliminated (Gil-Garcia and Dawes 2007). At the federal level, the Health Information Portability and Accountability

Act (HIPAA) impacted the information and services provided through the website. It includes provisions about security and privacy for health-related information. The Department of Health and other state agencies collected and maintained this type of information. OFT hosted much of this information through its data centers and therefore needed to be knowledgeable about HIPAA requirements and deadlines.

Finally, the civil service institution had two kinds of influences on the website. Similar to 29 other states, IT professionals in New York were not all members of the civil service. However, civil service rules about hiring and promoting highly influence the flexibility of state agencies to acquire and retain IT employees. First, it had an influence on the hiring process. According to civil service rules, employees had to begin working for the state in lower levels of employment, making it difficult to hire people with certain technical skills at higher levels. For instance, one of the respondents mentioned, "It is very difficult for us to be competitive when we hire. Right now, the kids coming out of school… they do not want to work for state government, because we pay probably half or quarter of what they can get in the private industry… so, they go somewhere else. We cannot be competitive in our starting salaries."

Second, civil service rules also had an impact on retaining people. Promotion was often based on both management skills and specific state tests. Some good technical people are very skilled in their work, but do poorly when taking tests or managing others, making it difficult for their supervisors to promote them. In addition, the content of the tests was frequently obsolete. For instance, some respondents mentioned that the tests still contained questions about programming with cards, programming with COBOL, and other topics that were hardly useful for the current web environment. An interviewee explained her perception of the effects of the civil service on the technology in use: "You are behind the curve in implementing new technologies; you're behind the curve in learning new technologies certainly. And it's not a cost-effective way to do business."

4.6 Environmental Conditions

A last crucial influence on the website outputs and outcomes were the environmental conditions. Political orientation and competition helped the NYS portal obtain the results described earlier. Following more than 20 years of Democratic governors, a Republican, George Pataki, was elected in 1998 with 52% of the votes. According to Holbrook and Van Dunk (1993), the Ranney Index of political competition presents New York as an almost-perfect-competition state between 1981 and 1988 (0.99 out of 1). At the district level, these authors found that New York was among the 15 states with the highest political competition between 1982 and 1986 (New York received a score of 47.68; the highest was 56.58 in North Dakota). However, during the gubernatorial election of 1998, the difference between the percentage of votes for Democrats and for Republicans was 22%, showing a clear shift to the Republican Party.

As mentioned earlier, the Governor's "Government Without Walls" initiative had a very important influence on the initial strategy and design of the NYS website. Some respondents mentioned that the governor's support and the creation of a statewide strategy could significantly change the current characteristics of the state website: "The governor has to think it's important; the governor has to want change." In contrast to other states, the New York State website had been primarily conceptualized and supported by the executive branch, not by the state legislature; therefore, the governor's support is essential. In fact, a respondent explained that "having the Governor's Office involved and having a cohesive team of all of us together now, is what made the difference of the successful changes and enhancements that took place."

From a normative point of view, citizen expectations should be one of the most important factors in shaping the design and content of state websites. Several respondents mentioned that the website was mainly to provide information and services to citizens. Similar to other situations in government, if the website could not satisfy citizens' needs and expectations, it was not accomplishing its objective and should be considered unsuccessful. Other respondents mentioned that businesses, local governments, and other stakeholders should have an influence on the state website functionality too.

Interviewees identified citizen expectations as one of the most important influences. In the words of a respondent, "Because after all, that is why the whole website exists. And so if that does not satisfy the citizens' expectations, it makes the website unsuccessful... If we don't have a pleased customer, we haven't satisfied our mission." For some of the respondents this influence was taking place and for others it was a normative requirement; that is, some believed citizen expectations still needed to have an influence on the website. For the first group, citizens were having an influence by not making new demands for the website. The website that existed in 2005 was not fancy or fully integrated, but it provided the information and services citizens needed. Therefore, citizens were not demanding a more sophisticated website at that point in time. However, respondents also recognized that the situation was changing rapidly and in the near future some changes to the website would be necessary: "The fact that people are becoming more sophisticated in their use of the Web; they know what to demand now." In fact, one of the leaders of OFT mentioned that citizens were increasingly using the web to conduct transactions as opposed to just looking for information.

Demographic factors were also an influence, since New York was the third most populous state in the US with about 19 million people in 2000. Therefore, it was also one of the biggest potential markets for government services. In 1999, median income per household was $43,400 and median income per family was about $51,700. In this same year, 14.6% of the population and 11.5% of families were considered to be below the poverty line. The population was highly educated with about 79% having completed high school or a higher degree and about 27% with at least a bachelor's degree. Computer ownership increased from 37% in 1998 to 49% in 2000. Similarly, the percentage of people with Internet access rose from 24% in 1998 to 40% in 2000.

Another important driver was the competition among states to be positioned among the top spots on several e-government rankings. State governments are well aware of these ranking systems. They were becoming knowledgeable about the factors that were evaluated in the different studies and some states were attempting to make progress in those relevant aspects.

Respondents mentioned that the size of the state economy is normally closely related to the size of the state budget and therefore had an indirect impact on the resources and capabilities of all agencies to design and manage their websites. For instance, one respondent said, "To the extent that there are dollars available to make improvements or to drive more towards the website certainly helps... I see dollars and resources as critical factors on what you can do." New York State is one of the largest state economies in the US. The government GSP was about $79.5 billion in 2000 and $81.2 billion in 2001. Total revenue in 2000 was about $111.5 billion. The number of state government jobs grew from 247,068 in 1998 to 251,245 in 2000. Similarly, the number of local government jobs increased from 996,848 in 1998 to 1,029,458 in 2000. Total earnings were about $13.6 billion for state government employees and about $48.6 billion for local government employees in 2000.

Another useful way to appreciate the size of the economy is by looking at the number of jobs and private earnings in several important industries such as education, communications, management, and engineering, among others. Total private earnings in education services jobs were about $9.9 billion in 2000 and the total number of jobs was 350,049, which positioned New York as number one in education service jobs. The total number of jobs in the electronic and other electric equipment industry was 88,593 and private earnings for this industry were about $6.2 billion in 2000. Similarly, the total number of jobs in the communications industry in 2000 was 125,652 and private earnings were about $11.9 billion. The total number of jobs in engineering and management services was 365,808 and their private earnings were about $19.5 billion in 2000.

4.7 Final Comments

In 2000, New York State began a systematic effort to integrate its government-wide website and present a more coherent image of state government on the Web. At that time, many NYS agencies not only had a presence on the Internet, but were also offering a great variety of services. A centralized approach would have been very difficult to implement. OFT, the state IT organization, was relatively new and its main functions were not website development and maintenance. Agencies were already developing and managing the great majority of online information and services. Agencies had technical capabilities and resources; OFT was not prepared to absorb all of these responsibilities and additional workload. Leaders at OFT decided that a decentralized approach would be a much more feasible and efficient way to manage the government-wide state website, and it worked very well for several years.

However, by 2005 the NYS website was facing the challenge of greater integration, at least virtually. According to some interviewees, the decentralized approach that helped New York to accommodate organizational diversity and agency autonomy needed rethinking. For instance, one respondent mentioned, "We think the website could be much, much better than it is." The NYS website continued to slowly evolve through more integrated prototypes, such as the small business portal. However, several leaders and managers at OFT thought that the website would need other changes very soon. One of the interviewees stated the following about the evolution of the state website: "It's not enough…it hasn't evolved since I've been here; it hasn't moved. There have been projects started and stuff for developing a real state Web portal, but not enough." These changes had to be guided by a more integrated vision, in which the state portal would be one of the central pieces. Usability and customization were seen as two other important elements. It was not clear how the decentralized approach would be modified in the following years to accommodate the next generation of government-wide websites, including Web 2.0 tools such as blogs, wikis, RSS feeds, and social media applications.

Several challenges lied ahead for the NYS Website. Nevertheless, the case clearly tells a story of e-government success. It describes how the government-wide website realizes several benefits (in terms of e-government success measures) while overcoming multiple challenges. Regarding benefits, the design of the portal was easy to use; people did not necessarily need to know which agency provided the information or service they wanted in order to find it on the website. In addition, the website services were available 24 h a day, 7 days a week. Another benefit is the possibility of understanding citizens' needs by receiving feedback through different online tools. Business had the ability to conduct transactions with the state electronically, avoiding some of the "red tape." Local governments also obtain some benefits from the website regarding several domains and transactions, since their relation with state government is continuous and involves multiple elements. Finally, an essential outcome for state agencies was the ability to communicate with their constituencies in a more effective way.

The benefits mentioned in this chapter were not easy to attain. There were several technical, organizational, and institutional challenges to the development of a more integrated, but decentralized government-wide website. For instance, the website suffered budget and efficiency pressures, while trying to ensure equal access to services for all people from the state. Also, the decentralized approach represented an important challenge of marketing and unifying the website image while truly aligning the agencies to a more integrated mission. They managed to offer ease of use and they established the banner as a visual for a common look and feel. In addition, since each agency develops their information, establishing clear rules and procedures for in-house and outsourced development was crucial and not an easy task.

As the chapter describes, other challenges were present and overcome by OFT and other NYS agencies in the development and management of a successful government-wide state website. The lessons derived from this case could be useful for governments that are starting their e-government efforts. They could also be relevant for governments that are redesigning their government-wide websites or are looking for new ways to deal with the day-to-day challenges present in government settings. This is particularly true for local governments around the world and government at the three levels (national, regional, and local) in many developing countries.

Chapter 5
Enacting the Government-Wide Indiana Website

Indiana was one of the first states in the US to build a government-wide state website. As of 2005, Indiana's website was the product of a long-term public–private partnership. Its IT functions have strong legislative underpinnings and its central IT agency exercises a relatively high degree of authority over agency-based IT functions. The present case describes a period in which Indiana's website used what was considered to be one of the most successful management strategies for a government website (Gil-Garcia and Hernandez-Tella 2010). Hence, it offers important lessons to public agencies, particularly for state and local governments from developed and developing nations that are just starting to deal with some of the same challenges or are working on new versions of their government-wide websites, potentially including Web 2.0 tools, social media, or open government strategies. Since the organizational and institutional arrangements are enduring and change very slowly, the main lessons will be relevant for many years in the future. Similar to the previous chapter, the case of Indiana's state website is described and analyzed following the main theoretical constructs presented in Chap. 2 and includes the following sections: (1) Enacted Technology, (2) Organizational Outputs and Outcomes, (3) Management Strategies and Practices, (4) Organizational Structures and Processes, (5) Institutional Arrangements, and (6) Environmental Conditions. At the end, the chapter provides some final comments about the experience of Indiana.

5.1 Enacted Technology

A marketing brochure states, "Belonging to Indiana state government, AccessIndiana is the brand name under which state agencies, boards, and commissions provide online services and information for citizens and businesses." Interviewees characterized Indiana's website in different ways. For example, one respondent mentioned that the goal is "citizen's service at the citizen's convenience, not at our

J. R. Gil-Garcia, *Enacting Electronic Government Success*,

Integrated Series in Information Systems 31, DOI: 10.1007/978-1-4614-2015-6_5,

convenience… And what that really meant was that we had to have 24 × 7 access, 365 [days a year]. We had to provide privacy and security, because people are not going to consider something convenient that puts them at risk. So privacy and security were very important to providing that kind of citizen convenience… And then through that convenience being able to drive down the cost of doing business with government, both for government and for the individual."

Talking about the mission, another interviewee described it as being "to provide access to citizens and businesses in an easy fashion. We do not want constituencies to have to know what agencies they need to interact with… At the same time the goal is to make it as cost effective as possible." From the view of leaders and managers, two main elements characterize the mission of Indiana's website. First, it should be able to produce cost-savings for both government agencies and website users. Second, it has to be able to help citizens, businesses, and other users to conveniently obtain the information and services they need. Reduced real costs and convenient high quality services are also seen as incentives for businesses and citizens to use Indiana's website.

By 2005, Indiana's website had a common look and feel (Gil-Garcia and Hernandez-Tella 2010). It was ordered in a three-column setup with two thinner columns on each side and a larger column in the middle (see Fig. 5.1). The middle column features services, either new ones or seasonal offerings such as filing taxes, hunting licenses, or fishing licenses. The column on the right contained direct links to information or services that people use the most and the column on the left was for site navigation.

Indiana's website was designed as a three-tier architecture: (1) presentation layer, (2) application layer, and (3) data layer. The main goal of this separation is to increase re-usability, portability, and scalability while reducing the complexity of managing the whole website. "The presentation layer is the user interface and is what the user sees… The application layer controls the business logic and applies that logic to the user input before passing a request to the data layer… The data layer performs the request and passes the results to the application layer, which may again apply business logic before delivering the result back to the presentation layer."[1]

Some agencies were already embracing specific technologies, so Indiana's website had to be ready to support these platforms and software. Hence, the staff attempted to be technology agnostic and remain open to many different technologies and programming languages. As an example of the variety of technologies used, the state IT office was planning to become a Microsoft driven shop, while the Bureau of Motor Vehicles was adopting the "dot.net" platform. Nevertheless, because of the kind of applications the AccessIndiana staff normally creates, in practice they could be considered a Java shop.

[1] From "Everything you ever needed to know about AccessIndiana www.IN.gov, but didn't know who to ask. A Primer on Indiana's Official Web Portal." Available at www.in.gov/itoc/html_site/architecture/guidelines.html.

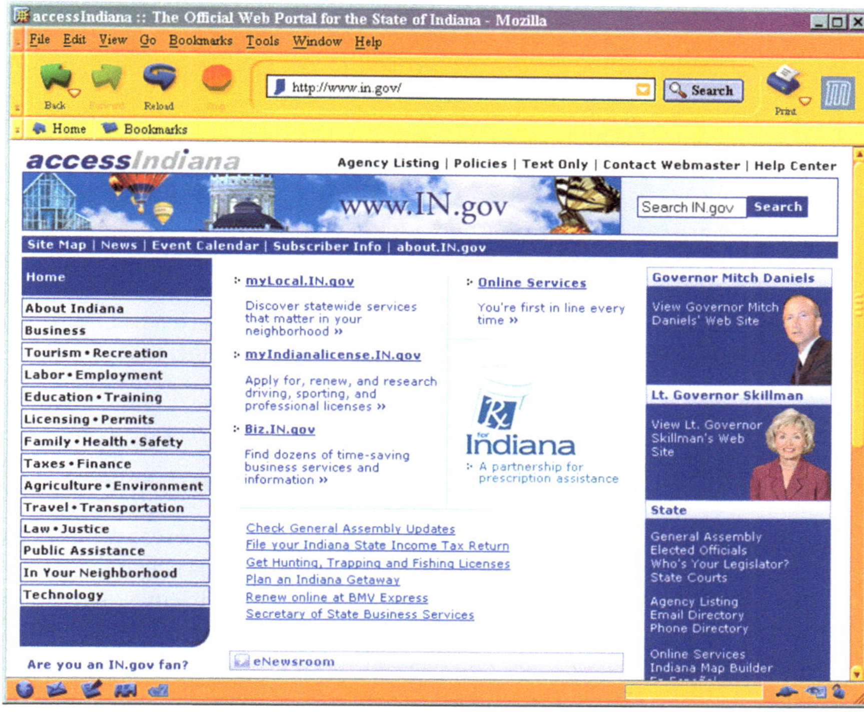

Fig. 5.1 Indiana Website (April, 2005)

Regarding service delivery, originally Indiana's home page was organized based on the user's knowledge about which agency he or she needed to interact with. On a window with a logo, a few categories were displayed (e.g., state, local, associations) and by clicking on a category the user accessed a list of available links (i.e., a list of all state agencies). Under such conditions it was difficult for users to find the information or service they needed. Therefore, by 2005 the homepage was driven more by functions than organizations. The left column had new categories that attempted to capture events, functions that users wanted to perform, or information they needed to find (e.g., finding a job, traveling, paying taxes). One respondent described it as "very functionally organized so that if you arrive at the AccessIndiana home page, you ought to be able to, very quickly, find the category of information that you need."

On Indiana's website, services and information were organized in fourteen categories: (1) Business, (2) Labor and Employment, (3) Licensing and Permits, (4) Taxes and Finance, (5) Agriculture and Environment, (6) Law and Justice, (7) Family, Health and Safety, (8) Public Assistance, (9) In Your Neighborhood, (10) Travel and Transportation, (11) Education and Training, (12) Tourism and Recreation, (13) Technology, and (14) About Indiana. The purpose of these categories was to help businesses, citizens, and other users easily find what they needed. They attempted to present information according to the functions that users want to perform. In addition, around 2002, Indiana partnered with Google to offer a search engine, which also helps users find what they need.

An important characteristic of Indiana's website is that all three branches of state government are represented on it (Gil-Garcia and Hernandez-Tella 2010). Citizens have access to information and services from the executive, legislative, and judicial branches through the same website. One of the respondents said, "Citizens of Indiana really do have a virtual one-stop shop. One place to go, no matter whom you need information from in state government." Legislation was an important factor in accomplishing this virtual co-location. In addition, searching for legislation is one popular service. Other services available were hunting and fishing licenses, renewing license plates, renewing a driver's license, renewing professional licenses, permits, and filing state taxes, among others.

5.2 Organizational Outputs and Outcomes

The technological features and the services in AccessIndiana resulted in several outcomes. According to West (2000, 2001, 2002, 2003, 2004), Indiana greatly improved from 2000 to 2001 and ranked among the top 15 states in e-government functionality for the years 2001–2004. The contract with Indiana Interactive was renewed in 2000 and it seems that this renewal had a positive effect on Indiana's 2001 ranking. Gant (2003a) describes a major redesign and other important policy and managerial changes that took place between 2000 and 2001. Indiana's Web portal was fully redesigned and organized in terms of functional categories, instead of government structures. Also, several guidelines and policies were created to improve the coordination and communication among the Office of the CIO, Indiana Interactive, and other state agencies.

The staff's rationale was that citizens do not know and do not have to know what part of government is responsible for certain information or services. Citizens and businesses requiring services do not necessarily differentiate between the judicial, executive, and legislative branches or between services provided by their state, their county, or their city (Gil-Garcia and Hernandez-Tella 2010). Therefore, in 2004 Indiana made the first applications for myLocal available online. There is a "local government" link on the home page (www.IN.gov). This page provides access to all local government websites and allows individuals to perform some transactions, such as paying property taxes. From a development point of view, the transactional services are like customizable templates that allow local governments to add their bank account number, name, and some additional information. These templates are available for all local governments in Indiana to use. An interviewee mentioned that, from a citizen perspective, "myLocal.gov is a place where anybody who might need government information but doesn't know exactly where to get it from, can go."

For every decision about the structure and content of Indiana's website, feedback from users was very important (Gil-Garcia and Hernandez-Tella 2010).

Businesses and citizens could always send e-mail messages with questions or suggestions. A live chat was also available in the portal and users could start a session to interact with a member of Indiana's website staff. At the end of a live chat session, like at the end of many services, the user was asked to fill out a short survey. Finally, there was an opportunity to share positive experiences through a service called FanMail. In addition, Indiana Interactive organized focus groups to get feedback before launching new services online. They also organized training sessions with law firms, banks, and other potential users to explain how the services work and get comments from them. Indiana Interactive staff attended trade shows and demoed several of their services to different audiences, including health professionals and human resource managers.

One of the most important benefits of Indiana's website is convenience for citizens, who can obtain information and services through the portal 24 h a day, 7 days a week. They do not have to stand in line in order to pay for government services or to obtain government forms. By 2005, the website was organized in such a way that users did not need to know precisely which agency they needed to interact with. They can easily find information and services they need using any computer with Internet access (Gil-Garcia and Hernandez-Tella 2010). The portal aims to offer more integrated solutions to specific audiences (e.g., the human resources portal).

A challenge to this level of convenience is language translation. By 2005 the portal used machine translation software, which provides only 60–70% accuracy. These levels may be enough for certain information and applications, but more accurate translations are necessary for others. In cases where the translation needs greater accuracy, the state had to make a decision about how to proceed: either build a dictionary repository to increase the accuracy or have the content manually translated. AccessIndiana was working on a Spanish version of the website in 2005, but the complexity of this initiative had delayed its implementation. One of the interviewees stated that initiatives like this one might require direct sponsorship from the governor.

Indiana's website attempts to be not only convenient and easy to use, but also to offer cost-saving solutions to most users. Using the website helps both citizens and state agencies to save money. Technology has the potential to reduce the cost of service provision, benefiting both the provider and the client. The services and fees are designed to meet users' needs and to help them to save money on costs like parking, gasoline, and traveling. According to one of the interviewees, fees are always lower than the total walk-in cost of the service at a state agency's office.

In terms of benefits for businesses, Indiana's website is clearly a cost-savings alternative (Gil-Garcia and Hernandez-Tella 2010). Businesses rely on the website because they save money and they can get the information and services they need faster. Additionally, many businesses used to spend a great deal of money and time on messenger services or dedicating staff resources to delivering and retrieving government documents. When asked about the benefits for businesses, one respondent mentioned, "Time is money, and the faster you can get something done, the more you have access to information, the more you can cut down that cycle and just have it finished, the better off you are. So, to me clearly [the benefit] is cost-savings." Indiana's website has helped businesses to reduce the time and cost to obtain specific services and information.

Greater participation in the democratic process is also a potential result, partly due to the convenience of having legislators' contact information, political appointees' e-mail addresses, legislative bills, and other information available online (Gil-Garcia and Hernandez-Tella 2010). One respondent declared that "the General Assembly has a really good website and it used more and more every single year to search for legislation and so that people can participate in their government." Citizens can be more informed and involved in state government actions through the website, and they have a sense that government is more open to the people. The availability of online information improves the perceived accessibility to representatives and government officials. Therefore, to a certain extent, it also helps to increase the perceived transparency and openness of state government, which is of increasing importance in today's political environment. Talking about the relationship between citizens and governments, one respondent said, "A web portal that works well creates a community that requires both sides to be responsible and accountable." Web portals have the potential to make state governments more accessible and accountable (Gil-Garcia and Hernandez-Tella 2010). Citizens' participation and involvement vary, but according to one of the interviewees, the website usage statistics show a positive trend regarding overall use of Indiana's website over time.

In terms of the interactions between Indiana's state website and local governments, we can identify at least two outcomes. First, like state agencies, local governments can provide information and services through Web portals. Therefore, local governments can take advantage of best practices developed at the state level, improving the provision of transactional services and overall efficiency at the local level. In addition, citizens are now more willing to interact with government through the web, including local governments. Second, similar to citizens and businesses, local governments are users of the information and services available on the state website and obtain similar benefits, such as convenience and cost-savings. They can also obtain some services, such as driving records or limited criminal histories, at either no cost or for a reduced fee (Gil-Garcia and Hernandez-Tella 2010).

5.3 Management Strategies and Practices

After mentioning some of the website's benefits, this section describes how the management strategies and practices relate to the results. In 1994, only two state agencies were providing some form of online services and very few had any type of presence on the web. It was then that a group of people from several state agencies started meeting regularly to talk about technology and the benefits it could bring to the State of Indiana. Initially they searched other states' strategies as alternatives and were interested in the public–private partnership developed by Kansas. In general terms, the partnerships consist of outsourcing the website development to a private company with the incentive of being able to charge convenience fees for commercially viable data. Since the public–private partnership model seemed to be a good and workable alternative for Indiana, the Intelenet Commission[2] issued a request for proposals. From the applicants, Indiana Interactive, Inc. (a wholly owned subsidiary of the NIC, Inc.) was selected as the manager of the state website (network manager). By December 1995, AccessIndiana was launched on the World Wide Web.

Identifying several commercially viable transactions was very important for the public–private partnership model, since it is funded through convenience fees that are applied to certain transactional services (Gil-Garcia and Hernandez-Tella 2010). Therefore, the portal started with driving records, which are used by insurance companies and other entities on a regular basis. Nevertheless, it was very risky to have a single source of revenue. Aiming for diversification of the sources of revenue, other potential transactions were explored and developed in the following years.

With help from the Governor's Technology Taskforce, AccessIndiana staff identified information and services that people were looking for on the website, but that Indiana was not providing. In order to gather this information, the taskforce reviewed other states' websites, discussed personal experiences among its members, and obtained information about the popularity of certain online services in other states, among other strategies. Through this process, the members of the taskforce identified a variety of potential services to offer. Indiana Interactive developed and made available on the Web some of the services the group identified, such as fishing licenses and driver's license renewals.

Indiana Interactive was in charge of the provision and management of the original and continuously expanded services. As the state network manager it has responsibility for daily operations, including design, application development, systems support, infrastructure, marketing, and customer service. The Enhance Data Access Review Committee (EDARC), which includes members from state agencies and some select citizens appointed by the Governor's Office, meets every other month. EDARC has the authority to evaluate Indiana Interactive's work and authorize fees for new online services. The general manager of AccessIndiana presents a report of the completed work and suggestions for next steps each month. The general manager also maintains regular meetings with the Office of the CIO to discuss the strategy for the website and to decide the next statewide priorities. The CIO in Indiana sits upon two legislatively mandated organizations: (1) the Information Technology Oversight Commission (ITOC) and (2) the Division of Information Technology (DIT). The ITOC was charged with activities such as IT

---

[2] The Intelenet Commission was chartered in 1986 by the Indiana Assembly as an Indiana corporate and policy body. The Intelenet Commission's mission is to provide cost-effective, current technology telecommunications network services and information gateway services to its public sector customers, comprised of state agencies, higher education institutions, K-12 school corporations, public libraries, local government entities, and other authorized users (Intelenet 2003).

planning, architecture standards, and policy setting for the state. DIT is an operations organization that provides centralized services to other agencies on a fee-for-service basis.

In the beginning, Indiana's website did not have a common look and feel, because each agency website was developed independently of the others. The only characteristic connecting them was the three-level URL to get to each of the different agencies (e.g., www.sos.IN.gov). All state agencies were required to use website domain names that ended with IN.gov. This situation was to be expected since the initial goal was just to get every agency online (Gil-Garcia and Hernandez-Tella 2010). As a next step, once every agency had some online presence, the Office of the CIO and Indiana Interactive started working towards two objectives: (1) applying a common look and feel across the state ("one site, one website") and (2) identifying and developing convenience-fee transactions. They set out to achieve these objectives through conversations with state agencies regarding the benefits and significance of having more dynamic information and providing electronic services to their constituencies.

According to legislation related to the portal, the judicial and legislative branches had the option of using AccessIndiana, but all agencies under the governor had to use the portal. Posting information at AccessIndiana is free for all three branches of government. Managing them as three separate streams of activity, Indiana Interactive has been able to respect the order and priorities of the governor, the legislators, and the judiciary regarding website services (Gil-Garcia and Hernandez-Tella 2010). This strategy is facilitated by the fact that each branch of government started their first transactional websites at AccessIndiana.

Based on Indiana Interactive's responsibilities and the inclusion of a multitude of agencies and the three branches of government, Indiana's website services relied on both outsourcing and direct provision from the Office of the CIO. In 2001, five states in the US entirely outsourced their website services and twenty-seven states entirely provided them directly. Indiana is one of thirty-one states in which the centralized IT organization directly managed portal development for agencies; in this specific case, through a formal relationship with Indiana Interactive (NASCIO 2002).

The AccessIndiana management strategy worked in accordance with its three-tier design, described in previous pages. The majority of the online transactions were hosted and managed at AccessIndiana in a centralized fashion, as well as most of the presentation layers. Likewise, most of the transactions used AccessIndiana's payment engine. Regarding the database layer of these applications, they were normally the responsibility of the respective agencies. Agencies had to pay to host their database layers and these databases were maintained in different locations. If the database layer was to be housed outside the agency or the central IT organization, they needed to get a waiver from the Information Technology Oversight Commission. Some of them were hosted at AccessIndiana, others were hosted at the Division of Information Technology, some agencies hosted them on their own servers, and others outsourced the hosting to a private company.

Most state agencies relied on Indiana Interactive for web applications development, particularly those that would be available through the portal. For this purpose, AccessIndiana staff met with state agencies to discuss the current state of their websites and potential new developments. Each agency presented its development request to AccessIndiana staff and discussed the priority and significance of their current and future projects. Upon acceptance of new projects, they were put on a list that works on a first come, first served basis. As mentioned before, this service was free for state government, including the executive, legislative, and judicial branches. Each branch had a separate priority list and in fact, as an interviewee explained, "We would never move legislative or judicial projects because of something the governor said. That was not acceptable."

If agencies needed an application faster (i.e., in order to meet a deadline), they could rely on their own resources to pay for its development. In these situations, they outsourced the development to another private company; when it was complete, AccessIndiana staff could web-enable and host it. In this way, all transactions were offered in one place and those agencies could still benefit from the free hosting of their presentation layers. The private vendor that developed the application had to follow statewide standards and detailed guidelines.[3] Some important elements included in these guidelines are architecture, common look and feel, privacy policy, technology standards, security, accessibility, and hosting. The use of these guidelines for vendors has been an important strategy to enable efficient administration and maintenance and to keep the website more consistent (Gil-Garcia and Hernandez-Tella 2010).

In general, the few initial pages of the portal were developed and managed by Indiana Interactive. AccessIndiana staff met with selected agencies and businesses to get their feedback on the portal. The Office of the CIO and other state agency representatives reviewed the proposed page. They were allowed to make suggestions about specific content changes and the overall structure of this initial page. Regarding the content of the main page, AccessIndiana staff proposes what to include, with an objective to change the content at least every quarter. In 2005 the content management process was done manually, but AccessIndiana was planning to acquire an automated tool in the near future. All other website pages can be updated by each agency through their own authorization process. If an agency does not have the necessary staff to do its own updates, AccessIndiana can help with this process. However, AccessIndiana staff must be directly involved in this process if it is a new fee-based service or if the modifications affect the current fee structure.

In 2005, there were three types of fees for fee-based transactional services. As an interviewee explained, "AccessIndiana as it exists today is similar to a toll road. If you drive on a toll road, you pay." First, instant access fees were used to

[3] For more information see the document called "Web-Based Computing Guidelines for Prospective Vendors," available at http://www.in.gov/dpoc/html_site/Policies/ITP_00-7_Web_Based_Guidelines.pdf.

cover the costs associated with processing a credit card or an electronic check. Second, enhanced access fees or convenience fees went to Indiana Interactive as the network manager of AccessIndiana. These fees were used to maintain the existing (free) services and to develop new projects. They were also used for management expenses such as marketing campaigns, AccessIndiana staff, new infrastructure, etc. Third, statutory fees always went back to the state agency and were the same as what agencies normally charge for providing certain kinds of services, as specified by law.

For some respondents there were clear differences between in-house and outsourced provision of services. For them, if the website is done in-house, it is subject to political forces such as the influence of legislators, the budget agency, and other powerful political actors. For example, in certain circumstances, one of these actors can re-allocate budget dollars initially allocated for website development. In contrast, when the state website is outsourced, there is a contract with a private company and a certain degree of protection from political forces. A public–private partnership model partially solves the budgetary and other issues linked to political forces.

For other respondents, these two types of responsibilities are very important because they are mutually supporting. For example, in Indiana the website was outsourced, a model that worked well because the state provided adequate support for the outsourcing company. The state protected the funding model and the structure that they put in place. Indiana Interactive, the Office of the CIO, and other state entities worked together to make AccessIndiana a successful initiative.

Convenience fees were the foundation of the AccessIndiana business model; therefore, it was important for Indiana to have an aggressive marketing strategy. As a respondent clearly stated, "If we have not built the service and we haven't marketed, we don't win." Another interviewee concurred: "You know the old saying 'build it and they will come' does not necessarily happen—marketing I think is key." For this model, the more people who use the website, the greater the amount of resources to continue developing and improving the information and services it provides. As with any other private company, Indiana Interactive needed to attract customers to stay in business. Attracting customers included identifying information and services that users really want, as well as some of the characteristics that they would like the applications to have. Surveys, focus groups, and other market identification strategies help shape the characteristics of a state website (Gil-Garcia and Hernandez-Tella 2010). All these strategies allowed Indiana to have "marketing pieces that are very directed [towards certain audiences]," as one interviewee pointed out.

In addition, marketing can help to create a sense of security. For instance, the use of the phrase "AccessIndiana: The Official Web Portal of the State of Indiana" assures users about the security of electronically interacting with the State of Indiana. All state agencies were required to use IN.gov in their URLs due to control and security considerations. This policy allowed people to easily verify the authenticity of the website and provides them with a sense of security about who they were interacting with online (Gil-Garcia and Hernandez-Tella 2010).

In addition, policies required that agencies host their presentation layer at AccessIndiana, which helped maintain the common look and feel and support the marketing and branding efforts. For all the mentioned reasons, marketing was very important for Indiana, as the respondents said, "That's the one thing that in Indiana we do very, very well" and "we are a market-driven organization."

In general, government-wide websites require complex inter-organizational processes and good communication and coordination mechanisms. However, in a public–private partnership model like AccessIndiana, communication between the vendor and the responsible state agency is crucial (Gil-Garcia and Hernandez-Tella 2010). Communication between the strategic level and the operational level was often difficult. In AccessIndiana, this communication had to take place on two levels: at the operational level between webmasters, graphic designers, etc. and also at the strategic level between the CIO and the general manager. The communication channels should flow not only from top to bottom, but also from bottom to top. Communication from the operational level to the strategic level was the most challenging for AccessIndiana. Although the information at the operational level could be useful in making better decisions, it generally did not flow as frequently as necessary. On this matter a respondent argued the importance of "making sure we do keep those lines of communication open, because the minute you don't, you're in big trouble."

Coordination among all the actors involved in the management and development of the website was important. In order to maintain a more integrated website, it was necessary for AccessIndiana staff to work together with state agencies, vendors, business users, legislators, courts, and other important stakeholders. For this process, AccessIndiana designed different ways to develop and manage transactional services for state agencies.

Another challenge for AccessIndiana was building consensus about the strategic direction of the site. Creating overall strategies is a combination of taking into account what the website can do for all state agencies and other stakeholders and what the state agencies need and want from the website (Gil-Garcia and Hernandez-Tella 2010). As one respondent said, "It is a mixture of listening and leading… and you cannot do one or the other, you have to do both, because there are some people who are going to give you things that you are going to be doing. Other people who just start looking for you to provide leadership because they have no idea and you have to be able to satisfy both of those to build consensus."

5.4 General Organizational Characteristics

All the strategies and management practices, because of the public–private partnership, relied on a relatively small number of employees. The total number of employees at the Office of the CIO was 185 in 2001, about 13% smaller than the US average of 213 employees (NASCIO 2002) and very few of them were directly related to the government-wide website. One respondent commented on how "the staff gr[ew] in a very gradual process and part of it was driven by us realizing our inefficiencies." Also connected to the public–private model, as stated by the interviewees, political influence had less of an impact on the website's budget.

In 2002, the percentage of the Office of the CIO's budget devoted to maintenance was 2%, while the national average was about 8%. Similarly, the percentage of resources from federal sources was 2% in Indiana, while the national average was 3.13% in 2002. The average budget for the centralized IT organization in the United States was about $68 million in 2001 and Indiana's budget for the Office of the CIO was $62.7 million (NASCIO 2002). Regarding budget issues, an interviewee argued, "How you manage is more important than how much money you have." However, there is a relationship between the budget and the things an organization can do. In the case of Indiana, the budget for maintenance did not have to be at the Office of the CIO. It could also be part of state agencies' budgets or AccessIndiana's budget.

Like about half of the states in the US, Indiana also provided accessibility and usability training for its IT employees. Training for IT employees was a very important factor in Indiana. This training was not necessarily technical, but also related to the acquisition of knowledge about architectural standards, the business model, strategy, and branding. As a respondent asserted, "It is a broad base of knowledge that is required." These trainings were important because they helped to build consensus and a common understanding among the actors involved in the statewide website. In addition, agencies normally updated their own pages. Having knowledge about HTML, Java, or other development and programming languages could be important for some state agencies. Agencies with knowledge about old technologies can sometimes be difficult to convince about the new alternatives. For all of these major changes, training in new technologies can be very helpful.

After its first 10 years, AccessIndiana entailed over 300,000 pages of information. The management of this content is difficult and requires work from many different actors. One respondent described the process: "We managed thirty million accesses a month; it's got a lot of traffic, a high expectation- it is managing chaos, for lack of a better word." In 2005 the content management was done manually, but it was commonly recognized that a website of this size needed a better approach, possibly using an automated content management tool. The challenge would be to convince all of the agencies and organizations involved to migrate to this new system (Gil-Garcia and Hernandez-Tella 2010). These actors are sometimes so adapted to the old systems and processes that they are very reluctant to change, even when they see advantages in the new alternatives.

Finally, the stability of the people responsible for the website seemed to be an important factor for the success of Indiana's website. While the average tenure of state CIOs is about 2 years, according to the National Association of State Chief Information Officers (NASCIO), by 2005 the former CIO of the State of Indiana had been in her position for 7 years. The general manager of Indiana Interactive had also been working for that company for a long time period—6 years. In addition to the leaders, several staff members also had a long tenure. A respondent mention how after 10 years the staff "evolved into a much more specialized group of professionals who each play a [specific] role."

5.5 Institutional Arrangements

Overall, institutional arrangements are specific aspects of government and they are essential to understand how information technologies could be useful. "When you work with or in government, you learn how government works," a respondent clearly stated. Laws, regulations, policies, and other rules are important aspects of how government works and how these characteristics could affect the success of e-government initiatives. Regarding how state laws and regulations shaped the development of the website, one interviewee answered, "Just AccessIndiana itself was created by legislation; all is driven by Indiana code so it very much shapes how things are organized and run."

Indiana had mandatory accessibility standards for state websites. Apart from requiring that the presentation layer be hosted at AccessIndiana, if a problem occurs at the back-end, Indiana Interactive can restrict access to the presentation layer until the problem is fixed and the application is running again. Since it offers transactions, security and privacy were especially important for Indiana's website. Several standards and guidelines regarding development, hosting, and other elements of the technological architecture work simultaneously to enhance convenience, but also to ensure security and privacy for the portal's users. In addition, some guidelines included information about required characteristics of the website and technology standards that state agencies have to use.

State and federal regulations were also important for Indiana. At the state level, AccessIndiana was created by legislation and some of its organizational and technological characteristics were shaped by Indiana code. As in any other government, many documents have to be signed and Indiana was one of the first states that adopted a law regarding digital signatures. One of the most important sources of revenue for AccessIndiana is driving records, as mentioned in the management strategies section. Although their main customers are insurance companies, courts also use driving records. For example, if a person is arrested for drunk driving and the case is going to court, the prosecutor needs to know that individual's previous driving record to make a better decision about the case. Some public institutions also need the service. For example, a school may need the record of a potential school bus driver. When that need arises, the record is provided for free to the public organization. The commissioner used to certify and sign all driving records before sending them to the courts, a process that took between 6 days and 2 weeks. A digital signature application was developed to streamline this process. With the new system, the driving records are electronically signed and the whole process takes only a few minutes. However, meeting all the requirements of the law is very expensive, making this solution infeasible for some online services (Gil-Garcia and Hernandez-Tella 2010). In many cases, adding a box that citizens can click to sign documents was a good solution. For other cases, legislative changes were necessary.

Credit card payments are also important for electronic services. Around 2002, the Indiana legislature passed a law authorizing state agencies to collect an additional fee for credit card payments. Before this time, agencies were not sure whether these additional fees were permitted. Originally, in order to obtain services that require a fee, users had to subscribe to the portal and they were billed at the end of the month. By 2005, agencies knew that if they were providing a service that required a fee, they could charge an additional amount to pay for it. Thanks to this development, agencies noticed that collecting fees was not as problematic as they thought and they became more interested in developing additional transactional services online. Finally, regarding accessibility, Indiana adopted most of the standards from section 508, which is a federal standard for accessibility. The state had a committee whose objective was making sure that accessibility guidelines were met.

Interviewees from Indiana described how executive orders creating and supporting the IT initiative were a relevant institutional factor, especially when they reflected real support from the governor. Garnering the governor's support was critical and one important way to obtain his support was to align all activities to his government agenda. As stated by one of the interviewees, "We proactively make sure that we are in line with the governor's agenda." In addition, the CIO needed to have the formal authority and responsibility to make change happen. Sometimes CIOs are good at negotiation and consensus building, but it is always more effective to have the necessary authority (Gil-Garcia and Hernandez-Tella 2010).

Similarly, another factor respondents mentioned was the involvement of agency stakeholders in direction setting. Involvement with and feedback from agency customers had been important factors, too. Formal and informal committees have been key to the success of the portal, because involved agencies become active designers and promoters of Indiana's website and its overall strategies. In addition, for the convenience-fee funding model, having partners in state government who were committed to the success of the website was very important.

Legislative involvement also played an important role in AccessIndiana. Regardless of the fact that Indiana did not have IT committees in its House of Representatives or Senate, the legislature was involved with AccessIndiana through the staff at the Legislative Services Agency (Gil-Garcia and Hernandez-Tella 2010). There was a committee of legislators, which oversaw the Legislative Services Agency and made requests to its staff about the website and other technology-related matters. The committee worked together with AccessIndiana staff in keeping the legislature's portion of the website up to date.

AccessIndiana helped legislators to conduct surveys of their constituencies. Sometimes the portal's staff met with legislators individually and talked about the services offered and how those services could be useful for the legislators' constituencies. Indiana Interactive staff was always working with the legislature, but individual legislators were normally not involved in decisions or actions about the whole website; most of their involvement was about their portion of the website.

Indiana interviewees believe that the state legislature needed to be involved in certain aspects of the website. For instance, in Indiana the business model was codified in law, which established greater certainty for all parties involved and provided continuity and long-term goals and strategies. For Indiana, the legislation was very general and did not restrict management flexibility. The legal framework clearly stated the goals, structure, and responsibilities for the website, but was broad enough to accommodate a decade of technological and organizational changes with relatively few modifications. The state legislature was not involved in the daily operations or in the strategic direction of the website. They established the framework and let Indiana Interactive staff do their jobs within AccessIndiana's governance structure. At the same time, legislators have been responsive to legislative issues in relation to the website operation, such as the use of credit cards to process transactions.

For IT professionals, civil service was not a limitation. Due to the public–private partnership, all employees of Indiana's website were formally working for Indiana Interactive, a private company. Therefore, in Indiana IT professionals were not members of the civil service. In fact, for these employees, personnel management had the flexibility, competitiveness, and other advantages of private sector organizations.

5.6 Environmental Conditions

Outside the organization and apart from the institutional arrangements, several environmental conditions presented and influenced the portal outcomes and outputs—for instance, Indiana's political orientation and competition. According to Holbrook and VanDunk (1993), the Ranney Index presents Indiana as a state with relatively high political competition between 1981 and 1988 (0.86 out of 1). At the district level, these authors found that Indiana was among the states with high political competition between 1982 and 1986 (Indiana received a score of 44.59, while the highest score was 56.58 in North Dakota). In the gubernatorial election of 2000 the percentage of votes for Republicans was 42 and 57% for Democrats, a 15% difference. The governor in 2000 was from the Democratic Party, but the Republican candidate won the 2004 gubernatorial election.

Political competition has an influence on the attitudes of politicians toward citizens' expectations. The more political competition, the more responsive politicians are to their constituencies. Electronic government is not different in this respect. One of the respondents clearly described this influence: "The more competition there is for the office, the more those office holders are going to be responsive and try to do things that are cutting edge."

Interviewees believed citizens' expectations about electronic transactions were increasing. As citizens' experiences with private sector companies were changing, what they expected and wanted from interacting with government agencies was also changing. For some respondents, this shift was already happening and governments had to adapt to this new situation: "More and more these days you get people begging for things to be online, which is really helpful in knowing what should be the next really big application." From this view, providing online services was no longer a choice, but a requirement. Similar to any other democratically driven policy, if politicians wanted to be elected, they had to understand and meet citizens' expectations about electronic services and information availability.

In this new reality, rankings helped AccessIndiana staff obtain information about what other states were doing and how the site could be improved. The staff reviewed the Center for Digital Government's rankings when planning a redesign, among other activities. They focused on the websites that ranked highly and looked for areas for improvement based on the differences and similarities between those websites and AccessIndiana. In addition, AccessIndiana had relied on user focus groups to identify how they thought about organizing the site. They also did focus groups to understand what services people were willing to pay for and what price they thought was reasonable, among other issues related to transactional services and fees.

Based on its convenience fee business model, Indiana's population was seen as the potential market. In 2000 Indiana had a population of about 6 million people, close to the national average of 5.6 million. While much smaller than New York, Indiana was still a big potential market for e-government services. In 1999, median income per household was $41,567 and median income per family was $50,261. In this same year, 9.5% of the population and 6.7% of families were considered below the poverty line. About 82% of its highly educated population had completed high school or a higher degree and about 19% had at least a bachelor's degree. Finally, computer ownership increased from 44% in 1998 to 49% in 2000. Similarly, the percentage of people with Internet access rose from 26% in 1998 to 39% in 2000. For a convenience fee model such as AccessIndiana, the size of the population is important. Using the state population and the kinds of services they needed, Indiana Interactive could better assess the feasibility of new services and their likelihood of becoming a strong revenue base.

Similar to the state's population, the overall size of the economy had an influence on the portal's success. Many of the indicators for the State of Indiana, which is a medium-size state economy, are close to the US national average for all states. For instance, the government GSP was about $19.3 billion in 2000 and $20.9 billion in 2001 (the national average was $23 and $24 billion, respectively). The number of state government jobs grew slightly from 108,867 in 1998 to 110,610 in 2000. Similarly, the number of local government jobs increased from 248,361 in 1998 to 255,369 in 2000. Total earnings were about $3.8 billion for state government employees and about $9.6 billion for local government employees in 2000. Indiana's total revenue in 2000 was about $20.5 billion.

The number of jobs and private earnings in several important industries, such as engineering and education, is also a useful way to appreciate the size of the economy. The total number of jobs in engineering and management services was 68,143 and private earnings were about $2.3 billion in 2000. Total private earnings in education services jobs were about $1.1 billion in 2000, with about 60,000 jobs. The total number of jobs in the communications industry in 2000 was 23,751 and private earnings were about $1.2 billion. Similarly, the total number of jobs in the electronic and other electric equipment industry was 52,858 and private earnings for this industry were about $2.7 billion in 2000.

5.7 Final Comments

AccessIndiana is without a doubt a story of e-government success. Indiana Interactive and the Office of the State CIO faced multiple challenges and were able to overcome all of them. There are clearly some important lessons for other state governments, but also for governments at all levels (national, regional, and local) in developed and developing countries around the world. The first big decision for Indiana was outsourcing the government-wide website development to a private company, particularly the transactional services. When the public–private partnership started, one of the main challenges was the absence of a common look and feel. In addition, since AccessIndiana provided services to the three branches of government, it had to be cautious to give equal service quality to all; which they managed by having separate priority lists for each of the three branches and within each list they establish a first come, first served policy. Similar to any other private company, Indiana Interactive needed to attract customers to stay in business. They develop an aggressive marketing strategy that was successful. Finally, a very important challenge for Indiana's Website was communication, coordination, and building consensus about the strategic direction of the site. This was even more important given the public–private partnership model and the diversity of the stakeholders involved in the decision-making processes.

Despite the challenges mentioned in the previous paragraphs and throughout the chapter, there were also important benefits. In terms of success measures, AccessIndiana brought enhance active public participation and transparency, delivered more and more efficient services, which also translated into costs savings, and improved service quality. For example, businesses and citizens could always send e-mail messages with questions or suggestions; and this feedback was used to improve the usability and usefulness of the website. Also, one of the most important benefits of Indiana's website is convenience for citizens, who can obtain information and services through the portal 24 h a day, 7 days a week. In addition to convenience, the website offers cost-saving solutions to most users, particularly businesses. Regarding local governments, at least two benefits can be clearly identified. They can use some services in the portal, which have been design for them and their interactions with state agencies. They could also provide some services to their citizens and other constituencies through the state website, taking advantage of best practices developed at the state level.

Hence, the public–private partnership model was successful for the state of Indiana. AccessIndiana also dealt with state politics without getting too entangled with any one of the branches of government (Gil-Garcia and Hernandez-Tella 2010). A respondent stated the perceived success of the portal: "We're one of the few things that is widely recognized as a positive." One example was the management of new application development on a first come, first served basis. The governor could only change the priority of the projects within the executive branch; his office could not affect the order of projects from the judicial or legislative branches.

Similarly, there was an automated system for press releases. Executive agencies, legislative bodies, and courts could use the system to post their press releases on the website. One of the respondents mentioned that prior to 2005, one of the caucuses released multiple negative postings about some of the governor's initiatives. The Office of the Governor called and asked why that was happening. AccessIndiana's response was that the caucus was using the system very frequently and the Governor's Office could do the same and post their own press releases. By focusing attention on the automated system and providing a solution to the Governor's Office, AccessIndiana was able to avoid direct intervention of the executive branch in the website's operations. Finally, AccessIndiana could not be used for campaign material. Campaign-related sites have to be separate from the portal and cannot be linked from it. In the words of an interviewee, "Typically the portal is able to stay out of politics."

Managers and leaders of AccessIndiana widely recognized that it is relatively easy to create a good interface for a legacy system or a cumbersome back-office process. Nevertheless, future website improvements have to address bureaucratic work processes that are not always as efficient or linked together as they might be in an ideal situation (Gil-Garcia and Hernandez-Tella 2010). In order to obtain the benefits from an efficient government and have a more integrated website, this type of change is essential. Regarding future challenges, one interviewee said, "With the Web... it's never done. It's always evolving."

Chapter 6
Understanding Electronic Government Success: Discussion and Implications

As mentioned before, this study focuses on the complex relationships between information technologies and social structures in government settings. It provides a better understanding of e-government success by including multiple factors and theorizing about their interrelationships and their effects on the characteristics of the enacted technology and its organizational outputs. It also explains some of the mechanisms through which these effects take place, leading to important theoretical and practical implications. I want to clarify that the theoretical framework was developed based on a broad conceptualization of the e-government phenomenon and, therefore, could be applied to different e-government initiatives. Government-wide websites are just one instance of a much broader e-government phenomenon. The rationale for selecting government-wide websites is explained at the end of Chap. 2.

This chapter is organized in three main sections. Section 6.1 summarizes the main theoretical and methodological contributions of the study. Section 6.2 provides a detailed account of the main results from the qualitative and quantitative analyses. This section also presents some direct quotes from the interviews to give the reader a sense of the importance of the different concepts and relationships from the perspective of public managers. Finally, Section 6.3 presents some practical recommendations derived from this research.

6.1 The Enactment of Electronic Government Success: Theoretical and Methodological Contributions

This section highlights some of the theoretical contributions and methodological innovations of this research. The objective is to clearly state how this study, using a comprehensive theoretical framework and a mixed-method research strategy, can offer advantages to understanding e-government success in particular, and advance

J. R. Gil-Garcia, *Enacting Electronic Government Success*, Integrated Series in Information Systems 31, DOI: 10.1007/978-1-4614-2015-6_6,

the field of digital government in general. I argue that the contributions highlighted in this section help to better characterize and understand the phenomenon of e-government success. Theoretically, this study draws upon and extends institutional theory—specifically, the technology enactment framework—by incorporating concepts from recent studies on technology and organization, as well as theoretical elements from other integrative approaches. Methodologically, the book reports on one of the first systematic, sequential-explanatory mixed-method studies in the field of e-government success.

6.1.1 Theoretical Contributions

The book attempts to explain the effects of organizational structures and processes and institutional arrangements on the information technology used by government agencies. According to Fountain (1995, 1999, 2008), the technology enactment framework pays attention to the relationships among information technology, organizations, embeddedness, and institutions. The book proposes variables to measure each of the different constructs relevant to institutional theory and tests the relationships hypothesized by Fountain's framework. Finally, the study also proposes some adjustments and extensions to the original framework in a theory building effort.

One of the theoretical contributions of this research is testing a technology enactment model through the use of quantitative and qualitative empirical evidence. Consistent with the technology enactment framework, this study shows that organizational factors have a direct effect on the enacted technology, but institutional arrangements do not. However, government agencies are embedded in institutional arrangements and other contextual factors that shape the organizational characteristics and management strategies and practices; therefore, institutional arrangements have an important indirect influence on the enacted technology (Battilana et al. 2009; Cordella and Iannacci 2010; Fountain 2001a, 2008; Hassan and Gil-Garcia 2008; Heeks and Bailur 2007; Kraemer et al. 1989; Lu et al. 2008; Luna-Reyes and Gil-Garcia 2011; Scott 2010a; Wry et al. 2010). This indirect influence is not necessarily minor; in fact, it could be even more important than other direct effects. However, the results from this research show that a change in the institutional arrangements would have an important effect on e-government success only if some organizational structures and processes are also adjusted. Section 6.2 in this chapter describes these relationships in more detail.

The theoretical model developed in this study explains for the first time the technology enactment process at the state level and is probably the first ensemble-view theoretical model for this level of government. From the analysis, it appears that state government settings are similar to but not identical with federal agencies (Fountain 2001a, c) or local governments (Kraemer et al. 1989). Fountain's original model describes how, at the federal level, all the effects of the environment are filtered and represented in the institutional arrangements. In contrast, the process model of computing change suggests that environmental factors directly influence management actions in local governments. This study found that at the state level, some environmental influences directly affect management practices, while others have an indirect effect on both management strategies and practices and general organizational characteristics through their direct influence on institutional arrangements. This finding may be a reflection of different degrees of flexibility and responsiveness to environmental pressures in different levels of government, specifically in the way they deal with IT initiatives.

As mentioned before, the ensemble-view posits that in order to study the information technology and organization phenomenon, researchers should explore not only the technological artifacts, but also the social structures around those artifacts (Orlikowski and Iacono 2001). For digital government researchers, the object of study can be characterized as a complex socio-technical network that includes not only technological artifacts, but also people, physical spaces, social relationships, public policies, and environmental constraints, among other important elements. Taking this more comprehensive view, this study identified and analyzed the impact of three environmental conditions: political orientation, potential e-government demand and citizens' expectations, and availability of resources for the state government as a whole. This integrative approach showed the impact of these environmental conditions not only on the enacted technology and its results (outputs and outcomes), but also on some organizational factors and institutions in which the technological artifacts are embedded. This approach is an extension of the technology enactment framework and provides initial explanations of the mechanisms through which these effects take place.

The new theoretical framework proposed in this book deals with some of the limitations that have been identified in Fountain's original framework and which were mentioned in Chap. 2. For example, this new framework is much more specific at the measurement level and can be used for prediction and hypothesis testing. In fact, this book uses quantitative analysis to test some hypotheses, which could be interpreted both at the construct and at the indicator level. Second, this new framework was developed and tested using a systematic mixed-method research strategy, providing more evidence from the 50 states in the US and two in-depth case studies. In addition, the framework has been used and proofed useful to study other levels of government and a different national context (Gil-Garcia and Luna-Reyes 2009; Herrera and Gil-Garcia 2010; Luna-Reyes and Gil-Garcia 2011; Luna-Reyes et al. 2007b, 2008, 2009; Puron Cid and Gil-Garcia 2004).

Third, I agree that the framework is good at explaining organizational politics, but this study provides evidence of its usefulness for understanding IT management and institutional influences too. In fact, one of the advantages of this integrative model is that it can interpret the e-government success phenomenon in a very comprehensive way and considers multiple influences. Fourth, by incorporating socio-technical aspects, this new framework presents a better explanation of how agents overcome organizational challenges and institutional barriers, clearly moving beyond social determinism. Finally, this framework does not ignore previous integrative theories such as the socio-technical approach. In fact, as mentioned several times in the book, the proposed theoretical model enriches the technology enactment framework by incorporating important concepts and relations from the process model of computing change and environmental approaches to organizations. In this way, the new framework builds upon previous integrative models and takes advantage of their complementarities.

6.1.2 Methodological Innovations

This study uses a nested research design, which combines statistical analysis with two in-depth case studies (Cresswell 2003; Cresswell and Tashakkori 2007; Gil-Garcia and Pardo 2006; Johnson et al. 2007; Molina-Azorín 2011; Tashakkori and Teddlie 1998, 2003; Verdegem and Verleye 2009). The study begins with a statistical analysis using organizational, institutional, and contextual factors as independent variables. The result is a new way to quantitatively operationalize Fountain's enactment framework. An overall score representing e-government success in terms of the functionality of government-wide websites is the ultimate dependent variable. Based on the statistical results, two cases were selected (New York and Indiana) and case studies were developed using semi-structured interviews and document analysis. Government-wide websites are good cases to use because they include a great variety of IT tools and applications and they have been widely adopted.

In terms of the statistical analysis, the book presents one of the first applications of partial least squares (PLS) to an e-government success study. PLS is a structural equations modeling (SEM) technique that allows for estimating the measurement model and the structural model simultaneously. The use of this sophisticated statistical strategy helped to test the relationships between e-government success and different factors influencing it, as well as some of the relationships between the factors to allow for the exploration of some indirect effects. The ability to explore multiple causal relationships simultaneously helps to understand the e-government phenomenon in more detail, without isolating some relationships that are deeply intertwined in the real world (Barclay et al. 1995; Esposito et al. 2010; Gil-Garcia 2008; Henseler et al. 2009; Hulland 1999; Tenenhaus et al. 2005).

6.2 Understanding Electronic Government Success: Factors and Mechanisms

As mentioned before, the first component of this study included the development and testing of a theoretical model based on Fountain's technology enactment framework and the process model of computing change. The statistical results were enriched with information from two in-depth case studies. This section presents the main findings of the study and discusses not only the relevance or statistical significance of the variables, but also some of the mechanisms through which different

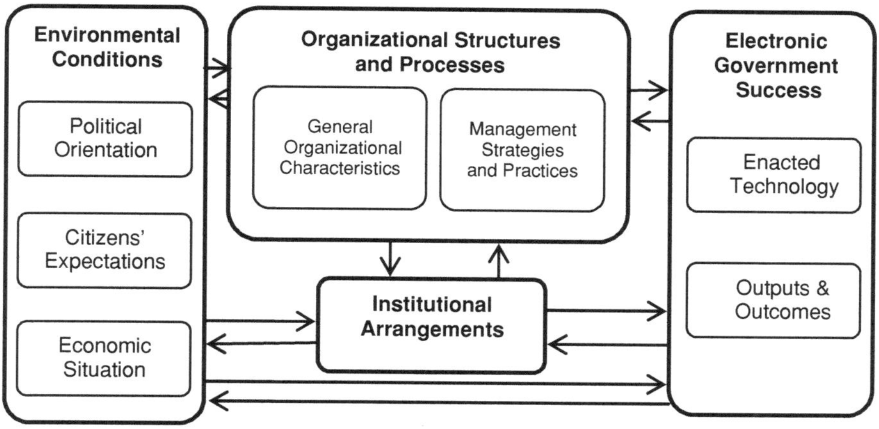

Fig. 6.1 Enacting electronic government success (proposed theoretical model)

factors have an effect on e-government success, represented by the functionality of government-wide websites. Findings are organized according to the theoretical constructs included in the proposed technology enactment model (see Fig. 6.1).

In terms of the statistical analysis, this research found three factors that directly influence the success of e-government initiatives: management strategies and practices, general organizational characteristics, and availability of financial resources. Therefore, this research provides evidence of the importance of organizational structures and processes such as size of the IT organization, budget allocation, IT training, in-house development, outsourcing, and a marketing strategy for the development of functional government-wide websites. It shows that other factors like the involvement of the legislature, state civil service, source of authority of the CIO, size of the state economy, and demographic factors representing both the potential demand and citizens' expectations for these websites are also important. Following, I describe the main results in terms of each of the different theoretical constructs and their relationships with e-government success (enacted technology and organizational outputs and outcomes).

Even though both cases are considered successful by external evaluations, their individual stories were very different. Indiana started its website development about 5 years earlier than New York and adopted a relatively centralized approach to online services. In contrast, when New York started its efforts towards integrating a government-wide website, many state agencies were already providing a great variety of online information and services. Therefore, a decentralized approach was more appropriate and feasible. The following subsections describe the quantitative results, but also the similarities and differences between the two case studies in terms of the main theoretical constructs and their observed indicators: (a) enacted technology, (b) organizational outputs and outcomes, (c) managerial strategies and practices, (d) general organizational characteristics, (e) institutional arrangements, and (f) environmental conditions. As background

Table 6.1 Mission of the government-wide websites in Indiana and New York

Mission	
Indiana	AccessIndiana should be able to produce cost-savings for government agencies, but also for users. It also has to be able to help citizens, businesses and other users to conveniently obtain the information and services they need
New York	To help citizens, businesses, local governments, state employees, and other stakeholders, to get the information and services they need in a more effective and convenient fashion

information, Table 6.1 shows the stated missions of both government-wide websites. It is clear they have important common elements.

6.2.1 Enacted Technology

As explained in Chap. 2, Fountain (2001a) contends that the enacted technology can be understood as the perception, design, implementation, and use of objective technologies, such as the Internet and different pieces of hardware and software. Therefore, two elements could represent the enacted technology: the technological features of the current system and the way in which different users take advantage of the technology's characteristics (Fountain 2001a; Hassan and Gil-Garcia 2008). These features and their potential results in terms of organizational outputs and outcomes could be seen as e-government success. In this case, enacted technology refers to certain characteristics of the e-government initiative such as hardware, software, functionality, usability, or accessibility, but also to the derived social relations and diverse uses.

For the statistical analysis, government-wide websites are used as an instance of a broader e-government phenomenon and their functionality serves as a proxy for e-government success. The case studies provide a broader characterization of e-government success, including some organizational outputs and outcomes. Electronic services (transactions) are emphasized in all four state website functionality assessments used in the statistical analysis, but they are not the only factors to consider. In fact, two of the measures in this construct, overall state ranking and e-commerce score, included other relevant elements such as types of online information, a usability assessment, e-mail responsiveness, privacy, and security, among others. The other two indicators were the number of e-commerce systems and the number of online services. Table 6.2 shows the scores of the four measures for the states of New York and Indiana.

The fact that all four indicators clearly loaded in the same factor and presented a good composite reliability score (see the statistical analysis in Chap. 3) shows that elements other than the number of online transactions are less heavily weighted in the more complex measures or that they are highly correlated with the rest of the elements included in the composite measures. Therefore, either electronic services are very good representations of government-wide website

Table 6.2 Indiana and New York government-wide website functionality

Measures	Indiana		New York	
	Score	Rank	Score	Rank
Overall state electronic government ranking	52.30	1	45.80	7
Electronic commerce score	75.00	8	66.67	15
All score	29.00	16	27.10	25
Number of e-commerce systems	7	19	8	10
Number of online services	7	10	9	1

functionality as a whole or in these rankings they have been considered the most important measures in comparison with other elements also included in the scores.

While the State of New York is one of the largest and most populous in the US, it was the last major state to create a centralized IT agency (around 1997), following decades of almost complete decentralization of IT functions and services. The NYS website demonstrates how a large and diverse state government with a long history of decentralized IT management goes about creating a high quality statewide website (Gil-Garcia and Dawes 2007). Part of the NYS website was hosted by private vendors, while the rest was hosted by the Office for Technology. Most agency websites were hosted internally and the majority of the content was updated by the respective agencies. Even though the Assembly and the Senate have their own pages, they are linked to the state website.

New York's strategy aimed to get the information or service a person is interested in available using the least possible number of "clicks." The portal was organized in categories to provide initial guidance to visitors. The design of the portal was easy to use; people did not necessarily need to know which agency provided the information or service they wanted in order to find it on the website. At the same time, the website was seen as an opportunity for NYS to save resources and improve citizen satisfaction with state government services and information. The website services were available 24 h a day, 7 days a week. As of 2005, many services could be paid for using a credit card or other electronic payment method. Many government forms were available as PDF files, but due to accessibility issues they were also usually available in other formats (e.g., HTML).

In contrast, Indiana was one of the first states in the US to build a government-wide state website. As of 2005, Indiana's website was the product of a long-term public–private partnership. Its IT functions have strong legislative underpinnings and its central IT agency exercises a relatively high degree of authority over agency-based IT functions. Through feedback and watching the competition, Indiana aimed to keep fresh and updated services for all the different stakeholders. AccessIndiana brought enhanced public participation and transparency and delivered more efficient services, which translated to cost reductions and significantly improved service quality. Another prominent characteristic was that all three branches of government were represented on the same government-wide state website. Hence, Indiana had to be cautious about giving equal service quality to all, which they managed by having separate priority lists for each of the three branches and establishing a first come, first served policy within each list.

Although it was hard in the beginning, AccessIndiana achieved a common look and feel with time. A singular crucial feature of AccessIndiana was its function driven approach, with the menus organized by audiences or events instead of government units. The users do not require knowledge about which agency they need to interact with. One of the most important benefits of Indiana's website is convenience for citizens, who can obtain information and services through the portal 24 h a day, 7 days a week. In addition, around 2002, Indiana partnered with Google to offer a search engine, which also helps users find what they need.

6.2.2 Organizational Outputs and Outcomes

Future research should develop more comprehensive measures of government-wide website functionality, which should include online services, but also information quality, responsiveness, consistency, applications, and other equally important elements. In addition, e-government success should be measured using not only characteristics of the enacted technology, but also organizational outputs and outcomes. Examples of these potential results have been mentioned in previous studies and are cost reductions, improved decision making processes, better coordination, higher customer satisfaction, and broadened professional networks (Andersen and Dawes 1991; Bandyopadhyay and Sattarzadeh 2010; Gil-Garcia et al. 2009; Gorla et al. 2010; Kuan and Chau 2001; Petter et al. 2008; Roldán and Leal 2003; Walton 1989). The results of the statistical analysis and the cases clearly identified some outputs and outcomes: (1) user convenience, (2) cost-savings, (3) enhanced communication, (4) feedback as a way to improve the website, (5) benefits for local governments, (6) productivity and improved internal operations, and (7) virtual integration. Figure 6.2 summarizes the organizational benefits identified in this study and the recipients of those benefits.

User Convenience. According to the evolutionary perspective, in the transactional stage the portal allows users to personalize it and access is organized according to people's needs instead of government functions or structures. The portal allows users to make electronic payments via secure sites, which facilitates transactions like payment of taxes, fines, and fees (Economides and Terzis 2008; Fedorowicz et al. 2009; Sancak and Güleç 2010; Tan and Benbasat 2009), which is very convenient for citizens and other users. Convenience could be understood in at least two different ways: (1) access to information and services 24 h a day, 7 days a week and (2) access to information and services without having to visit a government office.

One of the primary focuses of the NYS website was convenience for its users. People could get information more easily and they could find very diverse information and services in one place at anytime, from any location. As of 2005, people did not necessarily need to know which agency provided the information or service they wanted in order to find it on the website. Information was organized according to categories and these categories were designed to help citizens,

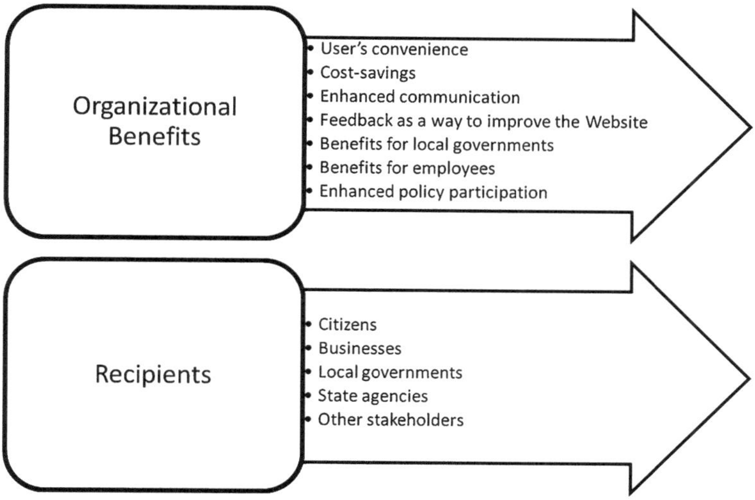

Fig. 6.2 Main government-wide website benefits and recipients

businesses, and other potential audiences navigate through NYS government. A large amount of information and services were available through the website 24/7. People could get information more easily and they could find very diverse information and services in one place, thereby increasing the convenience for businesses, citizens, and other stakeholders.

AccessIndiana also offered information and services 24 h a day, 7 days a week. Users did not have to stand in line in order to pay for government services or to obtain government forms. The portal aimed to offer easier and more integrated solutions to specific audiences every day. The staff's rationale was that citizens do not know and do not have to know what part of government is responsible for certain information and services. Citizens and businesses requiring services do not necessarily differentiate between the judicial, executive, and legislative branches or between services provided by their state, their county, or their city. They should be able to easily find the information and services they need from any computer with Internet access.

Cost-savings. Besides convenience, the government-wide websites offered cost-saving solutions to most users. As mentioned earlier, the implementation and use of information and communication technologies in government has mostly been driven by the persistent need to reduce costs (Bandyopadhyay and Sattarzadeh 2010; Baqir and Iyer 2010; Chwelos et al. 2010; Markaki et al. 2010; OECD 2003; Rahman 2010). Many of the e-government initiatives related to efficiency fall in the e-management component, such as payment processes, procurement, payroll, and human resources management (Fedorowicz et al. 2009; Fleming et al. 2010; Joseph and Ezzedeen 2009; Langford 2010; Seifert and Chung 2009). Although it was not the only factor identified, nor necessarily the most important, cost reductions and savings were important results.

In general, NYS government agencies were looking for online alternatives that could help them to save money and provide better services. A cost-savings justification was important because e-government initiatives were competing for resources with other priorities such as education, health, and public safety, among others. However, there was a perception that cost-savings were not comparable to the private sector. This disparity was associated with government's restrictions on going totally online because of inequality concerns, among other reasons.

Indiana's website attempted to be not only convenient and easy to use, but also to offer cost-saving solutions to most users. Using the website helps both citizens and state agencies to save money. The services and fees are designed to meet users' needs and to help them to save money on costs like parking, gasoline, and traveling. In terms of benefits for businesses, Indiana's website is clearly a cost-savings alternative. Businesses rely on the website because they save money and they can get the information and services they need faster. Additionally, many businesses used to spend a great deal of money and time on messenger services or dedicating staff resources to delivering and retrieving government documents. Indiana's website has helped businesses to reduce the time and cost to obtain specific services and information.

Enhanced Communication. Communication is a very important benefit from the use of information technologies in government settings (Gil-Garcia et al. 2006). The promise of greater public participation cannot be achieved without the development of efficient communication channels between citizens and public officials (Yao et al. 2010; Zissis et al. 2009). Creating new communication channels is a critical component of participation: "An essential function of e-government is the access and exchange of information. E-Government sites allow governments to offer new ways to interact with the government, such as email, online meetings and forums for voicing opinion, online transactions, and online voting" (Jaeger 2005, p. 703).

An essential outcome for state agencies in New York was their ability to communicate with their constituencies in a more effective way. As one respondent noted, "I think all agencies realize that the use of their websites is a very significant communications media for them." More importantly, state portals not only provide electronic services and communicate administrative information; they also have the potential to help government show a more integrated and consistent image to citizens, businesses, and other stakeholders, strengthening democratic values and mechanisms. Enhanced communication is definitely an important outcome of e-government initiatives.

In Indiana, citizens and businesses could send e-mail messages or access a live chat to interact with a member of AccessIndiana's staff. Since the website included work, services and information from the legislature, the judiciary, and local governments, citizens were more informed and involved in state government actions, which also enabled greater participation in the democratic process. The availability of online communication improves the perceived accessibility to representatives and government officials. Therefore, to a certain extent, it also helps to increase the perceived transparency and openness of state government, which is of increasing importance in today's political environment.

Feedback as a way to improve the website. Public participation, transparency, openness, and accountability should be seen as important ways to measure the success of e-government initiatives (Bertot et al. 2008; Chircu 2008; Pina et al. 2009, 2010). Participation is important only if government is really paying attention to what citizens, businesses, and other stakeholders are saying. There are many ways to use feedback from public participation. At the higher end, governments could use feedback to develop more effective public policies and make joint decisions with the public. To trigger these efforts and convince citizens to participate, government can start with small and easy steps like improving their websites based on the comments and suggestions they receive.

Both states relied on user feedback to improve the characteristics of the technology, as well as the outputs and outcomes of their government-wide websites. In New York, most pages within the portal had an option for citizens to provide feedback using an online form. Through this option, citizens could ask questions about where to find specific information on the website. However, they could also offer their opinions about how to improve the functionality of the website. These opinions were taken into consideration as the website evolved. For example, if there were many questions about a particular topic, OFT tried to make that section of the portal clearer or to add more information.

For every decision about the structure and content of Indiana's website, feedback from users was very important. For instance, Indiana Interactive organized focus groups to get feedback before launching new services online. They also organized training sessions with law firms, banks, and other potential users to explain how the services work and get comments from them. There was also an opportunity to share positive experiences through a service called FanMail. Finally, Indiana Interactive staff attended trade shows and demoed several of their services to different audiences, including health professionals and human resource managers. Clearly AccessIndiana staff members listen to their users and were always willing to act upon their requests, comments, and suggestions.

Benefits for Local Governments. Information technologies in government have the potential to facilitate relationships between government agencies, different levels of government, and even among the executive, legislative, and judicial branches (Bandyopadhyay and Sattarzadeh 2010; Joia 2008; Lux Wigand 2010; Makedon et al. 2010; Moflesh et al. 2009; Zarei and Ghapanchi 2008). This study identifies some particular benefits for local governments in their relationships with state agencies and their own constituencies.

Local governments in New York could get benefits that were qualitatively different, since they usually do not perform one-time transactions like citizens (e.g., renewing a driver's license or filing taxes). They needed to perform frequent transactions with the state and to report information to multiple state agencies on a regular basis. Thus, in New York the benefits for local government were related to having online applications that help them with their daily relationships with the state and their respective processes or work flows.

In contrast, in Indiana local governments could take advantage of the portal as a user with all the same outcomes, as well as for launching their own services for their constituencies. First, similar to citizens and businesses, local governments are users of the information and services available on the state website and obtain similar benefits, such as convenience and cost-savings. In Indiana, they can also obtain some services, such as driving records or limited criminal histories, at either no cost or for a reduced fee. Second, like state agencies, local governments can provide information and services through AccessIndiana. Therefore, local governments can take advantage of the developments at the state level, improving the provision of transactional services and overall efficiency at the local level.

Productivity and Improved Internal Operations. A government can improve its internal management through better use of information technologies in the workplace (Christensen and Laeliggreid 2010; Gascó 2007; Jun and Weare forthcoming; Kim et al. 2009; Lux Wigand 2010; Olbrich 2010). This situation was identified in New York State. In fact, from the perspective of the interviewees, NYS government achieved important benefits from the website and related Internet technologies, such as efficiency, effectiveness, and citizen satisfaction. A respondent mentioned "It would definitely make the state workforce more productive, because the state employees could customize their desktop to use the applications that they truly need on a daily basis."

Virtual Integration of the All Branches of Government. E-democracy initiatives involve much more than online voting, referring also to communication exchange between citizens and elected officials (Davis et al. 2002). In addition, Dawes (1996) identified more comprehensive public information and an integrated government image as political benefits from government IT initiatives. Indiana's government-wide website allowed for a more integrated political interaction since it entails all branches of government. Greater participation in the democratic process was a potential result partly due to the convenience of having legislators' contact information, political appointees' e-mail addresses, legislative bills, and other information available online. One respondent declared that "the General Assembly has a really good website and it is used more every single year to search for legislation and so that people can participate in their government." Virtual integration of the different branches of government should be seen as a success measure, when applicable, since it constitutes an important initial step towards a real virtual state (Gil-Garcia and Martinez-Moyano 2007; Gottschalk 2009; Klievink and Janssen 2009b; Moflesh et al. 2009; Ojha et al. 2011; Sancak and Güleç 2010; Ubaldi and Roy 2010).

6.2.3 Management Strategies and Practices

Organizational factors consist of characteristics, processes, structures, and relationships that take place within an organizational setting, including the project, organizational, and individual levels (Angelopoulos et al. 2010; Baqir and Iyer 2010; Chang et al. 2001; Davenport 1993; Gil-Garcia and Helbig 2006; Hossain et al. forthcoming; Joseph 2010; Rorissa et al. 2010; Seneviratne 1999; Umble et al. 2003; Yang and Maxwell 2011). Following the theoretical model presented in previous chapters, this study includes two organizational-level influences (or categories of success factors): (1) management strategies and practices and (2) general organizational characteristics. Management strategies and practices are clearly important factors of e-government success. Strategies such as outsourcing, marketing, or centralized website services have a direct influence on the success of e-government initiatives.

As mentioned in Chap. 2, the process model of computing change is based on socio-technical systems theory (Bostrom and Heinen 1977; Dawes 2009; Esteves and Joseph 2008; Kraemer et al. 1989; Lyytinen and Newman 2008; Maxwell and Dawes 2009; Pasmore 1988; Sittig and Singh 2010). It distinguishes between the environment, management actions, and computing conditions (Kraemer et al. 1989). External and internal components are hypothesized to have a direct impact on management action and indirect influence on the computing package. The main role of managers in this model is to transform environmental opportunities and constraints into computing policies. Therefore, the model acknowledges the important role of management strategies and practices. Following, several strategies are briefly discussed in terms of the statistical analysis and the two cases.

In-house and Outsourced Responsibilities. Previous studies have identified at least two main problems related to an IT project's goals and objectives. One is found in the lack of alignment between the IT project and organizational goals (Dawes and Nelson 1995; Janssen forthcoming; Meijer and Thaens 2010; Ubaldi and Roy 2010; Valdés et al. 2011). IT initiatives should be consistent with overall mission and goals of the organization. A second problem refers to the existence of multiple, and sometimes conflicting, goals in the public sector as an additional inter-organizational factor (Dawes and Pardo 2002). These two situations are many times reflected in the strategies used by the IT organization. For instance, development strategies (e.g. outsourced or not) should be aligned to the organizational goals and they require high coordination and commitment among participants.

In the quantitative analysis, the "website services are outsourced only" and the "only the IT organization directly provides website services" indicators were both statistically significant with a negative direct effect on government-wide website functionality. Hence, in-house and outsourced responsibilities are important, but depending on organizational needs and goals, it is necessary to develop an appropriate combination of these two strategies. First, agencies are clearly able to shape the characteristics of their own websites. Their commitment to the website is reflected in the quality and currency of the information and services provided. For government-wide websites, coordination is a key issue and clear definition of responsibility is essential for this coordination to be successful. Second, IT initiatives often involve outsourcing. In these situations, the contractual requirements and the technical and organizational capabilities of vendors will have an impact on the success of the initiative. Establishing standards and detailed guidelines could be an important component for dealing with these potential differences. Good coordination through regular meetings is another important element to take into consideration.

In New York, outsourcing was mainly used in some individual agency websites, including the Governor's Office. The management of the portal was an in-house responsibility at OFT and coordination among state agencies and vendors was very important. In Indiana, Indiana Interactive managed the portal and most transactional services. Even in this primarily outsourced environment, however, respondents said that in-house responsibilities were extremely important. The role of the Office of the CIO and other governance structures within the state had helped Indiana Interactive to do its part of the job.[1] Support and commitment from state partners were two important elements for a public–private partnership model to work well. For instance, strategic and operational staff from the Office of the CIO and Indiana Interactive had regular meetings to discuss progress and future directions.

Finally, some respondents said that these two responsibilities were individually important, but their interrelationships were more important. If both in-house and outsourced staff were responsible for the website, these two groups must be committed and work together in order to have a successful government-wide website. They also need solid management strategies and a supportive legal framework. Some interviewees from Indiana commented that these two types of responsibilities are significant because they are mutually supporting. While the website was outsourced, the model worked well because of the adequate support the state provided for the outsourcing company. On the same matter, respondents from New York agreed that it was crucial that these responsibilities were clearly defined in order to ensure better coordination.

Marketing Strategy. Marketing efforts help to identify information and services that users want, as well as some of the characteristics that they would like the applications to have. More generally, end-user involvement is considered a key success factor for government IT initiatives (Baqir and Iyer 2010; Chen 2010; Garson 2003a; Gil-Garcia and Pardo 2005; Klievink and Janssen 2009b; Mahler and Regan 2003; Markaki et al. 2010; Mills et al. 2010; Morgeson III and Mithas 2009; Rorissa et al. 2010; Tan and Benbasat 2009; West and Berman 2001). Surveys, focus groups, and other market identification strategies can greatly shape the characteristics of a government-wide website (e.g., services, content, design, etc.). In the statistical analysis, the "number of marketing media and intensity of marketing" indicator was statistically significant with a direct positive effect on the success of e-government. In addition, the marketing of the website was one of the most frequently mentioned factors associated with its success.

Both cases identified marketing as an important factor but for different reasons. New York State did not market its website very much, which some respondents attributed to the fact that there was not much to market. In addition, since OFT did not have the necessary resources to promote the site by itself, some respondents mentioned that all agencies should be part of the marketing effort. However, for

[1] The role of these organizations and governance structures could be thought of as related to the recently proposed concept of "infocracy" (Criado 2010).

the NYS respondents, marketing was much more about communicating to the public the information and services they already have, instead of using it as a way to better understand citizens' interests and needs. They believed New York should market much more aggressively so that people knew about the website and the information and services they could obtain from it.

For AccessIndiana, due to the convenience-fee approach, aggressive marketing was extremely important. Marketing efforts lead to more usage of the website, and more usage leads to more resources to continue developing AccessIndiana. As any other private company, Indiana Interactive needs to attract customers in order to continue in business. Consistent with this, from the time it was created, AccessIndiana searched for users' feedback through diverse lines of communication, including focus groups and training sessions. Marketing was therefore a key element of AccessIndiana's overall strategy. In fact, one of the four main areas in the organizational structure of Indiana Interactive was marketing.

Role of the IT organization in providing portal development for agencies . The complexity and newness of technology can greatly affect the results of government information technology initiatives (Barki et al. 1993; Carroll et al. 2006; Choudhari et al. 2011; Garson 2003a; Ghapanchi et al. 2008; Gil-Garcia and Helbig 2006; Joseph 2010; Rahman 2010; Sancak and Güleç 2010; Weerakkody et al. 2009). A certain degree of centralization of systems development and guidance from the central IT organization can help to mitigate some of the problems related to complexity and newness of the technology. Many times, particularly small agencies do not have the technical expertise to develop e-government applications and they need help and support from the IT organization. In the statistical analysis, the "IT organization directly manages portal development for agencies" indicator was not statistically significant. However, given that this analysis uses the complete population of states, the results can still be interpreted, but they apply only to our population of US states. "IT organization directly manages portal development for agencies" has a positive effect on government-wide website functionality.

The New York State website was managed through a combination of outsourcing and in-house development. Most of the web pages, including online transactions, were developed and managed directly by state agencies. Website hosting and content management were not centralized, so each agency decided which strategy to follow (in-house, outsourcing, or a combination of both) (Gil-Garcia and Dawes 2007). As a result, it was very important to attain a clear definition of roles and a common understanding of goals in order to ensure better coordination and, as a result, a more effective and consistent government-wide website. OFT played a small, but very important role in guiding small agencies in their development efforts.

In contrast, in Indiana, the few initial pages were developed and managed by Indiana Interactive and most state agencies relied on AccessIndiana for web applications development. Hence, in order to keep the same look and feel and a more integrated website, coordination was crucial for Indiana's state website. Despite a more centralized approach, building consensus about the overall strategy was a challenge for Indiana. The public–private partnership had to be able to listen and lead at the same time. Also, when state agencies in Indiana needed an application faster than AccessIndiana can deliver, they outsourced the development to another private company. But as a policy, the private vendor had to follow statewide standards and detailed guidelines.

Increasing the offer of services. Improving service quality has been widely recognized as a potential result of e-government initiatives (Baqir and Iyer 2010; Gil-Garcia and Helbig 2006; Luna-Reyes et al. 2010; Lux Wigand 2010; Markaki et al. 2010; Rorissa et al. 2010; Sancak and Güleç 2010). Governments can explicitly look for increasing the number of services or improving their quality. One of the first statewide goals for the New York State website was to create more services. The Office for Technology (OFT) began with a review of all the services that the individual state agencies offered and the development of a strategy to move them online. The main objective was to have a main page or state portal from which people could have access to information and services NYS agencies provide. Working with many other agencies, OFT identified services that were not online, but that agencies planned or wanted to make available via the portal. OFT prioritized these applications and created a "top 75" list. These 75 applications were tracked over time to evaluate their progress in being offered online. This list was reviewed and modified during quarterly meetings between OFT and state agency representatives for several years. These meetings continue, but after 2005 they are now held annually.

Identifying several commercially viable transactions was very important for the public–private partnership model in Indiana, since it is funded through convenience fees that are applied to certain transactional services. Therefore, the portal started with driving records, but it was very risky to have a single source of revenue. With help from the Governor's Technology Taskforce, AccessIndiana staff identified information and services that people were looking for on the website, but that Indiana was not providing. In order to gather this information, the taskforce reviewed other states' websites, discussed personal experiences among its members, and obtained information about the popularity of certain online services in other states, among other strategies. Through this process, the members of the taskforce identified a variety of potential services to offer.

6.2.4 General Organizational Characteristics

Organizational factors can promote or hinder the results of government IT initiatives (Dawes and Pardo 2002; Gil-Garcia and Pardo 2005; Luna-Reyes et al. 2007b). More specifically, the characteristics of IT organizations in government have an effect on e-government success. The number of people working for the IT organization, the budget revenue sources from federal funds, and training in certain areas such as accessibility and usability were identified as important in the statistical analysis. In addition, although not statistically significant in this study, there appears to be a relationship between management strategies and practices and general organizational characteristics. Future studies should focus on the nature (recursive or non-recursive) and strength of this relationship, as well as its overall impact on e-government success.

Some examples of organizational factors are understanding strategic goals, the project management approach, the length of the project, the extent of change in business processes, and the lack of implementation guidelines (Angelopoulos et al. 2010; Baqir and Iyer 2010; Chang et al. 2001; Davenport 1993; Gil-Garcia and Helbig 2006; Hossain et al. forthcoming; Joseph 2010; Rorissa et al. 2010; Seneviratne 1999; Umble et al. 2003; Yang and Maxwell 2011). The size of the project and the diversity of the users or organizations involved are also important success factors in government IT initiatives (Barki et al. 1993; Davis 1982; Dawes and Pardo 2002; Gil-Garcia and Helbig 2006; McFarlan 1981).

Size of the Centralized IT Organization. Size can be a challenge when it refers to the diversity of users and organizations involved. In addition, organizational politics can be more difficult to overcome in large projects if the diversity of personal interests leads to resistance and conflict (Barrett and Greene 2000; Dawes and Pardo 2002; Gil-Garcia and Helbig 2006; McFarlan 1981; Rocheleau 2003). In contrast, size can also be understood as an organizational capability, because human resources help the organization to achieve some of its goals and objectives. In the statistical analysis, the "number of people working for the IT organization" as a measure of size was a significant indicator with a positive direct effect on government-wide website functionality. It also has an indirect impact through its direct impact on the management strategies and practices.

The case of New York illustrated that a decentralized approach needs less centralized management, but the same or more coordination between the centralized IT office and other agencies. Each state agency had a "publisher" to introduce content to their own sites for its development. OFT worked as an administrator and allocated some time to focus on website development and maintenance. The number of OFT employees was important for small agencies that depended on them for their applications development. However, respondents agreed that the absolute number of employees in the IT organization is not as important as having human resources specifically dedicated to the website and adequate to the demands of the overall strategy. These human resources can be available at the central IT organization, at other state agencies, at private companies that manage outsourced services, or through a combination across these different organizations.

The case of Indiana showed that the size of the IT organization is less important than the overall strategy and good communication channels with the other state agencies. It also demonstrated that having a few people fully dedicated to the website is highly effective. The public–private partnership model allowed AccessIndiana's staff to be specialized and concentrated on the development of the government-wide website, while the agency's personnel could work with them towards a specific idea or initiative. Indiana Interactive and the Office of the CIO were responsible for the overall strategy and each individual agency could decide how much time to dedicate to their information and services.

Financial Resources . Previous studies argue that financial resources are not always a highly influential factor, but they are a necessary one. Due to budget limitations, sometimes managers are bound to develop innovative financial schemes and partnerships to implement e-government initiatives (Ahn 2011; Bandyopadhyay and Sattarzadeh 2010; Chen and Thurmaier 2008; Dawes and Nelson 1995; Dawes and Pardo 2002; Fountain 2001c; Gil-Garcia and Pardo 2005; Luna-Reyes et al. 2010; Rorissa et al. 2010; Wyld 2009). Budget allocation in terms of the "percentage of the IT budget revenue sources from federal funds" was statistically significant with a direct positive effect on government-wide website functionality. It has also an indirect positive effect through its direct effect on management strategies and practices. State website financial arrangements and their importance vary according to different business models and management approaches. Although relevant in the statistical analysis, the percentage of federal resources was not clearly important in the cases. This could be because most federal resources are used for specific IT projects and initiatives and they are rarely applied to the government-wide website.

Therefore, in general terms, the availability of federal resources may be more important for agencies other than the centralized IT organization. As mentioned before, federal resources are normally linked to specific programs and sometimes these programs include the development of a new system or application or the acquisition of information technologies. Although the State of New York had no federal resources for the centralized IT office, they mentioned that would be desirable and useful for their website. In fact, some individual state agencies had developed systems or services using federal grants. The percentage of federal resources in Indiana's IT budget was below the national average. However, due to its public–private partnership model, resources could come from other state agencies, but also from AccessIndiana's convenience fees. In fact, respondents in Indiana mentioned that in some cases federal resources and their respective requirements could delay the development of certain web applications.

Budget for Website Maintenance. Previous studies show that budget allocation has an impact on IT initiatives (Ashurst et al. 2008; Berlin et al. 2009; Gulati et al. 2010; Keil et al. 1998; Norris 1999; Rahman 2010; Rosacker and Olson 2008b; Weinstein and Jaques 2010). For instance, the budget for website maintenance is directly related to the ability to keep the content up-to-date. However, in the statistical analysis, "percentage of the IT office budget devoted to maintenance" was not statistically significant and the sign for this indicator was negative. For the specific population of the states in the US, this outcome could mean that states that are using more resources for maintenance are states with old and deteriorated infrastructures. Therefore, their capacity to develop and manage the government-wide website is diminished. In contrast, resources for the portal's maintenance were recurrently mentioned in both cases. Respondents emphasized that the way in which financial resources are managed is more important than how much money is available. However, they also recognized that there is a clear relationship between the size of the budget and how many things an agency can do with its website. In both cases, some maintenance was done by each state agency, and therefore all agencies also needed some resources to keep their information and applications up-to-date.

New York's OFT had resources above the national average. But, only 6% of its budget was used for maintenance. The budget for maintenance was important in both case studies. For New York, part of this budget was necessary at the Office for Technology, because it manages the portal and some of the initial pages. However, due to the decentralized approach, website maintenance was important not only for OFT, but also for every state agency. Regarding budget issues, one interviewee asserted, "Government is always so behind. And I know why it is—funds. If you don't have the money to keep up with the technology, you've got to work with the technology you've got." In contrast, the percentage of the Office of the CIO's budget devoted to maintenance was 2% in Indiana, while the national average was about 8%. For Indiana, the maintenance of the portal and most of the maintenance of online services were the responsibility of Indiana Interactive; therefore, in Indiana, the budget for maintenance did not necessarily have to be at the Office of the CIO. It could also be part of state agencies' budgets or AccessIndiana's budget.

Specialized Training. Previous studies have demonstrated that, similar to projects in non-technology areas, staff skills are a very important success factor in IT initiatives (Bandyopadhyay and Sattarzadeh 2010; Caffrey 1998; Dawes and Pardo, 2002; Ferro and Sorrentino 2010; Ghapanchi et al. 2008; Jain and Kesar 2011; Joseph 2010; Pavlichev 2004; Schelin 2004). Website design and development require certain skills that are not always readily available in a state's IT workforce. Training could help to acquire the necessary technical skills. In addition, training can also help to communicate other organizational messages regarding the business model in place, overall strategies, accessibility, security, usability, and other standards. Specialized IT training is important not only for the centralized IT organization, but for all state agencies, because they often create, manage, and update their own information and services. In the statistical analysis, the indicator "state provides accessibility training for IT professionals," which was used as a proxy of more general training opportunities and programs, was significant and had a direct positive effect on government-wide website functionality. It also had an indirect positive effect through its direct influence on management strategies and practices.

New York and Indiana provided specialized training for IT employees. For Indiana the training was particularly important, because in addition to the technical, it also included the acquisition of knowledge about architectural standards, their business model, overall strategy, and branding. In contrast, the New York State website had become a training challenge. Due to the independent development of agency websites during the initial years, the IT organization had no standard skills in the workforce, causing important limitations to the state website as a whole (Gil-Garcia and Dawes 2007).

Despite these differences, specialized training for state IT employees was recognized as a success factor in both cases. The specific skills deemed important varied in different contexts. For example, in Indiana, in order to meet specific deadlines, some agencies decided to outsource the development to other private companies. For these agencies, contracting and negotiating skills were important. Others may develop the application themselves. For these other agencies, certain technical skills were needed. In addition, specialized training in old technologies was sometimes necessary to support legacy systems, but was not as useful as training in new technologies, especially if the state wanted to migrate from those old technologies to greater use of the web.

Stability of Leadership. Respondents in Indiana identified an additional success factor, which was the stability of leadership. According to the National Association of State Chief Information Officers (NASCIO), the average tenure of state CIOs was about 2 years. The former CIO of the State of Indiana was in her position for 7 years and the general manager of Indiana Interactive had been working for that company for 6 years. In addition to the leaders, several staff members also had a long tenure. Respondents in Indiana considered that stability of the people responsible for the website as an important factor for the success of AccessIndiana. A respondent mention how after 10 years, the staff "evolved into a much more specialized group of professionals who each play a [specific] role."

Stakeholders Involvement. An additional success factor identified by respondents in Indiana was the involvement of agency stakeholders in direction setting. Involvement with and feedback from agency customers had been important factors. Formal and informal committees have been key to the success of the portal, because involved agencies become active designers and promoters of Indiana's website and its overall strategies. In addition, for the convenience-fee funding model, having partners in state government who were committed to the success of the website was very important. They not only help to understand their needs and develop new services, but they also influence the direction and overall mission of the government-wide website. Collaboration and trust within government IT projects have been identified as positive and related to advanced stages of e-government (Chen 2010; Gottschalk 2009; Pardo et al. 2006; Ubaldi and Roy 2010; Williams et al. 2010; Zheng et al. 2009).

6.2.5 Institutional Arrangements

Institutional arrangements can be conceived of as laws, norms, and meaning systems that constrain the way people act in organizational settings (Scott 2001). The current literature recognizes the importance of understanding and, in some cases, changing the institutional framework as a way to improve the conditions for e-government initiatives (Bandyopadhyay and Sattarzadeh 2010; Dawes and Nelson 1995; Fletcher 2004; Gil-Garcia and Helbig 2006; Gulati et al. 2010; Harris 2000; Landsbergen and Wolken 2001; NGA 1997; Rosacker and Rosacker 2010; Rose and Grant 2010; Sagheb-Tehrani 2010; Ubaldi and Roy 2010). A better understanding of government institutional arrangements could lead to more realistic expectations about government IT projects. Public managers can be more aware of the importance of institutions and develop better strategies for dealing with institutional constraints and taking advantage of institutional enablers, as well as adjusting their own and other stakeholders' expectations about the potential and limitations of electronic government.

In the statistical analysis, institutional arrangements seem to be affected by all three environmental conditions, but this construct is not as well explained as some of the other constructs (R-square = 0.22). This suggests that contextual factors, other than the ones included in the analysis, affect institutions, making institutional arrangements difficult to understand or predict. In addition, institutional arrangements are significant predictors of two very important factors associated with e-government success: (1) general organizational characteristics and (2) management strategies and practices. The statistical analysis and the case studies confirmed how civil service rules, executive orders, legislative committees, IT standards, and other state and federal regulations have an impact on government-wide website functionality.

Civil Service. The flexibility in the management of human resources greatly influences the success of e-government in terms of the characteristics of the technology and the potential organizational outputs and outcomes (Bandyopadhyay and Sattarzadeh 2010; Gil-Garcia and Helbig 2006; Gulati et al. 2010; Harris 2000; Landsbergen and Wolken 2001; Rosacker and Rosacker 2010; Rose and Grant 2010; Sagheb-Tehrani 2010; Ubaldi and Roy 2010). The civil service is a powerful institution that affects the hiring, promotion, and demotion of public servants. This is particularly important for government IT projects (Dawes 1996). In the statistical analysis, the indicator "state IT professionals are members of the civil service only" was statistically significant, but its particular effect on government-wide website functionality was negative.

Important differences exist between the cases of New York and Indiana. In states that have outsourced the management of their web portal, such as Indiana, many of the necessary staff worked for the outsourcing company, which has more flexibility in hiring, assignments, and compensation. The centralized IT organization still plays an important role, but it is less operational and more strategic in nature. Therefore, due to the public–private partnership, all employees of Indiana's website were formally working for Indiana Interactive, a private company. Therefore, for them personnel management had the flexibility, competitiveness, and other advantages of private sector organizations.

On the contrary, since some New York IT professionals were part of the Civil Service, according to its rules employees had to begin working for the state in lower levels of employment, making it difficult to hire people with certain technical skills at higher levels. It was also hard to get and keep the best staff members in order to be competitive. For instance, promotion was often based on both management skills and specific state tests; poor performance on these tests, which frequently had obsolete content, made it difficult for supervisors to promote some good technical people.

Executive Orders and the Authority of the CIO. CIOs should have enough authority to organize the government-wide IT function and to coordinate all agencies toward common overarching goals (Dawes and Nelson 1995; Dawes and

Pardo 2002; Fountain 2001c; Gil-Garcia and Pardo 2005; Marijn Janssen forthcoming; Meijer and Thaens 2010; Ubaldi and Roy 2010; Valdés et al. 2011). This authority could be given by laws, executive orders, and other mechanisms. In the case of executive orders, they can also be related to the support the CIO has from the governor, which is also a very important success factor. In the statistical analysis, the indicator "state has executive orders/directives as the only way to establish authority for CIO offices" was statistically significant, with a particular positive effect on government-wide website functionality.

Interviewees from Indiana and New York mentioned legislation, executive orders, and governor's support as relevant success factors for IT initiatives. In the case of New York, the executive orders referring to the state CIO influenced the website by allowing a more coordinated strategy. Respondents from New York agreed that support from the governor was essential. This perception of support could provide the CIO with greater authority to enforce directives and policies in relation to website development and maintenance. As noted before, the Governor's initiative "Government without Walls" had a very important influence on the initial strategy and design of New York State website. Also, the existence of a CIO in the state represented a formal attempt to develop an overarching and more coordinated IT strategy. This coordination could take place through some degree of managerial centralization and through the creation of statewide policies and standards.

In Indiana, there was legislation that supported the actions of the CIO and the partnership with Indiana Interactive. However, some respondents from Indiana said executive orders were important since they reflect support from the governor. Garnering the governor's support was critical and one important way to obtain his support was to align all activities to his government agenda. As stated by one of the interviewees, "We proactively make sure that we are in line with the governor's agenda." In addition, the CIO needed to have the formal authority and responsibility to make change happen. Formal and informal committees were a key strategy to the success of AccessIndiana, because involved agencies become active designers and promoters of AccessIndiana and its overall strategies, following the lead of the state CIO. Sometimes CIOs are good at negotiation and consensus building, but it is always more effective to have the necessary formal authority.

Legislative IT Committees. There are some potential challenges derived from intergovernmental relationships and the formal checks and balances among the different branches of government (Burbridge 2002; Cresswell et al. 2002; Criado 2009; Dawes et al. 2009; Dawes and Pardo 2002; Eynon and Margetts 2007; Fedorowicz et al. 2007; Gil-Garcia and Helbig 2006; Gil-Garcia and Pardo 2005; Jaeger 2002; Kwon et al. 2009; Pardo et al. 2008b; Rocheleau 2003). However, there are also great advantages to having the support and involvement of not only the executive branch, but also the legislature in IT initiatives. In the statistical analysis, the indicator "state has an IT specific Legislative Committee in the Senate" was statistically significant and its specific effect on government-wide website functionality was positive, confirming the relevance of legislative support.

In contrast, neither New York nor Indiana had IT committees in their House of Representatives or State Senate. However, interviewees agree that legislative participation and involvement are important success factors.

The relationship between New York State's executive and legislative branches is limited to the legislature's ability to impose statewide IT standards. Particularly, in relation to the government-wide website, the NYS legislature had the power to mandate the provision of certain information or services online and to impose standards about privacy, security, accessibility, usability, etc. While some specific legislation was passed, there were no specific committees for IT in either house of the legislature. Even though important acts have had an impact on the success of the portal, apart from those the involvement of the legislature is very low.

In Indiana the legislature played a very important role and legislators' information was part of the government-wide state website. Since AccessIndiana includes the legislative branch, the communication and involvement between the two were constant and proximate. Also, regardless of the fact that Indiana did not have IT committees in the House or Senate, the legislature was involved with AccessIndiana through the staff at the Legislative Services Agency and worked together in keeping the legislature's portion of the website up-to-date. Indiana interviewees believe that the involvement of the state legislature was definitely necessary in certain aspects of the website. In fact, their participation had been important for the portal's progress when specific legislation was needed, as it was in the case of the use of credit cards.

Accessibility, Usability, and Other IT Standards. Theory mentions information technology policies and standards as a key success factor for e-government initiatives (Garson 2003a; Gil-Garcia 2004; Gil-Garcia and Pardo 2005; Kim and Kim 2003; Milner 2000). The development of government-wide IT policies and standards can provide an adequate framework for the initiatives to be successful (Gil-Garcia and Pardo 2005). More specifically, recent studies identify privacy and security concerns as important influences for government IT initiatives (Baqir and Iyer 2010; Carter and McBride 2010; Duncan and Roehrig 2003; Joshi et al. 2002; Luna-Reyes and Gil-Garcia 2003a; Milner 2000; Rorissa et al. 2010; Rose and Grant 2010; Sancak and Güleç 2010; Zhao et al. 2010). In the statistical analysis, the indicator related to mandatory accessibility standards was not statistically significant. However, as mentioned before, the results could be interpreted as applicable to the population of states that we are using in the analysis. Therefore, mandatory accessibility standards as a proxy of more general IT standards have a positive effect on government-wide website functionality. The cases also confirmed this positive influence.

In New York, most of the integration effort came from a Governor's initiative and few things in relation to the website are in New York State code. Most of the guidelines and standards were policies developed by executive agencies. However, in 2004, the State Legislature released a statewide policy and standards for web accessibility. These standards were applicable to information available on any public state website and any web-based application that an agency develops. The NYS accessibility standards were partially based on section 508 of the

Rehabilitation Act, which is a federal guideline on accessibility. Security was also a significant issue covered by statewide policy. The Office of Cyber Security and Critical Infrastructure Coordination developed an overarching security policy for the state. Additionally, each agency had its own security policy. Finally, the Internet Privacy Act required every state agency website to include a privacy policy, including the portal. OFT created a model policy and many agencies used that model.

AccessIndiana and its governance structure were supported by legislation. From the very beginning, the website effort had a clear but flexible legal framework. For instance, agencies were required to participate in the website and meet certain requirements. Apart from requiring that the presentation layer be hosted at AccessIndiana, if a problem occurs at the back-end, Indiana Interactive can restrict access to the presentation layer until the problem is fixed and the application is running again. With regard to security and privacy, several standards and guidelines regarding development, hosting, and other elements of the technological architecture were established to ensure security and privacy for website users.

State and Federal Regulations. The existence of a federal system, such as in the United States, presents additional challenges regarding laws and regulations (Creswell et al. 2002; Criado 2009; Dawes et al. 2009; Eynon and Margetts 2007; Fedorowicz et al. 2007; Gil-Garcia and Helbig 2006; Jaeger 2002; Kwon et al. 2009; Pardo et al. 2008b). Governments at the lower levels have to pay attention to their own laws and regulations, but also to the laws and regulations of the higher levels of government. In this case, when developing their information systems and applications, states have to consider state laws and regulations, but also the federal legal framework. This is particularly important in some policy domains such as health.

In Indiana, state and federal regulations were important. At the state level, some characteristics were shaped by Indiana code, and the electronic signature appears as an example of state law. As in any other government, many documents have to be signed and Indiana was one of the first states that adopted a law regarding digital signatures. In many cases, adding a box that citizens can click to sign documents was a good solution. For other cases, legislative changes were necessary. Regarding how state laws and regulations shaped the development of the website, one interviewee answered, "Just AccessIndiana itself was created by legislation; all is driven by Indiana code so it very much shapes how things are organized and run."

Similarly, despite limited involvement from the state legislature, state and federal regulations had a significant effect on the NYS website. At the state level, the Electronic Signatures and Records Act (ESRA) had some important implications for IT applications in general. At the federal level, the Health Information Portability and Accountability Act (HIPAA) impacted the information and services provided through the website. It includes provisions about security and privacy for health-related information. The Department of Health and other state agencies collected and maintained this type of information. OFT hosted much of this information through its data centers and therefore needed to be knowledgeable about HIPAA requirements and deadlines.

6.2.6 Environmental Conditions

As mentioned before, Kraemer et al. (1989) propose a model based on the socio-technical systems theory. They recognize that both environmental determinism and managerial voluntarism offer partial explanations of the use of IT in organizations. With respect to managerial voluntarism, they state "after extensive empirical study, we were forced to conclude that the role of managers in computing change in organizations was much less clear than expected. Something other than management policy was playing a major role" (Kraemer et al. 1989, p. 2). The study reported in this book shows that management strategies and practices are important, but they are interrelated and partially explained by other success factors. These results suggest that both environmental conditions and management strategies are important in understanding e-government success.

Numerous environmental factors constitute the context of organizations. Academics and experts in organizational theory have developed different ways to understand the impact of the environment on organizations, as well as how organizations attempt to modify their environments (Aldrich 1979; Burke 2011; Gil-Garcia and Helbig 2006; Gulati et al. 2010; Hannan and Freeman 1989; Liao et al. 2011; Pfeffer and Salancik 1978; Scott 1998). More specifically, within information systems research, the essential role of environmental variables in shaping the way information technology is designed and used in organizations is widely accepted (Kuan and Chau 2001; Laudon 1985; Menachemi et al. 2011; Rahman 2010; Robey et al. 2008; Sila 2010). The next paragraphs describe the results of the environmental conditions identified as part of this research.

Overall Size of the Economy. Availability of financial resources has been identified as an important success factor for government IT initiatives (Bandyopadhyay and Sattarzadeh 2010; Baqir and Iyer 2010; Chwelos et al. 2010; Markaki et al. 2010; OECD 2003; Rahman 2010). In this study, this availability is represented by the overall size of the state economy. The indicator was statistically significant with a positive direct effect on government-wide website functionality. One possible explanation for the direct effect is the fact that many large agencies develop their own websites from program budgets. Therefore, centralized IT organizations are important, but generating IT capabilities and specific funding for other state agencies seems to be equally essential for e-government success. State agencies need resources to develop and manage information and services included in their websites. The overall size of the economy is normally related to the state budget. For traditional bureaucratic organizations, the state budget is almost the only source of revenue and, therefore, it is closely related to their capabilities to develop programs and projects, including web applications and other government information technologies.

The relation between the overall size of the economy and the budget was clearly observed in New York. The state budget not only impacted OFT, but also all other state agencies. In a highly decentralized model like New York, resources for all state agencies (or the lack of them) can greatly affect the quality of the government-wide website. In contrast, for Indiana the overall size of the economy was relevant but in a different way. The size of the economy was identified as closely related to the size of the population and therefore the size of the potential market for e-government services. For Indiana Interactive, as for any private company, the size of the market was important to assess the feasibility of certain services. By looking at the population and the kinds of services they need, Indiana Interactive could better assess the possibility of new services and their likelihood to become a strong revenue base. One respondent mentioned that in small states it may be more difficult to find a strong revenue base to create and grow a government-wide website like AccessIndiana.

Political Factors. Previous research mentions that political factors have an impact on organizations and IT projects in particular (Ahn 2011; Alvarez and Hall 2004; Baqir and Iyer 2010; Eynon and Margetts 2007; Gil-Garcia and Helbig 2006; Lee et al. 2009; Rorissa et al. 2010; Sancak and Güleç 2010). More specifically, some authors argue that external pressures such as competition or politics may affect the results of the IT initiative (Bellamy 2000; Bozeman and Bretschneider 1986; Chengalur-Smith and Duchessi 1999; Laudon 1986; Nour et al. 2008). In the statistical analysis, the political orientation indicator was statistically significant. Political orientation did not have a direct impact on e-government success, but affected other important constructs such as "Management Strategies and Practices" and "Institutional Arrangements," resulting in an indirect effect on the functionality of government-wide websites.

In New York, following more than 20 years of Democratic governors, a Republican, George Pataki, was elected in 1998 with 52% of the votes. As mentioned earlier, the Governor's "Government Without Walls" initiative had a very important influence on the initial strategy and design of the NYS website. Some respondents mentioned that the governor's support and the creation of a statewide strategy could significantly change the current characteristics of the state website. In contrast to other states, the New York State website had been primarily conceptualized and supported by the executive branch, not by the state legislature; therefore, the governor's support is essential. In fact, a respondent explained that "having the Governor's Office involved and having a cohesive team of all of us together now, is what made the difference of the successful changes and enhancements that took place this past year." Political influences were clearly important for New York.

In 2000, the Indiana governor was from the Democratic Party, but the Republican candidate won the 2004 gubernatorial election. Political competition has an influence on the attitudes of politicians toward citizens' expectations. One of the respondents clearly described this influence: "The more competition there is for the office, the more those office holders are going to be responsive and try to do things that are cutting edge." However, in general, AccessIndiana was able to stay out of politics and the political influences were much smaller than in New York.

Demographic Factors as a Proxy of E-Government Demand and Citizen's Expectations. Similar to "Political Orientation," demographic factors as a proxy for e-government demand and citizens' expectations did not have a direct impact on e-government success. However, it is statistically significant and its indicators (income, education, computer ownerships, and internet access) were found to be indirectly associated with the functionality of government-wide websites through their direct effects on institutional arrangements and management strategies and practices. Citizens' expectations were also identified as an important factor in both cases. From a normative point of view, citizen expectations should be one of the most important factors in shaping the design and content of state websites and citizens are now expecting better services (Baqir and Iyer 2010; CEG 2001; Gil-Garcia and Helbig 2006; Gurría 2008; Luna-Reyes et al. 2010; Markaki et al. 2010; Rorissa et al. 2010; Sancak and Güleç 2010). Several respondents mentioned that the website was mainly there to provide information and services to citizens.

In Indiana, interviewees believed citizens' expectations about electronic transactions were increasing. As citizens' experiences with private sector companies were changing, what they expected and wanted from interacting with government agencies was also changing. For some respondents, this shift was already happening and governments had to adapt to this new situation. From this view, providing online services was no longer a choice, but a requirement. Similar to any other democratically driven policy, if politicians wanted to be elected, they had to understand and meet citizens' expectations about electronic services and information availability.

Similar, during the interviews in New York, citizens' expectations were identified as one of the most important influences; in the words of a respondent, "Because after all, that is why the whole website exists. And so if that does not satisfy the citizens' expectations, it makes the website unsuccessful... If we don't have a pleased customer, we haven't satisfied our mission." For some of the respondents this influence was taking place and for others it was a normative requirement; that is, some believed citizen expectations still needed to have an influence on the website. For the first group, citizens were having an influence by not making new demands for the website. However, respondents also recognized that the situation was changing rapidly and in the near future some changes to the website would be necessary.

Competition Among States. Besides citizen's expectations, competition among states also drives them to progress, because they want to be positioned among the first places on several e-government rankings. They pay attention to the winners in order to obtain new ideas for improvement. More generally, current or best practices reviews are also strategies for increasing the success of government IT initiatives (Bellamy 2000; Bozeman and Bretschneider 1986; Detlor et al. 2010; Gil-Garcia and Pardo 2005; Lee et al. 2011; Lee 2009; Nour et al. 2008; Pina et al. 2009). In Indiana, rankings were important to obtain information about what other states were doing and how AccessIndiana could be improved. The staff reviewed the Center for Digital Government's rankings when planning a redesign, among other activities. They focused on the websites that ranked highly and looked for areas for improvement based on the differences and similarities between those websites and AccessIndiana. For New York, this factor was clearly seen as an influence and served as a driver to be positioned among the top spots on e-government rankings. As mentioned earlier, several individuals and organizations were developing and reporting these rankings and state governments were well aware of them. States were becoming knowledgeable about the factors that were evaluated in the different studies and some states were attempting to make progress in those relevant aspects.

6.3 Some Practical Recommendations

This section provides some practical recommendations for government IT professionals. Most of the findings and lessons are technology-independent and, therefore, could apply to other forms of e-government. While new challenges have emerged in recent years, they are still very similar and even more relevant, since the old problems have not been solved yet. The same factors and problems that were present before are present today, with added complexity in terms of new applications, tools, goals, objectives, etc. Therefore, this book helps to deal with today's challenges and problems in terms of government-wide websites and other information technologies in government settings. Although solutions are moving slowly, the following recommendations could help in achieving higher degrees of success in government IT initiatives.

Given that the recommendations come from both the quantitative and the qualitative analyses, I wanted to have flexibility in terms of presentation. Therefore, this section is organized using a framework originally proposed by Andersen and Dawes (1991), which represents technology, management, policy, and context as the main aspects or factors to take into consideration for government IT initiatives (Fig. 6.3). These factors map very well with the theoretical constructs of the technology enactment framework proposed in this book: (1) management is clearly linked to "General Organizational Characteristics" and "Management Strategies and Practices"; (2) policy could be understood as "Institutional Arrangements"; (3) context is a more general concept, but in this case equivalent to "Environmental Conditions"; and (4) technology, which is similar to "Objective Technology" and "Enacted Technology." The elements are broad in scope and allow for a good presentation of the practical recommendations.

6.3.1 Technology

Although many of these recommendations are already suggested in many IT design guides, they are also included here because they constitute one of the relevant components in this model, but also because they are supported in the empirical data, which is not always true for some design guidelines.

Develop and Enforce a Common Look and Feel. Having a government-wide common look and feel has been recognized as very positive. This increases the level of trust of citizens, businesses, and other stakeholders. It is also good in terms of having easy to use information for government constituencies. From the decentralized approach in NYS, since over 170 services were already online, the first statewide goal was not only to create more services, but also to help citizens and businesses find

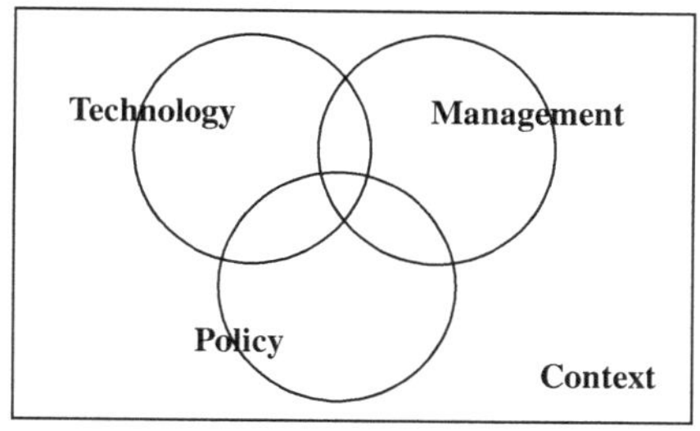

Fig. 6.3 Important success factors for government IT initiatives [Adapted from Andersen and Dawes (1991, pp. 225–353). Used by permission of M.E. Sharpe, Inc.]

the existing services and information on the web. Also, one of the first goals for Indiana was to have a common look and feel across all government agencies. Hence, all state agencies were required to use website domain names that ended with IN.gov: "one site, one website." In both cases, the common look and feel was considered a must and IT managers developing government-wide websites and other applications should seriously consider this recommendation.

Position Information and Services to be Found Using the Least Number of "Clicks". Finding the necessary information and services is very important for citizens, businesses, and other government users. To have the information organized so that it is easy to find at the least number of "clicks" could help users to have a better experience with government websites. For instance, in New York the portal had five general sections and it was then organized in categories at the left hand side of the screen, which provided initial guidance to site visitors. Under each of these categories are a number of links to specific information and services. Most of these links went directly to specific applications or forms. The design had the main objective of allowing visitors to get to the information or service they needed using the fewest possible number of "clicks." Similarly, Indiana's design was ordered in a three-column setup, featuring services and direct links to information or services that people use the most.

Provide Options to the Users to Find What They Need. These options could be presented using multiple menus, organized in different ways. The use of search engines is also a must. The NYS website had five sections plus categories which provided initial guidance to site visitors. It also had a search engine that could look for information within the portal database. The Indiana homepage was driven more by functions than organizations. The left column had new categories that attempted to capture events, functions that users wanted to perform, or information they needed to find (e.g., finding a job, traveling, paying taxes). One respondent described it as "very functionally organized so that if you arrive at the AccessIndiana home page, you ought to be able to, very quickly, find the category of information that you need." Not all users are the same, so providing multiple options to find the same information is always recommendable.

Include Links to Other Government Branches and Levels. The government-wide website could become the single window for all interactions with government in a broader sense, by providing links to other levels of government, as well as the legislative and judicial branches (depending on the actual government system). For example, the New York website also included pages that many different agencies within the executive branch had collaboratively developed. The Senate and the Assembly had their own pages, but were also linked to the state portal. In contrast, in Indiana's website all three branches of state government are represented, so citizens have access to information and services from the executive, legislative, and judicial branches through the same government-wide website. One of the respondents said, "Citizens of Indiana really do have a virtual one-stop shop. One place to go, no matter whom you need information from in state government."

Secure a Great Window of Availability for Users. For websites, this availability normally means the closest possible to 24 h a day, 7 days a week. Access is important because it generates convenience for citizens, businesses, and other stakeholders. For example, in Indiana one respondent mentioned that the goal was "citizen's service at the citizen's convenience, not at our convenience... And what that really meant was that we had to have 24 × 7 access, 365." Similarly, in New York the website offered a large amount of information and services 24 h a day, 7 days a week. People could get information more easily and they could find very diverse information and services in one place, thereby increasing the convenience of government for businesses, citizens, and other stakeholders. IT managers should secure this window of availability for users, either by concentrating on infrastructure, by creating a well-established contract (including levels of service), or using other means.

Implement a Strategy to Understand Users' Needs. It is widely recognized that having feedback from users improves systems and applications. This feedback also helps to have more people actually using the systems. Both cases collected feedback and used it to improve their information and services. For example, on most pages from the NYS website, there was an option for citizens to provide feedback using an online form. Similarly, in Indiana citizens and businesses could send e-mail messages or access a live chat to interact with a member of AccessIndiana's staff. Collecting feedback from users and having a strategy to use it are both important. Generating false expectations regarding how government would use the feedback for potential improvements could be equally negative to not listening to users at all.

Develop and Follow Privacy and Security Policies. Privacy and security concerns greatly influence government IT initiatives and must be adequately addressed. In New York, for example, every state agency website was required to display a privacy policy, including the portal. OFT created a model policy and many agencies used that model. For instance, if the personal record of an individual was disclosed, that person had to be notified. In Indiana, since it offers transactions, security and privacy were especially important for the website. Several standards and guidelines regarding development, hosting, and other elements of the technological architecture were established to ensure security and privacy for the portal's users.

Attempt to be Technology Agnostic. Similar to many other e-government initiatives, government-wide websites require the collaboration of multiple organizations. Each of these organizations could be using totally different hardware, software, and programming languages. Hence, IT staff members should be as capable and technology agnostic as possible. For instance, OFT developed the first NYS government-wide website. It was built as an index and database in Cold-Fusion, software developed by Macromedia. Part of the NYS website was hosted by private vendors, while the rest was hosted by OFT. Most agency websites were hosted internally and the majority of the content was updated by the respective agencies. Similarly, in Indiana, some agencies were already embracing specific technologies, so Indiana's website had to be ready to support these platforms and software. Hence, the staff attempted to remain open to many different technologies and programming languages. The development of IT standards can help with this situation, but there will always be a certain degree of technological diversity.

6.3.2 Management

Strategically Combine Outsourcing and In-House Development. It seems clear from the results of this study that neither in-house development nor outsourcing alone improve the success of e-government in general and the functionality of government-wide websites in particular. There are important limitations of these two strategies when they are applied to e-government initiatives embedded in highly complex environments. A thoughtful combination of in-house development and outsourcing appears to be the best strategy to follow. In both cases, in-house and outsourced staff members were responsible for the government-wide website. These two groups must be committed and work together in order to be successful. They also need solid management strategies and a supportive legal framework. Establishing standards could be an important component for dealing with these mixed situations. As interviewees from Indiana commented, these two types of responsibilities are very important because they are mutually supporting.

Foster State Government and Vendor Commitment. For a government IT initiative to be successful, both the state government and vendors have to be committed and work together in a coordinated fashion. For the case of New York, both the relationship with the vendor and the governor's support was crucial. The contractual requirements and the technical and organizational capability of the vendor had an impact on the characteristics of the government website. Commitment from the governor's office is reflected in the budget and through the creation of statewide policies and standards. The perception of support could provide the CIO with greater authority to enforce directives and policies in relation to website development and maintenance. Similarly, in a public–private partnership model like AccessIndiana, communication between the vendor and the responsible state agency is crucial. In order to maintain a more integrated website, it was also necessary for AccessIndiana staff to work together with other vendors when they were developing specific applications for some state agencies.

Clearly Define Roles , Responsibilities, and Management Mechanisms. Clear definition of responsibilities and management mechanisms are very important in complex settings in which state agencies and private companies may work together for a common goal. In NYS, due to the distributed approach, the coordination of all the different agencies was not always easy. OFT played the role of web administrator and coordination took place through the e-commerce/e-government coordinators in each state agency. It was very important that all responsibilities were clearly defined in order to ensure better coordination. People involved in website development and management should have a common understanding and goals in order to effectively work together. Having a public–private partnership model like AccessIndiana made communication also very important. It was necessary for AccessIndiana staff to work together with state agencies, vendors, business users, legislators, courts, and other important stakeholders. For this process, AccessIndiana designed different ways to work with them in a coordinated fashion.

Secure Enough Human Resources Dedicated to the IT Initiative. Having enough human resources dedicated to the initiative is essential. It is not only about the number of people working for the IT organization, but actually how many members of the staff are truly dedicated to the e-government initiative. For example, in New York, due to the decentralized approach, the number of employees at OFT was most important for some small agencies that rely on them for their website development. OFT also had many other functions and the website was a very small part of its work. Very few employees at OFT worked on website development and maintenance, but that didn't matter as long as some were dedicated to the website and that they could keep it functional. Similarly, Indiana, because of the public–private partnership, relied on a relatively small number of employees, but a few of them were directly assigned to the government-wide website.

Look for Adequate Skills or Good Training Options. Adequate skills or available training options are important factors that can help to develop functional government-wide websites that are interesting, flexible, and to certain degree unique. New York State provided accessibility and usability training for IT employees, since for them it is closely related to website design and development. IT employees learned new ways to design web pages; for example, they came to learn that accessibility did not mean that the website had to contain only text—a common misconception. Training for IT employees was also a very important factor in Indiana. This training was not necessarily technical, but also related to the acquisition of knowledge about architectural standards, the business model, strategy, and branding. In Indiana, it helped to build consensus and a common understanding among the actors involved in the website.

Develop an Appropriate Marketing Strategy. The marketing strategy seems to be positively related to the success of e-government. Marketing efforts such as surveys and focus groups can help to increase awareness and identify information and services that users really want, as well as some of the characteristics that they would like the applications to have. For example, in NYS the marketing strategy strengthened the general goal of building an online state presence. As part of this effort to create a brand for NYS and a homogenous image for the website, a uniform banner was created. The banner was functional and people could click on its picture and four buttons and go to different sections of the state portal. Indiana had a different marketing story because convenience fees were the foundation of the AccessIndiana business model. The more people who use the website, the greater the amount of resources to continue developing and improving the information and services it provides. Attracting customers included identifying information and services that users really want.

Centralize Some Aspects of Application Development. Finally, a certain degree of development centralization also seems to have a positive effect on the functionality of government-wide websites. The strategy of Indiana includes the centralization of the development and management of most online transactional services and this seems to contribute to the success of AccessIndiana. Even in NY with its decentralized approach, OFT had the responsibility of providing centralized technology services for other state agencies and to a certain extent to local government agencies, with a focus on infrastructure. It seems that a certain degree of centralization is useful.

6.3.3 Policy

Obtain Support from the Legislature. Government institutional frameworks are very important in shaping organizational characteristics and management strategies and practices. However, promoting institutional change in government settings is not a simple task. Obtaining support from the legislature and other stakeholders is always an essential strategy. Creating the conditions for legislative involvement with the IT initiative could help with this strategy. For New York, even if the website was "kind of below the radar with regard to legislation" as an interviewee commented, the NYS legislature had the power to mandate the provision of certain information and services online and to impose statewide IT standards. In addition, state and federal regulations had a significant effect on the government-wide website. Legislative involvement played an even more important role in Indiana. Formal and informal committees have been key to the success of the portal, because involved agencies become active designers and promoters of Indiana's website and its overall strategies. The legislature was involved with AccessIndiana through the staff at the Legislative Services Agency who work together in keeping the legislature's portion of the website up-to-date. New legislation has also been passed when needed.

Promote Flexibility in the Management of Human Resources. In this study, having all the IT employees as members of the state civil service seems to be negatively related to e-government success. This may be an indication of the degree of managerial flexibility and may show that more flexibility could lead to better results. Governments could try to have laws and regulations that promote more flexibility in the selection, hiring, and promotion of their IT staff. In addition, public managers should understand and strategically manage the rules of the civil service. Civil service rules clearly influence the flexibility of state agencies to hire, retain, and promote IT employees in New York. For example, promotion was often based on both management skills and specific state tests. Some good technical people are very skilled in their work, but do poorly when taking tests or managing others, making it difficult for their supervisors to promote them. In addition, the content of the tests was frequently obsolete. In contrast, in Indiana IT professionals were employees of Indiana Interactive, so staff management had the flexibility, competitiveness, and other advantages of the private sector.

Secure Support from the Governor and High Executives. Not surprisingly, having executive support appears to be positively related to e-government success. In the case of the states, the support from the governor is probably the most important one. For example, in New York the fact that the authority of the CIO came from executive orders was perceived as support from the Governor. This perception of support could provide the CIO with greater authority to enforce directives and policies in relation to website development and maintenance. Similarly, interviewees from Indiana described how executive orders creating and supporting the IT initiative were a relevant success factor, especially when they reflected real support from the governor. Direct or indirect support from the governor should be secured for IT initiatives to increase their probabilities of success.

Establish and Institutionalize Government-wide IT Standards. Statewide standards for accessibility, usability, security, and other relevant aspects could lead to better government IT initiatives. Both New York and Indiana had mandatory IT standards for state websites. These included several standards and guidelines regarding development, hosting, and other elements of the technological architecture that work simultaneously to enhance convenience, but also to ensure security and privacy for the potential users.

6.3.4 Context

Develop a Detailed Diagnosis of the IT Initiative's Environment. Dealing with the environment is always difficult, but necessary. Government IT initiatives do not happen in a vacuum; environmental conditions have an important effect on their design, implementation, and use. Public managers should develop a detailed diagnosis of the IT initiative's environment at the beginning of every e-government project. In order to have a more comprehensive diagnosis, they could use existing tools and guides for making decisions about IT investments or for implementing IT initiatives in government. Currently, there are several examples of these tools; Gil-Garcia and Pardo (2005) discuss the advantages and limitations of four of them.

Use Contingency Thinking and Planning. It is clear that political, social, and economic factors can affect organizational and institutional arrangements and, consequently, the success of e-government initiatives. Although they could do little to influence environmental conditions, public managers should be aware of these direct and indirect effects on e-government success and take them into consideration when making IT investment and implementation decisions. Contingency thinking when planning and managing e-government initiatives is a good recommendation to follow. It is true that there is no way to know all the possible problems and deviations in advance, but developing good scenarios and plans for facing contingencies could greatly improve the probabilities of success of e-government initiatives.

Chapter 7
Conclusions

E-government is a socio-technical phenomenon whose importance has rapidly increased in recent years. It is a dynamic phenomenon since it refers to government information technologies that are always changing. For instance, in the last few years governments have started to incorporate Web 2.0 tools, social media applications, and open government strategies. All these current and emergent technologies have the potential to at least partially solve some of the problems found in current bureaucracies: low quality of services, inefficiencies, lack of transparency, low citizen participation, and the lack of a unified vision of citizen needs. Despite this potential, practical experience and research have shown that e-government initiatives are not easy to implement. In fact, the failure rates reported by different entities, including consulting companies, associations of government officials, and international organizations, seem to indicate that these initiatives are clearly more complex than other administrative reform efforts. Therefore, understanding e-government success is critically important. Drawing on the qualitative and quantitative analyses performed as part of this research, this chapter presents the main conclusions of the study.

Overall, this study clearly demonstrates that e-government as a phenomenon is more than the technology—it includes powerful social and organizational aspects. In addition, achieving e-government success is not an easy task and the results are influenced by multiple factors such as management strategies and practices, organizational characteristics, institutions, and environmental conditions. E-government initiatives do not exist in a vacuum; they are profoundly embedded in social structures. Understanding organizational structures and processes, institutional arrangements, and environmental conditions is clearly important for developing a comprehensive and accurate framework for e-government success. In addition, simultaneously analyzing multiple variables and their relationships provides a better and more complete characterization of this phenomenon, in contrast to most previous studies that considered one or a few variables in isolation and missed other important variables and their interplays.

J. R. Gil-Garcia, *Enacting Electronic Government Success*,
Integrated Series in Information Systems 31, DOI: 10.1007/978-1-4614-2015-6_7,

Some of the findings refer to exploring and establishing relationships between e-government success and multiple types of factors. Other results attempt to provide initial explanations of the influence mechanisms and dynamics found in different contexts. General organizational characteristics, management strategies and practices, and availability of financial resources were found to be statistically significant success factors. These three variables have a direct effect on e-government success and together account for approximately 46% of the variance in functionality. Therefore, this research provides evidence of the importance of organizational structures and processes such as size of the IT organization, budget structure, IT training, in-house development, outsourcing, and a marketing strategy for the development of functional websites. Future research should test to what extent these factors are also important determinants of success in emerging tools and applications, such as social media, Web 2.0, and open government initiatives. Since the technology is changing rapidly, but the organizational structures and the institutions in government change very slowly, it is expected that many of the factors identified here should also be important for emergent and future technologies.

In addition, the statistical results show that management practices are important, but they are interrelated and partially explained by other factors such as political orientation and institutional arrangements. Therefore, this study suggests that both environmental factors and management strategies are important in understanding e-government success. Particularly, institutional arrangements seem to be affected by all three contextual factors in this model, and are significant predictors of both general organizational characteristics and management strategies and practices. Understanding institutions and their effects on e-government success is also a very important task to accomplish in future studies. This research should include the interrelationships between institutions and other variables such as management strategies and practices and environmental conditions.

It seems clear that there is no one path to e-government success. The two case studies included in this research had very different histories, managerial approaches, and division of labor among actors. They were embedded in different institutional frameworks and were influenced by different economic, social, and political factors. However, both states managed to develop highly functional government-wide websites that provide good information and a great number of electronic services to citizens, businesses, and other stakeholders. Therefore, there is not a single combination of factors that results in e-government success. For the State of Indiana, the public–private partnership model was successful. It had a clear management strategy and the goal of being a one-stop shop. In contrast, New York State performed a systematic effort to integrate its government-wide website, but leaders decided that a decentralized approach would be a much more feasible and efficient way to manage the state website, which worked very well for several years. Both government-wide websites were considered successful by external evaluations. Future research should include more cases and assess their similarities and differences in terms of paths to success.

In addition, this study uncovered several instances of parallel stories, in which actors from the two case studies mentioned the same factors as important, but for different reasons. For instance, marketing of the website was considered a very important factor in both cases. However, for New York State marketing was solely a way to communicate the existence of the website to potential users and make them aware of the information and services already available. For Indiana, marketing was an important element of their overall strategy and was used to understand their market of potential users. Through marketing, Indiana Interactive staff members were able to identify information and services that citizens, businesses, or other stakeholders needed. In addition, they gathered useful information for the design and content of specific online government services. Marketing has been a much more strategic tool for Indiana than for New York, but equally useful and important for both states. Future studies should explore how marketing and other management strategies are enacted (perceived and used) by other government agencies, including the national, regional, and local levels.

Similarly, the overall size of the state economy was an important factor in the statistical analysis, but the reasons were different for the two cases. In New York, the overall size of the economy was closely related to the size of the state budget and therefore to financial resources available for e-government projects. The story of Indiana seems to be more complex. They perceived a high correlation between the overall size of the state economy and the total population of the state. Both are, in some ways, measures of state size. For Indiana, the most important thing was the size of the population as a potential market. New York had a more government budget-centric approach, while Indiana, as expected because of the public–private partnership model, acted more like a private company by analyzing the potential demand of their products and services. Nonetheless, in both states the overall size of the economy was seen as important by interviewees. Future research should analyze other factors that are perceived as important by public managers, but whose importance could be explained in very different ways.

These two examples of marketing and the size of the state economy show that the mechanisms of causality can be relatively different, even in cases in which the variables seem to be basically the same. The environment in which organizations are embedded greatly influences how certain factors affect e-government success. Depending on the context and the specific strategy followed by IT leaders, similar factors affect e-government initiatives in different ways. Theoretically, this situation could lead to explanations that initially appear different or contradictory, but that in essence are explaining different phenomena. The study of the effects of environmental variables on the perceptions and actual impacts of different success factors should also be considered for future research efforts. They should include additional environmental variables that represent the context of e-government initiatives in the best possible way.

It is also important to clarify that some e-government success factors are important by themselves, but the way people think about them and use them strategically may be even more important than their presence in a specific situation. For example, some managerial strategies such as marketing and outsourcing were found important in both cases. However, for New York they were things that happened over time without strategic focus or conscious choice by managers.

In contrast, Indiana had a clear strategy from AccessIndiana's initial creation and the design of its governance structure. They have leveraged legislative involvement, marketing, outsourcing, training, and other strategies with a clear vision of what they were trying to achieve. The presence of the factor is important, but the strategy and the intentions behind it were key to the success of AccessIndiana. Theoretically, it seems clear that environmental forces and organizational structures are important, but managerial actions and strategies are also determinants of e-government success. Future research should study other government strategies and attempt to disentangle the actual impact of multiple individual variables, given that managers normally implement several strategies at the same time and for the same or different purposes.

The technology enactment process is complex and recursive in nature. Through this study, two important interactions were evident. First, from the discussion above, environmental forces and managerial action are intertwined and their separate impacts are difficult to disentangle. Different mixtures of managerial strategies, organizational structures, and contextual factors can lead to similar results. Similarly, we can expect that combinations of similar factors could lead to very different results. Second, there is a dynamic interplay between information technologies and the social structures around them. Organizational, institutional, and contextual factors truly have the potential to shape information technologies in government settings. Over time, these information technologies can also have an impact on all types of factors (e.g., new legislation, re-organizations, changing citizens' expectations). In this respect, e-government is not different from other types of IT initiatives. Recent research in information systems recognizes this recursive nature of information technologies in organizational settings and this applies to digital government as well. Organizational characteristics and institutional arrangements affect electronic government, but the specific features and applications of e-government also have an impact on organizational and institutional factors, leading to differentiated levels of e-government success. The framework presented in this book is mainly based on evidence from the US. I have also applied this integrative framework to understand federal, state, and local government IT initiatives in Mexico. Future research should apply it to other national realities and contexts.

Overall, there is an increasingly strong consensus among researchers and practitioners around the idea that problems in adopting and implementing e-government are not only about the complexity of technology. E-government success factors are also related to organizational, behavioral, institutional, socio-structural, and cultural aspects. However, most of the current work about these relationships is anecdotal in nature and more studies with solid empirical evidence are needed. The study presented in this book provides evidence of the influence of different organizational, institutional, and contextual factors on the success of e-government. The relative impact of these factors may be different according to specific initiatives and environmental conditions. However, it is clear that their interrelationships are very important and studying them in isolation (as many previous studies have done) may lead to limited understanding of the overall processes and results. Digital government research seeks to be both theoretically sound and practically useful. In order to clearly establish this link, researchers should develop theoretical frameworks with a more integrative and comprehensive view of social phenomena. Future studies should emphasize these dynamic interactions and continue the development of more comprehensive and accurate models of e-government success.

E-government success is a theoretical and practical concern. Theoretically, there are relatively few comprehensive efforts to understand information technologies in government settings. This study integrates insights from the technology enactment framework, the process model of computing change, and environmental approaches to organizational theory to generate necessary knowledge about e-government success. Comprehensive research has the potential to more accurately capture the real complexity of social phenomena and can provide a better explanation of complex situations. These comprehensive approaches also have the opportunity to integrate elements of previous theories that look at specific subcomponents of the social phenomenon of interest. Thus, they can be used to present a picture of the potential intersections and complementarities of different approaches to the same phenomenon. Therefore, comprehensive approaches could help to integrate previous knowledge about e-government success into a single and more powerful explanation. Since this study used government-wide websites as an instance of the broader e-government phenomenon, future research should apply this framework to other e-government initiatives, including Web 2.0 tools, cloud computing applications, and inter-organizational information integration, among others.

Practically, public managers at all levels of government are attempting to increase their probabilities of success in e-government initiatives. This study clearly shows the complexities and challenges of e-government. Public managers and other decision-makers can influence some of the factors analyzed in this research. They can increase their success rates by modifying some organizational structures and processes, or even by engaging other stakeholders in institutional changes. Therefore, in order to increase e-government success, public managers are important actors in promoting a necessary government reform. This reform would include significant changes in institutional arrangements and organizational structures, as well as overall strategies and objectives. In contrast, other factors are enduring characteristics of governments and their jurisdictions. Public managers should be aware of these environmental factors and adjust their expectations and strategies accordingly. They should also use contingency thinking in the planning and management of e-government projects. Understanding the complexity of e-government and the context in which it is embedded could help to set more realistic goals and develop better e-government strategies. Future studies should assess the effectiveness of different tools and strategies that help to deal with the environment and develop successful e-government initiatives.

Finally, I want to emphasize that the results of this study are not only theoretically sound and practically useful, but they are also relevant and timely. First, the theoretical model is intended for and could be used to analyze any type of e-government initiative. In fact, the theory proposed in this book could be useful for understanding any government information technology: old, current, or future. Since some of the challenges government IT initiatives face are very similar, studying one type of initiative could help to understand many others. Second, even the specific results about government-wide websites are very relevant, because websites are not disappearing or being substituted, at least in the short run. Instead, they are being expanded through the addition of new features, applications, and tools. The conclusions and lessons derived from this study are not technology-specific and can help to understand other technologies and applications, as well as how they are being developed and managed in different government settings. Finally, there are many local governments around the world that are just starting their own e-government efforts, including launching government-wide portals. The conclusions and lessons derived from this study are directly relevant and useful to them, as well as for agencies at the three levels of government (national, regional, and local) in many developing countries. Therefore, this book is clearly an important theoretical and practical contribution to the emergent field of electronic government and also to several of its related disciplinary traditions. I also expect this book to be useful for developing the next generation of e-government initiatives, which should create value for governments, citizens, businesses, and the society as a whole.

Appendix I
Research Design and Methods

This appendix describes the research design and methods used in this study. First, it explains the logic of the overall mixed method approach. This explanation is followed by a detailed description of each method, the statistical analysis, and the case studies, including the unit of analysis, sample, variables, data collection procedures, tools for analysis, and, when applicable, validity and reliability tests. The appendix ends with a section dedicated to the potential limitations of the research.

As mentioned earlier in the book, the objective of this study is to understand the complex relationships between e-government success as the dependent variable and (1) organizational structures and processes, (2) institutional arrangements, and (3) environmental conditions as independent variables. The research uses government-wide state websites as an example of e-government initiatives. Following a bidirectional and dynamic causality perspective consistent with the ensemble view proposed by Orlikowski and Iacono (2001), the study is guided by two interrelated questions:

1. To what extent are e-government initiatives, shaped by different organizational structures and processes, institutional arrangements, and environmental conditions?
2. To what extent are organizational structures and processes, institutional arrangements, and environmental conditions affected by the existence and characteristics of e-government initiatives?

A. Nested Research Design as an Explanatory Mixed Method Approach

Authors from different disciplines recommend the use of multiple methods to study complex social phenomena (Bennet 2002; Brewer and Hunter 1989; Cresswell 2003; Gil-Garcia and Pardo 2006; Hammond 2005; Heeks and Bailur

J. R. Gil-Garcia, *Enacting Electronic Government Success*, Integrated Series in Information Systems 31, DOI: 10.1007/978-1-4614-2015-6,

2007; Johnson et al. 2007; Newman and Benz 1998; Niehaves 2010; Rademacher 2001; Saxton et al. 2007; Scholl et al. 2006; Shin 2010; Soffer and Hadar 2007; Verdegem and Verleye 2009; Wang and Liao 2008; Weerakkody et al. 2009). For example, Mingers (2001, 2003) contends that there are various reasons for using a combination of research methods from an information systems (IS) perspective, but he also notes the scarcity of such multi-method work in the IS literature. Since multi-method approaches commonly refer to the use of both qualitative and quantitative methods in conducting research, the challenges and advantages of mixed method strategies seem to be equally important for the study of e-government phenomena (Carbo and Williams 2004; Gil-Garcia and Pardo 2006; Heeks and Bailur 2007; Niehaves 2010; Potnis 2010; Ringle et al. 2010; Soffer and Hadar 2007; Vélez-Rivera et al. 2010). The following paragraphs explain some of these challenges and advantages.

There are five principal advantages of multi-method approaches (Gil-Garcia and Pardo 2006): (1) enable discovery; (2) triangulate results; (3) provide a more comprehensive approach to the phenomenon; (4) validate methods; and (5) allow researchers to ask a broader set of questions. The first advantage, often considered a capstone, is how a multi-method approach enables the discovery of new or paradoxical factors that could foster future research (Hoyles et al. 2005; Tashakkori and Teddlie 1998). The promise of discovering and confirming unexpected outcomes may be the main reason to undertake such costs and complexity. Validating interpretations through triangulation of the results is another key advantage. It is useful at the single-study and the multiple-study review level (Gil-Garcia and Pardo 2006; Hammond 2005; Sammons et al. 2005; Tashakkori and Teddlie 1998).

A multi-method approach helps to obtain full answers, increase the robustness of our understanding, and potentially gain a better overall explanation of the phenomenon being studied (Mingers 2001). It partially solves the weaknesses of individual research methods and also validates those methods, since it assumes that doing research is a process (Gil-Garcia and Pardo 2006). An additional advantage of using a multi-method approach is that researchers can expand their scope of study, including many aspects of the phenomenon (Cresswell 2003; Cresswell and Tashakkori 2007; Gil-Garcia and Pardo 2006; Johnson et al. 2007; Molina-Azorín 2011; Tashakkori and Teddlie 1998; Abbas Tashakkori and Teddlie 2003; Verdegem and Verleye 2009).

Nevertheless, the use of a multi-method approach results in several challenges as well (Gil-Garcia and Pardo 2006): (1) availability of multi-method research knowledge; (2) incompatibility between methods; (3) costs of multi-method studies; and (4) publication, reputation, and tenure pressures. A first challenge to overcome is attaining trained people capable of developing this kind of research. Once experts are found, not all quantitative and qualitative methods are easily combined, an argument derived from the perceived differences between these two methods (Reichardt and Cook 1979). However, in recent years researchers have come to consider them compatible and complementary approaches (Brannen 2005). In addition, conducting research demands time and resources. Therefore, as a general rule, using a multi-method approach requires more time and more resources.

The elevated costs affect the researcher's decision about using several methods, in addition to the pressure to publish their research as a single-method study (Cresswell and Tashakkori 2007; Gil-Garcia and Pardo 2006; Mertens 2011; Mingers 2001; Reidl et al. 2007; Shin 2010; Soffer and Hadar 2007).

Acknowledging these advantages and challenges, this study uses a nested research design in order to disentangle the complex relationships between the functionality of government-wide websites (representing e-government success) and several organizational characteristics, institutional arrangements, and environmental conditions (Baker 2009; Batini et al. 2009; Dawes et al. 2009; Gil-Garcia 2006; Gil-Garcia and Pardo 2006; Puron Cid et al. 2009). Nested analysis is a multi-method approach that encompasses statistical tests and thick analysis research (Collier et al. 2003; Coppedge 2001; Cresswell 2009; Lieberman 2003). With the use of both types of research approaches, the study attempts to avoid some of the weaknesses and challenges resulting from each individual method while gaining the benefits of both (Gil-Garcia 2005b; Gil-Garcia and Pardo 2006; Johnson et al. 2007; Luk 2009; Soffer and Hadar 2007; Tseng et al. 2008; Verdegem and Verleye 2009).

This study begins with a statistical analysis where the dependent variable is an overall score representing the functionality of government-wide state websites as an example of e-government success. The independent variables are several organizational characteristics, institutional arrangements, and environmental conditions. Then, based on the statistical results, two cases are selected based on their position in the general ranking of website functionality (which includes four different measures) and their relative fitness to the statistical model (residuals). For the two selected states (New York and Indiana), case studies were developed in order to complement the results of the statistical analysis using semi-structured interviews and document analysis. The cases used a purposive sample of key informants involved in the management and development of government-wide state websites.

B. Statistical Analysis

It is generally accepted that statistical analysis has the potential to generalize findings from a sample to its population. In this research the complete population is used. Therefore, the practical significance is almost as important as the statistical significance. The main objective is to explain the current situation regarding e-government success in the states, not to make inferences about a larger population. However, e-government initiatives share relevant characteristics and, therefore, the results of the statistical analysis are potentially interesting and useful for understanding other e-government initiatives and other national realities.

This section begins by listing the main data sources for the study. Then, as described in Chap. 3, this section shows a summary table with the operationalization of each of the constructs. It also describes the PLS statistical technique and how it was applied to this study. Finally, it details how the validity and reliability of the statistical models were evaluated.

1. Data Sources

Information about all 50 states in the US was gathered from available published sources. Indicators for the dependent variable represent the success or functionality of government-wide state websites as the enacted technology. As mentioned before, the independent variables include several organizational structures and processes, institutional arrangements, and environmental conditions. Table A.1 summarizes the main data sources.

2. Operationalization of Constructs Tables

According to the theoretical model described in previous chapters, the relevant constructs for this research are (1) electronic government success, (2) organizational structures and processes, (3) institutional arrangements, and (4) environmental conditions. The following tables summarize how each of the constructs was operationalized and reflect the same information that is in Chap. 3 in text form (Tables A.2, A.3, A.4, A.5, A.6, A.7).

3. Data Analysis Using Partial Least Squares

This section introduces and explains the statistical technique used in the study: Partial least squares (PLS). A structural equation modeling (SEM) approach was appropriate due to the nature of the complex relationships among the variables (Gil-Garcia 2005a). SEM has become the ultimate strategy in validating instruments and testing linkages between constructs (Henseler et al. 2009). The most popular variety of SEM is covariance-based and is represented by models developed using computer programs such as LISREL (Fornell and Bookstein 1982; Joreskog 1978), AMOS (Byrne 2001), or EQS (Bentler 1985). SEM attempts to understand the causal relationships between theoretical constructs and how well each construct is captured by its indicators or manifest variables (see Fig. A.1).

Partial least squares (PLS) is a SEM statistical approach for modeling complex multivariable relationships among observed and latent variables (Esposito et al. 2010). As a SEM technique, PLS can simultaneously test the structural model (relationships between constructs) and the measurement model (relationships between indicators and their corresponding constructs) (Barclay et al. 1995; Gil-Garcia 2008; Hulland 1999; Tenenhaus et al. 2005). It produces loadings from reflective constructs to their indicators, standardized regression coefficients between constructs, weights to formative constructs from their indicators, and coefficients of multiple determination (R-squared) for endogenous constructs (dependent variables) (Gefen et al. 2000; Gil-Garcia 2008).

The PLS technique was developed as an alternative to covariance-based SEM (Esposito et al. 2010). Its objective is not to explain or generalize causal relationships, but to predict multiple events represented by theoretical constructs (Chin 1998). PLS is based on the variance of the dependent variables that is

Table A.1 Main data sources

Source	Variable
State and federal e-government in the United States, 2001 (D.M. West 2001)	Overall e-government ranking
The digital state 2001 (Lassman 2002)	E-commerce score
The book of the states 2002 (CSG 2002)	Number of online services
	Percentage of votes for the democrat and republican parties in previous gubernatorial election (1997–2000)
	Governor's political affiliation (D,R, Other) in 2000
	Personal income per capita for 1999
	Total state revenue
	Total state debt
NASCIO compendium of digital government in the states 2002 (NASCIO 2002)	Number of e-commerce systems
	Number of people working for statewide IT
	Percentage of IT budget from federal funds
	IT office budget for maintenance
	Number of marketing media and intensity
	Outsourced/directly portal websites services
	IT central manages directly portal development
	Existence of mandatory accessibility standards
	State IT professionals members of the civil service
	State relies on executive ordersor directives to establish authority for CIO offices
	State has an IT legislative committee in the senate
Census 2000, U.S. Census bureau and the state and local sourcebook (Governing 2003)	Income measures
	Education
	Computer ownership
	Internet access
U.S. bureau of economic analysis	Government gross state product
	Number of state jobs
	Private earnings in several industries (state and local government, education, communication and more)

Table A.2 Operationalization of the "electronic government success" construct (measurement model)

Construct	Government-wide website functionality
Indicators	Overall state e-government ranking (score)
	Digitalstate e-commerce score
	Number of e-commerce systems
	Number of online services

Table A.3 Operationalization of the "organizational structures and processes" constructs (measurement model)

Construct	General organizational characteristics	Management strategies and practices
Indicators	Number of people working for the IT organization (Size)	Website services are entirely outsourced
	Percentage of the IT budget revenue sources from federal funds	Number of marketing media and intensity of marketing
	State provides accessibility training for IT professionals	Only the IT organization directly provides website services
	Percentage of the IT office budget devoted to maintenance	IT organization directly manages portal development for agencies

Table A.4 Operationalization of the "institutional arrangements" construct (measurement model)

Construct	Institutional arrangements
Indicators	State has mandatory accessibility standards for state web sites
	State has executive orders/directives as the only way to establish authority for CIO offices
	State has an IT specific legislative committee in the Senate
	State IT professionals are members of the civil service only

Table A.5 Operationalization of the "environmental conditions" construct—demographic factors (measurement model)

Construct	Demographic factors
Indicators	Median income per family (1999)
	Median income per household (1999)
	Percentage of population for whom poverty status is determined (1999)
	Percentage of households with Internet access (2000)
	Percent of families below poverty level (1999)
	Percentage of population 25 years and over with bachelor's degree or higher education (2000)
	Percentage of households with computers (2000)
	Personal income per capita (1999)
	Percentage of households with Internet access (1998)
	Gross state product per capita (2000)
	Percentage of households with computers (1998)
	Percentage of population 25 to 34 years with bachelor's degree or higher (2000)
	Percentage of population 25 years and over with high school or higher education (2000)
	Percentage of population 25 years and over with less than 9th grade education (2000)

Table A.6 Operationalization of the "environmental conditions" constructs—voting preferences (measurement model)

Construct	Voting preferences
Indicators	Governor was democrat in 2000
	Governor was republican in 2000
	Percentage of votes for the democratic party in the previous gubernatorial election (1997–2000)
	Percentage of votes for the republican party in the previous gubernatorial election (1997–2000)

Table A.7 Operationalization of the "environmental conditions" constructs—overall size of the economy (Measurement Model)

Construct	Overall size of the economy
Indicators	Local government private earnings (2000)
	Government and government enterprises private earnings (2000)
	State government private earnings (2000)
	Government gross state product (2000)
	Number of local government jobs (2000)
	Number of engineering and management services jobs (2000)
	State total revenue (2000)
	Number of government and government enterprises jobs (2000)
	Engineering and management services private earnings (2000)
	Number of state government jobs (2000)
	Number of jobs in the communications industry (2000)
	Communications industry private earnings (2000)
	Number of educational services jobs (2000)
	Number of electronic and other electric equipment jobs (2000)
	Electronic and other electric equipment private earnings (2000)
	Educational services private earnings (2000)
	Total state debt (2000)

accounted for by their corresponding independent variables (Gil-Garcia 2005a). There are certain conditions under which PLS is much more appropriate than its covariance-based counterpart. Falk and Miller (1992) classify these conditions into four groups: (1) theoretical conditions, (2) measurement conditions, (3) distributional conditions, and (4) practical conditions.

Theoretical conditions refer to whether a strong theory about the phenomenon already exists (Gil-Garcia 2005a). Three situations are identified in this group (Falk and Miller 1992, p. 5): (1) "hypotheses are derived from macro-level theory in which all relevant variables are not known"; (2) "relationships between theoretical constructs and their manifestations are vague"; and (3) "relationships between constructs are conjectural." For instance, in "hard modeling," as Falk and Miller (1992) call it, the systems must include all the relevant variables. If the researcher fails to consider them all, biased estimates will occur. When using PLS,

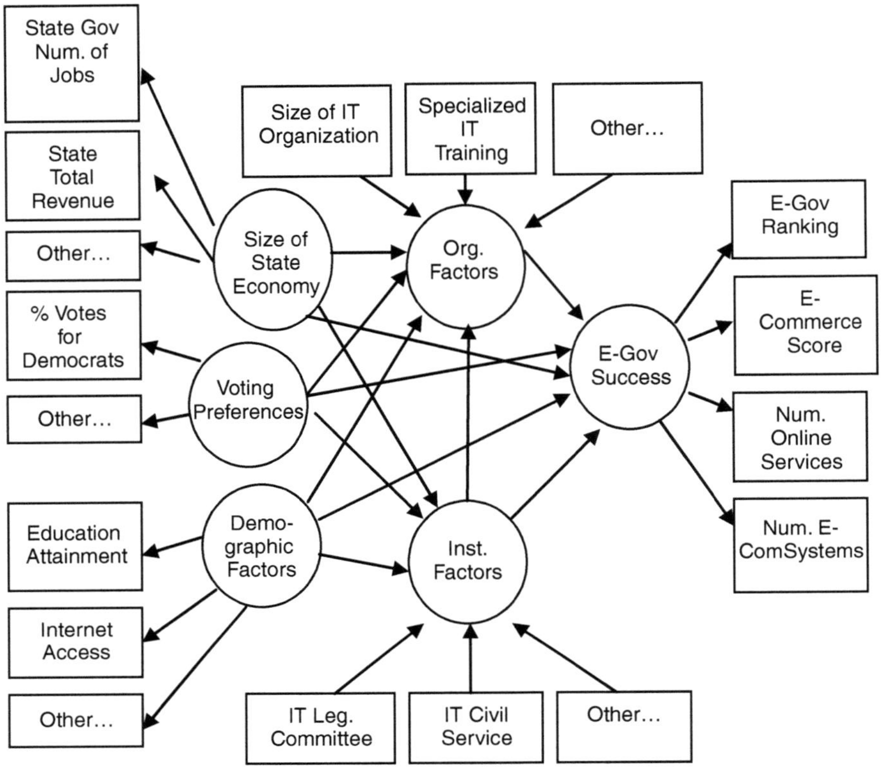

Fig. A.1 Initial high-level conceptual model for PLS analysis

such risk is avoided by "arguing not for invariant structural parameters, but for the best prediction of a specified set of variables" (Falk and Miller 1992, p. 8).

PLS was introduced as a soft modeling technique in order to emphasize the difference in methodology for estimating SEM. "Soft" refers to the general "ability of PLS to exhibit greater flexibility in handling various modeling problems in situations where it is difficult or impossible to meet the hard assumptions of more traditional multivariate statistics. Within this context, soft is only attributed to distributional assumptions and not to the concepts, models, or the estimation techniques" (Esposito et al. 2010, p. 2).

Measurement conditions refer to the characteristics of the data and their relationships with both manifest and latent variables (Falk and Miller 1992; Gil-Garcia 2005a). Falk and Miller (1992, p. 6) have identified three measurement conditions: (1) "some of the manifest variables are categorical or they represent different levels of measurement"; (2) "manifest variables have some degree of unreliability"; and (3) "residuals on manifest and latent variables are correlated." In social science research, the presence of variables with different levels of measurement (i.e., categorical, ordinal, interval) in a single problem is common.

PLS can integrate multiple levels of measurement. In addition, as a consequence of the use of an iterative algorithm, identification is not a problem in PLS (Barroso et al. 2010). Typically in SEM, unreliability and heteroscedasticity can lead to identification issues and it becomes necessary to limit the number of parameters the researcher estimates (Falk and Miller 1992). PLS can be a powerful method of analysis because of the minimal demands on measurement scales (nominal, ordinal, and interval scaled variables are permissible) and residual distributions.

PLS can also be a more appropriate technique for one very important distributional condition, when "data come from non-normal or unknown distributions" (Falk and Miller 1992, p. 6). As Falk and Miller (1992) explain, population parameters converge with maximum likelihood estimates when the sample size is very large. But that characteristic presumes knowledge of the underlying distributions. If the wrong distribution is assumed, then the estimates are not consistent.

In contrast, "given any distribution, PLS produces the best set of predictive weights" (Falk and Miller 1992, p. 11). Basic statistical knowledge points out how small samples do not always meet normality and homogeneity assumptions. Nevertheless, the present method accommodates them by making less strict assumptions about the distribution of the data (Hair et al. 1998). When comparing PLS and maximum likelihood (ML), Vilares et al. (2010, p. 303) concluded that "practitioners should use PLS as a preferable choice over ML methods when using skewed data [since they] may more likely obtain accurate coefficient estimates and achieve a better understanding of the structures underlying the data they have collected".

In addition, according to Chin (1998), the PLS sample size should be 10 times whichever is greater: (1) the larger number of structural paths going to an endogenous construct or (2) the larger number of indicators in a formative construct. However, this may vary depending on the actual effect sizes and the distribution of the sample (Barclay et al. 1995; Chin 1998; Chin and Newsted 1999; Gefen et al. 2000; Gil-Garcia 2008). For instance, after a Monte Carlo simulation, Chin and Newsted (1999, p. 335) affirm that "overall, the results show that the PLS approach can provide information about the appropriateness of indicators at [a] sample size as low as 20".

Finally, Falk and Miller (1992, p. 6) suggest three practical conditions: (1) non-experimental research designs are used; (2) "a large number of manifest and latent variables are modeled"; and (3) "too many or too few cases are available." Such conditions refer to the design and limitations of the research in which a SEM technique will be applied (Gil-Garcia 2005a, 2008). For example, sample size raises two issues: one regarding the ratio of the number of cases to the number of variables in the model and a second focuses on the model fit indices. The first problem becomes obvious when, for instance, in a regression analysis the number of subjects equals the number of variables. PLS responds with an efficient data reduction system and could at times be even less strict than a multiple regression model.

Besides, "frequently, the chi-square statistic is used to evaluate the 'goodness fit' of the model. This statistic is sensitive to the sample size. As the sample size increases beyond 300, models will be rejected as having poor fit to the data. When the number of cases is less than 60, the statistic is not powerful enough to reject most models" (Falk and Miller 1992, p. 12). PLS does not have a widely accepted overall fit index and relies on fit indices that individually indicate the variance accounted for in the endogenous constructs of the model (Falk and Miller 1992).

Further, PLS can be used for exploratory purposes, which is not generally acceptable when using other SEM techniques (Gil-Garcia 2005a). Rather than searching for causal mechanisms, the PLS technique seeks optimal linear predictive relationships, thus privileging a prediction-relevance discovery process to the statistical testing of causal hypotheses (Esposito et al. 2010). On this matter, Chin (1998, p. 295) states that "although PLS can be used for theory confirmation, it can also be used to suggest where relationships might or might not exist and to suggest propositions for testing later". As Mahmood et al. (2004, p. 20) summarize: "The PLS technique imposes minimal demand on measurement scales, sample sizes, and residual distribution, [hence] it is often used to test and validate exploratory models". When the research model is not based on strong theory, an exploratory "theory development" approach is more appropriate (Gefen et al. 2000).

PLS can be particularly useful in situations where the researcher has the complete population, instead of a representative sample, because the main purpose is not to make inferences to a population, but to predict the values of the dependent variables based on the corresponding independent variables (Falk and Miller 1992). Even so, the increased popularity of PLS path modeling within the research community is likely motivated by its explorative and predictive capacity. In fact, "PLS is recommended in an early stage of theoretical development in order to test and validate exploratory models" (Henseler et al. 2009, p. 282).

In a review of the use of PLS path modeling, Henseler et al. (2009) summarized the method's advantages and they converge with some of the conditions initially proposed by Falk and Miller (1992): (1) "delivers latent variable scores, i.e. proxies of the constructs, which are measured by one or several indicators (manifest variables)"; (2) "avoids [the] small sample size problem and can therefore be applied in some situation when other methods cannot"; (3) "can estimate very complex models with many latent and manifest variables"; (4) "has less stringent assumptions about the distribution of variables and error terms"; and (5) "can handle both reflective and formative measurement models" (Henseler et al. 2009, p. 283).

In PLS, the relationship between a construct and its indicators can be modeled as either reflective or formative (Barclay et al. 1995; Gefen et al. 2000; Gil-Garcia 2008). Reflective indicators are also known as effect indicators and formative indicators are also known as cause or induced indicators (Bollen 1989). Reflective indicators are commonly used in the social sciences. They are gathered to be unidimensional and correlated with each other and to measure the same underlying phenomenon (Chin 1998; Esposito et al. 2010; Gefen et al. 2000; Gil-Garcia 2008). In contrast, formative indicators are conceived as causes of the underlying construct and they represent different dimensions of the construct; therefore, there is no assumption of homogeneity or unidimensionality of the block (Esposito et al. 2010; Gefen et al. 2000; Gil-Garcia 2008). No clear cut-off has been established for choosing to model constructs as formative or reflective and this choice represents the best judgment of researchers (Chwelos et al. 2001).

For the measurement model (outer model), formative and reflective indicators must be treated differently. For formative indicators, traditional measures of validity are not appropriate since they are not expected to be correlated with each other (Chin 1998; Esposito et al. 2010). However, Bollen (1989, p. 222) contends that validity is "the strength of the direct structural relation between a measure and a latent variable" and, therefore, validity of formative constructs can be evaluated by looking at the size and significance of the weights (Gil-Garcia 2008).

In reflective constructs, indicators linked to the same latent variable should covary: "Changes in one indicator imply changes in the other. Moreover, internal consistency has to be checked, i.e. each block is assumed to be homogeneous and unidimensional" (Esposito et al. 2010, p. 49). In this respect, there are two important aspects that need evaluation: convergent and discriminant validity (Gefen et al. 2000). Assessments of convergent validity include an examination of indicator reliability, composite reliability, and average variance extracted (Chin 1998; Fornell 1982; Gefen et al. 2000; Gil-Garcia 2008). In order to assess discriminant validity, "the average variance extracted should be greater than the variance between the construct and other constructs in the model (i.e., the squared correlation between two constructs)" (Barroso et al. 2010, p. 434).

The structural model represents the relationships between constructs that are being hypothesized. Since PLS lacks a well-established overall fit measure, coefficients of determination (R-squares) and paths (statistical and practical significance) together indicate overall goodness of fit for the model. R-squares are measures of the variance in endogenous constructs, accounted for by other constructs that were hypothesized to have an effect on them. Therefore, they can be interpreted as R-squares in regression analysis (Chin 1998; Gil-Garcia 2008). The emphasis is more on the accuracy of the predictions than on the accuracy of estimation (Esposito et al. 2010).

4. Tests of Validity and Reliability of the PLS Models

This subsection refers to the process employed for evaluating the validity and reliability of the PLS models. It includes some brief explanations that are complementary to the text in the statistical analysis chapter and a series of tables with the more detailed results. The purpose of this section is to provide the readers with more information about the evaluation of the PLS models and to present the actual data for readers to use their own judgment about the measurement and structural PLS results.

There has been established that there is no clear cut-off for choosing to model constructs as formative or reflective. I evaluated the sensitivity of the structural parameters to the modeling preference. One model with only formative constructs (when possible) and one model with only reflective constructs were developed.

Table A.8 Reflective construct correlations and square root of AVE for the full model

	Government-wide website functionality	Voting preferences	Demographic factors	Overall size of the economy
Government-wide website functionality	0.771	–	–	–
Voting preferences	−0.152	0.848		–
Demographic factors	0.034	0.081	0.829	–
Overall size of the economy	0.473	−0.024	0.124	0.954

In both cases the results were qualitatively the same: no paths gained or lost in statistical significance and no significant path changed in sign. Chwelos et al. (2001) argue that this process can be used to show that the results are not an artifact of the researcher's modeling decisions.

PLS does not directly provide significance tests. Significance levels for loadings, weights, and paths were calculated through bootstrapping (Davison and Hinkley 2003; Henseler et al. 2009).[1] Two hundred bootstrap samples (200) were used to empirically calculate standard errors and evaluate statistical significance. The following tables show the results of several tests performed in order to assess validity and reliability for the full and refined models: (1) correlations and square root of AVE for the full model (Table A.8), (2) loadings and cross loadings for the full model (Table A.9), (3) correlations and square root of AVE for the refined model (Table A.10), and (4) loadings and cross loadings for the refined model (Table A.11). These tables complement the text provided in the statistical analysis of Chap. 3 and should help the reader to better understand the evaluation of validity and reliability that was performed (Tables A.10, A.11).

C. Case Studies

Using the multi-method research strategy already described, the statistical analysis was followed by two case studies. This section explains the selection of the cases, describes the data collection procedures, and very briefly discusses the analysis of the qualitative data. The purpose of the case studies as a qualitative strategy was to contribute to a theoretical model that can capture the complexity of two comparable, but different realities. In addition, the cases complement the analysis by uncovering and describing some of the mechanisms by which organizational, institutional, and contextual variables affect e-government success. The use of case studies is a well-known technique for obtaining rich and detailed information about specific phenomena (Becker et al. 2009; Gibbert et al. 2008; Gieber et al. 2010;

[1] For an overview of bootstrapping techniques and applications, see Mooney and Duval (1993).

Table A.9 Indicators loadings and cross loadings for the full model

Indicator in reflective construct*	Government-wide website functionality	Voting preferences	Demographic factors	Overall size of the economy
Overall quality of e-government services	**0.8315**	−0.164	0.089	0.486
Number of online services	**0.8267**	−0.109	−0.088	0.439
Number of e-commerce systems	**0.7108**	−0.047	−0.052	0.361
Quality of e-commerce	**0.7048**	−0.144	0.172	0.177
Governor was democrat in 2000	−0.126	**0.9069**	0.052	−0.007
Governor was republican in 2000	0.068	**−0.8545**	−0.089	0.040
Percentage of votes for democratic party	−0.224	**0.8461**	0.029	−0.004
Percentage of votes for republican party	0.030	**−0.7794**	−0.142	0.044
Median income per family (1999)	0.112	0.103	**0.9332**	0.223
Median income per household (1999)	0.117	0.137	**0.9217**	0.265
Percent of population in poverty (1999)	−0.009	−0.054	**−0.8844**	0.089
Households with internet access (2000)	−0.079	0.179	**0.8838**	0.066
Percent of families in poverty (1999)	0.002	−0.035	**−0.8673**	0.110
Percentage of population with bachelors	0.024	0.044	**0.8609**	0.228
Households with computers (2000)	−0.054	0.121	**0.8393**	−0.008
personal income per capita (1999)	0.107	−0.034	**0.8253**	0.357
Households with internet access (1998)	−0.003	0.234	**0.8206**	0.082
Gross state product per capita (2000)	0.046	0.059	**0.7994**	0.317
Households with computers (1998)	−0.011	0.136	**0.7784**	−0.013
Population 25 to 34 with bachelor's degree	0.114	−0.043	**0.7734**	0.231
Population with complete high school	−0.080	−0.026	**0.7275**	−0.291
Population—less than 9th grade education	0.104	−0.015	**−0.6457**	0.359
Local government private earnings (2000)	0.460	−0.025	0.094	**0.9910**
Government and GE private earnings (2000)	0.472	0.006	0.097	**0.9903**
State government private earnings (2000)	0.509	0.002	0.092	**0.9895**
Government gross state product (2000)	0.475	0.006	0.087	**0.9877**
Number of local government jobs (2000)	0.483	−0.045	0.044	**0.9864**
Engineering and management jobs (2000)	0.441	−0.018	0.150	**0.9839**
State total revenue (2000)	0.465	−0.008	0.105	**0.9838**
Government and GE jobs (2000)	0.492	−0.011	0.042	**0.9828**
Engineering and management private earnings (2000)	0.425	−0.030	0.191	**0.9778**
Number of state government jobs (2000)	0.537	0.008	0.018	**0.9643**
Jobs in the communications industry (2000)	0.417	−0.054	0.103	**0.9554**
Communication industry private earnings (2000)	0.366	−0.049	0.167	**0.9366**
Number of educational services jobs (2000)	0.474	−0.080	0.195	**0.9341**
Electronic and electric equip. jobs (2000)	0.392	0.058	0.089	**0.9201**
Electronic and EE private earnings (2000)	0.316	0.088	0.110	**0.8888**
Educational services private earnings (2000)	0.443	−0.107	0.217	**0.8790**
Total state debt (2000)	0.422	−0.070	0.246	**0.8586**

* Indicator names were truncated to accommodate to this format. Complete indicator names are available in Tables A.5, A.6 and A.7

Table A.10 Reflective construct correlations and square root of AVE for the refined model

	Government-wide website functionality	Voting preferences	Demographic factors	Overall size of the economy
Government-wide website functionality	0.771			
Voting preferences	−0.146	0.850		
Demographic factors	0.028	0.087	0.831	
Overall size of the economy	0.472	−0.024	0.111	0.954

Table A.11 Indicators loadings and cross loadings for the refined model

Indicator in reflective construct*	Government-wide website functionality	Voting preferences	Demographic factors	Overall size of the economy
Overall quality of e-government services	**0.8309**	−0.163	0.081	0.485
Number of online services	**0.8276**	−0.103	−0.094	0.438
Number of e-commerce systems	**0.7121**	−0.040	−0.053	0.362
Quality of e-commerce	**0.7031**	−0.137	0.173	0.176
Governor was democrat in 2000	−0.126	**0.9052**	0.051	−0.006
Governor was republican in 2000	0.068	**−0.8635**	−0.090	0.039
Percentage of votes for democratic party	−0.224	**0.8320**	0.031	−0.003
Percentage of votes for republican party	0.030	**−0.7952**	−0.147	0.044
Median income per family (1999)	0.111	0.105	**0.9240**	0.223
Median income per household (1999)	0.116	0.139	**0.9137**	0.265
Households with internet access (2000)	−0.080	0.183	**0.8912**	0.067
Percent of population in poverty (1999)	−0.007	−0.058	**−0.8863**	0.089
Percent of families in poverty (1999)	0.003	−0.039	**−0.8712**	0.110
Percentage of population with bachelors	0.024	0.045	**0.8618**	0.228
Households with computers (2000)	−0.054	0.126	**0.8509**	−0.007
Households with internet access (1998)	−0.004	0.239	**0.8306**	0.082
Personal income per capita (1999)	0.107	−0.032	**0.8107**	0.356
Households with computers (1998)	−0.012	0.140	**0.7942**	−0.012
Gross state product per capita (2000)	0.045	0.061	**0.7842**	0.316
Population 25 to 34 with bachelor's degree	0.114	−0.043	**0.7672**	0.230
Population with complete high school	−0.081	−0.020	**0.7437**	−0.291
Population—less than 9th grade education	0.105	−0.019	**−0.6596**	0.360
Local government private earnings (2000)	0.460	−0.026	0.082	**0.9909**
Government and GE private earnings (2000)	0.472	0.004	0.085	**0.9904**
State government private earnings (2000)	0.509	< 0.001	0.079	**0.9893**
Government gross state product (2000)	0.475	0.004	0.075	**0.9879**
Number of local government jobs (2000)	0.483	−0.047	0.032	**0.9866**
Engineering and management jobs (2000)	0.441	−0.020	0.138	**0.9846**
State total revenue (2000)	0.465	−0.008	0.093	**0.9837**
Government and GE jobs (2000)	0.492	−0.013	0.030	**0.9831**
Engineering and management private earnings (2000)	0.426	−0.032	0.179	**0.9783**

(continued)

Table A.11 (continued)

Indicator in reflective construct*	Government-wide website functionality	Voting preferences	Demographic factors	Overall size of the economy
Number of state government jobs (2000)	0.537	0.005	0.005	**0.9645**
Jobs in the communications industry (2000)	0.417	−0.056	0.091	**0.9554**
Communication industry private earnings (2000)	0.366	−0.050	0.156	**0.9363**
Number of educational services jobs (2000)	0.474	−0.079	0.181	**0.9331**
Electronic and electric equipment jobs (2000)	0.393	0.056	0.079	**0.9217**
Electronic and EE private earnings (2000)	0.316	0.085	0.101	**0.8908**
Educational services private earnings (2000)	0.443	−0.106	0.203	**0.8777**
Total state debt (2000)	0.422	−0.070	0.231	**0.8567**

* Indicator names were truncated to accommodate to this format. Complete indicator names are available in Tables A.5, A.6 and A.7

Hardy and Williams 2008; Lee 1989; Löfgren 2007; Luk 2009; Reidl et al. 2007; Rocheleau 2007; Walsham 1995; Weerakkody et al. 2007; Weerakkody et al. 2009; Yin 2003). The main selection criteria for case studies were the differences in government-wide state website functionality and the relative fit to the PLS statistical model. However, other criteria were also considered in order to have a more robust comparison of the cases. These criteria are described in the following section. Following academic conventions for qualitative approaches, semi-structured interviews were conducted with different actors in each case to understand its specific structure and dynamics (Gil-Garcia 2005a). An analysis of formal documents complemented and contrasted the information obtained through the interviews.

1. Selection of cases

Two states were selected using the results of the PLS statistical analysis. Different alternatives for the selection of the cases were explored. First, the two case studies could have different fitness to the model (one with low residuals and another with high residuals), but similar e-government success outcomes (websites with high functionality). In this scenario, the objective would be to look for new variables that were not included in the original statistical model and might help to explain the quality or functionality of state websites. This alternative would also help to explain some of the causal mechanisms in two very different cases and provide insights about the importance of each variable, as well as the processes and mechanisms that took place and were relevant in each of the cases.

As a second alternative, we could consider two case studies with relatively good fit to the model (low residuals), but different website outcomes (substantial differences in functionality). In this case, the objective of the case studies would mostly be to understand the process of causality in the two cases and to corroborate the causal relationships. Simply put, it would explain why these variables are relevant in

Table A.12 Ranking of states according to website functionality

Rank	State	Functionality
1	Michigan	1.888
2	Washington	1.585
3	Texas	1.524
4	Indiana	1.442
5	Maine	1.260
6	New York	1.233
7	Pennsylvania	1.090
8	Louisiana	1.017
9	Ohio	0.947
10	Florida	0.900

Florida was eliminated from the remaining steps because this state did not provide information to one of our main data sources (NASCIO, 2002); therefore, its residuals are not the results of the complete empirical model.

determining the functionality or quality of government-wide state websites and identifying the mechanisms through which their influence occurs.

This study uses the first alternative to contribute to a better understanding of the relationships among different factors and between these factors and the success of government-wide websites. Future studies could systematically test the new knowledge generated in this research.

The selection process followed the logic of a nested research design. As a first criterion, the functionality of the government-wide state websites was taken into consideration. As mentioned in the statistical analysis chapter, this construct was measured using four different indicators from different sources: West (2001), Lassman (2002), NASCIO (2002), and CSG (2002). Since the only year in which all four measures were available was 2001, that year was used for the statistical analysis. Using PLS-Graph as the analytical software, both measurement and structural parameters were calculated; the states with the highest functionality are presented in Table A.12.

The second criterion was the relative fit to the model as represented by the size of the residuals. Once identified, the high functionality states were divided into two groups: states with high residuals and states with low residuals (see Table A.13). In this research, high residuals are defined as scores of 0.5 or more. As explained before and in accordance with the logic of nested research, we need one state from each of these groups.

Based on the fact that the study only includes high performers, a third criterion was added for one of the two cases: improvement. This criterion was measured as the positive change or number of positions gained in the West ranking from 2000 to 2001, which should offer some interesting insights about how poorly performing states managed to greatly improve in one year. There are three states in this situation: Indiana, Maine, and Louisiana (see Table A.14).

Likewise, the comparability of the states was a decisive factor for the case studies, since the theoretical model should explain differences and similarities in

Table A.13 Groups of states according to website functionality and size of residuals

Low residual states	Residuals	High residual states	Residuals
Texas	0.0307	Maine	1.3676
New York	0.4478	Washington	1.1478
Michigan	0.4726	Louisiana	1.0973
		Indiana	0.9543
		Pennsylvania	0.6369
		Ohio	0.5939

Table A.14 States with great improvement from 2000 to 2001

State	Improvement from 2000
Indiana	+20
Maine	+14
Louisiana	+13

relatively comparable settings. The states' managerial capability was considered more relevant than similar population or geographical area. Therefore, I consulted the Government Performance Project conducted by the Maxwell School of Citizenship and Public Affairs at Syracuse University. This project gives the states report cards on capital management, information technology, financial management, human resources, and managing for results. We looked for pairs of states with similar profiles (average grades).

Different case study selections appear depending on the criteria taken into consideration. Focusing on the functionality and the relative fit to the model only, Washington and Michigan seem to be the best options. Plus, these two states were comparable, since they show similar management capacity according to the Government Performance Project. In contrast, keeping functionality and relative fit, but adding improvement as another important criterion, two new options emerge: Indiana and Texas or Indiana and New York. In order to ensure a good degree of comparability, Indiana and New York were selected as the best alternatives for case studies, since they have more similar management profiles than Indiana and Texas according to the Government Performance Project. Table A.15 shows a summary of the first three alternatives and the criteria that they met.

Taking all four criteria into consideration, Indiana and New York were the best alternatives for the case studies. They have both developed highly functional government-wide websites. From the PLS model, we know that New York has low residuals and Indiana has high residuals. Indiana experienced high improvement from 2000 to 2001, while New York was very stable in this period. According to the Government Performance Project, they have similar management capacities, so they could be considered comparable settings.

Finally, states were selected because there were already interesting integrative frameworks based on local governments (Kraemer et al. 1989) and federal agencies (Fountain 2001c). This study considers some particularities of the state

Table A.15 Summary of alternatives for the case studiescase studies

Criterion	Indiana—New York	Indiana—Texas	Washington—Michigan
Functionality	*	*	*
Relative fit	*	*	*
Improvement	*	*	
Comparability	*		*

level and, therefore, contributes to the development of a more comprehensive and integrative theoretical framework. In addition, Gant and Gant (2002) argue that, "A web portal serves as the integrated gateway into the state government website and provides visitors with a single point of contact for online service delivery within the state." According to this relatively loose definition of a government portal, all states in the US have developed e-government portals or government-wide websites to provide online services to their constituencies. Therefore, statistical and comparative analyses were possible.

2. Data collection procedures

This subsection provides a brief description of the data collection procedures for the qualitative portion of this research. It includes some details on how the semi-structured interviews and the analysis of formal documents were performed.

Semi-structured Interviews. The unit of analysis was the organization, but observations were conducted at the individual level. Some key informants were selected for each case study: people with deep knowledge about the government-wide website, the organization, and the institutional environment in the state. Their knowledge helped the researcher to learn about the technological features of the state website in particular and the characteristics of the organization in general. Interviewees include website developers, vendors, project managers, chief information officers (CIOs), and content owners from other state government agencies.

The cases used a purposive sample representative of the relevant social groups. Using semi-structured interviews, the objective was to obtain enough information about the case to understand the causes and problems related to the success of the government-wide website. Special attention was paid to defining *what* happened and *which* factors they consider most important in each case and *why*. These factors were compared with the ones mentioned in the literature and with the results of the statistical analysis.

After obtaining the authorization of the head of the Office for Technology (OFT) in New York State and the general manager of AccessIndiana, several employees involved in the development and management of the state websites were selected as key informants. An introduction letter was sent to them. This introduction letter explained the objectives of the study and asked them to participate as interviewees.

In New York, most respondents have had long careers in state government and several also have experience in local government and the private sector. Most interviewees also have backgrounds related to information technology management, telecommunications, systems development, technology auditing, or public relations. A total of nine interviews with ten interviewees were held for leaders and managers from the centralized IT organization and four programmatic agencies.

In Indiana, leaders, managers, and developers from the Office of the CIO and Indiana Interactive were interviewed, for a total of four interviews. Most of the respondents have had careers in the private sector or state government. Some also have experience working for non-profit organizations. Most respondents have educational backgrounds related to business management, information technology management, marketing, or systems development.

The original plan was to interview the same number of people in Indiana and New York. However, the gubernatorial election took place in Indiana at the end of 2004 and key people in state agencies were replaced. I was able to interview the former CIO and individuals from Indiana Interactive who were responsible for Indiana's website during the period covered in this study, from about 2000 to 2005. Several interviews conducted by Gant between 2000 and 2001 were used to enrich the information and complement the initial knowledge about AccessIndiana's context and evolution. Two documents resulting from these early interviews were also reviewed and considered for the analysis. They are currently available on the Center for Technology in Government website: (1) a case study (Gant 2003a) and (2) an essay on coordination and communication in collaborative service delivery systems (Gant 2003b).

Analysis of Formal Documents. For the two selected case studies, a document analysis was also conducted. This analysis included official documents such as (1) executive orders, (2) strategic plans and other planning and evaluation documents, (3) statewide policies, (4) the organization mission and objectives, (5) the organization chart, and (6) internal formal rules, among others.

3. Analysis of Qualitative Data

There are many ways to analyze qualitative data (Bennet et al. 2006; Reidl et al. 2007; Soffer and Hadar 2007; Verdegem and Verleye 2009), from completely interpretative techniques to mainly positive analysis. Being a multi-method approach, this study attempts to take advantage of the complementarities of quantitative and qualitative data. Therefore, the qualitative data is mainly used to explain some of the process and causal mechanisms for the variables identified in the quantitative analysis.

First, all interviews were transcribed and placed in a text-processing software. Then the interviews were carefully and systematically reviewed, looking for instances of the constructs and indicators included in the statistical analysis, particularly the ones that were statistically significant. The researcher then compiled all of those instances and analyzed the context in which each one took place, paying special attention to the process and the causal mechanisms between e-government success and each of the independent variables (organizational structures and processes, institutional arrangements, and environmental conditions). Finally, the situations with more empirical evidence were selected to be included in the results of this study and as the explanations for the variables already identified as significant in the PLS analysis. At the end of this appendix, the reader can find an example invitation letter for the interviews and the complete interview protocol.

D. Potential Limitations of the Research Design

As described in Section A, the use of a multi-method approach presents important advantages. This section mentions some of the limitations of this research that are a consequence of the chosen research methods and discusses the ways the study addresses some of these limitations. It also attempts to show how the combination of methods and the use of some strategies helped to partially deal with these limitations. Finally, this section suggests some ideas for future research based on those limitations.

Statistical Analysis. Using quantitative methods is a way to achieve a good level of external validity or generalizability. Researchers can make valid inferences of results obtained from a representative sample to a larger population. Statistical techniques allow for the calculation of numerical coefficients that represent the relationships between dependent and independent variables. In the statistical analysis, the researcher had a limited capacity to assess the validity and reliability of the secondary data due to the lack of detailed definitions of the terms and information about the actual questions that were asked. For this study, previous research and expert judgment were used to ensure face validity and standard measures of indicator and composite reliability were also performed. These procedures contributed to produce valid and reliable results. However, future research should explore potential variations in the results using survey techniques in which items are carefully defined and consistently measured.

One important criticism of e-government research is that academics and experts appear to "do little more than sit at their PCs. Per se, this does not invalidate research but large tranches of data, events, opinions, etc., are inaccessible to such researchers. This might, for example, explain the absence from some research of the human, social, and political elements that more easily become apparent during direct contact with data subjects and settings: on average those who had clearly left their office took a balanced socio-technical perspective on e-government; those who had not generally saw technology as the main change driver" (Heeks and Bailur 2007, p. 257).

Another aspect observed in the literature, due to a shift of focus from technological to managerial and organizational issues, is that qualitative research methods have become increasingly useful. Hence, quantitative methods have lost importance during the past decade. "IS researchers have become more interested in obtaining scientific knowledge in real world settings and thus they attribute more importance to external validity of research findings than to internal validity" (Reidl et al. 2007, p. 3). By systematically combining quantitative and qualitative methods, the present study attempts to avoid some of the limitations and take advantage of the strengths of individual methods and approaches.

In addition, in this study, the resulting coefficients are not calculated from a representative sample, but from the complete population. In fact, as explained before, the objective of PLS is to obtain both measurement and structural coefficients that maximize the predictive power of the model using the available raw data and are not necessarily used to generalize causal relationships to a larger population. PLS path modeling does not have less stringent assumptions about the representativeness of the sample, but could be used for complete populations too (Gil-Garcia 2008; Henseler et al. 2009). A limitation results from the data itself, since only state executive branch organizations are included. The context and organizational culture could be very different from other public organizations. Consequently, the results can be fully extended only to our population of state IT organizations and government-wide websites.

On this same matter, since the environment of public organizations is complex and heterogeneous, a single research effort cannot cover all relevant contextual factors. This study included three important environmental influences and provided evidence of their impact on e-government success, on organizational structures and processes, and on institutional arrangements. From the results presented in this research, it seems clear that certain environmental conditions have interrelationships with other success factors and, therefore, different impacts on e-government success. In order to have a more comprehensive understanding of e-government, other factors such as political competition, demographic composition, or cultural orientation and their interrelationships should be taken into consideration for future studies.

Interviews and case studies. Interviews in particular and case studies in general can provide good qualitative data. They are designed to delve into an environment and to find specific details about each case. They are not designed for generalizing, but to obtain lessons that can be applied to similar realities, which has been called transferability (Bernard 2000). The main limitation of this method is that it does not have high external validity (Niehaves 2010; Reidl et al. 2007; Tseng et al. 2008). However, some scholars have shown that well-developed qualitative techniques can obtain highly valid results (Becker et al. 2009; Brower et al. 2000; Lee 1999; Luk 2009; Shin 2010; Verdegem and Verleye 2009; Walsham 1995; Weerakkody et al. 2009). Two cases were used to enrich this study. The cases were carefully and systematically selected and the interviews were conducted in accordance with academic conventions. However, case studies do not produce generalizable results. In this research they were used to uncover some of the mechanisms by which the effects found in the statistical analysis took place in specific contexts. They produced rich and detailed information about two different realities.

Internal validity is also a potential limitation of the interviews. It is difficult to establish causality with only a few cases and without a clear idea about which variables are important. An experimental design would be necessary to do that. In addition, trust in informants is important because we cannot be sure that interviewees are answering the questions accurately, particularly when dealing with sensitive topics. Self-reporting is a consistently problematic issue in interviews (Bernard 2000). However, in this study we were not asking about health, income, or other sensitive data; therefore, this concern may not have a major impact on the research.

The lessons derived from the cases can be useful not only to explain the statistical results, but also to understand how they play out in different settings in order to develop useful strategies. Additional case studies are needed to better explain the differences and similarities in the technology enactment process in different government settings. In order to have a complete range of possibilities, some of these additional cases should represent situations in which the functionality of the government-wide website is poor.

Analysis of Formal Documents. Document analysis focuses on information from formal documents and records. To some extent, the problem of self-reporting is minimized because written documents do not change their content over time. The limitation of document analysis is that we cannot be sure that people in the organization actually follow the rules or that their actual behavior is similar to what is written in the documents (Bowen 2009; Heeks and Bailur 2007). Another limitation of document analysis is its lack of external validity. Document analysis is often used in case studies and it is difficult to generalize the findings to other organizations. However, document analysis, like interviews, provides deeper insights about one or a few cases and identifies lessons that could be applicable to similar realities (Luk 2009; Niehaves 2010; Weerakkody et al. 2009). In this study, the analysis of formal documents was useful to complement the information obtained during the interviews. It was also useful to triangulate the findings and strengthen the overall results of this research.

Multi-Method Design. Every research project has some advantages and some limitations. This project attempts to emphasize its strengths and to deal with its weaknesses. As mentioned before, the general strategy of the study is to avoid the individual limitations of single research methods and apply a systematic multi-method approach. This study pursues the advantages of both statistical analysis and its external validity and the rich information gathered from case studies. The interviews can provide information that could not be included in the statistical analysis. Similarly, document analysis can provide information that it is almost impossible to collect with other research methods. Through document analysis, the researcher has access to historical information and official documents. It is possible to learn the formal goals, written rules, functions, objectives, hierarchical structure, and other key organizational details.

This study combines these different methods. Using rigorous quantitative methods provides a high level of external validity. However, the overall objective is not only to establish the relationships among the dependent and independent variables, but also to know to what extent, in which situations, and why these relationships were important for e-government success. Case studies with interviews and document analysis were very important for this purpose. Interviews provide the perspectives of self-reported behavior. In contrast, document analysis provides a good sense of the formal rules and functions of the different organizations and relevant sub-units. By using several methods, this study can avoid some of the disadvantages of each single research method and benefit from their complementary strengths and results.

The combination of methods used in this study provides a methodologically strong research design by taking advantage of the strengths of each single method and minimizing their weaknesses. A general assessment of the hypothesized relationships (statistical analysis) and a detailed explanation of their mechanisms and dynamics in real life settings (case studies) are the overall results of this research. Future research should attempt to develop a longitudinal design to clearly explain the evolution and causal relationships between e-government success and some of the variables identified in this study. A quantitative and/or qualitative longitudinal approach would allow a more rigorous assessment of causality and provide generalizable findings on the dynamics and evolution of these complex interrelationships.

Invitation Letter Example

Dear Mr./Ms. (Last Name),

I am an Associate Professor at *Centro de Investigación y Docencia Económicas* interested in government information strategy and management. Currently, I am conducting interviews as part of a research project on the impact of different organizational, institutional, and contextual factors on the characteristics of government-wide state websites.

Early this week I interviewed (Name) as part of this research. He recommended you as someone who should also be interviewed about this topic. I am writing to request an hour of your time sometime in the next few weeks to participate in an interview about the (state) web site. The interview topics include historical development of the state web site, policies, management strategies and organizational resources. Your experience, opinions, and perceptions will make an important contribution to this research. You can be sure that I will keep all information confidential and nothing will be attributed to you without your permission.

If you are willing to be interviewed, please let me know when would be a good time for an appointment. Thank you for considering this request. I look forward to talking with you.

Sincerely,
Dr. J. Ramon Gil-Garcia, MPA
Associate Professor, Public Administration Department
Director, Data Center for Applied Research in Social Sciences
Centro de Investigación y Docencia Económicas (CIDE)
Carretera México-Toluca No. 3655, Col. Lomas de Santa Fe,
C.P. 01210, México, D.F., MEXICO
Tel.: +52 55 5727-9800 Ext. 2311
E-mail: joseramon.gil@cide.edu
www.cide.edu

J. R. Gil-Garcia, *Enacting Electronic Government Success*,
Integrated Series in Information Systems 31, DOI: 10.1007/978-1-4614-2015-6,

Interview Protocol Example

ENACTING ELECTRONIC GOVERNMENT SUCCESS
Principal Investigator: J. Ramon Gil-Garcia, Centro de Investigación y Docencia Económicas (CIDE)

INTERVIEW PROTOCOL

Introduction

Good morning, my name is Ramon Gil-Garcia. I am an Associate Professor at Centro de Investigación y Docencia Económicas (CIDE), and these interviews constitute an important component of a research project. This research attempts to understand how different factors affect the quality or functionality of state websites.

I would like to thank you again for accepting this interview and for allowing me to talk to other people at (name of the IT organization). This research will greatly benefit from your experiences and opinions about the (name of the state) website.

(The consent form will or has been provided to the interviewee.) Before we begin the interview, I need to make sure you have had a chance to read this consent form. (Hand interviewee form).

The purpose of this form is to inform you about your rights as a research participant. You can be sure that I will keep all information confidential and nothing you say will be attributed to you without your permission (Allow time for reading.)

Do you have any questions? (Answer any that are asked.) I'll take one copy, and you keep a copy for yourself.

If this is OK with you, I will place the tape recorder and the microphone in a suitable place. Taping is very important because it gives me much more accurate notes than I can take by hand. As I said in my email, the interview will last about 1 hour.

J. R. Gil-Garcia, *Enacting Electronic Government Success*,
Integrated Series in Information Systems 31, DOI: 10.1007/978-1-4614-2015-6,

Interview Questions

Let's take the first 5 minutes to talk about your job: Please, can you give me a brief description of your job title and major responsibilities?	
Prompts	Your role in the website management/development/use Your formal education Your professional background

Now, I would like to turn your attention into the state website. Historically, what is the origin and evolution of the state website?	
Prompts	How was it started? How has it evolved? Costs logistical problems

Please, could you talk to me about the mission and goals of the state website?	
Prompts	provision of services management improvement political image

Please, could you describe the main characteristics of the state web site such as the services it offers, technical features and so on?	
Prompts	technical features, services provided customers, audiences, user-satisfaction management strategy

Was the initial design of the website affected by the governor's policy agenda? If so, how?	
Prompts	governor's initiative examples of other political factors were legislators involved

Similarly, how have state laws and regulations shaped the development of the state website? What about the effect of any federal laws?	
Prompts	technical characteristics privacy accessibility usability

What are some of the most important policies governing the web site?

Prompts	security, privacy technical standards data ownership content management

Could you describe how the website is managed? Who does what, how are decisions made, how are vendors used, etc.?

Prompts	Participation of different actors Decisions about content, REVIEW AND APPROVAL STEPS Key people or organizations, how do they participate? Outsourcing, how much? What kind of work? How is the decision to include something in the website made?

Please, could you describe a normal day in YOUR OFFICE/this unit in relation to the state website?

Prompts	management, use, development

What do you think are the most difficult challenges in managing the website? Why?

Prompts	people organizational problems regulatory constraints resources: IT Personnel, Equipment, Software, Budget

What do you think are the most important benefits from the web site? Why?

Prompts	for people for private sector for the state government other stakeholders

Finally, please think about how state government as a whole uses web sites. I would like to ask you to rate the following factors according to their importance in shaping the characteristics of the state websites (allow time for filling).
Please, could you tell me why these factors are the most important?

Do you have any comments that you would like to add to this interview?

Are there any reports or evaluations or other documents about the state web site that you can share with me or that I can look for on the web?

Is there anyone else you think I should be talking to?

Someone who could add another important perspective on these topic?

Should I contact them directly and can I mention that you recommended that I talk to them?

End/Thanks

Thank you very much for your time.
I may need to contact you again for clarification. Would this be OK with you?
Would you like me to send you a summary of the results when they are ready?

References

6, P (2001) E-governance. Do digital aids make a difference in policy making? In: Prins JEJ (ed) Designing e-government. On the crossroads of technological innovation and institutional change. Kluwer Law International, The Hague, Netherlands, pp 7–27
Abdel-Hamid TK, Madnick SE (1990) The elusive silver lining: how we fail to learn from software development failures. Sloan Manag Rev 32:39–48
Abuali A, Alawneh A, Mohammad H (2010) Factors and rules effecting in e-government. Eur J Sci Res 39(2):169–175
Ahn MJ (2011) Adoption of e-communication applications in U.S. municipalities: the role of political environment, bureaucratic structure, and the nature of applications. Am Rev Public Adm. doi:10.1177/0275074010377654
Ahn MJ, Bretschneider S (2011) Politics of e-government: e-government and the political control of bureaucracy. Public Adm Rev 71(3):414–424
Åkesson M, Edvardsson B (2008) Effects of e-government on service design as perceived by employees. Manag Serv Qual 18(5):457–478
Al-Busaidy M, Weerakkody V (2011) E-government services in Oman: an employee's perspective. Electron Gov Int J 8(2/3):185–207
Al Nagia E, Hamdan M (2009) Computerization and e-government implementation in Jordan: challenges, obstacles and successes. Gov Inf Q 26(4):577–583
Aldrich HE (1979) Organizations and environments. Prentice Hall, Englewood Cliffs
Alshawi S, Alalwany H (2009) E-government evaluation: citizen's perspective in developing countries. Inf Technol Dev 15(3):193–208
Alter S (2010) Integrating sociotechnical and technical views of e-services. e-Service J 7(1):15–42
Alvarez MR, Hall TE (2004) Point, click, and vote: the future of internet voting. Brookings Institution Press, Washington
Ambite JL, Arens Y, Bourne W, Feiner S, Gravano L, Hatzivassiloglou V et al (2002) Data integration and access. In: McIver WJ, Elmagarmid AK (eds) Advances in digital government. Technology, human factors, and policy. Kluwer Academic Publishers, Norwell, pp 85–106
Amenta E, Ramsey KM (2010) Institutional theory. In: Leicht KT, Jenkins JC (eds) Handbook of politics: state and society in global perspective. Springer, New York, pp 15–39
Amoretti F (2007) International organizations ICTs policies: e-democracy and e-government for political development. Rev Policy Res 24(4):331–344
Ancarani A (2005) Towards quality e-service in the public sector: the evolution of web sites in the local public service sector. Manag Serv Qual 15(1):6–23
Andersen DF, Belardo S, Dawes SS (1994) Strategic information management: conceptual frameworks for the public sector. Public Prod Manag Rev 17:335–353 (Summer)

J. R. Gil-Garcia, *Enacting Electronic Government Success*,
Integrated Series in Information Systems 31, DOI: 10.1007/978-1-4614-2015-6,

Andersen DF, Dawes SS (1991) Government information management. A primer and casebook. Prentice Hall, Englewood Cliffs
Andersen KN, Henriksen HZ, Medaglia R, Danziger JN, Sannarnes MK, Enemærke M (2010) Fads and facts of e-government: a review of impacts of e-government (2003–2009). Int J Public Adm 33(11):564–579
Andersen KV (2006) E-Government: five key challenges for management. Electron J e-Gov 4(1):1–8
Andersen KV, Henriksen HZ (2006) E-government maturity models: extension of the Layne and Lee model. Gov Inf Q 23(2):236–248
Anderson PT (2009) Strategic organization development: an invitation to the table. In: Yaeger TF, Sorensen PF (eds) Strategic organization development: managing change for success. Information Age Publishing, Charlotte, pp 97–114
Angelopoulos S, Kitsios F, Kofakis P, Papadopoulos T (2010) Emerging barriers in e-government implementation. In: Wimmer MA, Chappelet J-L, Janssen M, Scholl HJ (eds) Electronic government (Proceedings of the 9th IFIP WG 8.5 international conference, EGOV 2010). Springer, Berlin
Angelopoulos S, Kitsios F, Papadopoulos T (2010b) New service development in e-government: identifying critical success factors. Transform Gov People Process Policy 4(1):95–118
Apostolou D, Mentzas G, Stojanovic L, Thoenssen B, Lobo TP (2011) A collaborative decision framework for managing changes in e-government services. Gov Inf Q 28(1):101–116
Ashurst C, Doherty NF, Peppard J (2008) Improving the impact of IT development projects: the benefits realization capability model. Eur J Inf Syst 17:352–370
ASPA (2001) American Society for Public Administration Home Page. www.aspanet.org. Retrieved from 12 May 2002
Assar S, Boughzala I, Boydens I (2011) Back to practice, a decade of research in e-government. In: Assar S, Boughzala I, Boydens I (eds) Practical studies in e-government: best practices from around the world. Springer, New York, pp 1–12
Azad B, Faraj S (2008) Making e-government systems workable: exploring the evolution of frames. J Strateg Inf Syst 17(2):75–98
Badri MA, Alshare K (2008) A path analytic model and measurement of the business value of e-government: an international perspective. Int J Inf Manag 28(6):524–535
Baer M, Leenders RTAJ, Oldham GR, Vadera AK (2010) Win or lose the battle for creativity: the power and perils of intergroup competition. Acad Manag J 53(4):827–845
Baker DL (2009) Advancing e-government performance in the United States through enhanced usability benchmarks. Gov Inf Q 26(1):82–88
Ballou DP, Tayi GK (1999) Enhancing data quality in data warehouse environments. Commun ACM 42(1):73–79
Bandyopadhyay A, Sattarzadeh SD (2010) A challenging e-journey along the silk road: lessons learnes from e-governments in China and India. In: Reddick CG (ed) Comparative e-government. Springer, New York, pp 116–138
Banerjee U (1984) Information management in government. Prometheus Books, NY
Bannister F (2007) The curse of the benchmark: an assessment of the validity and value of e-government comparisons. Int Rev Adm Sci 73(2):171–188
Bannister F, Connolly R (2011) The trouble with transparency: a critical review of openness in e-government. Policy Internet 3(1)
Baqir MN, Iyer L (2010) E-government maturity over 10 years: a comparative analysis of e-government maturity in select countries around the world. In: Reddick CG (ed) Comparative e-government. Springer, New York, pp 3–22
Barclay D, Thompson R, Higgins C (1995) The partial least squares (PLS) approach to causal modeling: personal computer adoption and use as an illustration. Technol Stud 2(2):285–309
Barki H, Rivard S, Talbot J (1993) Toward an assessment of software development risk. J Manag Inf Syst 10:203–223
Barley SR (1990) The alignment of technology and structure through roles and networks. Adm Sci Q 35(1):61–103

Barrett K, Greene R (2000) Powering up: how public managers can take control of information technology. Congressional Quarterly Press, Washington

Barroso C, Cepeda CG, Roldán JL (2010) Applying maximum likelihood and PLS on differente sample sizes: studies on SERVQUAL model and employee behavior model. In: Esposito VV, Chin WW, Henseler J, Wang H (eds) Handbook of partial least squares: concepts, methods, and applications. Springer, Heidelberg, pp 427–447

Bartis E, Mitev N (2008) A multiple narrative approach to information systems failure: a successful system that failed. Eur J Inf Syst 17:112–124

Barzilai-Nahon K, Scholl HJ (2010) Siblings of a different kind: e-government and e-commerce. In: Wimmer MA, Chappelet J-L, Janssen M, Scholl HJ (eds) Electronic government (Proceedings of the 9th IFIP WG 8.5 international conference, EGOV 2010). Springer, Berlin, pp 25–37

Batini C, Viscusi G, Cherubini D (2009) Gov qual: a quality driven methodology for e-government project planning. Gov Inf Q 26(1):106–117

Battilana J, Leca B, Boxenbaum E (2009) How actors change institutions: towards a theory of institutional entrepreneurship. Acad Manag Ann 3:65–107

Baumgarten J, Chui M (2009) E-government 2.0. McKinsey Gov 4:26–31

Baxter G, Sommerville I (2011) Socio-technical systems: from design methods to systems engineering. Interact Comput 23(1):4–17

Becker J, Niehaves B, Krause A (2009) Shared service center vs. shared service network: a multiple case study analysis of factors impacting on shared service configurations. In: Wimmer MA (ed) EGOV 2009. Springer, Berlin, pp 115–126

Bekkers VJJM, Homburg VMF (2005) The information ecology of e-government. IOS Press, Amsterdam

Bélanger F, Carter L (2009) The impact of the digital divide on e-government use. Commun ACM 52(4):132–135

Bellamy C (2000) The politics of public information systems. In: Garson GD (ed) Handbook of public information systems. Marcel Dekker, New York, pp 85–98

Bellamy C, Taylor JA (1996) New information and communication technologies and institutional change. The case of the UK criminal justice system. Int J Public Sect 9(4):51–69

Benjamin RI, Rockart JF, Morton MSS, Wyman J (1984) Information technology: a strategic opportunity. Sloan Manag Rev 25(3):3–10

Bennet A (2002) Where the model frequently meets the road: combining statistical, formal, and case study methods. Paper presented at the American political science association conference, Boston, MA

Bennet TJ, Brower RS, Mason RM (2006) Organizational fields and the diffusion of information technologies within and across the nonprofit and public sectors. A preliminary theory. Am Rev Public Adm 36(4):437–454

Bentler PM (1985) Theory and implementation of EQSEQS: a structural equations program. BMDP Statistical Software, Los Angeles

Berger PL, Luckmann T (1966) The social construction of reality: a treatise in the sociology of knowledge. Anchor Books, New York

Berleur J, Nurminen MI, Impagliazzo J (eds) (2006) Social informatics: An information society for all? In remembrance of Rob Kling. Springer, Berlin

Berlin S, Raz T, Glezer C, Zviran M (2009) Comparison of estimation methods of cost and duration in IT projects. Inf SoftwTechnol 51(4):738–748

Bernard R (2000) Social research methods: qualitative and quantitative approaches. Sage Publications, Newbury Park

Bertot JC, Jaeger PT (2006) User-centered e-government: challenges and benefits for government web sites. Gov Inf Q 23(2):163–168

Bertot JC, Jaeger PT, Grimes JM (2010) Using ICTs to create a culture of transparency: e-government and social media as openness and anti-corruption tools for societies. Gov Inf Q 27(3):264–271

Bertot JC, Jaeger PT, McClure CR (2008) Citizen-centered e-government services: benefits, costs, and research needs. Paper presented at the international conference on digital government research (dg.o)
Best JD (1997) The ditigal organization. Wiley, New York
Bijker WE, Hughes TP, Pinch TJ (eds) (1987) The social construction of technological systems: new directions in the sociology and history of technology. MIT Press, Cambridge
Bijker WE, Law J (2000) Shaping technology/building society. Studies in sociotechnical change. The MIT Press, Cambridge
Bissessar AM (2010) The challenge of e-governance in a small, developing society: the case of Trinidad and Tobago. In: Reddick CG (ed) Comparative E-Government. Springer, New York, pp 313–329
Bloomfield BP, Hayes N (2009) Power and organizational transformation through technology: hybrids of electronic government. Organiz Stud 30(5):461–487
Blumer H (1962) Society as social interaction. In: Rose AM (ed) Human behavior and social processes: an interactionist approach. Houghton Mifflin, Boston, pp 179–192
Boland RJ (1985) Phenomenology: a preferred approach to research on information systems. In: Mumford E, Hirschheim R, Fitzgerald G, Wood-Harper T (eds) Research methods in information systems. Elsevier Science Publishers, Amsterdam
Bollen KA (1989) Structural equations with latent variables. Wiley, New York
Bostrom RP, Gupta S, Thomas D (2009) A meta-theory for understanding information systems within sociotechnical systems. J Manag Inf Syst 26(1):17–48
Bostrom RP, Heinen SJ (1977) MIS problems and failures: a socio-technical perspective. Part II: the application of socio-technical theory. MIS Q 1(4):11–28
Bourquard JA (2003) What's up with e-government?. http://www.ncsl.org/programs/pubs/slmag/2003/303egov.htm. Retrieved from 6 April 2005
Bowen G (2009) Document analysis as a qualitative research method. Qual Res J 9(2):27–40
Bozeman B, Bretschneider S (1986) Public management information systems: theory and prescriptions. Public Adm Rev 46:475–487
Brainard LA, McNutt JG (2010) Virtual government-citizen relations: informational, transactional, or collaborative? Adm Soc 42(7):836–858
Brandt L, Gregg V (2010) History of digital government research in the United States. In: Chen H-G, Brandt L, Gregg V, Traunmüller R, Dawes S, Hovy E, Macintosh A, Larson CA (eds) Digital government: e-government research, case studies, and implementation. Springer, New York, pp 203–218
Brannen J (2005) Mixing methods: the entry of qualitative and quantitative approaches into the research process. Int J Soc Res Method 8(3):173–184
Bretschneider S (2003) Information technology, e-government and institutional change. Public Adm Rev 63(6):738–741
Brewer J, Hunter A (1989) Multimethod research. A synthesis of styles. SAGE Publications, Newbury Park
Brinton MC, Nee V (1998) The new institutionalism in sociology. Stanford University Press, Stanford
Brower RS, Abolafia MY, Carr JB (2000) On improving qualitative methods in public administration research. Adm Soc 32(4):363–397
Brown MM (2000) Mitigating the risk of information technology initiatives: best practices and points of failure for the public sector. In: Garson GD (ed) Handbook of public information systems. Marcel Dekker, New York, pp 153–163
Brown MM, Brudney JL (2004) Achieving advanced electronic government services: opposing environmental constraints. Public Perform Manag Rev 28(1):96–114
Bryson JM, Berry FS, Yang K (2010) The state of public strategic management research: a selective literature review and set of future directions. Am Rev Public Adm 40(5):495–521
Burbridge L (2002) Accountability and MIS. Public Perform Manag Rev 25(4):421–423
Burke WW (2011) Organization change: theory and practice, 3rd edn. Sage, Thousand Oaks

Butler T (2003) An institutional perspective on developing and implementing intranet- and internet-based information systems. Inf Syst J 13(3):209–232

Bwalya KJ, Healy M (2010) Harnessing e-government adoption in the SADC region: a conceptual underpinning. Electron J e-Gov 8(1):23–32

Byrne MB (2001) Structural equation modeling with AMOS: basic concepts, applications and programming. Lawrence Earlbaum Associates, New Jersey

Caffrey L (1998) Information sharing between and within governments. Commonwealth Secretariat, London

Campbell J, McDonald C, Sethibe T (2009) Public and private sector IT governance: identifying contextual differences. Australasian J Inf Syst 16(2):5–18

Carbo T, Williams JG (2004) Models and metrics for evaluating local electronic government systems and services. Electron J e-Gov 2(2):95–104

Carr D (2010) Time and technology: addressing changing demands. In: Shea CM, Garson GD (eds) Handbook of public information systems. CRC Press, Boca Ranton, pp 261–272

Carroll JM, Rowlands B, Standing C, Frampton K, Smith R (2006) A Framework for redesigning information systems development methodologies to enhance global information infrastructure. Paper presented at the European and mediterranean conference on informations systesm (EMCIS)

Carter L, McBride A (2010) Information privacy concerns and e-government: a research agenda. Transform Gov People Process Policy 4(1):10–13

Carugati A, Morelli C, Giangreco A (2010) Socio-materiality as lens to study IT driven change. In: D'Atri A, Saccà D (eds) Information systems: people, organizations, institutions, and technologies. Physica Verlag, Berlin

Caves RW, Walshok MG (1999) Adopting innovations in information technology. The California municipal experience. Cities 16(1):3–12

CEG (2001) e-Government. The next American revolution. The Council for Excellence in Government, Washington

Cicourel AV (1964) Method and measurement in sociology. Free Press, New York

Cicourel AV (1974) Cognitive sociology. Free Press, New York

Clegg S (2010) The state power and agency: missing in action in institutional theory. J Manag Inquiry March 19(1):4–13

Clegg S, Dunkerley D (1980) Organization, class, and control. Routledge, London

Coakes E (ed) (2011) Knowledge development and social change through technology: emerging studies. IGI Global, Hershey

Collier D, Seawright J, Brady HE (2003) Qualitative versus quantitative: What might this distinction mean? Qual Methods Newsletter Am Political Sci Assoc Organ Sect Qual Methods 1(1):4–7

Collins HM (1987) Expert Systems and the science of knowledge. In: Bijker WE, Hughes TP, Pinch T (eds) The social construction of technological systems. The MIT Press, Cambridge

Contractor NS, Monge PR, Leonardi PM (2011) Multidimensional networks and the dynamics of sociomateriality: bringing technology inside the network. Int J Commun 5:682–720

Cook M, Dawes SS, Juraga D, Werthmuller DR, Pagano CM, Schwartz BF (2004) Bridging the enterprise: lessons from the New York state-local internet gateway prototype. Center for Technology in Government, University at Albany, SUNY, Albany

Cook M, LaVigne M (2002). Making the local e-gov connection. www.urbanicity.org/FullDoc.asp?ID=36. Retrieved from 24 May 2002

Cook ME, LaVigne MF, Pagano CM, Dawes SS, Pardo TA (2002) Making a case for local e-government. Center for Technology in Government, Albany

Coppedge M (2001) Explaining democratic deterioration in Venezuela through nested induction. Paper presented at the annual meeting of the American political science association, San Francisco, 2–5 Sept 2001

Cordella A (2007) E-government: towards the e-bureaucratic form? J Inf Technol 22(3):265–274

Cordella A, Iannacci F (2010) Information systems in the public sector: the e-government enactment framework. J Strateg Inf Syst 19(1):52–66
Corradini F, Falcioni D, Polini A, Polzonetti A, Re B (2010) Designing quality business processes for e-government digital services. In: Wimmer MA, Chappelet J-L, Janssen M, Scholl HJ (eds) Electronic government (Proceedings of the 9th IFIP WG 8.5 international conference, EGOV 2010). Springer, Berlin, pp 424–435
Council AC (2008) Audti report 2008: city of Austin's e-government initiative. Office od the City Auditor, Austin
Cresswell AM, Connelly D (1999) Reconnaissance study. Developing a business case for the integration of criminal justice information. Center for Technology in Government, Albany
Cresswell AM, Pardo TA (2001) Implications of legal and organizational issues for urban digital government development. Gov Inf Q 18:269–278
Cresswell AM, Pardo TA, Thompson F, Canestraro DS, Cook M, Black L et al. (2002) Modeling intergovernmental collaboration: a system dynamics approach. In: Proceedings of the 35th Hawaiian international conference on system sciences. IEEE Computer Society Press, Los Alamitos, CA
Cresswell AM, Pardo TA, Thompson F, Zhang J (2002) Trust and networking: knowledge sharing in the public sector. Paper presented at the academy of management conference
Cresswell JW (2003) Research design. Qualitative, quantitative, and mixed methods approaches. SAGE Publications, Thousand Oaks
Cresswell JW (2009) Research design. Qualitative, quantitative, and mixed methods approaches. Sage Publications, Thousand Oaks
Cresswell JW, Tashakkori A (2007) Editorial: developing publishable mixed methods manuscripts. J Mixed Methods Res 1(2):107–111
Criado JI (2009) Gobierno Electrónico en Latinoamerica. Aproximación desde una Perspectiva Intergubernamental. Estado, Gobierno y Gestión Pública. Revista Chilena de Administración Pública 14
Criado JI (2010) The politics of e-government in Spain: between recent innovations and old inertias. In: Reddick CG (ed) Comparative e-government. Springer, New York, pp 275–297
Criado JI, Ramillo MC (2003) e-Government in practice. An analysis of web site orientation to the citizens in Spanish municipalities. Int J Public Sect Manag 16(3):191–218
CSG (2002) The book of the states, 2002 edn, vol 34. The Council of State Governments, Lexington, KY
Cunliffe A (2010) Retelling tales of the field: in search of organizational ethnography 20 years on. Organ Res Methods 13(2):224–239
Cunningham M (1999) It's all about business needs. Doc World 4(5):34
Currie W (2009) Contextualising the IT artefact: towards a wider research agenda for IS using institutional theory. Inf Technol People 22(1):63–77
Chadwick A (2003) Bringing e-democracy back in: why it matters for future research on e-governance. Soc Sci Comput Rev 21(4):443–455
Chadwick A, May C (2003) Interaction between states and citizens in the age of internet:" e-government" in the United States, Britain and the European Union. Gov Int J Policy Adm 16(2):271–300
Chan CML, Lau Y, Pan SL (2008) E-government implementation: a macro analysis of Singapore's e-government initiatives. Gov Inf Q 25(2):239–255
Chang A-M, Kannan PK (2008) Leveraging web 2.0 in government. IBM Center for the Business of Government, Washington
Chang S, Gable G, Smythe E, Timbrell G (2001) A Delphi examination of public sector ERP implementation issues. Paper presented at the international computer information systems conference, Brisbane, Australia

Charalabidis Y, Lampathaki F, Askounis D (2010) Emerging interoperability directions in electronic government. In: Popplewell K, Harding J, Poler R, Chalmeta R (eds) Enterprise Interoperability IV: making the internet of the future for the future of enterprise. Springer, London, pp 419–428

Chen T, Zhang J, Lai K-K (2009) An integrated real options evaluating model for information technology projects under multiple risks. Int J Project Manag 27(8):776–786

Chen Y-C (2010) Citizen-centric e-government services: understanding integrated citizen service information systems. Soc Sci Comput Rev 28(4):427–442

Chen Y-C, Hsieh J-Y (2009) Advancing e-governance: comparing Taiwan and the United States. Public Adm Rev 69(S1):S151–S158

Chen Y-C, Thurmaier K (2008) Advancing e-government: financing challenges and opportunities. Public Adm Rev 68(3):537–548

Chengalur-Smith I, Duchessi P (1999) The initiation and adoption of client-server technology in organizations. Inf Manag 35:77–88

Chin WW (1998) The partial least squares approach for structural equation modeling. In: Marcoulides GA (ed) Modern methods for business research. Lawrence Erlbaum Associates, Mahwah

Chin WW, Newsted PR (1999) Structural equation modeling analysis with small samples using partial least squares. In: Hoyle RH (ed) Statistical strategies for small sample research. Sage Publications, Thousand Oaks

Chircu AM (2008) E-government evaluation: towards a multidimensional framework. Electron Gov Int J 5(4):345–363

Choudhari RD, Banwet DK, Gupta MP (2011) Assessment of risk in e-governance projects: an application of product moment correlation and cluster analysis techniques. Electron Gov Int J 8(1):85–102

Choudhury S, Kumar S (2009) E-governance: tool for e-democracy and citizen empowerment in the horizon of information technology era in developing society in India, Nepal and Bangladesh. In: Sahu GP, Dwivedi YK, Weerakkody V (eds) E-government development and diffusion: inhibitors and facilitators of digital democracy. IGI Global, Hershey

Choudrie J, Ghinea G, Weerakkody V (2004) Evaluating global e-government sites: a view using web diagnostic tools. Electron J e-Gov 2(2):105–114

Christensen T, Laeliggreid P (2010) Civil servants' perceptions regarding ICT use in Norwegian central government. J Inf Technol Politics 7(1):3–21

Chun SA, Shulman S, Sandoval R, Hovy E (2010) Government 2.0: making connections between citizens, data and government. Inf Polity 15(1/2):1–9

Chutimaskul W, Funilkul S, Chongsuphajaisiddhi V (2008) The quality framework of e-government development. Paper presented at the 2nd international conference on theory and practice of electronic governance

Chwelos P, Benbasat I, Dexter AS (2001) Research report: empirical test of an EDI adoption model. Inf Syst Res 12(3):304–326

Chwelos P, Ramirez R, Kraemer KL, Melville NP (2010) Does technological progress alter the nature of information technology as a production input? New evidence and new results. Research note. Inf Syst Res 21(2):392–408

Damanpour F, Schneider M (2009) Characteristics of innovation and innovation adoption in public organizations: assessing the role of managers. J Public Adm Res Theory 19(3):495–522

Danziger JN (2004) Innovation in innovation? The technology enactment framework. Soc Sci Comput Rev 22(1):100–110

Danziger JN, Kraemer KL (1985) Computerized data-based systems and productivity among professional workers: the case of detectives. Public Adm Rev 45(1):196–209

Davenport E (2008) Social informatics and sociotechnical research—a view from the UK. J Inf Sci 34(4):519–530

Davenport E, Horton K (2006) Rethinking e-Government Research: The 'ideology-artefact complex. Paper presented at the 6th IFIP international conference on e-commerce, e-business, and e-government (13E 2006), Turku, Finland, 11–13 Oct 2006
Davenport T (1993) Process innovation: reengineering work through information technology. Harvard Business School Press, Boston
Davis FD (1989) Perceived usefulness, perceived ease to use, and user aceptance of information technology. MIS Q 13(3):319–340
Davis GB (1982) Strategies for information requirements determination. IBM Syst J 21:4–30
Davis S, Elin L, Reeher G (2002) Click on democracy: the internet's power to change political apathy into civic action. Westview Press, Cambridge
Davison AC, Hinkley DV (2003) Bootstrap methods and their application, 2nd edn. Cambridge University Press, New York
Dawes SS (2002) Government and technology: user, not regulator. J Public Adm Res Theory 12:627–631
Dawes SS (2010) Introduction to digital government research in public policy and management. In: Chen H-G, Brandt L, Gregg V, Traunmüller R, Dawes S, Hovy E, Macintosh A, Larson CA (eds) Digital government: e-government research, case studies, and implementation. Springer, New York, pp 103–126
Dawes SS, Cresswell AM, Pardo TA (2009) From "need to know" to "need to share": tangled problems, information boundaries, and the building of public sector knowledge networks. Center for Technology in Government, Albany
Dawes SS, Pardo TA (2008) Critical issues and practical challenges of it tools for policy analysis and program evaluation. Center for Technology in Government, Albany
Dawes SS (1996) Interagency information sharing: expected benefits, manageable risks. J Policy Anal Manag 15(3):377–394
Dawes SS (2008) The evolution and continuing challenges of e-governance. Public Adm Rev 68(S1):S86–S102
Dawes SS (2009) Governance in the digital age: a research and action framework for an uncertain future. Gov Inf Q 26(2):257–264
Dawes SS, Helbig N (2010) Information strategies for open government: challenges and prospects for deriving public value from government transparency. In: Wimmer MA, Chappelet J-L, Janssen M, Scholl HJ (eds) Electronic government (Proceeding of the 9th IFIP WG 8.5 international conference, EGOV 2010) Springer, Berlin, pp 50–60
Dawes SS, Nelson MR (1995) Pool the risks, share the benefits: partnership in IT innovation. In: Keyes J (ed) Technology trendlines, technology success stories from today's visionaries. Van Nostrand Reinhold, New York, pp 125–135
Dawes SS, Pardo T, DiCaterino A (1999) Crossing the threshold: practical foundations for government services on the world wide web. J Am Soc Inf Sci 50(4):346–353
Dawes SS, Pardo TA (2002) Building collaborative digital government systems. Systematic constraints and effective practices. In: McIver WJ, Elmagarmid AK (eds) Advances in digital government. Technology, human factors, and policy. Kluwer Academic Publishers, Norwell, pp 259–273
Dawes SS, Pardo TA, Cresswell AM (2004) Designing electronic government information access programs: a holistic approach. Gov Inf Q 21(1):3–23
Dawes SS, Préfontaine L (2003) Understanding new models of collaboration for delivering government services. Commun ACM 46(1):40–42
Dawson P, Daniel L (2010) Understanding social innovation: a provisional framework. Int J Technol Manag 51(1):9–21
De Angelis F, Polzonetti A, Tapanelli P (2010) Policy makers and performance management in e-government domain. Paper presented at the 4th international conference on theory and practice of electronic governance (ICEGOV), Beijing, China
de Bruijn H, Herder PM (2009) System and actor perspectives on sociotechnical systems. IEEE Trans Syst Man Cybern 39(5):981–992

De' R, Sarkar S (2010) Rituals in e-government implementation: an analysis of failure. In: Wimmer MA, Chappelet J-L, Janssen M, Scholl HJ (eds) Electronic government (Proceedings of the 9th IFIP WG 8.5 international conference, EGOV 2010), Springer, Berlin, pp 226–237

Deephouse C, Mukhopadhyay T, Goldenson D, Kellner M (1995) Software processes and project performance. J Manag Inf Syst 12(3):187–205

DeLone W, Mclean E (1992) Information systems success: the quest for the dependent variable. Inf Syst Res 3(1):60–95

DeLone W, Mclean E (2003) The DeLone and McLean model of information systems success: a 10 year update. J Manag Inf Syst 19(4):9–30

Demeester M (1999) Cultural aspects of information technology implementation. Int J Med Informatics 56(1–3):25–41

Denzin NK (ed) (2008) Studies in symbolic interaction. Emerald Group Publishing, Bingley

DeSanctis G, Poole MS (1994) Capturing the complexity in advanced technology use: adaptive structuration theory. Organ Sci 5(2):121–147

DeSanctis G, Poole MS, Zigurs I, DeSharnais G, D'Onofrio M, Gallupe B et al (2010) The Minnesota GDSS research project: group support systems, group processes, and outcomes. J Assoc Inf Syst 9(10/11):551–608

Detlor B, Finn K (2002) Towards a framework for government portal design: the government, citizen and portal perspectives. In: Grönlund Å (ed) Electronic government: design, applications and management. Idea Group Publishing, Hershey

Detlor B, Hupfer ME, Ruhi U (2010) Internal factors affecting the adoption and use of government websites. Electron Gov Int J 7(2):120–136

Detlor B, Hupfer ME, Zhao L, Ruhi U (2009) Successful community municipal portal diffusion: internal government factors and individual perceptions. Paper presented at the Americas conference on information systems (AMCIS)

Dickerson VC (2010) Positioning oneself within an epistemology: refining our thinking about integrative approaches. Fam Process 49(3):349–368

Dimaggio P, Markus HR (2010) Culture and social psychology converging perspectives. Soc Psychol Q 74(4):347–352

dos Santos EM, Reinhard N (forthcoming) Electronic government interoperability: Identifying the barriers for frameworks adoption. Soc Sci Comput Rev. doi:10.1177/0894439310392196

Dover G, Lawrence TB (2010) A gap year for institutional theory: integrating the study of institutional work and participatory action research. J Manag Inquiry 19(4):305–316

Drogkaris P, Gritzalis S, Lambrinoudakis C (2010) Transforming the Greek e-government environment towards the e-gov 2.0 era. In: Andersen KN, Francesconi E, Grönlund Å, van Engers TM (eds) Electronic government and the information systems perspective (Proceedings of the 1st international conference, EGOVIS 2010), Springer, Berlin, pp 142–149

Duchessi P, Chengalur-Smith I (1998) Client/server benefits, problems. Best practices. Commun ACM 41(5):87–94

Duncan GT, Roehrig ST (2003) Mediating the tension between information privacy and information access: the role of digital government. In: Garson GD (ed) Public information technology: policy and management issues. Idea Group Publishing, Hershey, pp 94–119

Dutta A (2008) A new perspective in understanding the role of information technology features in technology use pattern. VIKALPA 33(1):55–68

Eason K (2009) Before the internet: the relevance of socio-technical systems theory to emerging forms of virtual organisation. Int J Sociotechnology Knowl Dev 1(2):23–32

Ebbers WE, Pieterson WJ, Noordman HN (2008) Electronic government: rethinking channel management strategies. Gov Inf Q 25(2):181–201

Ebbers WE, van Dijk JAGM (2007) Resistance and support to electronic government, building a model of innovation. Gov Inf Q 24:554–575

Economides AA, Terzis V (2008) Evaluating tax sites: an evaluation framework and its application. Electron Gov Int J 5(3):321–344

Edmiston KD (2003) State and local e-government: prospects and challenges. Am Rev Public Adm 33(1):20–45
Elliott A (2010) Theories of structuration. In: Elliott A (ed) The Routledge companion to social theory. Routledge, New York, pp 86–101
Eric S, Kraemer KL, Dedrick J (2008) IT diffusion in developing countries. Commun ACM 51(2):43–48
Esposito VV, Chin WW, Henseler J, Wang H (2010a) Perspectives on partial least squares. In: Esposito VV, Chin WW, Henseler J, Wang H (eds) Handbook of partial least squares. Concepts, methods and applications. Springer, Heidelberg, pp 1–22
Esposito VV, Trinchera L, Amato S (2010b) PLS path modeling: from foundations to recent developments and open issues for model assessment and improvement. In: Esposito VV, Chin WW, Henseler J, Wang H (eds) Handbook of partial least squares. Concepts, methods, and applications. Springer, Heidelberg, pp 47–82
Estermann B, Riedl R, Neuroni AC (2009) "Integrated" and "transcendent" e-government: keys for analyzing organizational structure and governance. Paper presented at the 10th annual international conference on digital government research (dg.o)
Esteves J, Joseph RC (2008) A comprehensive framework for the assessment of eGovernment projects. Gov Inf Q 25(1):118–132
Eynon R, Margetts H (2007) Organizational solutions for overcoming barriers to eGovernment. Eur J ePractice 1:73–86
Ezz I, Papazafeiropoulou A, Serrano A (2009) Challenges of interorganizational collaboration for information technology adoption: insights from a governmental financial decision-making process in Egypt. Inf Technol Dev 15(3):209–223
Falk RF, Miller NB (1992) A primer for soft modeling. The University of Akron, Akron
Fasanghari M, Habibipour F (2009) E-government performance evaluation with fuzzy numbers. Paper presented at the international association of computer science and information technology - spring conference (IACSIT-SC)
Fedorowicz J, Gelinas UJ Jr, Gogan JL, Williams CB (2009) Strategic alignment of participant motivations in e-government collaborations: the internet payment platform pilot. Gov Inf Q 26(1):51–59
Fedorowicz J, Gogan JL, Culnan MJ (2010) Barriers to interorganizational information sharing in e-government: a stakeholder analysis. Inf Soc Int J 26(5):315–329
Fedorowicz J, Gogan JL, Williams CB (2007) A collaborative network for first responders: lessons from the CapWIN case. Gov Inf Q 24:785–807
Feldman MS, Orlikowski WJ (forthcoming) Theorizing practice and practicing theory. Organ Sci. doi:10.1287/orsc.1100.0612
Feldman SS, Horan TA (forthcoming) Collaboration in electronic medical evidence development: a case study of the social security administration's MEGAHIT system. Int J Med Informatics
Ferro E, Sorrentino M (2010) Can intermunicipal collaboration help the diffusion of e-government in peripheral areas? Evidence from Italy. Gov Inf Q 27(1):17–25
Finger M (2010) What role for government in e-government? J E-Gov 33(4):197–202
Fleming ED, Kuo C-C, White RE (2010) Funding e-procurement initiatives in US government agencies: challenges, models, and trends. Int J Procure Manag 3(3):231–246
Fletcher PD (2002) The government paperwork elimination act: operating instructions for an electronic government. Int J Public Adm 25(5):723–736
Fletcher PD (2004) Portals and policy: implications of electronic access to U.S. federal government information and services. In: Pavlichev A, Garson GD (eds) Digital government: principles and best practices. Idea Group Publishing, Hershey, pp 52–62
Fletcher PT, Bretschneider SI, Marchland DA, Rosenbaum H, Berto JC (1992) Managing information technology: transforming county governments in the 1990s. School of Information Studies, Syracuse University, Syracuse
Fornell C (1982) A second generation of multivariate analysis: methods, vol 1. Praeger, New York, NY

Fornell C, Bookstein FL (1982) Two structural equation models: LISREL and PLS applied to consumer exit-voice theory. J Mark Res 19(4):440–452
Fornell C, Larcker DF (1981) Evaluating structural equation models with unobservable variables and measurement error. J Mark Res 18:39–50
Fortin DR, Westin S, Mundorf N (1997) On the predispositions toward information technology: a three-way cross-cultural study. Telematics Inform 14(2):145–157
Foteinou G-B, Pavlidis G (2010) E-government: from actors to interrelations. Int J Electron Gov 3(3):319–331
Fountain JE (1995) Enacting technology: an institutional perspective. John F. Kennedy School of Government, Harvard University, Cambridge
Fountain JE (1999) The virtual state: toward a theory of federal bureaucracy in the 21st century. In: Kamarck EC, Nye JSJ (eds) Democracy.com? Governance in a networked world. Hollis Publishing, Hollis
Fountain JE (2001a) Building the virtual state. Information technology and institutional change. Brookings Institution Press, Washington
Fountain JE (2001b) Public sector: early stage of a deep transformation. In: Litan R, Rivlin A (eds) The economic payoff from the internet revolution. Brookings Institution Press, Washington
Fountain JE (2001c) Toward a theory of federal bureaucracy in the 21st century. In: Kamarck EC, Nye JSJ (eds) Governance.com: democracy in the information age. Brookings Institution Press, Washington
Fountain JE (2005) Central issues in the political development of the virtual state. Paper presented at the network society and the knowledge economy: Portugal in the global context
Fountain JE (2008) Bureaucratic reform and e-government in the United States: an institutional perspective national center for digital government
Fountain JE (2009) Bureaucratic reform and e-government in the United States: an institutional perspective. In: Chadwick A, Howard PN (eds) Routledge handbook of internet politics. Taylor & Francis Group, New York, pp 99–113
Fountain JE, Gil-Garcia JR (2006a) Comparing integrative models of technology and structure in government. Paper presented at the 2006 APPAM fall conference "tax and spend: designing, implementing, managing and evaluating effective redistributional policies", Madison, WI, 2–4 Nov 2006
Fountain JE, Gil-Garcia JR (2006b) Technology enactment theory: understanding the role of power, bureaucracy, and institutions in government information technology initiatives [POSTER]. Paper presented at the 2006 APSA annual meeting, Philadelphia, PA, 31 Aug–3 Sept 2006
Fourie I (2010) Social and political implications of data mining: knowledge management in e-government. Online Inf Rev 34(1):194–195
Friedman VJ, Rogers T (2009) There is nothing so theoretical as good action research. Action Res 7(1):31–47
Frissen PHA (1999) Politics, governance and technology. A postmodern narrative on the virtual state. Edwards Elgar, Cheltenham
Fulk J, Gould JJ (2009) Features and contexts in technology research: a modest proposal for research and reporting. J Comput-Mediat Commun 14(3):764–770
Galindo F (2002) e-Government trust providers. In: Grönlund Å (ed) Electronic government: design, applications, and management. IDEA Group Publishing, Hershey, pp 121–150
Ganapati S (2011) Uses of public participation geographic information systems applications in e-government. Public Adm Rev 71(3):425–434
Gant DB, Gant JP, Johnson CL (2002) State web portals: delivering and financing e-service. The PricewaterhouseCoopers Endowment for The Business of Government, Arlington, VA
Gant JP (2003a) Delivering e-government services through the access indiana information network. Center for Technology in Government, University at Albany, SUNY, Albany
Gant JP (2003b) Information sharing, communications, and coordination in e-government collaborations. Center for Technology in Government, University at Albany, SUNY, Albany

Gant JP (2004) Digital government and geographic information systems. In: Pavlichev A, Garson GD (eds) Digital government: principles and best practices. Idea Group Publishing, Hershey

Garfinkel H (1967) Studies in ethnomethodology. Prentice Hall, Englewood Cliffs

Garson DG (2003a) Symposium on the theory of technology enactment in Jane Fountain's (2001) building the virtual state: an introduction. Soc Sci Comput Rev 21(4):409–410

Garson GD (2000a) Information systems, politics, and government: leading theoretical perspectives. In: Garson GD (ed) Handbook of public information systems. Marcel Dekker, New York

Garson GD (2003b) Public information technology: policy and management issues. Idea Group Publishing, Harrisburg

Garson GD (2003c) Toward an information technology research agenda for public administration. In: Garson GD (ed) Public information technology: policy and management issues. Idea Group Publishing, Hershey, pp 331–357

Garson GD (2004) The promise of digital government. In: Pavlichev A, Garson GD (eds) Digital government: principles and best practices. Idea Group Publishing, Hershey, pp 2–15

Garson GD (ed) (2000b) Handbook of public information systems. Marcel Dekker, New York

Gascó M (2007) Civil-servants′ resistance toward e-government development. In: Anttiroiko AV, Mälkiä M (eds) Encyclopedia of digital government. Idea Group, Hershey, pp 190–195

Gaudino S, Moro G (2010) Evaluation of an e-government project: which are the barriers to e-government integration? Int J Technol Policy Manag 10(1/2):53–72

Geels FW (2010) Ontologies, socio-technical transitions (to sustainability), and the multi-level perspective. Res Policy 39(4):495–510

Gefen D, Straub DW, Boudreau M-C (2000) Structural equation modeling and regression: guidelines for research practice. Commun AIS 4(7):1–80

Ghapanchi A, Albadvi A, Zarei B (2008) A framework for e-government planning and implementation. Electron Gov Int J 5(1):71–90

Gibbert M, Ruigrok W, Wicki B (2008) What passes as a rigorous case study? Strateg Manag J 29:1465–1474

Giddens A (1984) The constitution of society. University of California Press, Berkeley and Los Angeles

Gieber H, Leitner C, Orthofer G, Traunmüller R (2010) Taking best practice forward. In: Chen H-G, Brandt L, Gregg V, Traunmüller R, Dawes S, Hovy E, Macintosh A, Larson CA (eds) Digital government: e-government research, case studieas and implementation. Springer, New York, pp 203–218

Gil-Garcia JR (2004) Information technology policies and standards: a comparative review of the states. J Gov Inf 30(5):548–560

Gil-Garcia JR (2005a) Enacting state websites: a mixed method study exploring e-government success in multi-organizational settings. Unpublished Doctoral Dissertation University at Albany, State University of New York, Albany

Gil-Garcia JR (2005b) Exploring the success factors of state website functionality: an empirical investigation. Paper presented at the National Conference on Digital Government Research, Atlanta

Gil-Garcia JR (2006) Enacting state websites: a mixed method study exploring e-government success in multi-organizational settings. Paper presented at the 39th Hawaii international conference on system sciences (HICSS), Hawai'i, USA 4–7 January 2006

Gil-Garcia JR (2008) Using partial least squares in digital government research. In: Garson GD, Khosrow-Pour M (eds) Handbook of research on public information technology. Idea Group Inc, Hershey

Gil-Garcia JR, Arellano-Gault D, Luna-Reyes LF (2010) Gobierno electrónico en México (2000–2006): una visión desde la Nueva Gestión Pública. Paper presented at the 11th annual international digital government research conference, Puebla, Mexico

Gil-Garcia JR, Canestraro D, Costello J, Baker A, Werthmuller D (2008) Fostering innovation in electronic government: benefits and challenges of XML for web site management. University of Albany, Center for Technology in Government SUNY, Albany

Gil-Garcia JR, Costello J, Pardo TA, Werthmuller D (2007a) Invigorating website management through XML: an e-government case from New York State. Int J Electron Gov 1(1):52–78

Gil-Garcia JR, Chengalur-Smith I, Duchessi P (2007b) Collaborative e-government: impediments and benefits of information-sharing projects in the public sector. Eur J Inf Syst 16(2):121–133

Gil-Garcia JR, Chun SA, Janssen M (2009) Government information sharing and integration: combining the social and the technical. Inf Polity 14(1/2):1–10

Gil-Garcia JR, Dawes SS (2007) The New York state website: accommodating diversity through a distributed management structure. In: Rocheleau B (ed) Case studies in digital government. Idea Group Inc, Hershey, pp 230–246

Gil-Garcia JR, Hassan S (2008) Structuration theory and government IT. In: Garson DG, Khosrow-Pour M (eds) Handbook of research on public information technology. IGI Global, Hershey, pp 361–375

Gil-Garcia JR, Helbig N (2006) Exploring e-government benefits and success factors. In: Anttiroiko A-V, Malkia M (eds) Encyclopedia of digital government. Idea Group Inc, Hershey, pp 803–811

Gil-Garcia JR, Helbig N, Ferro E (2006) Is it only about internet access? An empirical test of a multi-dimensional digital divide. Paper presented at the Fifth International Conference on Electronic Government, Krakow, Poland, 4–8 Sept 2006

Gil-Garcia JR, Hernandez-Tella FR (2010) AccessIndiana: managing a web site through a successful public-private partnership. In: Downey E, Ekstrom CD, Jones MA (eds) E-government website development: future trends and strategic models. IGI Global, Hershey

Gil-Garcia JR, Luna-Reyes LF (2003) Towards a definition of electronic government: a comparative review. In: Mendez-Vilas A, Mesa Gonzalez JA, Mesa Gonzalez J, Guerrero Bote V, Zapico Alonso F (eds) Techno-legal aspects of the information society and new economy: an overview. Formatex, Badajoz

Gil-Garcia JR, Luna-Reyes LF (2006) Integrating conceptual approaches to e-government. In: Khosrow-Pour M (ed) Encyclopedia of e-commerce, e-government and mobile commerce. Idea Group Inc, Hershey

Gil-Garcia JR, Luna-Reyes LF (2007) Modelo Multidimensional de Medición del Gobierno Electrónico para América Latina y el Caribe. Retrieved from www.eclac.org

Gil-Garcia JR, Luna-Reyes LF (2008) Una Breve Introducción al Gobierno Electrónico: Definición, Aplicaciones y Etapas. Revista de Administración Pública XLIII(2):49–72

Gil-Garcia JR, Luna-Reyes LF (2009) Fostering the information society through collaborative e-government: digital-community centers and the e-learning program in Mexico. In: Meijer A, Boersma K, Wagenaar P (eds) ICTs, Citizens and governance: after the hype. IOS Press, Amsterdam, pp 99–118

Gil-Garcia JR, Martinez-Moyano IJ (2004) Exploring e-government evolution: the influence of systems of rules on organizational action. Paper presented at the Pre-ICIS egovernment workshop, international conference on information systems

Gil-Garcia JR, Martinez-Moyano IJ (2007) Understanding the evolution of e-government: the influence of systems of rules on public sector dynamics. Gov Inf Q 24(2):266–290

Gil-Garcia JR, Pardo TA (2005) E-government success factors: mapping practical tools to theoretical foundations. Gov Inf Q 22(2):187–216

Gil-Garcia JR, Pardo TA (2006) Multi-method approaches to digital government research: value lessons and implementation challenges. Paper presented at the 39th Hawaii international conference on system sciences (HICSS), Hawai'i, USA, Jan 4–7 2006

Gil-Garcia JR, Schneider C, Pardo TA, Cresswell AM (2005) Interorganizational information integration in the criminal justice enterprise: preliminary lessons from state and county initiatives. Paper presented at the 38th Hawaii international conference on system sciences (HICSS), Mãnoa, Hawai, 3–6 Jan 2005

Glaser G, Torrance AL, Schwartz MH (1983) Administrative applications. In: Ralston A, Reilly ED (eds) Encyclopedia of computer science and engineering. Van Nostrand Reinhold, New York, pp 23–40

Goffman E (1961) Encounters: two studies in the sociology of interaction. Bobbs-Merrill, New York

Goffman E (1974) Frame analysis. Harper and Row, New York

Golubchik L (2002) Scalable data collection for internet-based digital government applications. In: McIver WJ, Elmagarmid AK (eds) Advances in digital government technology, human factors, and policy. Kluwer Academic Publishers, Norwell

Gonzalez P, Adenso-Diaz B, Gemoets LA (2010) A cross-national comparison e-government success measures: a theory-based empirical research. Paper presented at the Americas conference on information systems, Lima, Peru

Gorla N, Somers TM, Wong B (2010) Organizational impact of system quality, information quality, and service quality. J Strategic Inf Syst 19(3):207–228

Gottschalk P (2009) Maturity levels for interoperability in digital government. Gov Inf Q 26(1):75–81

Gøtze J, Christiansen PE, Mortensen RK, Paszkowski S (2009) Cross-national interoperability and enterprise architecture. Informatica 20(3):369–396

Governing (2003) State and local sourcebook 2003. Governing, the Magazine of States and Localities, Washington

Grant G, Chau D (2005) Developing a generic framework for e-government. J Global Inf Manag 13(1):1–30

Greenhalgh T, Stones R (2010) Theorising big IT programmes in healthcare: Strong structuration theory meets actor-network theory. Soc Sci Med 70(9):1285–1294

Grgecic D, Rosenkranz C (2008) Information systems change and social interaction: a research agenda. Paper presented at the 18th European conference on information systems, Pretoria, South Africa 4–6 June 2008

Griffin D, Trevorrow P, Halpin E (2007) Developments in e-government. A critical analysis. IOS Press, Amsterdam

Grimsley M, Meehan A (2007) e-government information systems: evaluation-led design for public value and client trust. Eur J Inf Syst 16:134–148

Grönlund Å (2010) Ten years of e-government: the 'end of history' and new beginning. In: Electronic government (Proceedings of the 9th IFIP WG 8.5 international conference, EGOV 2010), Berlin, Springer (pp 13–24)

Grönlund Å (ed) (2001) Electronic government: design, applications, and management. IDEA Group Publishing, Hershey

Grönlund Á, Horan TA (2004) Introducing e-gov: history, definitions, and issues. Commun Assoc Inf Syst 15:713–729

Groznik A, Kovačič A, Trkman P (2008) The role of business renovation and information in e-government. J Comput Inf Syst 49(1):80–88

Groznik A, Trkman P (2009) Upstream supply chain management in e-government: the case of Slovenia. Gov Inf Q 26(3):459–467

Gulati GJ, Yates DJ, Tawileh A (2010) Towards e-participation in the Middle East and northern Europe. In: Reddick CG (ed) Comparative e-government. Springer, New York, pp 71–91

Gupta MP (2010) Tracking the evolution of e-governance in India. Int J Electron Gov Res 6(1):46–58

Gurría A (2008) Building the public services of tomorrow with, for and around customers. Retrieved from http://www.oecd.org/document/26/0,3343,en_2649_34565_41527450_1_1_1_3447,00.html

Hair JF Jr, Anderson RE, Tatham RL, Black WC (1998) Multivariate data analysis. Prentice Hall, Upper Saddle River

Hall RH (2002) Organizations structures, processes, and outcomes. Upper Saddle River, Prentice Hall

Hammond C (2005) The wider benefits of adult learning: an illustration of the advantages of multi-method research. Int J Soc Res Methodol 8(3):239–255
Hanna NK (2011) Transforming government and building the information society: challenges and opportunities for the developing world. Springer, New York
Hannan MT, Freeman JH (1989) Organizational ecology. Harvard University, Cambridge
Hardy C (2010) Textualizing technology: knowledge, artifact, and practice. In: Phillips N, Sewell G, Griffiths D (eds) Technology and organization: essays in honour of Joan Woodward, vol 29. Emerald Group Publishing, New York, pp 247–258
Hardy CA, Williams SP (2008) E-government policy and practice: a theoretical and empirical exploration of public e-procurement. Gov Inf Q 25(2):155–180
Hardy CA, Williams SP (2011) Assembling e-government research designs: a transdisciplinary view and interactive approach. Public Adm Rev 71(3):405–413
Harklau L (2011) Approaches and methods in recent qualitative research. In: Hinkel E (ed) Handbook of research in second language teaching and learning, vol 2. Taylor and Francis, New York, pp 175–189
Harris ND (2000) Intergovernmental cooperation in the development and use of information systems. In: Garson GD (ed) Handbook of public information systems. Marcel Dekker, New York, pp 165–177
Harrison T, Pardo TA, Gil-Garcia JR, Thompson F, Juraga D (2007) Geographic information technologies, structuration theory, and the world trade center crisis. J Am Soc Inf Sci Technol 58(14):2240–2254
Hassan HS, Shehab E, Peppard J (2011) Recent advances in e-service in the public sector: state-of-the-art and future trends. Bus Process Manag J 17(3):526–545
Hassan S, Gil-Garcia JR (2008) Institutional theory and e-government research. In: Garson GD, Khosrow-Pour M (eds) Handbook of research on public information technology. Idea Group Inc, Hershey
Hatch MJ (1997) Organization theory modern, symbolic, and posmodern perpectives. Oxford University Press, Oxford
Heeks R (1999) Reinventing government in the information age. International practice in IT-enabled public sector reform. Routledge, New York
Heeks R (2001) Understanding e-governance for development. The University of Manchester, UK
Heeks R (2003) Success and failure rates of egovernment in developing/transitional countries: overview. www.egov4dev.org/sfoverview.htm
Heeks R (2005) Implementing and managing egovernment: an international text. SAGE Publications, Thousand Oaks
Heeks R (2006) Implementing and managing e-government. Sage Publications, London
Heeks R, Bailur S (2007) Analyzing e-government research: perspectives, philosophies, theories, methods, and practice. Gov Inf Q 24(2):243–265
Helbig N, Dawes S, Mulki FH, Hrdinová J, Cook ME, Edwards T (2009a) International digital government research: a reconnaissance study (1994–2008) -updated. Center for Technology in Government, Albany
Helbig N, Gil-Garcia JR, Ferro E (2009b) Understanding the complexity of electronic government implications from the digital divide literature. Gov Inf Q 26(1):89–97
Henseler J, Ringle CM, Sinkovics RR (2009) The use of partial least squares path modeling in international marketing. Adv Int Mark 20:277–319
Herrera L, Gil-Garcia JR (2010) Implementation of e-government in Mexico: the case of infonavit. In: Assar S, Boughzala I, Boydens I (eds) Practical studies in e-government: best practices from around the world. Springer, New York, pp 29–48
Heshusius L, Ballard K (eds) (1996) From positivism to interpretivism and beyond: tales of transformation in educational and social research. Teachers College Press, New York
Heydebrand WV (1977) Organizational contradictions in public bureaucracies: toward a Marxian theory of organizations. Sociol Q 18:83–107

Hiller JS, Bélanger F (2001) Privacy strategies for electronic government. In: Abramson MA, Means GE (eds) E-government 2001. Rowman and Littlefield Publishers, Lanham, pp 162–198
Hirschheim R, Newman M (1991) Symbolism and information systems development: myth. Metaphor Magic Inf Syst Res 2(1):29–62
Ho AT-K (2002) Reinventing local governments and the e-government initiative. Public Adm Re 62(4):434–444
Hogrebe F, Blinn N, Nüttgens M (2009) Survey of e-government portals in European capitals and large cities: a benchmarking study of G2B-services. In: Wimmer MA, Scholl HJ, Janssen M, Traunmüller R (eds) Electronic government (Proceedings of the 8th international conference, EGOV 2009), Springer, Berlin
Holbrook TM, Van Dunk E (1993) Electoral competition in the American states. Am Political Sci Rev 87(4):955–962
Holden SH, Norris DF, Fletcher PD (2003) Electronic government at the local level: progress to date and future issues. Public Perform Manag Rev 26(4):325–344
Holmes D (2001) E. Gov e-business strategies for government. Nicholas Brealey Publishing, London
Holstein JA, Gubrium JF (eds) (2008) Handbook of constructionist research. Guilford Press, New York
Holtzner B, Marx JH (1979) Knowledge application: the knowledge system in society. Allyn and Bacon, Boston
Holland CP, Light B, Kawalek P (1999) Focus issue on legacy information systems and business process change: introduction. Commun AIS 2(9)
Homburg VMF, Snellen TMI (2007) Will ICTs finally reinvent government? The mutual shaping of institutions and ICTs. In: Pollit C, van Thiel S, Homburg VMF (eds) The new public management in Europe: adaptation and alternatives. Palgrave Macmillan, Houndmills, pp 135–148
Hong EK (2009) Information technology strategic planning. IT Professional 11(6):8–15
Hood C, Margetts H (2007) The tools of government in the digital age. Palgrave, London
Hoque F, Walsh LM, Mirakaj DL, Bruckner J (2011) The power of convergence: linking business strategies and technology decisions to create sustainable success. AMACOM, New York
Hornnes E, Jansen A, Langeland Ø (2010) How to develop an open and flexible information infrastructure for the public sector? In: Wimmer MA, Chappelet J-L, Janssen M Scholl HJ (eds) Electronic government (Proceedings of the 9th IFIP WG 8.5 international conference, EGOV 2010), Springer, Berlin, pp 301–314
Hossain MD, Moon J, Kim JK, Choe YC (forthcoming) Impacts of organizational assimilation of e-government systems on business value creation: a structuration theory approach. Electron Commerce Res Appl doi:10.1016/j.elerap.2010.1012.1003
Hovy E (2008) Data and knowledge integration for e-government. In: Chen H, Brandt L, Gregg V, Traunmüller R, Dawes S, Hovy E, Macintosh A, Larson CA (eds) Digital government: e-government research, case studies, and implementation. Springer, New York, pp 219–231
Howcroft D, Light B (2010) The social shaping of packaged software selection. J Assoc Inf Syst 11(3):122–148
Hoyles C, Küchemann D, Healy L, Yang M (2005) Students' developing knowledge in a subject discipline: insights from combining quantitative and qualitative methods. Int J Soc Res Methodol 8(3):225–238
Hrdinová J, Helbig N, Peters CS (2010) Designing social media policy for government: eight essential elements. Center for Technology in Government, University at Albany, The Research Foundation of State University of New York, Albany
Hrdinová J, Helbig N, Raup-Kounovsky A (2009) Enterprise IT governance in state government: state portals. Center for Technology in Government, Albany
Hsu JS-C, Chan C-L, Liu JY-C, Chen H-G (2008) The impacts of user review on software responsiveness: moderating requirements uncertainty. Inf Manag 45(4):203–210

Hu G, Pan W, Lu M, Wang J (2009) The widely shared definition of e-government: an exploratory study. Electron Libr 27(6):968–985
Hu G, Pan W, Wang J (2010) The distinctive lexicon and consensual conception of e-Government: an exploratory perspective. Int Rev Adm Sci 76(3):577–597
Huang J, Galliers RD (2011) The importance of rhetoric in conceptualising IS adoption. J Enterp Inf Manag 24(3):219–223
Hughes M (2011) The challenges of informed citizen participation in change. Transforming Gov People Process Policy 5(1):68–80
Hulland J (1999) Use of partial least squares squares in strategic management research: a review of four recent studies. Strateg Manag J 20(2):195–204
Hunter SD III (2010) Same technology, different outcome? Reinterpreting Barley's technology as an occasion for structuring. Eur J Inf Syst 19:689–703
Hussin H, Kassim ES (2010) Assessing government to business services performance: The role of human and organizational factors. Paper presented at the Pacific Asia conference on information systems (PACIS)
Hwang S-D, Choi Y, Myeong S-H (1999) Electronic government in South Korea: conceptual problems. Gov Inf Q 16(3):277–285
Iannacci F (2010) When is an information infrastructure? Investigating the emergence of public sector information infrastructures. Eur J Inf Syst 19:35–48
IDABC (2003) UN publishes global e-government report. Retrieved April 6, 2005, from http://europa.eu.int/idabc/en/document/1740/5652
Iivari J, Hirschheim R, Klein HK (1998) A paradigmatic analysis contrasting information systems development approaches and methodologies. Inf Syst Res 9(2):164–193
Iivari J, Isomäki H, Pekkola S (2009) The user–the great unknown of systems development: reasons, forms, challenges, experiences and intellectual contributions of user involvement. Inf Syst J 20(2):109–117
Inkinen TA (2010) Does size or geography matter? Empirical Analysis of finnish local government services on the internet. In: Reddick CG (ed) Comparative e-government. Springer, New York, pp 615–637
Intelenet C (2003) Financial statements- Unaudited
Iris V, Ramesh V, Glass RL (2002) Research in information systems: An empirical study of diversity in the discipline and its journals. J Manag Inf Syst 19(2):129–174
Irwin A (2011) The SAGE handbook of sociolinguistics. In: Johnstone B, Wodak R, Kerswill PE (eds) The SAGE handbook of sociolinguistics. Sage, Thousand Oaks, pp 100–112
Jackson P, Klobas J (2008) Building knowledge in projects: a practical application of social constructivism to information systems development. Int J Project Manag 26(4):329–337
Jaeger PT (2002) Constitutional principles and e-government: an opinion about possible effects of Federalism and separation of powers on e-government policies. Gov Inf Q 19:357–368
Jaeger PT (2005) Deliberative democracy and the conceptual foundations of electronic government. Gov Inf Q 22:702–709
Jaeger PT, Bertot JC (2010) Transparency and technological change: ensuring equal and sustained public access to government information. Gov Inf Q 27(4):371–376
Jain V, Kesar S (2011) E-government implementation challenges at local level: a comparative study of government and citizens' perspectives. Electron Gov Int J 8(2/3):208–225
Jansen A, Løvdal E (2009) Can ICT reform public agencies? In: Wimmer MA Scholl HJ, Janssen M, Traunmüller R (eds) Electronic government (Proceedings of the 8th international conference, EGOV 2009), Springer, Berlin pp 88–102
Janssen D, Rotthier S, Snijkers K (2004) If you measure it they will score: an assesment of international egovernment benchmarking. Inf Polity 9:121–130
Janssen M (2008) Exploring the service-oriented enterprise: drawing lessons from a case study. Paper presented at the 41st Hawaii international conference on system sciences (HICSS)
Janssen M (forthcoming) Sociopolitical aspects of interoperability and enterprise architecture in e-government. Social Sci Comput Rev doi:10.1177/0894439310392187

Janssen M, Klievink B (2010) Gaming and simulation for transforming and reengineering government: towards a research agenda. Trans Gov People Process Policy 4(2):132–137
Janssen M, Kuk G, Wagenaar RW (2008) A survey of web-based business models for e-government in the Netherlands. Gov Inf Q 25:202–220
Jarque Uribe CM (1998) Aplicación de la Nuevas Tecnologías en las Administraciones Públicas. Revista de Administración Pública 99:1–23
Jarrahi MH (2010) A structurational analysis of how course management systems are used in practice. Behav Inf Technol 29(3):257–275
Jayatilaka B, Hirschheim R (2009) Changes in IT sourcing arrangements: an interpretive field study of technical and institutional influences. Strategic Outsourcing Int J 2(2):84–122
Jenster PV (1987) Firm performance and monitoring of critical success factors in different strategics contexts. J Manag Inf Syst 3(3):17–33
Jiang J, Klein G (2000) Software development risks to project effectiveness. J Syst Softw 52:3–10
Johnson BR, Onwuegbuzie AJ, Turner LA (2007) Toward a definition of mixed methods research. J Mixed Methods Res 1(2):112–133
Johnson CL (2007) A framework for pricing government e-services. Electron Commer Res Appl 6(4):484–489
Johnson DG, Wetmore JM (eds) (2009) Technology and society: building our sociotechnical future. MIT Press, Cambridge
Joia LA (2008) The impact of government-to-government endeavors on the intellectual capital of public organizations. Gov Inf Q 25(2):256–277
Jones MR, Karsten H (2008) Giddens's structuration theory and information systems research. Manag Inf Syst Q 32(1):127–158
Joreskog KG (1978) Structural analysis of covariance and correlation matrices. Psychometrika 43:443–477
Joseph BK (2010) E-Government adoption landscape Zambia: context, issues and challenges. In: Reddick CG (ed) Comparative e-government, Springer, pp 241–258
Joseph RC, Ezzedeen SR (2009) E-government and e-HRM in the public sector. In: Torres-Coronas T, Arias-Oliva M (eds) Encyclopedia of human resources information systems: challenges in e-HRM. IGI Global, Hershey, pp 272–277
Joshi JBD, Aref WG, Ghafoor A, Spafford EH (2001) Security models for web-based applications. Commun ACM 44(2):38–72
Joshi JBD, Ghafoor A, Aref WG, Spafford EH (2002) Security and privacy challenges of a digital government. In: McIver WJ Jr, Elmagarmid AK (eds) Advances in digital government technology, human factors, and policy. Kluwer Academic Publishers, Norwell, pp 121–136
Jun K-N, Weare C (forthcoming) Institutional motivations in the adoption of innovations: the case of e-government. J Public Adm Res Theory
Kanat IE, Özkan S (2009) Exploring citizens' perception of government to citizen services: a model based on theory of planned behaviour (TBP). Transform Gov People Process Policy 3(4):406–419
Kang S, Gearhart S (2010) E-government and civic engagement: How is citizens' use of city web sites related with civic involvement and political behaviors? J Broadcast Electron Media 54(3):443–462
Kaplan D, Krishnan R, Padman R, Peters J (1998) Assessing data quality in accounting information systems. Commun ACM 41(2):72–77
Kavanaugh A, Perez-Quinones MA, Tedesco JC, Sanders W (2010) Toward a virtual town square in the era of web 20. In: Hunsinger J, Klastrup L, Allen M (eds) International handbook of internet research. Springer, Dordrecht, pp 279–294
Keil M, Cule PE, Lyytinen K, Schmidt R (1998) A Framework for identifying software project risks. Commun ACM 41(11):76–82
Kelly S, Gibson N, Holland CP, Light B (1999) Focus issue on legacy information systems and business process change: a business perspective of legacy information systems. Commun AIS. 2(7)

Kennedy A, Coughlan JP, Kelleher C (2010) Business process change in e-government projects: the case of the Irish land registry. Int J Electron Gov Res 6(1):9–22

Khalil OEM (2011) e-Government readiness: Does national culture matter? Gov Inf Q 28(3): 388–399

Khan GF, Moon J, Park HW, Swar B, Rho JJ (2010) A socio-technical perspective on e-government issues in developing countries: a scientometrics approach. Scientometrics 87(2):267–286

Kim D-Y, Grant G (2010) E-government maturity model using the capability maturity model integration. J Syst Inf Technol 12(3):230–244

Kim S, Kim D (2003) South Korean public officials' perceptions of values, failure, and consequences of failure in e-government leadership. Public Perform Manag Rev 26(4):360–375

Kim S, Kim HJ, Lee H (2009) An institutional analysis of an e-government system for anti-corruption: the case of OPEN. Gov Inf Q 26(1):42–50

King JL, Lyytinen K (eds) (2006) Information systems: the state of the field. Wiley, Chichester

Klein HK, Hirschheim R (1983) Issues and apoproaches to appraising technological change in the office: a consequentialist perspective. Technol People 2:15–42

Klievink B, Janssen M (2009a) Realizing joined-up government—dynamic capabilities and stage models for transformation. Gov Inf Q 26(2):275–284

Klievink B, Janssen M (2009b) Realizing joined-up government: dynamic capabilities and stage models for transformation. Gov Inf Q 26(2):275–284

Kling R (1993) Organizational analysis in computer science. Inf Soc 9(2):71–87

Kling R (2000) Learning about information technologies and social change: the contribution of social informatics. Inf Soc 16(3):217–232

Kling R, Lamb R (2000) IT and organizational change in digital economies: a sociotechnical approach. In: Brynjolfsson E, Kahin B (eds) Understanding the digital economy data, tools, and research. The MIT Press, Cambridge

Kling R, Rosenbaum H, Hert C (1998) Social informatics in information science: an introduction. J Am Soc Inf Sci 49(12):1047–1052

Kling R, Schacchi W (1982) The web of computing: computer technology as social organization. Adv Comput 21:1–90

Klischewski R (2011) Architectures for tinkering? Contextual strategies towards interoperability in e-government. J Theor Appl Electron Commer Res 6(1):26–42

Klischewski R, Scholl HJ (2008) Information quality as capstone in negotiating e-government integration, interoperation and information sharing. Electron Gov Int J 5(2):203–225

Kraemer KL, Danziger JN (1984) Computers in the work environment. Public Adm Rev 44(1):32–42

Kraemer KL, Dedrick J (1997) Computing and public organizations. J Public Adm Res Theory 7(1):89–112

Kraemer KL, Dutton WH, Northrop A (1980) The management of information systems. Columbia University Press, New York

Kraemer KL, King JL (1986) Computing and public organizations. Public Adm Rev 46:488–496 (Special Issue)

Kraemer KL, King JL (2003) Information technology and administrative reform: will the time after e-government be different? Paper presented at the heinrich reinermann schrift fest, post graduate school of administration, Speyer, Germany, 29 Sept 2003

Kraemer KL, King JL, Dunkle DE, Lane JP (1989) Managing information systems. Change and control in organizational computing. Jossey-Bass, San Francisco

Kramer KL, King JL (2003) Information technology and administrative reform: Will the time after e-government be different? Irvine, CA (Unpublished manuscript)

Kuan KKY, Chau PYK (2001) A perception-based model for EDI adoption in small businesses using a technology-organization-environment framework. Inf Manag 38:507–521

Kunstelj M, Vintar M (2004) Evaluating the progress of e-government development: a critical analysis. Inf Polity 9:131–148

Kwon H, Pardo TA, Burke GB (2009) Interorganizational collaboration and community building for the preservation of state government digital information: lesson from NDIIPP state partnershipr initiative. Gov Inf Q 26:186–192

La Porte TM, Demchak CC, DeJong M (2002) Democracy and bureaucracy in the age of the web. Empirical findings and theoretical speculations. Adm Soc 34(4):411–446

Lai VS, Mahapatra RK (1997) Exploring the research in information technology implementation. Inf Manag 32(4):187–201

Landsbergen D Jr, Wolken G Jr (2001) Realizing the promise: government information systems and the fourth generation of information technology. Public Adm Rev 61(2):206–220

Langford J (2010) E-government, service transformation, and procurement reform in Canada. In: St.Amant K (eds) IT outsourcing: concepts, methodologies, tools, and applications. IGI Global, Hershey, PA, pp 1360–1370

Langford J, Roy J (2009) Building shared accountability into service transformation partnerships. Int J Public Policy 4(3/4):232–250

Lassman K (2002) The digital state 2001. The Progress & Freedom Foundation, Washington

Laudon KC (1985) Environmental and institutional models of system development: a national criminal history system. Commun ACM 28(7):728–740

Laudon KC (1986) Dossier society. Value choices in the design of national information systems. Columbia University Press, New York

Laudon KC, Laudon JP (2003) Management information systems. Prentice Hall, Upper Saddle River

Laudon KC, Westin AF (1986) A longitudinal model of information systems development: IRS, FBI, and SAA. School of Business Administration, New York University, New York

LaVigne M (2002) Electronic government: a vision of a future that is already here. Syracuse Law Rev 52(4):1243–1251

Layne K, Lee J (2001) Developing fully functional e-government: a four stage model. Gov Inf Q 18(2):122–136

Leavitt HJ (1965) Applied organizational change in industry: structural, technical and humanistic approaches. In: March JG (ed) Handbook of organizations. Rand McNally, Chicago

Lee AS (1989) A scientific methodology for MIS case studies. MIS Q 13(1):33–50

Lee AS (1999) Rigor and relevance in MIS research: beyond the approach of positivism alone. MIS Q 23(1):29–33

Lee C-p, Chang K, Berry FS (2011a) Testing the development and diffusion of e-government and e-democracy: a global perspective. Public Adm Rev 71(3):444–454

Lee J-N (2001) The impact of knowledge sharing, organizational capability and partnership quality on IS outsourcing success. Inf Manag 38:323–335

Lee J (2010a) 10 year retrospect on stage models of e-government: a qualitative meta-synthesis. Gov Inf Q 27:220–230

Lee J, Kim HJ, Ahn MJ (2011b) The willingness of e-government service adoption by business users: The role of offline service quality and trust in technology. Gov Inf Q 28(2):222–230

Lee JW, Rainey HG, Chun YH (2009) Of politics and purpose: political salience and goal ambiguity of us federal agencies. Public Adm 87(3):457–484

Lee JY (2010b) The development of e-government capabilities: framework for government. In: Rahman H (ed) Handbook of research on e-government readiness for information and service exchange: utilizing progressive information communication technologies. IGI Global, Hershey, pp 1–20

Lee K-S (2009) A final flowering of the developmental state: the IT policy experiment of the Korean information infrastructure, 1995–2005. Gov Inf Q 26(4):567–576

Lee KR, Lee K-S (2009) The Korean government's electronic record management reform: the promise and perils of digital democratization. Gov Inf Q 26(3):525–535

Lenk K (2006) E-government in Europe. Uniform solutions for all countries? Inf Polity 11(3):189–196

Lenk K, Traunmüller R (2001) Broadening the concept of electronic government. In: Prins JEJ (ed) Designing e-government on the crossroads of technological innovation and institutional change. Kluwer Law International, The Hague, pp 63–74
Leonardi PM (2009a) Crossing the implementation line: the mutual constitution of technology and organizing across development and use activities. Commun Theory 19(3):278–310
Leonardi PM (2009b) Why do people reject new technologies and stymie organizational changes of which they are in favor? Exploring misalignments between social interactions and materiality. Hum Commun Res 35(3):407–441
Leonardi PM (2010) Digital materiality? How artifacts without matter, matter. First Monday. 15(6/7). Available at http://firstmonday.org/htbin/cgiwrap/bin/ojs/index.php/fm/article/view Article/3036
Leonardi PM, Barley SR (2008) Materiality and change: challenges to building better theory about technology and organizing. Inf Organ 18(3):159–176
Leonardi PM, Barley SR (2010) What's under construction here? Social action, materiality, and power in constructivist studies of technology and organizing. Acad Manage Ann 4:1–51
Leung TKP, Adams J (2009) Explaining IT usage in government through "resistance to change". J Chin Entrepreneurship 1(3):176–192
Liao C, Chuang S-H, To P-L (2011) How knowledge management mediates the relationship between environment and organizational structure. J Bus Res 64(7):728–736
Lieberman E (2003) Nested analysis in cross-national research. APSA CP Newsletter ASPA Comp Politics Sect 14(1):17–20
Liu J, Tan Y-H (2010) Realising collaborative government-to-business business models: the case of the authorised economic operator. Electron Gov Int J 7(4):330–345
Lock A, Strong T (eds) (2010) Social constructionism: sources and stirrings in theory and practice. Cambridge University Press, Cambridge
Löfgren K (2007) The government of e-government. Public Policy Adm 22(3):335–352
Loukis E, Charalabidis Y (2011) Why do eGovernment projects fail? Risk factors of large information systems projects in the Greek public sector: an international comparison. Int J Electron Gov Res 7(2):59–77
Lu J, Shambour Q, Xu Y, Lin Q, Zhang G (2010) BizSeeker: a hybrid semantic recommendation system for personalized government-to-business e-services. Internet Res 20(3):342–365
Lu Y, Tsang EWK, Peng MW (2008) Knowledge management and innovation strategy in the Asia Pacific: toward an institution-based view. Asia Pac J Manag 25(3):361–374
Lu Y, Xiang C, Wang B, Wang X (2011) What affects information systems development team performance? An exploratory study from the perspective of combined socio-technical theory and coordination theory. Comput Hum Behav 27(2):811–822
Luk SCY (2009) The impact of leadership and stakeholders on the success/failure of e-government service: using the case study of e-stamping service in Hong Kong. Gov Inf Q 26(4):594–604
Luna-Reyes LF, Andersen DF, Richardson GP, Pardo TA, Cresswell AM (2007) Emergence of the governance structure for information integration across governmental agencies: a system dynamics approach. Paper presented at the 8th annual international conference on digital government research (dg.o), Philadelphia, 20–23 May 2007
Luna-Reyes LF, Gil-Garcia JR (2003a) E-government security, privacy and information access: some policy and organizational trade-offs. Paper presented at the international conference on public participation and information technologies 2003 (ICPPIT03), Cambridge, MA, 10–12 Nov 2003
Luna-Reyes LF, Gil-Garcia JR (2003b) eGovernment & internet security: some technical and policy considerations. Paper presented at the national conference on digital government research, Boston, MA, 18–21 May 2003
Luna-Reyes LF, Gil-Garcia JR (2011) Using institutional theory and dynamic simulation to understand complex e-Government phenomena. Gov Inf Q 28(3):329–345

Luna-Reyes LF, Gil-Garcia JR, Cruz CB (2007b) Collaborative digital government in Mexico: some lessons from federal Web-based interorganizational information integration initiatives. Gov Inf Q 24(4):808–826

Luna-Reyes LF, Gil-Garcia JR, Estrada-Marroquín M (2008) The impact of institutions on interorganizational IT projects in the Mexican federal government. Int J Electron Gov Res 4(2):27–42

Luna-Reyes LF, Hernandez García JM, Gil-Garcia JR (2009) Hacia un Modelo de los Determinates de éxito de los portales de Gobierno Estatal en México. Gestión y Política Pública. XVIII(2): 307–340

Luna-Reyes LF, Pardo TA, Gil-Garcia JR, Navarrete C, Zhang J, Mellouli S (2010) Digital government in North America: a comparative analysis of policy and program priorities in Canada, Mexico and the United States. In: Reddick CG (ed) Comparative e-government. Springer, New York, pp 139–160

Luna-Reyes LF, Zhang J, Gil-Garcia JR, Cresswell AM (2005) Information systems development as emergent socio-technical change: a practice approach. Eur J Inf Syst 14(1):93–105

Lux Wigand DF (2010) Adoption of web 2.0 by Canadian and US governments. In: Reddick CG (ed) Comparative e-government. Springer, New York, pp 161–181

Lyytinen K, King JL (2006) Nothing at the center?: academic legitimacy in the information systems field. In: King JL, Lyytinen K (eds) Information systems: the state of the field. Wiley, England, pp 233–266

Lyytinen K, Newman M (2008) Explaining information systems change: a punctuated socio-technical change model. Eur J Inf Syst 17:589–613

Maali F, Cyganiak R, Peristeras V (2010) Enabling interoperability of government data catalogues. In: Electronic government (Proceedings of the 9th IFIP WG 8.5 international conference, EGOV 2010), Springer, Berlin, pp 339–350

Macintosh A, Malina A, Farrell S (2002) Digital democracy through electronic petitioning. In: McIver WJ, Elmagarmid AK (eds) Advances in digital government technology, human factors, and policy. Kluwer Academic Publishers, Norwell

Madnick SE, Wang RY, Lee YW, Zhu H (2009) Overview and framework for data and information quality research. J Data Inf Qual 1(1):1–22

Mahler J, Regan PM (2003) Developing intranets for agency management. Public Perform Manag Rev 26(4):422–432

Mahmood MA, Bagchi K, Ford TC (2004) On-line shopping behavior: cross-country empirical research. Int J Electron Commer 9(1):9–30

Makedon F, Loukis E, Ford J (2010) Electronic support of government-to-government negotiation and collaboration for the design and implementation of new policies. Int J Appl Syst Stud 3(3):264–282

Manning P, Smith G (2010) Symbolic interactionism. In: Elliott A, Mendelson D (eds) The Routledge companion to social theory. Routledge, New York, pp 37–55

Mansell R, Silverstone R (eds) (1996) Communication by design. The politics of information and communication technologies. Oxford University Press, London

March JG, Olsen JP (1989) Rediscovering institutions: the organizational basis of politics. Free Press, New York

Margetts H (2003) Electronic government: method or madness? Paper presented at the inaugural lecture, School of Public Policy, University College of London, 13 Feb 2003

Margetts H (2009) The internet and public policy. Policy Internet 1:1–21

Mariscal J (2003) Digital divide in Mexico. Centro de Investigación y Docencia Económicas, Mexico City

Markaki OI, Charilas DE, Askounis D (2010) Evaluation of the impact and adoption of e-government services in the Balkans. In: Reddick CG (ed) Comparative e-government. Springer, New York, pp 91–114

Markus ML (1983) Power, politics and MIS implementation. Commun ACM 26:430–444

Markus ML (2005) Technology shaping effects of e-collaboration technologies: Bugs and features. Int J E-Collab 1(1):1–23
Markus ML, Robey D (1988) Information technology and organizational change: causal structure in theory and research. Manag Sci 34(5):583–598
Markus ML, Silver MS (2008) A foundation for the study of IT effects: a new look at DeSanctis and Poole's concepts of structural features and spirit. J Assoc Inf Syst 9(10/11):609–632
Mars M, Scott RE (2010) Global e-health policy: a work in progress. Health Aff 29(2):237–243
Maumbe BM, Owei V, Alexander H (2008) Questioning the pace and pathway of e-government development in Africa: a case study of South Africa's cape gateway project. Gov Inf Q 25(4): 757–777
Maxwell T, Dawes SS (2009) Public governance as a socio-technical system: from concept to application. Paper presented at the 10th annual international conference on digital government research (dg.o)
McClure CR, Sprehe T, Eschenfelder K (2000) Developing web site performance measures for federal agency websites. Educational Resources Information Clearinghouse (ERIC), Syracuse, NY
McFarlan FW (1981) Portfolio approach to information systems. Harvard Bus Rev 59:142–150
McNabb DE, Barnowe JT (2009) Trends shaping public sector transformation: knowledge management, e-government and enterprise architecture. J Inf Knowl Manag 8(1):25–34
McNeal R, Hale K, Dotterweich L (2008) Citizen-government interaction and the internet: expectations and accomplishments in contact, quality, and trust. J Inf Technol Politics 5(2): 213–229
Mead GH (1938) The philosophy of act. University of Chicago Press, Chicago
Means G, Schneider D (2000) Meta-capitalism: the e-business revolution and the design of 21st century companies and markets. Wiley, New York
Meijer A, Thaens M (2010) Alignment 2.0: strategic use of new internet technologies in government. Gov Inf Q 27(2):113–121
Melin U (2009) The enterprise system as a part of an organization's administrative paradox. J Enterp Inf Manag 23(2):181–200
Melin U, Axelsson K (2009) Managing e-service development—comparing two e-government case studies. Transform Gov People Process Policy 3(3):248–270
Menachemi N, Shin DY, Ford EW, Yu F (2011) Environmental factors and health information technology management strategy. Health Care Manag Rev 36(3):275–285
Meneklis V, Douligeris C (2008) Technological integration: evidence of processes of structuring in governmental organizations. Paper presented at the 2nd international conference on theory and practice of electronic governance, Cairo, Egypt, 1–4 Dec 2008
Meneklis V, Douligeris C (2010) Studying the interaction of the epistemology in e-government, organization studies and information systems. In: Sideridis AB, Patrikakis CZ (eds) Next generation society. Technological and legal issues, vol 26. Springer, Berlin, pp 79–86
Mergel IA, Schweik CM, Fountain JE (2009) The transformational effect of web 2.0 technologies on government. Available at SSRN: http://ssrn.com/abstract=1412796
Mertens DM (2011) Publisihing mixed methodsmethods research. J Mixed Methods Res 5(1):3–6
Milner EM (2000) Managing information and knowledge in the public sector. Routledge, New York
Miller DW (2008) Facilitator effects on the process of GSS appropriation: opening the "black box". Rev Bus Inf Syst 12(4):57
Millerand F, Baker KS (2010) Who are the users? Who are the developers? Webs of users and developers in the development process of a technical standard. Inf Syst J 20(2):137–161
Mills A, Carter L, Belanger F (2010) Conceptualizing public service value in e-government services. Paper presented at the Americas conference on information sciences
Mingers J (2001) Combining IS research methods: towards a pluralist methodology. Inf Syst Res 12(3):240–259
Mingers J (2003) The paucity of multimethod research: a review of the information systems literature. Inf Syst J 13(3):233–250

Miranda SM, Saunders CS (2003) The social construction of meaning: an alternative perspective on information sharing. Inf Syst Res 14(1):87–106

Misuraca GC (2009) e-Government 2015: exploring m-government scenarios, between ICT-driven experiments and citizen-centric implications. Technol Anal Strateg Manag 21(3):407–424

Mitev N (2009) In and out of actor-network theory: a necessary but insufficient journey. Inf Technol People 22(1):9–25

Moflesh S, Wanous M, Strachan P (2009) Understanding national e-government: the role of central government. Electron Gov Int J 6(1):1–18

Mölder B (2010) Mind ascribed: an elaboration and defence of interpretivism. John Benjamins Publishing Company, Philadelphia

Molina-Azorín JF (2011) The use and added value of mixed methods in management research. J Mixed Methods Res 5(1):7–24

Moon MJ (2002) The evolution of e-government among municipalities: rhetoric or reality? Public Adm Rev 62(4):424–433

Mooney CZ, Duval RD (1993) Bootstrapping. A nonparametric approach to statistical inference. Sage Publications, Newbury Park

Morgeson FV III, Mithas S (2009) Does e-government measure up to e-business? Comparing end user perceptions of U.S. federal government and e-business web sites. Public Adm Rev 69(4):740–752

Mukherjee I (2008) Understanding information system failures from the complexity perspective. J Soc Sci 4(4):308–319

Mumford E (2000) A socio-technical approach to systems design. Requir Eng 5(2):125–133

Mundkur A, Venkatesh M (2009) The role of institutional logics in the design of e-governance systems. J Inf Technol Politics 6(1):12–30

Myeong S, Choi Y (2010) Effects of information technology on policy decision-making processes: some evidences beyond rhetoric. Adm Soc 42(4):441–459

Naik N, Kim DJ (2010) An extended adaptive structuration theory for determinants and consequences of virtual team success. Paper presented at the international conference on system sciences (ICIS 2010), Saint Louis, Missouri, 12–15 Dec 2010

NASCIO (2002) NASCIO 2002 compendium of digital government in the states. National Association of State Chief Information Officers, Lexington

Nasim S, Sushil (2010) Managing continuity and change: a new approach for strategizing in e-government. Transform Gov People Process Policy 4(4):338–364

Navarra DD (2010) The architecture of global ICT programs: a case study of e-governance in Jordan. Inf Technol Dev 16(2):128–140

Nevo S, Nevo D, Ein-Dor P (2009) Thirty years of IS research: core artifacts and academic identity. Commun Assoc Inf Syst 25(1):221–242

Newman I, Benz CR (1998) Qualitative-quantitative research methodology. Exploring the interactive continuum. Southern Illinois University Press, Carbondale and Edwardsville

Newman M, Robey D (1992) A social process model of user-analyst relationships. MIS Q 16(2):249–266

Newman M, Rosenberg D (1985) System analysts and the politics of organizational control. OMEGA Int J Manag Sci 13(5):393–406

NGA (1997) Barriers to intergovernmental enterprise. National Governors Association, Washington

Niederman F, de Vreede G-J, Briggs RO, Kolfschoten GL (2008) Extending the contextual and organizational elements of adaptive structuration theory in GSS research. J Assoc Inf Syst 9(10/11):633–652

Niehaves B (2010) Open process innovation: the impact of personnel resource scarcity on the involvement of customers and consultants in public sector BPM. Bus Process Manag J 16(3):377–393

Norris DF (1999) Leading edge information technologies and their adoption: lessons from US cities. In: Garson GD (ed) Information technology and computer applications in public administration: issues and trends. Idea Group, Hershey, pp 137–156
Norris DF (2003) Building the virtual state ... or not: a critical appraisal. Soc Sci Comput Rev 21(4):417–424
Norris DF (2010) E-government... not e-governance... not e-democracy not now!: not ever?. Paper presented at the 4th international conference on theory and practice of electronic governance (ICEGOV), Beijing, China
Norris DF, Moon MC (2005) Advancing e-government at the grassroots: tortoise or hare. Public Adm Rev 65(1):64–75
Norris P (2001) Digital divide: civic engagement, information poverty, and the internet worldwide. Cambridge University Press, New York
North DC (1999) Institutions, institutional change, and economic performance. Cambridge University Press, New York
Northrop A, Kraemer KL, Dunkle DE, King JL (1990) Payoffs from computerization: lessons over time. Public Adm Rev 50(5):505–514
Nour MA, AbdelRahman AA, Fadlalla A (2008) A context-based integrative framework for e-government initiatives. Gov Inf Q 25(3):448–461
Noveck BS (2009) Wiki government: how technology can make government better, democracy stronger, and citizens more powerful. Brookings Institution Press, Washington
Nunes VT, Santoro FM, Borges MRS (2009) A context-based model for knowledge Management embodied in work processes. Inf Sci 179(15):2538–2554
O'Looney JA (2002) Wiring governments. Challenges and possibilities for public managers. Quorum Books, Westport
OECD (2003) The e-government imperative. Organisation for Economic Co-operation and Development, Paris
Ojha A, Tripathi R, Gupta MP (2011) E-government adoption and proliferation across different stages of evolution. In: Shareef MA, Kumar V, Kumar U, Dwivedi YK (eds) Stakeholder Adoption of e-government services: driving and resisting factors. IGI Global, Hershey, pp 137–150
Ojo A, Estevez E, Janowski T (2010) Semantic interoperability architecture for governance 2.0. Inf Polity 15(1/2):105–123
Olbrich S (2010) Implementing e-government locally - an empirical survey from the European Metropolitan area rhine-nechar. In: Reddick CG (ed) Comparative e-government. Springer, New York, pp 221–237
Orlikowski W (2000) Using technology and constituting structures: a practice lens for studying technology in organizations. Organ Sci 11(4):404–428
Orlikowski W, Baroudi JJ (1991) Studying information technology in organizations: research approaches and assumptions. Inf Syst Res 2(1):1–28
Orlikowski W, Gash D (1994) Technological frames: making sense of information technology in organizations. ACM Trans Inf Syst 12(2):174–207
Orlikowski WJ (1992) The duality of technology: rethinking the concept of technology in organizations. Organ Sci 3(3):398–427
Orlikowski WJ (2007) Sociomaterial practices: exploring technology at work. Organ Stud 28(9):1435–1448
Orlikowski WJ (2008) Using technology and constituting structures: a practice lens for studying technology in organizations. In: Ackerman MS, Halverson CA, Erickson T, Kellogg WA (eds) Resources, co-evolution and artifacts: theory in CSCW. Springer, London, pp 255–305
Orlikowski WJ (2010a) Practice in research: phenomenon, perspective and philosophy. In: Golsorkhi D, Rouleau L, Seidl D, Vaara E (eds) Cambridge handbook of strategy as practice. Cambridge University Press, Cambridge, pp 23–33
Orlikowski WJ (2010b) The sociomateriality of organisational life: considering technology in management research. Camb J Econ 341(1):125–141

Orlikowski WJ (2010c) Technology and organization: contingency all the way down. In: Phillips N, Sewell G, Griffiths D (eds) Technology and organization: essays in honour of Joan Woodward, vol 29. Emerald Group Publishing, Cambridge, pp 239–246

Orlikowski WJ, Iacono CS (2001) Research commentary: desperately seeking the "IT" in IT research–a call to theorizing the IT artifact. Inf Syst Res 12(2):121–134

Orlikowski WJ, Iacono CS (2006) Desperately seeking the 'IT' in IT research: a call to theorizing the IT artifact. In: King JL, Lyytinen K (eds) Information systems: the state of the field. Wiley, England, pp 19–42

Orlikowski WJ, Robey D (1991) Information technology and the structuring of organizations. Inf Syst Res 2(2):143–169

Orlikowski WJ, Scott SV (2008) Sociomateriality: challenging the separation of technology, work and organization. Acad Manag Ann 2:433–474

Osimo D (2008) Web 2.0 in government: Why and how? JRC scientific and technical reports, European commission, joint research centre, Institute for prospective technological studies. Available at ftp://ftp.jrc.es/pub/EURdoc/EURdoc/JRC45269.pdf

Packer M (2011) The science of qualitative research. Cambridge University Press, New York

Pache A-C, Santos F (2010) When worlds collide: the internal dynamics of organizational responses to conflicting institutional demands. Acad Manag Rev 35(3):455–476

Panagopoulos C (2004) Consequences of the cyberstate: the political implications of digital government in international context. In: Pavlichev A, Garson GD (eds) Digital government: principles and best practices. Idea Group Publishing, Hershey

Pardo TA, Cresswell AM, Zhang J, Thompson F (2001) Interorganizational knowledge sharing in public sector innovations. In: Best Paper Proceedings of the Academy of Management Conference. Academy of Management/Pace University, Briarcliff Manor

Pardo TA, Gil-Garcia JR, Burke B (2006) Building response capacity through cross-boundary information sharing: the critical role of Trust. Paper presented at the eChallenges 2006 Conference, Barcelona, Spain (October 25–27)

Pardo TA, Gil-Garcia JR, Burke B (2007) (March 23–27). *IT-Enabled Collaboration in Intergovernmental Settings: Lessons from the Response to the West Nile Virus Outbreak.* Paper presented at the 68th ASPA National Conference, Washington, DC

Pardo TA, Gil-Garcia JR, Burke GB (2008a) Building response capacity through cross-boundary information sharing: the critical role of trust. Suny

Pardo TA, Gil-Garcia JR, Burke GB (2008b) Sustainable cross-boundary information sharing. In: Chen H, Brandt L, Gregg V, Traunmüller R, Dawes S, Hovy E, Macintosh A, Larson CA (eds) Digital Government: e-government research, case studiescase studies, and implementation. Springer, New York, pp 421–438

Pardo TA, Gil-Garcia JR, Luna-Reyes LF (2010) Collaborative governance and cross boundary information sharing: enviosioning a networked and IT-enabled public administration. In: O'Leary RO, Van Slyke D, Kim S (eds) The future of public administration, public management and public service around the world: the minnowbrook perspective. Georgetown University Press, Washington, pp 129–140

Pardo TA, Nam T, Burke GB (forthcoming) E-government interoperability: interaction of policy, management, and technology dimensions. Social Sci Comput Rev. doi:10.1177/0894439310392184

Pardo TA, Scholl HJ (2002) Walking atop the cliffs: avoiding failure and reducing risk in large scale e-government projects. Paper presented at the 35th Annual Hawaii international conference on system sciences, Hawaii

Paré G, Bourdeau S, Marsan J, Nach H, Shuraida S (2008) Re-examining the causal structure of information technology impact research. Eur J Inf Syst 17:403–416

Parisopoulos K, Tambouris E, Tarabanis K (2009) Transformational government in Europe: a survey of national policies. In: Lytras MD, Damiani E, Carroll JM, Tennyson RD, Avison D, Naeve A, Dale A, Lefrere P, Tan F, Sipior J, Vossen G (eds) Visioning and engineering the knowledge society: a web science perspective (Proceedings of the second world summit on the knowledge society, WSKS 2009). Springer, Berlin, pp 462–471

Park R (2010) Effectiveness of e-government in delivering services. In: Reddick CG (ed) Citizens and e-government: evaluating policy and management. IGI Global, Hershey, pp 53–68

Pascual P (2009) E-government Asean Task Fors Undp-Apdip

Pasmore WA (1988) Designing effective organizations: the sociotechnical systems perspective. Wiley, New York

Pavlichev A (2004) The e-government challenge for public administration education. In: Pavlichev A, Garson GD (eds) Digital government: principles and best practices. Idea Group Publishing, Hershey

Peled A (2001a) Centralization or diffusion? two tales of online government. Adm Soc 32(6):686–709

Peled A (2001b) Do computers cut red tape? Am Rev Public Adm 31(4):414–435

Pentland BT, Feldman MS (2007) Narrative networks: patterns of technology and organization. Organ Sci 18(5):781–795

Pérez-Castillo R, de Guzmán I.G-R, Piattini M (forthcoming) A case study on business process recovery using an e-government system. Softw: Pract Experience. doi:10.1002/spe.1057

Persson, A, Goldkuhl G (2009) Joined-up e-government: needs and options in local governments. In: Wimmer MA, Scholl HJ, Janssen M, Traunmüller R (eds) Electronic government (Proceedings of the 8th international conference, EGOV 2009), Springer, Berlin pp 76–87

Peters BG (2001) Institutional theory in political science. The ‘New’ institutionalism. Continuum, London

Petter S, DeLone W, McLean E (2008) Measuring information systems success: models, dimensions, measures, and interrelationships. Eur J Inf Sys 17:236–263

Pettigrew AM (1977) Strategy formulation as a political process. Int Stud Manag Organiz 7(2):78–87

Pfeffer J (1982) Organizations and organization theory. Ballinger Publishing Company, Cambridge

Pfeffer J (1992) Managing with power: politics and influence in organizations. Harvard Business School Press, Cambridge

Pfeffer J, Salancik GR (1978) The external control of organizations: a resource dependence perspective. Harper & Row, New York

Phang CW, Kankanhalli A, Ang C (2008) Investigating organizational learning in eGovernment projects: a multi-theoretic approach. J Strategic Inf Syst 17(2):99–123

Pina V, Torres L, Royo S (2009) E-government evolution in EU local governments: a comparative perspective. Online Inf Rev 33(6):1137–1168

Pina V, Torres L, Royo S (2010) Is e-government leading to more accountable and transparent local governments? An overall view. Financial Account Manag 26(1):3–20

Pinch TJ, Bijker WE (1987) The social construction of facts and artifacts: or how the sociology of science and the sociology of technology might benefit from each other. In: Bijker WE, Hughes TP, Pinch TJ (eds) The social construction of technological systems. The MIT Press, Cambridge

Poole MS, Jackson M, Kirsch L, DeSanctis G (1998) Alignment of system and structure in the implementation of group decision support systems. Paper presented at the 1998 academy of management, San Diego, CA

Potnis DD (2010) Measuring e-Governance as an innovation in the public sector. Gov Inf Q 27: 41–48

Powell WW, DiMaggio PJ (1991) The new institutionalism in organizational analysis. University of Chicago Press, Chicago

Prasad A (2009) Understanding successful use of technology in organisations in developing countries: a structurational perspective. Electron J Inf Syst Dev Countries 37. Available from http://www.ejisdc.org/ojs2.../index.php/ejisdc/article/view/555

Prasad P (1993) Symbolic processes in the implementation of technological change: a symbolic interactionist study of work computerization. Acad Manag J 36(6):1400–1429
Pratchett L (2004) Electronic government in Britain. In: Eifert M, Püschel JO (eds) National electronic government: comparing governance structures in multi-layer administration. Routledge, London, pp 13–45
Prins C (2001) Electronic government variations on a concept. In: Prins JEJ (ed) Designing e-government on the crossroads of technological innovation and institutional change. Kluwer Law International, The Hague, pp 1–5
Prybutok VR, Zhang X, Ryan SD (2008) Evaluating leadership, IT quality, and net benefits in an e-government environment. Inf Manag 45(3):143–152
Puron Cid G, Gil-Garcia JR (2004) Enacting E-budgeting in Mexico. Public Finance Manag 4(2):182–217
Puron Cid G, Gil-Garcia JR, Pardo TA (2009) Longitudinal analysis of the effects of IT characteristicson web site ratings across state governments in the US (2001–2006). Paper presented at the 42st Hawaii international conference on system sciences (HICSS)
Rademacher R (2001) The changing profile of information systems research:1995–2000. J Comput Inf Syst 42(1):13–16
Rahman H (2010) Framework of e-governance at the local government level. In: Reddick CG (ed) Comparative e-government pp 23–47
Rashid N, Rahman S (2010) An investigation into critical determinants of e-government implementation in the context of a developing nation. In: Andersen KN, Francesconi E, Grönlund Å, van Engers TM (eds) Electronic government and the information systems perspective (Proceedings of the 1st international conference, EGOVIS 2010), Springer, Berlin, pp 9–21
Reddick CG (2004) A two-stage model of e-government growth: theories and empirical evidence for US cities. Government Inf Q 21:51–64
Reddick CG (2005) Citizen interaction with e-government: from the streets to servers? Government Inf Q 22(1):38–57
Reddick CG (2009a) The adoption of centralized customer service systems: a survey of local governments. Gov Inf Q 26(1):219–226
Reddick CG (2009b) Factors that explain the perceived effectiveness of e-government: a survey of United States city government information technology directors. Int J Electron Gov Res 5(2):1–15
Reddick CG (2010) Preface. In: Reddick CG (ed) Comparative e-government. Springer, New York
Redman TC (1998) The impact of poor data quality on the typical enterprise. Commun ACM 41(2):79–82
Reeve D, Petch J (1999) GIS organisations and people. A socio-technical approach. Taylor & Francis, London
Reichardt CS, Cook TD (1979) Beyond qualitative versus quantitative methods. In: Cook TD, Reichardt CS (eds) Qualitative and quantitative methods in evaluation research. Sage, Beverly Hills
Reidl R, Roitnmayr F, Schenkenfelder B (2007) Using the Structured-case approach to build theory in E-Government. Paper presented at the 40th Hawaii international conference on system science
Remus U, Wiener M (2010) A multi-method, holistic strategy for researching critical success factors in IT projects. Inf Syst J 20(1):25–52
Ribes D, Finholt TA (2009) The long now of technology infrastructure: articulating tensions in development. J Assoc Inf Syst 10(5):375–398
Riccucci N (2010) Public administration: traditions of inquiry and philosophies of knowledge. Georgetown University Press, Washington
Ringle CM, Sarstedt M, Mooi EA (2010) Response-based segmentation using finite mixture partial least squares partial least squares. Theoretical foundations and an application to American customer satisfaction index data. In: Stahlbock R (ed) Data mining, annals of information systems, vol 8. Springer, New York

Rittgen P (2008) Towards a meta-model for socio-instrumental pragmatism. In: Rittgen P (ed) Handbook of ontologies for business interaction. IGI Global, Hershey, pp 88–100
Roberts P, Henderson R (2000) Information technology acceptance in a sample of government employees: a test of the technology acceptance model. Interact Comput 12(5):427–443
Robey D (1987) Implementation and the organizational impacts of information systems. Interfaces 17:72–84
Robey D, Boudreau M-C (1999) Accounting for the contradictory organizational consequences of information technology: theoretical directions and methodological implications. Inf Syst Res 10(2):167–185
Robey D, Im G, Wareham JD (2008) Theoretical foundations of empirical research on interorganizational systems: Assessing past contributions and guiding future directions. J Assoc Inf Syst 9(9):497–518
Robey D, Sahay S (1996) Transforming work through information technology: a comparative case study of geographic information systems in county government. Inf Syst Res 7(1):93–110
Rocheleau B (1999) Building successful public management information systems: critical stages and success factors. Paper presented at the American society for public administration's 60th national conference, Orlando, FL
Rocheleau B (2003) Politics, accountability, and governmental information systems. In: Garson GD (ed) Public information technology: policy and management issues. Idea Group Publishing, Hershey, pp 20–52
Rocheleau B (2007) Case studies on digital government. Idea Group Publishing, Hershey
Roldán JL, Leal A (2003) A validation test of an adaptation of the DeLone and McLean's model in the Spanish EIS field. In: Cano JJ (ed) Critical reflections on information systems: a systemic approach. Idea Group Publishing, Hershey
Rorissa A, Demissie D, Pardo T (2011) Benchmarking e-Government: a comparison of frameworks for computing e-government index and ranking. Gov Inf Q 28(3):354–362
Rorissa A, Potnis DD, Demissie D (2010) A comparative study of contents of e-government service websites of Middle East and North African (MENA) countries. In: Reddick CG (ed) Comparative e-government. Springer, New York, pp 49–69
Rosacker KM, Olson DL (2008a) An empirical assessment of IT project selection and evaluation methods in state government. Project Manag J 39(1):49–58
Rosacker KM, Olson DL (2008b) Public sector information system critical success factors. Transform Gov: People, Process Policy 2(1):60–70
Rosacker KM, Rosacker RE (2010) Information technology project management within public sector organizations. J Enterp Inf Manag 23(5):587–594
Rose WR, Grant GG (2010) Critical issues pertaining to the planning and implementation of e-government initiatives. Gov Inf Q 27(1):26–33
Rosenbloom DH (1998) Public administration understanding management, politics, and law in the public sector. McGraw-Hill, New York
Ross A, Chiasson MW (2005) A call to (dis)order: an ethnomethodological study of information techonolgy "distruptions" in the courtrom. Inf Organ 15:203–227
Rowley J (2011) E-government stakeholders—who are they and what do they want? Int J Inf Manag 31(1):53–62
Roy J (2009) E-government and integrated service delivery in Canada: the province of Nova Scotia as a case study. Int J Electron Gov 2(2/3):223–238
Rutherford M (1999) Institutions in economics. The old and the new institutionalism. Cambridge University Press, New York
Ruuska I, Teigland R (2009) Ensuring project success through collective competence and creative conflict in public–private partnerships: a case study of Bygga Villa, a Swedish triple helix e-government initiative. Int J Project Manag 27(4):323–334
Saba HCI (2010) Social networking in government: opportunities and challenges

Sagheb-Tehrani M (2010) A model of successful factors towards e-government implementation. Electron Gov, Int J 7(1):60–74
Sammons P, Siraj-Blatchford I, Sylva K, Melhuish E, Taggart B, Elliot K (2005) Investigating the effects of pre-school provision: using mixed methods in the EPPE research. Int J Social Res Methodoloy 8(3):207–224
Sancak HÓ, Güleç S (2010) Towards e-government transformation in turkey: policy and implementation. In: Reddick CG (ed) Comparative e-government. Springer, New York, pp 331–352
Sandfort JR (2003) Exploring the structuration of technology within human service organizations. Adm Soc 34(6):605–631
Sandoval-Almazan R, Gil-Garcia JR (2010) Assessing local e-government: an initial exploration of the case of Mexico. Paper presented at the 4th international conference on theory and practice of electronic governance (ICEGOV), Beijing, China
Sandoval-Almazan R, Gil-Garcia JR (2008) Limitations of evolutionary approaches to e-government. In: Garson GD, Khosrow-Pour M (eds) Handbook of research on public information technology. Idea Group Inc, Hershey
Sarker S (2000) Toward a methodology for managing information systems implementation: a social constructivist perspective. Informing Sci 3(4):195–205
SAS (1990) SAS/Stat user guide. SAS Institute, Inc., Cary
Savvides S, Koutrakou VN (2010) The merger of health and technology for Europe's future. In: Nixon PG, Koutrakou VN, Rawal R (eds) Understanding e-government in Europe: issues and challenges. Routledge, New York, pp 186–201
Sawyer S, Tyworth M (2006) Social informatics: principles, theory, and practice. In: Berleur J, Nurminen MI, Impagliazzo J (eds) Social informatics: an information society for all? in remembrance of Rob Kling. Springer, New York, pp 49–62
Saxton ML, Naumer CM, Fisher KE (2007) 2-1-1 Information services: outcomes assessment, benefit-cost analysis, and policy issues. Gov Inf Q 24:186–215
Scavo C (2003) World Wide Web site design and use in public management. In: Garson GD (ed) Public information technology: policy and management issues. Idea Group Publishing, Hershey
Scott M, Robbins G (2010) Understanding e-government implementation from an NPM strategic reform perspective. Commun Assoc Inf Syst 27(1):493–516
Scott WR (1998) Organizations rational, natural, and open systems. Prentice Hall, Upper Saddle River
Scott WR (2001) Institutions and organizations, 2nd edn. Sage, Thousand Oaks
Scott WR (2010a) Institutions and Organizations: Ideas and Interests 3rd ed
Scott WR (2010b) Reflections: the past and future of research on institutions and institutional change. J Change Manag 10(1):5–21
Schelin SH (2003) E-government: an overview. In: Garson GD (ed) Public information technology: policy and management issues. Idea Group Publishing, Hershey, pp 120–137
Schelin SH (2004) Training for digital government. In: Pavlichev A, Garson GD (eds) Digital government: principles and best practices. Idea Group Publishing, Hershey
Schellong A (2007) Extending the Technology enactment framework. Harvard-Kennedy school of government
Scholl, H. J. (2002a). E-government: a special case of ICT-enabled Business, Albany, NY (Unpublished manuscript)
Scholl HJ (2002b) Executive briefing on electronic government and business process change. Center for Technology in Government, Albany
Scholl HJ (2008) Discipline or interdisciplinary study domain? challenges and promises in electronic government research. In: Chen H, Brandt L, Gregg V, Traunmüller R, Dawes S, Hovy E, Macintosh A, Larson CA (eds) Digital government: e-government research, case studies, and implementation. Springer, Boston, pp 21–41

Scholl HJ (2009) Profiling the EG research community and its core. In: Wimmer MA (ed) EGOV 2009, LNCS 5693. Springer, Berlin Heiderlberg, pp 1–12

Scholl HJ, Luna-Reyes LF (2011) Uncovering dynamics of open government, transparency, participation, and collaboration. Paper presented at the 44th Hawaii international conference on systems science

Scholl HJ, Mai JE, Fidel R (2006) Interdisciplinary analysis of digital government work (birds-of-a-feather session). Paper presented at the 7th International conference on digital government research

Schuppan T (2009) E-Government in developing countries: experiences from sub-Saharan Africa. Gov Inf Q 26(1):118–127

Schutz A (1967) Phenomenology of the social world. Northwestern University Press, Evanston

Seddon PB (1997) A re-specification and extension of the DeLone and McLean model of IS success. Inf Syst Res 8(3):240–253

Seddon PB, Staples S, Patnayakuni R, Bowtell M (1999) Dimensions of information system success. Commun AIS 2(20):17

Sefyrin J, Mörtberg C (2009) "We do not talk about this"–problematical silences in e-government. Electron J e-Government 7(3):259–270

Seidel S, Müller-Wienbergen F, Becker J (2010) The concept of creativity in the information systems discipline: past, present, and prospects. Commun Assoc Inf Syst 27(1):217–242

Seifert JW, Chung J (2009) Using e government to reinforce government citizen relationships: comparing government reform in the United States and China. Social Science Computer Review 27(1):3–23 February

Seneviratne SJ (1999) Information technology and organizational change in the public sector. In: Garson GD (ed) Information technology and computer applications in public administration: issues and trends. Idea Group Publishing, Hershey

Shachaf P, Rosenbaum H (2010) A structuration approach to online communities of practice: The case of Q&A communities. J Am Soc Inf Sci Tech 61(9):1933–1944

Shareef MA, Kumar U, Kumar V, Dwivedi YK (2009) Identifying critical factors for adoption of e-government. Electron Gov, Int J 6(1):70–96

Shay S (2008) Beyond social constructivist perspectives on assessment: the centring of knowledge. Teach High Edu 13(5):595–605

Shea CM, Garson GD (eds) (2010) Handbook of public information systems. CRC Press, Boca Raton

Shin D-H (2010) A socio-technical framework for cyber-infrastructure design: implication for Korean cyber-infrastructure vision. Technol Forecast Soc Chang 77(5):783–795

Sila I (2010) Do organisational and environmental factors moderate the effects of Internet-based interorganisational systems on firm performance? Eur J Inf Syst 19:581–600

Silcock R (2001) What is e-government? Parliamentary Affairs 54(1):88–101

Singh M (2009) Customer value via an Intranet: a case application of B2E at HCL technologies. Int J Inf Manag 29(6):497–501

Sismondo S (2009) An introduction to science and technology studies, 2nd edn. Blackwell Publishing, West Sussex

Sittig DF, Singh H (2010) A new sociotechnical model for studying health information technology in complex adaptive healthcare systems. BMJ Qual Saf 19(3):i68–i74

Smith ML (2010) Building institutional trust through e-government trustworthiness cues. Inf Technol People 23(3):222–246

Snellen TMI (2002) Electronic governance: implications for citizens, politicians and public servants. Int Rev Administrative Sci 68(2):183–198

Soffer P, Hadar I (2007) Applying ontology-based rules to conceptual modeling: a reflection on modeling decision making. Eur J Inf Syst 16:599–611

Somers MJ (2010) Using the theory of the professions to understand the IS identity crisis. Eur J Inf Syst 19(4):382–388

Southon G, Sauer C, Dampney K (1999) Lessons from a failed information systems initiative: issues for complex organizations. Int J Med Inf 55(1):33–46
Spirakis G, Spiraki C, Nikolopoulos K (2010) The impact of electronic government on democracy: e-democracy through e-participation. Electron Gov, Int J 7(1):75–88
Srivastava SC (2011) Is e-government providing the promised returns?: a value framework for assessing e-government impact. Transform Gov: People, Process Policy 5(2):107–113
Srivastava SC, Teo TSH (2008) The relationship between e-government and national competitiveness: the moderating influence of environmental factors. Commun Assoc Inf Syst 23(1):73–94
Stahl BC (2008) Information systems: critical perspectives. Routledge, New York
Stanforth C (2010) Analysing e-government project failure: comparing factoral systems and interpretative approaches. Center for development informatics
Star SL, Ruhleder K (1996) Steps toward an ecology of infrastructure: design and access for large information spaces. Inf Syst Res 7(1):111–134
State of the portal: a review of the 50 states'online offerings (2010) California: center for digital government
Stevenson M (2003) Internet democracy elusive report. Associated Press, New York November 5
Stillman L, Linger H (2009) Community informatics and information systems: can they be better connected? Inf Soc: Int J 25(4):255–264
Stowers G (2004) Issues in e-commerce and e-government service delivery. In: Pavlichev A, Garson GD (eds) Digital government: principles and best practices. Idea Group Publishing, Hershey
Streib G, Willoughby KG (2010) E-government as a public management reform: the experience in the United states. In: Shea CM, Garson GD (eds) Handbook of public information systems, 3rd edn. CRC Press, Boca Ranton, pp 171–186
Strong DM, Volkoff O, Johnson SA, Bar-On I, Pelletier L (2009) Electronic health records and the changing roles of health care professionals: a social informatics perspective. Paper presented at the Americas conference on information systems (AMCIS), Lima, Peru
Stryker S (2008) From mead to a structural symbolic interactionism and beyond. Annu Rev Sociology 34:15–31
Suddaby R (2010) Challenges for institutional theory. J Manag Inquiry 19(1):14–20
Swiss JE (2003) Information technology as a facilitator of results-based management in government. In: Garson GD (ed) Public information technology: policy and management issues. Idea Group Publishing, Hershey
Tan CW, Benbasat I (2009) IT mediated customer services in e-government: a citizen's perspective. Commun Assoc Inf Syst 24(1):175–198
Tapscott D, Williams AD, Herman D (2008) Government 2.0: transforming government and governance for the twenty-first century. Available at http://www.newparadigm.com/media/gov_transforminggovernment.pdf
Tashakkori A, Teddlie C (1998) Mixed methodology: combining qualitative and quantitative approaches. Sage, Thousand Oaks
Tashakkori A, Teddlie C (2003) Handbook of mixed methods in social and behavioral research. Sage, Thousand Oaks
Tatnall A (2010) Actor-network theory and technology innovation: advancements and new concepts. IGI Global, Hershey
Tayi GK, Ballou DP (1998) Examining data quality. Commun ACM 41(2):54–56
Taylor JA, Lips AMB (2008) The citizen in the information polity: exposing the limits of the e-government paradigm. Inf Polity 13(3/4):139–152
Taylor JA, Lips AMB, Organ J (2006) Freedom with information: electronic government, information intensity and challenges to citizenship. In: Chapman R, Hunt M (eds) Freedom of information: perspectives on open government in a theoretical and practical context. Ashgate, Aldershot

Tenenhaus M, Esposito VV, Chatelin Y, Lauro C (2005) PLS path modeling. Comput Stat Data Anal 48:159–205

Teo TSH, Srivastava SC, Jiang L (2008) Trust and electronic government success: an empirical study. J Manag Inf Syst 25(3):99–132

Thomas G, Fernández W (2008) Success in IT projects: a matter of definition? Int J Project Manag 26(7):733–742

Thomas JC, Streib G (2003) The new face of government: citizen-initiated contacts in the Era of e-government. J Public Administration Res Theor 13(1):83–101

Thomson JD (2009) Remodelled and restyled e-procurement–new power relationships down under. Electron J E-Government 7(2):183–194

Tilson D, Lyytinen K, Sørensen C (2010) Research commentary—digital infrastructures: the missing IS research agenda. Inf Syst Res 21(4):748–759

Tolbert CJ, Mossberger K, McNeal R (2008) Institutions, policy innovation, and e-government in the American states. Public Administration Rev 68(3):549–563

Traunmüller R (2010) Web 2.0 creates a new government. In: Andersen KN, Francesconi E, Grönlund Å, van Engers TM (eds) Electronic government and the information systems perspective (proceedings of the first international conference, EGOVIS 2010). Springer, Berlin, pp 77–83

Tripathi RP, Gupta MP, Bhattacharya J (2011) Identifying factors of integration for an interoperable government portal: a study in Indian context. Int J Electron Gov Res 7(1):64–88

Trkman P, McCormack K (2010) Estimating the benefits and risks of implementing e-procurement. IEEE Trans Eng Manag 57(2):338–349

Tsai N, Choi B, Perry M (2009a) Improving the process of e-government initiative: an in-depth case study of web-based GIS implementation. Gov Inf Q 26(2):368–376

Tsai W-H, Purbokusumo Y, Cheng JM-S, Tuan ND (2009b) E-government evaluation: the case of Vietnam's provincial websites. Electron Gov, Int J 6(1):41–53

Tseng PTY (2008) A study of e-government system effectiveness: applying structuration theory to context-aware ICT applications in public organisations. Int J Electron Bus 6(4):405–432

Tseng PTY, Yen DC, Hung YC, Wang NCF (2008) To explore managerial issues and their implication on e-government deployment in the public sector: lessons from Taiwan's Bureau of foreign trade. Gov Inf Q 25:734–756

Tsui E (2009, August 19–21) Blending content and process management technologies with Web 2.0 tools for effective e-information management. Paper presented at the government information forum Hong Kong

Ubaldi B-C, Roy J (2010) E-government and federalism in Italy and Canada—a comparative assessment. In: Reddick CG (ed) Comparative e-government, vol 25. Springer, Berlin, pp 183–199

Umble EJ, Haft RR, Umble MM (2003) Enterprise resource planning: Implementation procedures and critical success factors. Eur J Oper Res 146:241–257

UN & ASPA (2002) Benchmarking e-government: a global perspective. United Nations Division of Public Economics and Public Administration and the American Society for Public Administration, New York

United Nations (2010) United nations e-government survey 2010: leveraging e-government at a time of financial and economic crisis

UNPAN (2002) UNPAN e-government. Retrieved July 8, 2002, from www.unpan.org/egovernment.asp

Valdés G, Solar M, Astudillo H, Iribarren M, Concha G, Visconti M (2011) Conception, development and implementation of an e-government maturity model in public agencies. Gov Inf Q 28(2):176–187

van den Haak MJ, de Jong MDT, Schellens PJ (2009) Evaluating municipal websites: a methodological comparison of three think-aloud variants. Gov Inf Q 26(1):193–202 van Veenstra AF, Janssen M, Tan Y-H (2010) Towards an understanding of e-government induced change: drawing on organization and structuration theories. In: Wimmer MA, Chappelet J-L, Janssen M, Scholl HJ (eds) Electronic government (proceedings of the 9th IFIP WG 8.5 international conference, EGOV 2010). Springer, Berlin, pp 1–12

van Veenstra AF, Klievink B, Janssen M (2011) Barriers and impediments to transformational government: insights from literature and practice. Electron Gov, Int J 8(2/3):226–241

Vannoy SA, Salam AF (2010) Managerial interpretations of the role of information systems in competitive actions and firm performance: a grounded theory investigation. Inf Syst Res 21(3):496–515

Vélez-Rivera B, Rodríguez-Martinez M, Díaz W, Nuñez-Molina M, Rivera-Vega PI (2010) Multidisciplinary e-government research and education as a catalyst for effective information technology transfer. In: Chen H-G, Brandt L, Gregg V, Traunmüller R, Dawes S, Hovy E, Macintosh A, Larson CA (eds) Digital government: e-government research, case studies, and implementation. Springer, New York, pp 670–695

Verdegem P, Verleye G (2009) User-centered e-government in practice: a comprehensive model for measuring user satisfaction. Gov Inf Q 26(3):487–497

Vilares MJ, Almeida MH, Coehlo PS (2010) Comparison of likelihood and PLS estimators for structural equation modeling: a simulation with customer satisfaction data. In: Esposito VV, Chin WW, Henseler J, Wang H (eds) Handbook of partial least squarespartial least squares. Concepts methods and applications. Springer, Heidelberg, pp 289–305

Walker GH, Stanton NA, Salmon PM, Jenkins DP (2008) A review of sociotechnical systems theory: a classic concept for new command and control paradigms. Theor Issues Ergon Sci 9(6):479–499

Walsham G (1995) Interpretative case studies in IS research: nature and method. Eur J Inf Syst 4(2):74–81

Walsham G, Han C-K (1991) Structuration theory and information systems research. J Appl Syst Anal 17:77–85

Walton RE (1989) Up and running. Integrating information technology and the organization. Harvard Business School Press, Boston

Wang P (2010) Chasing the hottest IT: effects of information technology fashion on organizations. MIS Q 34(1):63–85

Wang YS, Liao YW (2008) Assessing e-government systems success:a validation of DeLone and McLean model of information systems success. Gov Inf Q 25:717–733

Warschauer M (2003) Technology and social inclusion: rethinking the digital divide. MIT Press, Cambridge

Waxer C (2011) CIOs struggle with social media's security risks. Journal

Weerakkody V, Dhillon G (2008) Moving from e-government to t-government: a study of process reengineering challenges in a UK local authority context. Int J Electron Gov Res 4(4):1–16

Weerakkody V, Dwivedi YK, Brooks L, Williams MD, Mwange A (2007) E-government implementation in Zambia:contributing factors. Electron Gov, Int J 4(4):484–508

Weerakkody V, Dwivedi YK, Kurunananda A (2009) Implementing e-government in Sri Lanka: lessons from the UK. Inf Technol Dev 15(3):171–192

Weigl T, Hartmann E, Jahns C, Darkow I-L (2008) Inter-organizational network structures in Russia: organizational changes from institutional and social embeddedness perspectives. Human Res Dev Int 11(2):151–165

Weinstein J, Jaques T (2010) Achieving project management success in the federal government. Management Concepts, Vienna

Weissenberger-Eibl MA, Teufel B (2011) Organizational politics in new product development project selection: a review of the current literature. Eur J Innov Manag 14(1):51–73

Wenjing L (2011) Government information sharing: principles, practice, and problems—an international perspective. Gov Inf Q 28(3):363–373

West DM (2000) State and federal e-government in the United states. Brown University, Providence

West DM (2001) State and federal e-government in the United states. Brown University, Providence
West DM (2002) State and federal e-government in the United states. Brown University, Providence
West DM (2003) State and federal e-government in the United states. Brown University, Providence
West DM (2004) State and federal e-government in the United states. Brown University, Providence
West DM (2005a) Digital government. Technology and public sector performance. Princeton University Press, Princeton
West DM (2005b) State and federal e-government in the United states. Brown University, Providence
West DM (2006) State and federal e-government in the United states. Brown University, Providence
West DM (2007) State and federal e-government in the United states. Brown University, Providence
West DM (2008) State and federal e-government in the United states. Brown University, Providence
West JP, Berman EM (2001) The impact of revitalized management practices on the adoption of information technology: a national survey of local governments. Pubic Perform Manag Rev 24(3):233–253
Whitson T, Davis L (2001) Best practices in electronic government: comprehensive electronic information dissemination for science and technology. Gov Inf Q 18(2):79–91
Whittington R (2010) Giddens, structuration theory and strategy as practice. In: Golsorkhi D, Rouleau L, Seidl D, Vaara E (eds) Cambridge handbook of strategy as practice. Cambridge University Press, Cambridge, pp 109–126
Williams CB, Fedorowicz J, Tomasino AP (2010) Governmental factors associated with statewide interagency collaboration initiatives. Paper presented at the 11th annual international digital government research (dg.o)
Williams MD (2008) E-government adoption in Europe at regional level. Transforming Gov: People, Process Policy 2(1):47–59
Willmott H (2011) "Institutional work" for what? Problems and prospects of institutional theory. J Manag Inquiry 20(1):67–72
Wiredu GO (2010) An institutional perspective on the challenges of information systems innovation in public organisations. In: Wimmer MA, Chappelet J-L, Janssen M, Scholl HJ (eds) Electronic government (proceedings of the 9th IFIP WG 8.5 international conference, EGOV 2010). Springer, Berlin, pp 97–108
Wry T, Greenwood R, Jennings PD, Lounsbury M (2010) Institutional sources of technological knowledge: a community perspective on nanotechnology emergence. In: Phillips N, Sewell G, Griffiths D (eds) Technology and organization: essays in honour of Joan woodward, vol 29. Emerald Group Publishing, Bingley, pp 149–176
Wu H, Ozok AA, Gurses AP, Wei J (2009) User aspects of electronic and mobile government: results from a review of current research. Electron Gov, Int J 6(3):233–251
Wu L-C, Wu L-H, Wen Y-F (2010) Interdisciplinary research of options theory and management information systems: review, research issues, and suggestions for future research. Ind Manag Data Syst 110(3):433–452
Wyld DC (2009) Moving to the cloud: an introduction to cloud computing in government. IBM center for the business of government, Washington
Yang K (2003) Neoinstitutionalism and e-government: beyond Jane fountain. Social Sci Comput Rev 21(4):432–442
Yang T-M, Maxwell TA (2011) Information-sharing in public organizations: a literature review of interpersonal, intra-organizational and inter-organizational success factors. Gov Inf Q 28(2):164–175
Yao Y, Lee YW, Hong P, Weng Z (2010) Power of information channels: participation in e-government discourse. Paper presented at the Americas conference on information systems (AMCIS)
Yildiz M (2007) E-government research: reviewing the literature, limitations, and ways forward. Gov Inf Q 24(3):646–665

Yin RK (2003) Case study research. design and methods. Sage Publications, Thousand Oaks
Yoo Y, Henfridsson O, Lyytinen K (2010) Research commentary—the new organizing logic of digital innovation: an agenda for information systems research. Inf Syst Res 21(4):724–735
Yu C–C, Janssen M (2010) The need for strategic management and business model design in government and public administration. Electron Gov, Int J 7(4):299–315
Zackariasson P, Boström G-O, Wilson TL (2009) Technology and change in the Swedish architectural industry. Competit Rev: Int Bus J Incorporating J Global Competit 19(1):46–62
Zanko M, Badham R, Couchman P, Schubert M (2008) Innovation and HRM: absences and politics. Int J Human Res Manag 19(4):562–581
Zarei B, Ghapanchi A (2008) Guidelines for government-to-government initiative architecture in developing countries. Int J Inf Manag 28(4):277–284
Zhang P, Scialdone MJ (2010, July 9–12) State of IT artifacts: an analysis of ICIS 2009 research papers. Paper presented at the Pacific Asia conference on information systems, Taipei, Taiwan
Zhao JJ, Zhao SY, Zhao SY (2010) Opportunities and threats: a security assessment of state e-government websites. Gov Inf Q 27(1):49–56
Zheng L, Yang T-M, Pardo TA, Jiang Y (2009) Understanding the "boundary" in information sharing and integration. Paper presented at the 42nd Hawaii international conference on system sciences
Ziegenfuss JT (2011) Analyzing changing organizational environments: methodological approach and the academic health center case. J Syst Inf Technol 13(1):81–97
Zillien N, Hargittai E (2009) Digital distinction: status-specific types of internet usage. Social Sci Q 90(2):274–291
Zissis D (2011) Securing e-government and e-voting with an open cloud computing architecture. Gov Inf Q 28(2):239–251
Zissis D, Lekkas D, Papadopoulou A-E (2009) Competent electronic participation channels in electronic democracy. Electron J E-Government 7(2):195–208
Zouridis S, Thaens M (2005) Reflections on the anatomy of e-government. In: Bekkers VJJM, Homburg VMF (eds) The information ecology of e-government. IOS Press, Amsterdam, pp 21–36
Zweers K, Planqué K (2001) Electronic government. From an organizational based perspective towards a client oriented approach. In: Prins JEJ (ed) Designing e-government on the crossroads of technological innovation and institutional change. Kluwer Law International, The Hague, pp 91–120

Index

J. R. Gil-Garcia, *Enacting Electronic Government Success*,
Integrated Series in Information Systems 31, DOI: 10.1007/978-1-4614-2015-6,

R

S

MIX
Papier aus verantwortungsvollen Quellen
Paper from responsible sources
FSC® C105338

If you have any concerns about our products,
you can contact us on
ProductSafety@springernature.com

In case Publisher is established outside the EU,
the EU authorized representative is:
Springer Nature Customer Service Center GmbH
Europaplatz 3, 69115 Heidelberg, Germany

Printed by Libri Plureos GmbH
in Hamburg, Germany